THE CHINESE MIND:

ESSENTIALS OF CHINESE PHILOSOPHY AND CULTURE

the Chinese Mind

Essentials of Chinese Philosophy and Culture

Charles A. Moore, editor
With the assistance of Aldyth V. Morris

HONOLULU

East-West Center Press

University of Hawaii Press

CHARLES A. MOORE, for many years senior professor of philosophy at the University of Hawaii, died in April, 1967, before his work on this volume was completed. Long an advocate of the promotion of greater tolerance between people of the East and West, Professor Moore was known internationally as the innovator and driving force behind the East-West Philosophers' Conferences, held in Honolulu in 1939, 1949, 1959, and 1964, which brought together some of the leading thinkers of the Orient and the Occident to exchange ideas and to enhance their understanding of other traditions.

Every effort has been made by those involved in finishing this book to maintain the high standards set by Professor Moore. A special recognition is owing to Professors Peter Lee, Lily Winters, Chung-ying Cheng, Edward H. Schafer, Mr. Shien-min Jen, and Mr. Chi-ping Chen for their help in preparing this posthumous work.

WINFIELD E. NAGLEY
Chairman
Department of Philosophy
University of Hawaii

Preface

THIS VOLUME is composed exclusively of chapters selected from the proceedings volumes resulting from the four East-West Philosophers' Conferences held at the University of Hawaii in 1939, 1949, 1959, and 1964.* Each of the chapters here was originally a paper presented at one of these conferences and discussed at that time. (Incidentally, some of the discussion which took place is included at the end of some of the papers, in the form of Questions and Answers.)

This volume—and two succeeding volumes on India and Japan —are intended both for the general reader and for the philosophy student and scholar. These are not textbooks as such, but are presented with this possibility strongly in mind, since they provide an excellent basis for courses in their respective fields. The papers are substantial and authoritative, but not overly technical, presentations on Chinese philosophy in general and also on specific aspects of Chinese life and culture in their philosophical and social contexts.

While this is essentially a reprint volume, the papers have been re-edited by their authors (except Hu Shih and E. R. Hughes, who are no longer living) and by the editor of this volume, and some changes in style, translation, transliteration, etc., have been

---

* The four volumes from which these papers are taken, all edited by Charles A. Moore, are: *Philosophy—East and West,* published by Princeton University Press (1944); and three published by the University of Hawaii Press, *Essays in East-West Philosophy: An Attempt at World Philosophical Synthesis* (1951); *Philosophy and Culture, East and West* (1962); *The Status of the Individual in East and West* (1967).

made. However, there are no major revisions of the substance of the papers.

An attempt has been made to bring about unity and consistency of style as far as possible, although the four volumes were not always consistent in style; in fact, within the same volume some of the authors themselves insisted on following different styles.

As in all the conference volumes, several editing difficulties were encountered. Among these are the usual ones of capitalization, hyphenation, italicizing, and transliteration from Oriental languages. Another concerned the order of names of Far Easterners mentioned in the text.

Far Eastern tradition calls for the family name to be given first, but this practice has been abandoned by some contemporary Asians; this results in confusion. Usually, classical names are given in traditional style, modern and contemporary names in Western style. The proper name-order will be found in the index in all cases.

The matters of capitalization and hyphenation in romanized Chinese are extremely difficult because competent scholars in the field are not in agreement as to what constitutes correct style. An effort to achieve uniformity and consistency has been made, but there are undoubtedly some discrepancies. An attempt to correct all such discrepancies will be made in the index.

The editor assumes responsibility for revising usage employed by some of the authors—and common usage—in cases of published items which are in fact articles or chapters or parts of standard works. These are enclosed within quotation marks and are not italicized. (There are some unavoidable discrepancies here.)

On matters of detail:

(1) The fear is that there is too much capitalization—because some of the authors strongly wished it that way. Usually, the capital letter is used for "ambiguous" terms when they refer to metaphysical ultimates, the lower-case when reference is to empirical matters. For example, the Buddha, but *buddha*-nature, *buddha-dharma*, etc.; Heaven and heaven, Ying-Yang for the school, but *yin* and *yang* for the two forces in Nature, and so on. In some cases authors insisted otherwise and the editor complied.

(2) Dates (sometimes varying slightly because of personal interpretations) are given frequently so as to provide the unacquainted reader with a better historical sense of the development of ideas.

(3) Transliterated Chinese is often in the text or within parentheses to provide the opportunity for those who can to check interpretations given in the translations.

(4) In a few cases, common usage is observed rather than technically correct spellings.

(5) The same Chinese term or title is sometimes differently translated—in accordance with the preferences of the several authors but clarity is not thereby sacrificed. (One example is *li:* reason, law, principle, etc.)

(6) Alternate names are frequently used for some of the important thinkers whose views are described and explained here—their "true" name and their pen name, or adopted name, or honorific name. For example: Wang Shou-jen and Wang Yang-ming; Chu Hsi and Chu Yüan-hui; Ch'eng Hao and Ch'eng Ming-tao; Ch'eng I and Ch'eng I-ch'uan, etc. Double listings are provided in the index.

An alphabetical list of Chinese names, titles, terms, etc., with corresponding Chinese characters, is given as an appendix.

Appreciation is hereby extended to Professor Peter H. Lee of the University of Hawaii and Professor Edward H. Schafer of the University of California, Berkeley, for their great assistance in the most difficult matter of transliteration, to Mrs. Floris Sakamoto for work far beyond the call of duty, and to Princeton University Press for permission to republish Professor Wing-tsit Chan's "The Story of Chinese Philosophy," from *Philosophy—East and West* (1944, 1946).

Charles A. Moore

Honolulu
October 9, 1966

Contents

Contents (*continued*)

THE CHINESE MIND:

ESSENTIALS OF CHINESE PHILOSOPHY AND CULTURE

CHARLES A. MOORE   *Introduction:*
The Humanistic Chinese Mind

IN THE CONTEMPORARY world a knowledge of the basic principles of Chinese philosophy is indispensable for the educated man and for the philosopher, both in the West and throughout Asia. Simply to be educated requires that we understand the Chinese people and Chinese culture. To understand the contemporary world of Asia—and to be able to live at peace, or at war, if need be, with any other people—we must *know* them. This is impossible without a substantial knowledge of the fundamental characteristics and also the variety of points of view that constitute, in this case, the Chinese mind or Chinese philosophy. This necessitates understanding these principles in themselves and in their applications to the various aspects of Chinese life—its culture and civilization as a whole.

It has often been said that philosophy is more significant in China, in the life of even the common man, than in any other civilization in the history of the world. It has been said, too, that in China it is not necessary to be religious but it is necessary to be philosophical, or at least possessed of a knowledge of philosophy. For the Chinese, philosophy takes the place of religion—certainly for the educated and intellectual Chinese.

The philosopher, even the technical philosopher—not merely those who simply want to know and understand other peoples—must know the fundamentals of Chinese philosophy if he would be worthy of the title "philosopher." By definition, the philosopher must have, or at least seek, comprehensive knowledge of all the data of experience and reality if he is to accomplish the time-honored tasks of philosophy. Not only that, but Chinese philosophy has much in general point of view and in terms of many specific philosophical doctrines to contribute to the total magazine of the philosopher's mind, and to philosophy itself.

Dr. Hu Shih, the great Chinese intellectual and philosopher, has been quoted as saying that every people has a unique character in terms of which that particular people must be understood—and that this essential character or mind of a given people consists essentially of its deepest philosophical convictions. And this is certainly true. This volume follows this interpretation.

Here we have a series of what might be called living essays on various aspects of the Chinese mind, all written by authors of exceptional philosophical competence who also have a living knowledge and experience of the philosophy and culture they represent—an ideal combination for the presentation of studies and explanations which can and do reflect the academic and technical principles involved and also the living and practical significance of these principles in the lives of the Chinese people.

The over-all question of this volume is: What are the basic, and possibly the unique—the "rock-bottom"—characteristics of the Chinese philosophical tradition and of Chinese culture as based upon that thought-tradition? In a sense, however, it will be the reader's responsibility to determine what these basic principles of the Chinese philosophical tradition as a whole are in the light of the several less general and sometimes more specific treatments of particular problems, attitudes, and philosophical theories. No attempt is made to simplify the mind of the Chinese. From many angles, the Chinese mind, Chinese philosophy, and Chinese culture are very complex indeed—any simplification would necessarily be oversimplification and therefore falsification.

There is nothing "inscrutable" about the Chinese or Chinese mentality. However, there is much that is subtle, at first unclear, and, to a Westerner, sometimes even enigmatic and paradoxical. There are many gray areas. However—and this is part of the purpose (and achievement) of the chapters that follow—these sometimes puzzling, sometimes difficult, doctrines and points of view, are clarified for non-Chinese by experts who both know and have experienced, have lived, the essence of Chinese philosophy. They are steeped in the knowledge and wisdom of China, both academically (or intellectually) and personally.

In one way and at least to some extent, this volume makes an understanding of Chinese philosophy and the Chinese mind more difficult, not less. This is because it consists of a number of distinct chapters dealing with distinct and seemingly separate aspects of the over-all situation. There is a certain artificiality, and some actual inaccuracy, in approaching Chinese philosophy in this piecemeal manner. This questionable "compartmentalization" is used primarily for the sake of Westerners. In view of the manner and spirit of Western thought ever since Aristotle, Westerners have seemed to need departmentalization—analysis—of the totality of truth, experience, life, and philosophy itself into what the West has come to think of as the basic separate or at least separable aspects of the knowledge which the philosopher is seeking. This division of philosophical labor in the West and its strong tendency toward analysis are responsible for this manner of presenting the over-all picture in its various parts. And, since this volume is directed primarily to Westerners, this method has seemed to be advisable. However, it is not fully permissible, because Chinese philosophers, more than those in any other philosophical tradition, past and present, look at life and philosophy in its totality, not in its parts. Perhaps this manner of presentation will make for clarity in one sense; but it must not be forgotten that it is a questionable procedure, even though any other procedure would very probably be much more difficult for the Western reader. As a matter of fact, in some of these papers the reader will find overlapping of areas of study and of life. This is unavoidable.

There are many distinct systems in the history and totality of Chinese philosophy. Furthermore, in the course of its history many sub-systems and many individual so-called followers of particular systems have developed what could well be called new systems, thus adding greatly to the complexity and variety of the scope of Chinese philosophy. The tendency in China—as in India—is for later thinkers to consider themselves as mere commentators upon or followers of the major classical schools or of the great early thinkers. They are not necessarily followers in the strict sense of the word. They are guided, rather, by a sense of personal humility which prevents them from claiming originality despite the fact that their doctrines are sometimes so much out of harmony with the "original" that the creativity of their work is unmistakable.

All the papers here originated in and were presented at philosophical conferences devoted exclusively to the attempt—by comparative study—to bring about mutual understanding between the philosophies and philosophers of Asia and the philosophies and philosophers of the West. However, this volume is as exclusively as possible on the philosophies of China alone and is not specifically or directly a comparative study. Comparisons—similarities and contrasts, affinities and conflicts—are here, however, to be discovered, realized, and appreciated, or denied, by those who are interested in such philosophical relationships.

A further purpose underlying the conferences at which these papers were first presented was that of enriching the philosophical minds of all the major traditions involved in those discussions— China, India, Japan, and the West—and also in seeking out specific contributions from each tradition to the total perspective which is philosophy. In other words, we shall find here philosophical principles, basic convictions, and attitudes of mind without which the Chinese people and Chinese culture cannot be understood. But we shall also find an astounding number of vital, suggestive, even provocative new ideas, new perspectives, new methods, new attitudes. These are exciting in themselves. They demand serious consideration by substantial thinkers far beyond the reaches of the Chinese tradition. The expression "Western knowledge and Eastern wisdom" is far from being true or accurate. However, there are in the chapters to follow many examples of both the knowledge and the wisdom of one of the greatest philosophical traditions and one of the greatest cultures the world has ever known.

This volume is concerned with the entire range and scope of the Chinese philosophical tradition—except, as will be explained later, the Communist order of today. Both for understanding and for what China can contribute to Western philosophy and to the totality of the data of philosophy in terms of original and possibly unique ideas, it is essential that we know the entire range of the Chinese tradition. As has been so truly said, "To understand China, one must start at least as early as Confucius. One must consider the great thinkers because they have played a principal part in making China what she is. . . . One must know something about China's traditional thought even to understand Chinese Communist theory."

By way of some anticipatory suggestion, it might help to cite some of the interesting and exciting ideas and attitudes—to indicate, in advance, how very rewarding this experience can be. The following are among the most important basic principles of Chinese philosophy—and all of them find clear and authoritative explanation and defense in these studies.

(1) There is what might be considered the unique and certainly the fundamental *problem* of Chinese philosophy—and one great Chinese philosopher has said that the best clue to any philosophical tradition is the problem with which it is primarily concerned. This problem for Chinese philosophy is that of achieving "sageliness within and kingliness without," a truly significant concept and interestingly different from both the West and India in its twofold emphasis.

(2) There is the profound and all-pervading inseparability of philosophy and life and even of theory and practice—a major attitude of the Chinese philosophical mind, old and new.

(3) There is the universally recognized doctrine—and attitude—of humanism, which is unquestionably more pervasive and more significant in China than in any other philosophical tradition. "People come first in China." This attitude requires—and receives here—comprehensive treatment both in general and in its specific applications to the many affected sides of Chinese thought and life.

(4) There is the predominance of ethical consciousness—both inner and outer—as the essence of all human living and as the highest goal for man. In a very real sense, the ethical and the spiritual are one in China.

(5) There is the uniquely Chinese concept of spirituality—coupled with, and defining its expression in, the fullest possible development of the ethical character (and innate goodness) of man. Another unique concept and attitude.

(6) There is the very famous—and equally fundamental—but usually thoroughly misunderstood doctrine of filial piety, possibly the very essence of Chinese ethical and social life.

(7) There is the great emphasis upon man as a social being, with all the problems attendant to that interpretation, but without many of its alleged anti-individual connotations.

(8) There is what one writer has called "the art of social living in China," an attitude in and toward life in society which characteristically identifies Chinese thought in this area as distinct from that in all other cultures—an attitude which, by the way, Leibniz described as far superior to the Western, or Christian, way of civil life.

(9) There is, in spite of China's unquestioned emphasis upon the social nature of man, a deep respect for the individual, includ-

ing the fundamental concept of the original equality and the original goodness of all individuals—the two emphases being joined in China's typical attitude of harmony.

It is true that there is respect for the individual and his dignity and a sense of equality and "the democratic spirit," but all of these seem to be conceived of in a strictly Chinese—and therefore a unique—form and meaning. All men are originally and/or potentially and/or ultimately equal but not "actually" or literally equal. Qualitative and personal criteria seem to take precedence over actual individuality and equality. Only the sage, it seems at times, is a genuine individual—and very few attain this status, although it is open to all. Rights are either seriously neglected or have a decidedly secondary status relative to duties. And the "rights" of an individual are all but unthinkable if in fact they jeopardize society or the state. All this would seem to pose serious problems for the Westerner.

(10) There is the optimistic—and thoroughly democratic— doctrine of what is called the "universal attainability of sagehood."

(11) There is the already-mentioned supreme importance of philosophy and the lesser importance of religion—especially for the intellectual but also for all educated men.

(12) There is the pervasive theoretical and practical principle and ideal of harmony—a general Oriental characteristic of life and thought, but perhaps more fully developed and "implemented" in China than in any other tradition, Eastern or Western.

(13) There is the famous Chinese synthetic attitude—sometimes called "mere eclecticism," although it is much more than that. This doctrine applies the Chinese spirit of harmony in the realm of the intellect and in the realm of religion as well as in the practical and ethical life of man.

(14) Coupled with this is the somewhat difficult-to-understand attitude of "both-and"—as contrasted with the Western tendency to think in terms of "either/or," such that the fine lines of distinction and exclusiveness so typical of Western life and thought and even religion are not common to the Chinese mind.

(15) Along the same lines, there is the comprehensive attitude of tolerance, which pervades the Chinese mentality and Chinese society.

(16) In legal and political philosophy, too, one finds two of these fundamental elements—again in considerable disagreement with the West. One is the element of humanism, in which the

individual person is more important than the abstract rule (in law, as in ethics), and the concept of "both-and," or non-black-or-white. The other—also humanism—is the tendency toward rule by man rather than rule of law, although this is one area where much misunderstanding still seems to exist.

(17) Also in line with the general attitude of "both-and" and tolerance is the ethical attitude of moderation. The Golden Mean is vital to China, as it was to the Greeks. But there is also the "un-moderate" attitude of profound ethical sincerity of will.

(18) The Golden Rule is also fundamental despite its famous —and therefore ridiculously criticized—negative expression in Confucius.

(19) On the intellectual side, there is a great love of learning, and a demand for the fullest possible "investigation of things"—and, in seeming conflict with the doctrine of "both-and," the doctrine of the rectification of names, and living in accord with this rectification of names. Professor William Ernest Hocking has cited this attitude as one of the greatest contributions of Chinese philosophy and culture.

(20) There are two Neo-Confucian metaphysical considerations of rather special importance, especially because of their philosophical significance and also because of their possible uniqueness among the traditions of Asia, thus separating China from the other Asian traditions with which it is frequently—and so fallaciously— united in "*the* philosophy of *the* East." These are, first, the doctrine of the mutual necessity of the ultimate reason or principle of reality and the material element (or vital force) which necessitates the expression of the "absolute," if it can be called that, in the empirical world; and, second, the doctrine of the one in the many and the many in the one, and the impossibility of one without the other.

(21) And, finally, to keep this list from extending endlessly— there is the famous "argument" (an almost all-inclusive sorites) in one of the Confucian classics, in which, in brief, the investigation of things leads to sincerity of will, and that to personal moral integrity, and that to the well-established family, and that to the well-ordered state, and that to peace in the world—the essence of the argument, according to one interpretation, being that knowledge and the personal integrity of the individual constitute the root principle of all Chinese thought and culture.

In sum, the Chinese thought-and-culture tradition may be

characterized by humanism, by its emphases upon the ethical, the intellectual (primarily with relation to life and activity), the aesthetic, and the social (not necessarily in that order of importance), without any aversion to material welfare and the normal enjoyments of life—and with an inner tranquillity of spirit that pervades life in both prosperity and adversity, a tranquillity born of a sense of harmony with Nature and one's fellow men.

Each of these specific doctrines is interesting, significant, and possibly provocative in itself. And, taken together, they constitute the essentials of a unique and important philosophical tradition and a veritable storehouse of important ideas.

While we are concerned with a positive understanding of the Chinese philosophical mind and the Chinese character and with the positive recognition of interesting and valuable new ideas, there is also the necessity on the part of every Westerner to eliminate from his mind the many misunderstandings which have almost been bred into his knowledge and mentality by the distortions of the past and by the sheer ignorance of basic Chinese thought that has been prevalent throughout most of Western philosophical history. "Answers" to these many falsifications, or to many of them at least, will be found here, but sometimes only indirectly, to be seen and appreciated by the discerning. They may be missed or misunderstood unless one brings to this task a serious concern with fundamental accuracy of interpretation.

Among the many misunderstandings of Chinese thought and culture for which one will find corrective clarifications here are: that Chinese philosophy has no interest in metaphysics; that there is no logic in Chinese philosophy; that China is dominated by intuition—or mere common sense; that in China—as everywhere else in Asia!—philosophy and religion are identical; that Chinese philosophy and culture are pessimistic; that the individual is of no significance whatever in China, being dominated completely by the family and filial piety; that there is no genuine philosophy in China; that the very earliest philosophers—Confucius, Lao Tzu, and their contemporaries—are the essence of Chinese philosophy and that they, because of the "peculiar" ways in which they expressed their thought, are not genuine philosophers; that science and the scientific method are non-existent in China; and that Chinese philosophy has nothing to contribute either to the West or to philosophy as such. All of these and other equally false, sometimes even malicious, misapprehensions must be removed and corrected and revealed for the errors they are if one is to understand the Chinese mind. They must be answered pointedly and convincingly—and that is just what is done in the chapters in this volume.

Not to be considered necessarily as a misunderstood, but certainly as a very controversial, interpretation, is Professor F. S. C. Northrop's extremely well-known view of the Chinese philosophical and intellectual tradition as characterized by a "natural-history," a "pointing," a purely denotative attitude and method, as dominated by "concepts of intuition"—all of which characterizations set China off against the West, with its domination by "concepts by postulation," scientific method, etc. This view is indirectly challenged—at least by implication—in several of the papers in this volume and specifically and pointedly in the papers by E. R. Hughes and Hu Shih. This is a vital point and a vital problem in any attempt by the Westerner to achieve general and technical understanding of China and the Chinese mind, and here it receives responsible and penetrating examination from the Chinese point of view. In view of the great prominence given to Northrop's view over the years, special attention is called to its consideration here.

There is especially concentrated attention in this volume upon the status of the individual and the relationships among individuals and the relationship between the individual and the many aspects of thought and life and the many institutions of society and society itself which might seem to conflict with the dignity and significance of the individual. This emphasis is due to the fact that the contemporary world is probably more concerned with the problem of the status of the individual and his dignity as a human being than with any other single problem, and also because the status of the individual, especially in relation to the family, has long been one of the most misunderstood principles of Chinese life and thought. (There is, too, the involved question of the ultimate status of authority and freedom—and of rights and duties—in Chinese philosophy and culture as a whole.) In the light of the contemporary emphasis upon this problem—as well as its historical importance—and also in the light of the necessity of understanding the traditional Chinese point of view relative to the individual in relation to the family, to society, and to the state in the contemporary situation involving the communistic take-over in Mainland

China, this particular problem receives more attention than any other specific problem under study here—but no more than it deserves and demands.

This volume does not deal with the political philosophical development in mainland China since the communists assumed power. This entire movement, philosophically speaking, is so much a period of transition and is characterized by so much confusion that it simply cannot be examined or described intelligently and clearly. This is partly because of the effort of the communists to follow both Western communist doctrines and at the same time whatever in the Chinese tradition they can find (or interpret) to suit their purpose. Part of the confusion lies in the fact that communism is a Western doctrine, whereas tradition has such a solid foundation among the Chinese people. This volume is concerned with those Chinese philosophical concepts and attitudes which have been basic to the Chinese mind and to Chinese society for centuries as "rock-bottom" ideas, and which have guided China through many historical changes of conditions and even of attitudes—and through revolution after revolution.

It seems to be the thought of most free Chinese that the basic principles found in this volume are so strongly imbedded in the mind of the Chinese people, are so uniquely Chinese, and are so fundamentally sound that they will undoubtedly play a great part in the eventual restoration of China to its pre-communist intellectual and cultural stature. This conviction receives added support from the fact that historical fluctuations are almost intrinsic to the history of Chinese thought—but that the "rock-bottom" ideas of the great China—as Dr. Hu Shih calls them—will win out because they are the life blood of China and the Chinese people.

A prominent American scholar of China recently posed the question as to whether the contemporary situation in Mainland China (what he calls "modern China") "represents aggressive, expansionist communism or an ancient culture seeking to re-establish itself and its influence." The essays in this volume will provide the reader with ample knowledge and basic evidence to enable him to answer that question for himself. It is likely that he will decide to agree with another authoritative Sinologist who recently reported to the U.S. Congress that the communists are beginning to realize that "the world cannot be remade in a day"— especially in China where such a strong tradition has been accepted and lived for so many centuries.

WING-TSIT CHAN   *Chinese Theory*

and Practice, with Special Reference

to Humanism

IN ORDER to understand the relation between Chinese philosophical theories and practical affairs, it is necessary, first, to see what the Chinese have conceived that relation to be, and then to see how theory is related to actual practice. This paper is therefore divided into two parts: (1) the Chinese concepts of truth and (2) humanism in practice, humanism being taken as the most dominant doctrine.

It is often said that there is a closer relationship between philosophical theories and practice in China than in other lands. Whether this is true or not, it is certainly a fact that the relationship between philosophical doctrines and actual practice in China has been very close indeed. As to why this has been the case, it is sometimes said that the system that has dominated Chinese thought throughout most of Chinese history, namely, Confucianism, is the system that has controlled Chinese education, society, and government for some 2,000 years, and therefore there has been an unusually close affinity between theory and practice. It is also suggested that Chinese philosophers have not been much interested in abstract theories, and have, instead, directed their thinking chiefly to practical problems. There is also the theory that Chinese philosophy is essentially pragmatic and devoid of absolute, inflexible theories and is therefore more easily applicable to human affairs.

There is some element of truth in each of these assertions, but the matter goes much deeper. In order to find an adequate explanation of the practical character of Chinese philosophy, we must understand the Chinese concept of truth. First of all, truth is not understood as something revealed from above or as an abstract principle, however logically consistent, but as a discoverable and demonstrable principle in human affairs. In other words, the real test of truth is in human history. Therefore, when Confucius (551–479 B.C.) frequently referred to the legendary Sage-Emperors Yao and Shun and when he repeatedly looked to the past, he was looking for historical evidence of truth. If that was conservatism, it was only incidental to that search. The fact that China has had a long and continuous history in which Confucianism has had a long and continuous domination makes the belief in the close relationship between theory and practice all the more certain. In the history of Chinese philosophy, there has been a continuing controversy over the question whether principles are transcendent to or immanent in events. Roughly speaking, the school of Chu Hsi (1130–1200), which represents the rationalistic wing of Neo-Confucianism, insists that principles are inherent in things and events, while the school of Wang Yang-ming (Wang Shou-jen, 1472–1529), which represents the idealistic wing of Neo-Confucianism, insists that principles are inherent in the mind. However, they both agree that the validity of principles can be tested only in actual events. As a matter of fact, Chinese philosophers generally do not distinguish between reality and actuality. From the point of view of technical philosophy, this Chinese position lacks refinement, but the Chinese spirit of stressing the affinity of theories and practical affairs is clear.

Since truth can be discovered and tested only in events—and that means chiefly human events—it follows that the records of truth are found in historical documents. Confucius repeatedly looked to such records, whether written or not. Eventually these records came to constitute what may be called the Chinese Canon, notably the Four Books and the Five Classics.[1] It is generally understood that these Classics are the foundation stones of Confucian teachings. It is not so generally understood, however, that they have been regarded by most Confucians as histories also. They are not merely histories of changing human events but histories of events as the unfolding and functioning of eternal principles. The Chinese word for Classics, "ching," means constancy, that is, what is immutable and invariable. As Dr. Hu Shih has aptly remarked, the Chinese Classics have served China as a Natural Law, for they have exercised supreme authority over government, society, religion, and other aspects of Chinese culture.[2] Historically, the Classics were set up as authority by Confucian scholars in the second century B.C. for the purpose of checking the power of the emperor. They were advanced as the highest authority, even over and above that of the sovereign, whose power had been supposed to be absolute. In 124 B.C., a national university was established with five colleges corresponding to the Five Classics, each with fifty nationally prominent scholars attached to it. The simpler of the Four Books were required as texts in school education. From the beginning of the fourteenth century, the Classics were accepted as standard texts for the civil service examinations, on the basis of which civil officials were selected. Until 1905 they were regarded as the norm for all aspects of life. As such, they have provided China with a set of standards which are open to discussion and examination at all times. They have maintained the unity and harmony of Chinese culture and life for a remarkably long period. Most important of all, they have been living testimonies of the conviction that truth finds its validity primarily in history, and, as a Confucian would say, "can wait a hundred generations for a sage [to confirm it] without doubt." [3] At the same time, they grew to be so powerful as to dominate Chinese thought, restrict creative philosophical thinking, and discourage intellectual variety. At times, their study even degenerated into pure scholasticism. There can be no doubt that the belief in the supreme authority of the Classics delayed the advent of both the intellectual renaissance and natural science in China.

The fact that the Classics have been accepted as the highest standards for human activity implies that the eternal truths which they embody are essentially moral. This is another important aspect of the Chinese concept of truth. The Natural Law covers all events, so that all events, whether human or natural, have a moral character. When the Confucian of the second century B.C. advocated a philosophy of correspondence between political events and astronomical phenomena, they were not believers in astrology. To a great extent they were politically motivated, for they purposely utilized certain objective laws and events to control the emperor. Behind this political activity, however, there was the fundamental conviction about truth, that it is essentially moral. That is to say, all truths, whether evident in Nature or in human history, are meant for the purpose of moral cultivation. The Chinese make no absolute distinction between physical things and human activities, both being represented by the word "*shih.*" (Only the Whiteheadian term "event" approximates this word.) They both obey the same set of laws, of which the Moral Law is considered the ultimate. As a result, there has been very little discussion on the problem of truth and falsehood but much discussion on the problem of good and evil. In fact, the question of good and evil has been one of the most important in philosophical inquiry throughout Chinese history, whether in Confucianism, Taoism, or Buddhism. On the transcendental level, Buddhism denies the distinction between good and evil. Taoism to some extent does the same. And, under the influence of Buddhism and Taoism, Neo-Confucianism made similar assertions. But Chinese philosophers have been quick to add that the having of no distinction of good and evil in the transcendental state is itself good. As Ch'eng Hao's (Ch'eng Ming-tao, 1032–1085) famous saying has it, "Good and evil are natural principles. What is called evil is not originally evil." [4] And Chu Hsi added, "All natural principles are good." [5] It is significant to note that the term "*shih-fei*" (true or false) almost invariably has moral connotations.

However, it is not enough simply to read the Classics and learn the moral truths contained therein. Truth comes to life only when it is genuinely and concretely realized by one's person through actual polishing and training in human affairs. This is the concept of *t'i-jen,* or personally realizing and witnessing truth, a term that defies simple translation. It involves a critical and rational understanding of things, a personal conviction as to their meaning and significance, and, finally, an intuition of their ultimate reality. Such realization can come about only after rich experience in human affairs. One of the strongest advocates of such realization was the idealistic Neo-Confucian Wang Yang-ming. He was no Meditation Buddhist in Confucian disguise, as has been charged, for he always insisted that realization must be preceded by "always be doing something." [6] To him, ultimate truth is to be realized in the midst of human affairs and can be understood only in the light of human affairs. Of course, Wang, Ch'eng, and Chu were all talking about moral truths. But, then, to most Chinese philosophers, no truth is amoral.

This close relation between truth and experience is expressed in yet another concept, namely, the close relation between action and words. Confucius was one of the very first Chinese thinkers to lay equal emphasis on both. He always insisted that words and actions should correspond. He said, "I listen to a person's words and watch his action." [7] He also said, "What the superior man says can be carried out." [8] In *The Doctrine of the Mean* it is said, "A superior man's words correspond to his action, and his action corresponds to his words." [9] The whole doctrine of the rectification of names in ancient Chinese philosophy, as well as the whole extensive discussion on the correspondence between names and actuality [10] in ancient China, was ethical in intent rather than epistemological or metaphysical. In the entire Neo-Confucian movement, this equal emphasis on words and action was faithfully maintained. According to Ch'eng I (Ch'eng I-ch'uan, 1033–1107) and his elder brother, Ming-tao, efforts for the extension of knowledge (of which words are but expressions) and actual demonstration are to be exerted simultaneously. [11] Chu Hsi said, "Knowledge and action always require each other. It is like a person who cannot walk without legs although he has eyes and who cannot see without eyes although he has legs. With respect to order, knowledge comes first, and, with respect to importance, action is more important." [12] Again, he said, "The efforts of both knowledge and action must be exerted to the utmost. As one knows more clearly, he acts more earnestly, and, as he acts more earnestly, he knows more clearly." [13] The final result was Wang Yang-ming's famous doctrine of the unity of knowledge and action. He said, "Knowledge is the crystallization of the will to act, and action is the task of carrying out that knowledge; knowledge is the beginning of action, and action is the completion of knowledge." [14] Wang is usually credited with the innovation of the doctrine, but, while he was the first one to identify knowledge and action, the stress on their equal importance, and by implication on their mutual involvement, is an ancient one. Actually, in all this emphasis on the equality or identity of knowledge and action, the stress has always been on the side of action. This tradition can be traced to *The Book of History*, where it is said, "It is not difficult to know but difficult to act." [15] It was continued by Confucius, who taught that "the superior man acts before he speaks and afterwards speaks according to his actions." [16] We have already noted that to Chu Hsi action is more important than knowledge. When Sun Yat-sen turned the ancient doctrine around and said that "it is difficult to know but easy to act," he was really upholding the long tradition of emphasizing action.

From the above it is clear that in the Chinese tradition theories and practice have been thought of as complementary, interdependent, mutually penetrating, and even identical. Along with this conviction, or perhaps because of it, several significant developments have taken place in the history of Chinese thought. One is that in traditional China philosophy never became a separate discipline of study. This discipline came into existence only as a result of Western influence. Not that there has been no metaphysics. Neo-Taoist philosophy and much of Buddhist philosophy are highly metaphysical. But they are outside the main currents of Chinese thought. In the major tradition, philosophy was not set aside as an independent discipline but was regarded as a study of all human affairs in all their connections and ramifications. The word for philosophy, "che," means the same as the Greek "sophia." Etymologically it consists of the "mouth" and the "hand" (or the axe) as integral parts, thus suggesting words and action. But we are not sure of this etymology. At any rate, philosophy has been understood basically as wisdom. Among the Confucian Classics, the book that corresponds to philosophy is *The Book of Changes,* which was originally used for divination. To interpret Chinese philosophy as an outgrowth of ancient oracles is to miss the essential point. The connection between Chinese philosophy and divination has nothing to do with supernaturalism or revelation. Rather, divination performed the function of philosophy in early Chinese society because divination was a search for decisions for action, which is the very purpose of Chinese philosophy as the Chinese have understood it. In short, philosophy is dedicated to everyday life and ordinary action. Consequently, the Chinese did not develop a special terminology for philosophy different from everyday language and beyond the understanding of the simple man. As *The Doctrine of the Mean* puts it, the Way of the superior man "can be understood by the men and women of simple intelligence." [17] Major terms such as "*li*" (principle), "*ch'i*" (material force or matter-energy), "*yin,*" "*yang,*" "*jen*" (humanity), and so forth are ordinary words connected with various aspects of life, including art, government, medicine, and even cooking. To be sure, the Neo-Taoists and Buddhists used very technical philosophical terms, and some terms, e.g., "*ch'i,*" can become very technical, but they are exceptions rather than the rule.

Another interesting development parallel with or growing out of the close relation between theories and practice is that, aside from a few philosophers, notably Chuang Tzu (b. 369 B.C.), the

Taoist Kuo Hsiang (d. A.D. 312), and Neo-Taoist and Buddhist philosophers, all have been men active in social and political affairs. Confucius was, of course, the one who set the pattern. As was said of him, "If for three months he was not in government employment he would be at a loss," [18] so anxious was he for an active life. From Tung Chung-shu (*ca.* 176–104 B.C.) through Chu Hsi down to K'ang Yu-wei (1857–1927), with only a few exceptions, all prominent scholars have been active public figures. A typical case is that of Wang Yang-ming. After he started his public career at twenty-eight, all the rest of his life, with the exception of seven or eight years, was devoted to government service—as a magistrate, a governor, or a military governor suppressing several rebellions, and so forth. In our own day, Chinese philosophers have been intimately involved in social and political movements.

Because Chinese philosophers have emphasized action more than words, and because they themselves were dedicated to social and political action, few have shut themselves up in an ivory tower to write long treatises on philosophy or any theoretical subject. This explains the scarcity of such materials in the huge body of Chinese literature. More often than not, they have propounded their doctrines in conversations, letters, and official documents. Hence, the teachings of Confucius, Lao Tzu, and others are found in conversations. Books like the *Chuang Tzu* seem to consist of systematic essays. Actually, they are a series of conversations. The two most important works of Ch'eng Hao are his "Ting-hsing shu" (On Calming Human Nature) and "Shih-jen p'ien" (On Understanding *Jen* [Humanity]).[19] The former is part of a letter, and the latter is a conversation. Similarly, the most important piece of work by Wang Yang-ming is his *Records of Instructions for Practical Living*, which is recorded dialogues, especially the essay on "Pulling up the Root and Stopping up the Source," which is part of a letter included in the *Records*.[20] The source of Chu Hsi's philosophy is his conversations, recorded and published in 140 chapters.

These facts, that Chinese Philosophy finds its being and expression in the common life and common speech of the Chinese, that most Chinese philosophers have been active men, and that their philosophical works have been chiefly writings connected with actual living, should convince us that the close relationship between theories and practice is not just a conviction in China but a demonstrated fact. However, we need to examine at least one basic doctrine and see how it has actually been applied to practical affairs. In order to do so, we must find the most representative doctrine, one that has been prevalent over a long period of time and has been characteristic not only of Confucianism but of Taoism and Buddhism as well. Fortunately, such a doctrine is not difficult to find. Most students of Chinese thought will immediately mention humanism, for humanism is evident in all aspects of Chinese life, is characteristic of all three traditional systems, and has prevailed in China for many centuries.

The emergence of man as of supreme importance took place very early in Chinese history, probably before Confucius. During the Shang Dynasty (1751–1112 B.C.), spiritual beings exercised direct control over men and their affairs. By the Chou period (1111–249 B.C.), however, their influence gradually declined. The Mandate of Heaven, by which a ruler obtained his power to rule, used to be absolute but now came to be looked upon with misgiving. "The Mandate of Heaven is not constant," an early Chou poet declared.[21] He also said, "Never mind your ancestors! Cultivate your virtue." [22] The new emphasis was now on man and his moral character. The emphasis on human virtue instead of on the powers of spirits or the might of the Lord-on-High represented a radical transition from the Shang to the Chou. The conquest of the Shang must have required a great deal of ingenuity and ability, and the importance of man could not have failed to impress thinking men. New talents were needed for new trades and the building of new towns. Thus, the role of man became greater and greater. The time finally came when a slave became a prime minister. By 645 B.C., a prime minister had declared that "the way of Heaven is far away and the way of man is near," [23] and, in 547 B.C., some famous words were uttered that were to become the established expression for the traditional Chinese concept of immortality. "The best is to establish virtue," so went the words, "the next best is to establish achievement, and still the next best is to establish words. When these are not abandoned with time, it may be called immortality." [24]

It was Confucius, of course, who brought Chinese humanism to its climax. When he was asked about knowledge, he said it was to know man.[25] When he was asked about serving spirits, he answered, "If you cannot serve man, how can you know to serve spirits?" [26] When he was asked about wisdom, he said it was "to attend to the welfare of the people." [27] Confucius was so concerned with man that, when a stable was burned down, he asked only if any person was hurt and did not ask about the horses.[28] In government, he shifted its center from the rulers to the people, urging the feeding and educating of the people as the primary functions of government.[29] The traditional concept of the superior man meant superiority in blood, for the term *"chün-tzu"* literally meant sons of rulers. Confucius changed it to mean superiority in character. This radical change in concept practically amounted to a social revolution, and it definitely contributed to the steady decline of feudalism, which finally collapsed in the third century B.C. The climax of humanism can be summed up in this celebrated saying of Confucius: "It is man that can make the Way great and not the Way that can make man great." [30] His humanism is complete.

At this point we must immediately add that Confucian humanism does not imply in the least that the Supreme Being is either non-existent or unimportant. When he said, "Respect the spirits but keep them at a distance," [31] he merely wanted people to solve their own problems and direct their own destiny instead of depending on spirits or ancestors. Confucius clearly said that the superior man stands in awe of Heaven.[32] He said that at fifty he knew the will of Heaven.[33] While genuinely believing in a Supreme Being, Confucianism unmistakably teaches that man is the center of things.

It may be objected that, while Confucianism is unmistakably humanistic, Taoism is certainly naturalistic and Buddhism otherworldly. No one can deny naturalism in Taoism or otherworldliness in Buddhism. It is not generally realized, however, that both Taoism and Buddhism are humanistic also. It may be surprising, but it is true.

On the surface, the *Lao Tzu* (*Tao-te ching*) seems to teach withdrawal from the human world. Actually, at least a third of the book deals with the art of governing, including a few chapters on military operations.[34] Chuang Tzu did say that "man, compared to the myriad things, is like the tip of a hair upon a horse's skin." [35] He also urged us "not to violate the Way with the human heart or to assist Nature with man." [36] But three of the seven so-called "inner" chapters of the *Chuang Tzu*, which are considered to be the authentic chapters, deal with the mundane world, the ideal teacher, and the ideal ruler. The ideal being, to him as to Lao Tzu, is the sage, and is not one who withdraws from the human world. He takes no action (*wu-wei*), but, according to Kuo Hsiang, "By taking no action is not meant folding one's arms and closing one's mouth." [37] He also said, "Although the sage is in the midst of government, his mind seems to be in the mountain forest. . . . His abode is in the myriad things, but it does not mean that he does not wander freely." [38] His ideal is what the Taoists have called "sageliness within and kingliness without." [39] This ideal was accepted in later Confucianism as well. By following Nature, then, Taoism simply means to be natural, which does not mean to be any less human. After all, the main theme in the long development of Taoism, both as a philosophy and as a religion, has been the cultivation of a long life, an everlasting life if possible. This theme is prominent in both Lao Tzu and Chuang Tzu, and was even translated into action in the Taoist religion. For centuries, it tried various ways and means, including exercise, diets, medicine, and alchemy, in an effort to prolong life on earth.

As to Buddhism, most people agree that it has its otherworldly aspects. It is important to point out, however, that it was in an intensively humanistic atmosphere that Buddhism entered China and thrived. Consequently, from the very beginning, the Buddha was understood in human terms. In the treatise, "The Disposition of Error" (*Li-huo lun*) by Mou Tzu (second century A.D.?), perhaps the first Chinese treatise on Buddhism, there is repeated emphasis on the Buddha as a man of moral achievements, claiming that he "accumulated many virtues," "aimed at virtue," "was the progenitor of virtue," etc.[40] The Chinese translation for the Buddha's name, Śākyamuni, was "*neng-jen*," literally "the ability to be good." Temples dedicated to him were called "*jen-tz'u*," "temples of goodness."

To be sure, the Buddha has been worshipped in China as a deity. In fact, the Chinese people worship three Buddhas, or, rather, the Buddha in Three Bodies or three aspects. But the most popular Buddhist deity in China has been Avalokiteśvara or Kuan-yin, and Kuan-yin has been almost humanized. In India, from the third to the twelfth century, and in Japan today, he retains his transcendental and heavenly features, but in China he has been devoid of these qualities and has become a human figure, and, from the T'ang period (618–907) on, a woman, or the Goddess of Mercy, "Mother" to millions of devotees. In pictorial representations, the Indian rosaries are still present, but, more often than not, they are carried by a crane, a Chinese symbol for longevity. Kuan-yin holds a flower vase from which all kinds of blessings are poured over all of humanity. And these blessings are not *nirvāṇa*, a world transcending our own, but such human blessings as health, wealth, long life, and, most important of all, children. Instead of sitting in the high heavens looking upon us with compassion, she is likely to be sitting by a bamboo grove, carrying a baby or holding a fish basket. A story was even invented in the eleventh century that she was originally a girl who became a goddess because of her filial piety. Kuan-yin is so close to mankind as to be almost human.

The story of Chinese Buddhism is too complicated to go into here. It is often said, however, that the Pure Land and Meditation schools have provided Chinese Buddhism with a general pattern of practice. It is significant that in both these schools Buddhism has been humanized.

It sounds strange to say that the Pure Land school is humanistic, for to pray to be reborn in paradise means to get away from the human world. Nevertheless, man occupies a central position in this movement. Technically speaking, the school is not indigenous to China, for the doctrine was taught in India and the basic texts are Indian. But in spirit and character it is truly Chinese, and it now exists nowhere else but in China and Japan, in both of which it is the most popular Buddhist sect. While in India rebirth in the Pure Land meant a complete break with earthly life, which was considered a life of suffering, in the Chinese Pure Land school it means an extension of earthly living. There is no deprecation of mundane life. Human relations are continued in the Pure Land. This is why one should transfer his merits to his ancestors, and to the Buddhists this act is considered one of the most meritorious. One cannot help hearing here the ring of a Confucian note.

In the Meditation school the most important tenet is the belief that *buddha*-nature is inherent in one's own mind and that the best means to salvation is to look into one's mind to see *buddha*-nature there. This is what later Buddhists called "directly pointing to the human mind and becoming a *buddha* by seeing one's own nature." The result is the doctrine of salvation by oneself. What is more interesting, salvation is to be achieved here and now. And, most interesting of all, it is to be achieved "in this very body." One cannot help recalling that Confucians have always regarded the body as a gift from parents and, as such, as a sacred trust and therefore to be well taken care of, and, that for centuries, as has already been noted, the Taoists tried many ways to make the body suitable for everlasting life on earth.[41]

From the above it is clear that in China the note of humanism has been strong, not only in Confucianism, but in Taoism and Buddhism also. It is not necessary to argue any further that humanism is the keynote in Chinese thought. That keynote vibrates throughout Chinese history. What we need to do now is to see how this uncompromising humanism has affected Chinese practices and institutions. For this purpose we shall concentrate on two questions: (1) Has man in fact occupied a central position in Chinese institutions? (2) Has man in fact been regarded as important?

With respect to the central position of man in Chinese life, it is significant to note that man, rather than law, has been the controlling factor in Chinese political life. As early as Confucius, man was considered the most important element in government. "The administration of government depends on men," declared the Sage. "Let there be men, and the government will flourish," he said, "but, without men, government will decay and cease." [42] Up to our own time, government in Chinese history has been based on man rather than law or systems. Not that there were no laws or systems, but man was considered the deciding factor. Consequently, government officials were selected through an open competitive civil service examination which resulted in the institution of government by scholar-gentlemen, that is, government by the élite. Generally speaking, the record of these scholar-gentlemen has been a worthy one. It was good enough to be praised and imitated in eighteenth-century Europe. Nevertheless, it has given China a tremendous handicap in her transition from government by men to government by law, and personal considerations in Chinese government have been a curse.

Not only in government but also in art has man been the center in China. From its earliest days, Chinese poetry has been concerned with man's fortune and misfortune, his joys and sorrows, and his family and friends. It is man's sentiments that poets strive to express. This idea is stated more than once in the Classics. In *The Book of History* it is said that "poetry is to express the will." [43] This dictum is repeated in Tso's *Commentary* on *The Spring and Autumn Annals*.[44] And in *The Book of Rites* it is declared that "poetry is to express the will." [45] When Confucius said that the odes can arouse the mind, can help us observe social conditions, can assist us in living as a group, can express our feelings of dissatisfaction, and can help us fulfill the more immediate duty of serving our fathers and the remoter one of serving one's ruler, as well as becoming acquainted with the names of birds, animals, and plants,[46] he was describing the function of Chinese poetry that has been accepted in Chinese history ever since his time. It is true that there have been Nature poetry and religious poetry in China, but they are exceptions rather than the rule. While it has been the convention for poets to devote the first half of a poem to the description of natural scenery, the purpose is chiefly to create a mood for the expression of human sentiments in the latter half.

Like drama in many lands, Chinese drama had a religious origin and, consequently, in its early stages had supernatural characters and supernatural themes. But, as it developed, it quickly gave way to the portrayal of historical events and social life and the expression of sentiments. What is true of Chinese poetry and drama is also true of Chinese music, for it has always been a part of the poetic and dramatic arts.

It may be argued that in Chinese painting man occupies a rather insignificant place. In the traditional classification of painting, landscape and flowers-and-birds precede people-and-things. Landscape is the crowning art of China, in which the fundamental principles of art are embraced and the greatest artistic talents have been immortalized. It is truly the representative art of China. Here man seems to be subordinated to Nature, for human figures are usually very small, often incidental, and sometimes totally absent. This fact has led some Western writers to conclude that man is not important in China.

To understand the true meaning of Chinese landscape painting, however, one must understand its relation to poetry. It is well known to students of Chinese art that in Chinese painting there is poetry and in Chinese poetry there is painting, or, as Kuo Hsi (ca. 1085) put it, "Poetry is formless painting, and painting is poetry in visual form." In short, the two arts are not only related but identical as far as their ultimate functions are concerned. What is their function? It is none other than to express human sentiments of joy and sorrow, happiness and anger, and feelings of peace, nobility, loneliness, and so on. Chinese artists paint landscape for the same reason poets describe scenery in their poems. Their purpose is to refine the feelings, stimulate the mind, and create a mood so that when the reader or onlooker emerges from the mood, he becomes a nobler soul, a loftier spirit, a friendlier neighbor, a more pious son, in short, a better human being. There is no subordination of man to Nature in Chinese landscape painting. Neither is there escape from the human world.

Man is central, not only in Chinese government and the arts, but even in religion, which is supposed to be otherworldly and transcendental. This is not to deny that most Chinese Buddhists aspire to go to paradise, the "Pure Land." But, significantly, one of the most important transformations of Buddhism in China has been the change from the doctrine of salvation in *nirvāna* after death to the doctrine of salvation on earth and "in this very body," as we have pointed out. In spite of its acceptance of Buddhist concepts of heavens and hells, the Taoist religion has always held to the goal of everlasting life on earth. Immortals are believed to inhabit the high mountains. They may ascend to heaven, but, more often than not, they roam this earth and move among men, guiding them and helping them. The center of religion is the human world, where even man's own body becomes important.

These observations are quite general, but they are based on such broad facts as to convince us that man in fact occupies a central place in the various aspects of Chinese culture.

As to the importance of man as such, it is often asked why, if man is so important, has the idea of the individual not been developed in Chinese thought? In answer to this it must be stressed that the Western impression that the individual is undermined in traditional Chinese society comes partly from limited observation of Chinese social and political life and partly from an inadequate understanding of Chinese thought. Since marriage has traditionally been arranged by parents, property held in the name of the family, and for a long time in Chinese history the family, rather than the individual, was treated as a unit, it would seem that China has had no respect for the individual. Furthermore, since both Taoism and Buddhism deny the self and Confucianism teaches obedience, it seems that Chinese thought attaches little importance to the individual as such.

Such observations are superficial. While in traditional China the Chinese has had no personal choice in marriage, he has enjoyed absolute freedom in the choice of religion. There is a general regard for privacy, in religion as in other spheres of life. While property has been held in common, each son has had his inalienable right to inheritance. There was no individual vote guaranteed by a constitution, and yet in village meetings every male adult was a voting member by natural right. In the thirteen-century-long tradition of civil service examinations, the basis for the selection of government officials was individual merit rather than race, creed, economic status, sex, or age.

Whether Buddhism denies the individual is a moot point. However, in the Mahāyāna concept of *nirvāṇa*, it is described in terms of permanence, joy, the ego, and purity. The self is not really denied. Certainly most Chinese Buddhists aspire to individual, eternal existence in paradise. Taoism does advocate "having no self," and teaches that one must lose one's life in order to find it. Yet, the Taoist is the most rugged individualist among the Chinese. He would have as little government as possible. He would not be swayed by fear of other people's opinions. He meditates on Nature, not to overcome himself by it but to enjoy himself therein. Under Taoist influence Nature does seem to dominate in Chinese landscape painting where the human figure is dwarfed in the shadow of majestic mountains and rivers. But it is wrong to say that in Chinese landscape painting man is subjugated by Nature; the perspective is not intended to put man into oblivion, but to purify and harmonize his emotions and make him a better man. As to Confucianism, suffice it to quote from Confucius, who said, "Although the leader of three armies can be captured, the will of a common man cannot be destroyed," [47] and from Mencius, who declared, "All things are complete in the self." [48] Some years ago a group of Oxford scholars, being disturbed by the popular but mistaken belief that the individual was respected in the West but suppressed in the East, examined the idea in all cultures. This is what the editor of the symposium had to say: "It was stated that the individual had been discovered by Christianity. Now, apart from the question of what the Christian religion has done for the individual —admittedly a very great deal—there can be no doubt that the statement is not true to historical facts. The India that produced Buddhism, not to speak of the greater part of the *Bhagavadgita*, in the centuries before the Christian era, had plainly been awake to the individual and his soul. In China, from the fifth century [B.C.] on, there were remarkable discoveries made by all sorts of thinkers as to the nature of personality and its value to society." [49]

Actually, one of China's chief troubles in recent decades has been an excess of individualism. Everyone has his own opinion.

There have been far too many individualists who think they are above society. Teamwork and co-operative enterprise have been conspicuously lacking. This is the type of thing the communists have set out to destroy. The problem is whether they will destroy the individual himself in the process.

However, while the individual is fully considered as important, his importance is not to overshadow that of society. A balance of the two has to be maintained. In fact, the goal of moral discipline is exactly this balance. The highest ethical goal is humanity (*jen*). As Confucius taught, "The man of *jen,* wishing to establish his own character, also tries to help others to succeed." [50] This is an exceedingly important saying, one that is well known to any student of Confucianism. It is important, not only because it is a positive statement of the Golden Rule, but also because it expresses the central Chinese idea that a good man must also be a good member of society. Significantly, the Chinese character for *jen* consists of two parts, one meaning man himself and the other meaning many, that is, society. The interest of the individual and that of society are fully recognized, and so is the necessity of their adjustment. A basic institution has existed for centuries for this purpose, namely, the family. Among the functions of the family, surely one of the most important is its position as the intermediate point between the individual and the larger society. It is here that one is trained in the adjustments he will have to make throughout life as between himself and other men. This is the reason harmony has been stressed as a cardinal virtue for the family. How well the Chinese have succeeded in maintaining the balance between the individual and society and whether the family should continue to be the training ground for this adjustment in a modern democracy are important and interesting questions for discussions.

So far as our immediate question is concerned, the above observations cannot fail to lead to the conclusion that Chinese philosophy and practical affairs have been close both in theory and in fact.

In summary, from the Chinese concepts that truth can be discovered and tested only in events, that eternal truths are essentially moral, and that action and words are virtually identified, and from the fact that these concepts have resulted in humanism as the dominant system of Chinese thought, we are forced to the conclusion that Chinese philosophy and practical affairs have been close both in theory and in fact.

QUESTION: In your paper you have discussed Buddhism and Taoism at some length, and their place in Chinese life and thought is recognized. Nevertheless, it is hard to avoid the feeling that you have considered Confucianism the dominant system in Chinese history. Does this agree with the usual saying that the three systems of Confucianism, Buddhism, and Taoism have prevailed in parallel throughout much of Chinese history?

ANSWER: It is difficult to measure the influence of philosophical systems. Surely Taoism has exercised tremendous influence on Chinese art, religion, government, and philosophy of life, and Buddhism has contributed substantially to Chinese religion, philosophy, and art, especially sculpture. But there is no question that Confucianism, or, rather, Neo-Confucianism, has been the dominant system in China during the last 800 years. It has been the controlling system so far as government, education, literature, society, ethics, and non-institutional religion are concerned. It went through many phases and has various aspects, but its fundamental tenets have remained throughout the centuries. In all these, both Buddhism and Taoism have played a secondary role. Furthermore, the metaphysics, espistemology, and psychology of medieval Buddhism and Taoism were assimilated into Confucianism to constitute Neo-Confucianism in the eleventh and twelfth centuries. Finally, there has been no significant Buddhist or Taoist development in the last 800 years in institutions or in thought.

QUESTION: You have emphasized the Confucian teaching of correspondence between theory and practice, and yet it seems that Confucius taught occasional departure from theory. In *Analects* XIII. 18, for example, Confucius taught that it is not upright for a son to bear witness against his father's stealing a sheep but upright for him to conceal the misconduct of his father. How do you explain that?

ANSWER: This and other teachings have given rise to the impression that Confucian ethics is relative or determined by circumstances, especially family relatives. This is not true. Actually, Confucians and Neo-Confucians have always strongly stressed eternal moral principles. At the same time, they have been practical enough to take care of special situations. They have done this with the twofold doctrine of standard and expedient. Eternal principles are standard, while special situations require expedient measures. It is standard to be forthright and honest, but in this case it is expedient to conceal the father's misconduct. The reason for this is not to sacrifice moral principles in order to be filial or to submit to the father's will. Rather, it is to sacrifice honesty to preserve the greater value of family harmony. This is permissible as an expedient when small issues are involved, so long as the total human values are preserved. However, when fundamental issues are involved, even family relations must be sacrificed. This is illustrated by the classical example of Confucius' hero, the Duke of Chou (d. 1094 B.C.). He executed his own older and younger brothers who were plotting for the overthrow of the Chou Dynasty. The principle "to annihilate relatives for the sake of great moral principles" (*ta-i mieh-ch'in*) has been a fundamental one in Confucianism.

Notes

1. The Four Books are *The Analects* (*Lun yü*), *The Great Learning* (*Ta hsüeh*), *The Doctrine of the Mean* (*Chung yung*), and *The Book of Mencius* (*Mencius*); and The Five Classics (*wu ching*) are *The Book of History* (*Shu ching*), *The Book of Odes* (*Shih ching*), *The Book of Changes* (*I ching*), *The Book of Rites* (*Li chi*), and the *Spring and Autumn Annals* (*Ch'un ch'iu*).
2. "The Natural Law in the Chinese Tradition," *Natural Law Institute Proceedings*, V (1953), 133–141.
3. *Doctrine of the Mean*, XXIX. For an English translation, see Lin Yutang, ed., *The Wisdom of Confucius* (New York: The Modern Library, 1938), p. 29; also Wing-tsit Chan, *A Source Book in Chinese Philosophy* (hereafter *Source Book*) (Princeton: Princeton University Press, 1963), chap. 5.
4. *I-shu* (Surviving Works), IIA.lb; *Ts'ui-yen* (Pure Words), I.9b, II.13a-b, both in the *Erh-Ch'eng ch'üan-shu* (Complete Works of the Ch'eng Brothers), Ssu-pu pei-yao edition.
5. *Yü-lei* (Classified Conversations), IV.12b.
6. *Ch'uan-hsi lu* (Records of Instructions for Practical Living), secs. 87, 145, 147, 163, 170, 186, 188. For realization, see secs. 31, 66, 76, etc. For a complete English translation of the *Ch'uan-hsi lu*, see Wang Yang-ming, *Instructions for Practical Living, and Other Neo-Confucian Writings by Wang Yang-ming*, Wing-tsit Chan, trans. (New York: Columbia University Press, 1963).
7. *Analects*, V.9. For an English translation, see Arthur Waley, trans., *The Analects of Confucius* (London: George Allen & Unwin Ltd., 1938).

8. *Ibid.*, XIII.4. Similar equal emphasis on words and action is found in *ibid.*, XIV.4; XV.5; XVIII.8.
9. VIII.
10. See Fung Yu-lan, *A History of Chinese Philosophy*, Vol. I (Princeton: Princeton University Press, 1952), pp. 54, 59–63, 173, 204–206, 253–255, 302–311, 323–325, 332–335.
11. *Ts'ui-yen*, I.16.
12. *Chu Tzu ch'üan-shu* (Complete Works of Chu Hsi), III.8a–b.
13. *Ibid.*
14. *Ch'uan-hsi lu*, sec. 5.
15. See James Legge, trans., *The Shoo King* (Hong Kong: Henry Frowde, 1865), p. 258.
16. *Analects*, II.13. See also IV.24; IV.22; XIV.29.
17. XII.
18. *Book of Mencius*, IIIB.3.
19. *I-shu*, IIA.3a–b, and *Wen-chi* (Literary Works), III.1a–b, in the *Erh-Ch'eng ch'üan-shu*. For an English translation of the two essays, see Chan, *Source Book*, pp. 523–526.
20. *Ch'uan-hsi lu*, secs. 142–143.
21. *Book of Odes*, ode no. 235. For an English translation, see Arthur Waley, trans., *The Book of Songs* (New York: Houghton Mifflin Co., 1937).
22. *Ibid.*
23. *Tso chuan* (*Tso's Commentary on The Spring and Autumn Annals*), Duke Chao, 18th year. See James Legge, trans., *The Ch'un-Ts'ew* (Hong Kong: Henry Frowde, 1872).
24. *Ibid.*, Duke Hsiang, 24th year.
25. *Analects*, XII.22.
26. *Ibid.*, XI.11.
27. *Ibid.*, VI.20.
28. *Ibid.*, X.12.
29. *Ibid.*, XIII.9.
30. *Ibid.*, XV.28.
31. *Ibid.*, VI.20.
32. *Ibid.*, XVI.8; see also VI.26; IX.11; XIV.37.
33. *Ibid.*, XII.4.
34. XXXVI, LVII, LXVIII, LXIX, LXXVI.
35. *Chuang Tzu*, XVI; see Herbert A. Giles, trans., *Chuang Tzu, Mystic, Moralist, and Social Reformer* (2nd ed., rev., Shanghai: Kelly and Walsh, 1926), p. 202.
36. *Chuang Tzu*, VI; see Fung Yu-lan, trans., *Chuang Tzu, A New Selected Translation with an Exposition of the Philosophy of Kuo Hsiang* (Shanghai: Commercial Press, 1933), p. 113.

37. Commentary on the *Chuang Tzu,* XI.
38. *Ibid.,* I.
39. *Chuang Tzu,* XXXIII; cf. Giles, *op. cit.,* p. 439.
40. Seng-yu, ed., *Hung-ming chi* (Essays Elucidating the Doctrine), I.1B.2a. Ssu-pu pei-yao edition.
41. For a more extensive discussion on the Chinese humanization of Buddhism, see the writer's article, "Transformation of Buddhism in China," *Philosophy East and West,* VII, Nos. 3 & 4 (October, 1957–January, 1958), 107–116.
42. *Doctrine of the Mean,* XX.
43. See Legge, trans., *Shoo King,* p. 48.
44. Duke Hsiang, 27th year.
45. XIX.
46. *Analects,* XVII.9.
47. *Ibid.,* IX.25.
48. *Book of Mencius,* VIIB.14.
49. E. R. Hughes, ed., *The Individual in East and West* (London: Oxford University Press, 1937), pp. 3–4.
50. *Analects,* VI.28.

WING-TSIT CHAN   *The Story*

of Chinese Philosophy

CHINESE PHILOSOPHY is an intellectual symphony in three movements. The first movement, from the sixth to the second century B.C., was essentially a period of development of the three major themes of Confucianism, Taoism, and Moism, and the four minor ones of the Logicians, Neo-Moism, the Legalists, and Yin-Yang Interactionism, all with their contrasts and harmonies, to the accompaniment of the others of the "Hundred Schools." The second movement was characterized by the intermingling of the different motives which resolved into the dominant chord of medieval Chinese philosophy, while the note of Buddhism was introduced from India, giving it the effect of counterpoint. In the third movement, the longest of all, from the eleventh century to the present day, the characteristic notes of Chinese philosophy have been synthesized to transform the persistent chord of Confucianism into the long and unique melody which is Neo-Confucianism.

This analogy immediately suggests that there is consonance as well as dissonance among the main systems of Chinese thought, a significant fact to note particularly in the case of the ancient schools. The opposition between humanistic Confucianism and naturalistic Taoism is, at first sight, almost irreconcilable. But any complete distinction inevitably distorts the picture. Early Taoism is nearer to Confucianism than is generally understood, especially in its philosophy of life. Contrary to the popular belief that Lao Tzu taught the renunciation of life and society, his ethical doctrine was more akin to that of the world-wise Confucius than to Hinduism or Buddhism. This opinion is neither new nor personal, but a general one among native historians of Chinese philosophy. Both Dr. Hu Shih in his *The Development of the Logical Method in Ancient China* [1] and Professor Fung Yu-lan in his *A History of Chinese Philosophy* [2] interpreted Lao Tzu in a way quite different from that to which the West is accustomed. The main interest of Taoism and Confucianism is life, the chief difference being that in Taoism the preservation of life comes with following Nature, whereas in Confucianism the fulfillment of life comes with the full development of man.

Early Confucianism: Confucius, Mencius, Hsün Tzu, and the Chung yung

The movement of humanism began with Confucius (551–479 B.C.). It gained momentum in Mencius (327–289? B.C.) and Hsün Tzu (313–238? B.C.), and finally reached its climax in Neo-Confucianism. It is a story of more than two thousand years. It is the story of Chinese life and thought. From the time of Confucius to the present day, the chief spiritual and moral inspiration of the Chinese has been the Confucian saying: "It is man that can make the Way great, and not the Way that can make man great." [3]

To say that Confucius was humanistic is not to deny that the Sage showed a reasonable interest in religion. Confucius was, on the one hand, a reformer, a pioneer in universal education for all those who cared to come [4] and for people of all classes,[5] a man who traveled for fourteen years over many states in search of an opportunity to serve the rulers in order that the Moral Law (*Tao*, the Way)[6] might prevail. He was, on the other hand, a conformist, a man who "believed in and loved the ancients,"[7] a man who attempted to uphold the culture of Chou [8] of which the worship of Heaven and ancestors was an integral part. Consequently, he said: "The superior man stands in awe of . . . the Mandate of Heaven." [9] He believed that, "if the Way is to prevail, it is the Mandate of Heaven." [10] He himself offered sacrifices to his ancestors and "felt as if his ancestral spirits were actually present," saying, "If I do not participate in the sacrifice, it is as if I did not sacrifice at all." [11] Nevertheless, he frankly put the welfare of men before religion. His reluctance to discuss Heaven caused his pupils to say that his view of the Way of Heaven "cannot be heard." [12] He "never discussed strange phenomena, physical exploit, disorder, or spirit-

jen - humanity

ual beings." [13] When a pupil asked about serving spiritual beings and about death, he replied, "If we are not yet able to serve men, how can we serve spiritual beings? . . . If we do not yet know about life, how can we know about death?" [14]

From these it is evident that Confucius was a humanist even in religious matters; he was not a priest, much less the founder of the religion bearing his name. Man, and man alone, engaged his primary attention. This can be seen from the following passage:

The ancients who wished to manifest their clear character to the world would first bring order to their states. Those who wished to bring order to their states would first regulate their families. Those who wished to regulate their families would first cultivate their personal lives. Those who wished to cultivate their personal lives would first rectify their minds. Those who wished to rectify their minds would first make their wills sincere. Those who wished to make their wills sincere would first extend their knowledge. The extension of knowledge consists in the investigation of things. When things are investigated, knowledge is extended; when knowledge is extended, the will becomes sincere; when the will is sincere, the mind is rectified; when the mind is rectified, the personal life is cultivated; when the personal life is cultivated, the family will be regulated; when the family is regulated, the state will be in order; and when the state is in order, there will be peace throughout the world.[15]

This is a comprehensive program, but may be summed up in one word, namely, *"jen,"* humanity. This is the central idea in the Confucian system, around which the whole Confucian movement developed. Confucius neither defined nor analyzed *jen*. It is even recorded in *The Analects* (*Lun yü*) that he "seldom" talked about it.[16] Although 55 out of the 498 chapters of *The Analects* are devoted to a discussion of humanity, the Master viewed the matter with such high seriousness that he gave the impression of having seldom discussed the subject.

The statement nearest to a definition of *jen* is that it "consists in mastering oneself and returning to propriety (*li*)." [17] This practically amounts to the entire Confucian philosophy, since *jen*, so defined, involves the realization of the self and the creation of a social order. Specifically, "humanity" consists in "being respectful in private life, being serious in handling affairs, and being loyal in dealing with others." [18] A man "who is strong, resolute, simple, and slow to speak" is "near" to humanity.[19] Again, "One who can practice five things wherever he may be, is humane . . . namely, earnestness, broadness, truthfulness, diligence, and generosity." [20]

"The man of humanity," Confucius said, "wishing to establish his own character, also seeks to establish the character of others. Wishing to succeed, he also seeks to help others succeed." [21] In a word, to be a man of humanity is to "love all men." [22]

Such a man of humanity is what Confucius called the "superior man," who is the combination of "the man of humanity who has no worry, the man of wisdom who has no perplexities, and the man of courage who has no fear." [23] He regards "righteousness as the substance of everything. He practices it according to the principle of propriety. He brings it forth in modesty. And he carries it to its conclusion with faithfulness." [24] He "restrains himself in matters of sex when his blood and vital force are strong. When he reaches maturity and his blood and vital force are full of vigor, he restrains himself in matters of strife. When he reaches old age and his blood and vital force have already weakened, he restrains himself in matters of acquisition." [25] He aims at nine things. "In the use of his eyes, his object is to see clearly. In the use of his ears, his object is to listen distinctly. In expression, his object is to be warm. In appearance, his object is to be respectful. In speech, his object is to be sincere. In handling affairs, his object is to be serious. In doubt, he wishes to ask. In anger, he wishes to think of the resultant difficulties. In the face of gain, he thinks of righteousness." [26] He does not do anything contrary to the principle of propriety,[27] wants to be slow in word but diligent in action,[28] and thinks of righteousness instead of profit.[29] He enjoys the pleasure derived from the due ordering of rituals and music, from talking about the good points of others, and from friendship with many virtuous men.[30] He would give up wealth and rank but endure poverty and mean position for the sake of moral principles.[31] He does not do to others what he does not want others to do to him,[32] "repays hatred with uprightness and repays virtue with virtue." [33] He exercises filial loyalty to his parents, to the point of never disobeying but adhering strictly to the principle of propriety in serving them when they are alive and sacrificing to them when they are dead.[34] He is respectful to his superiors.[35] In short, he is a perfect man.

This emphasis on humanism in Confucius is supreme. It underlies all his political, educational, aesthetic, and even his logical doctrines. People are to be ruled by the good examples of the rulers, guided by virtue, and regulated by the principles of propriety,[36] and the object of government is to bring wealth and education to the people and security to the state.[37] Knowledge is "to know men." [38] The superior man "studies to reach the utmost of the Way." [39] Poems are "to stimulate your emotions, to broaden your observation, to enlarge your fellowship, and to express your grievances." "They help you in your immediate service to your parents and in your more remote service to your ruler. They widen your acquaintance with the names of birds, animals, and plants." [40] Even the "rectification of names," the nearest Confucian approach to logic, is to be carried out along humanistic lines. For example, music does not mean merely bells and drums,[41] for names, when rectified, have a practical flavor. So, to rectify names in a state means: "Let the ruler *be* a ruler, the minister *be* a minister, the father *be* a father, and the son *be* a son." [42]

This humanism is complete. But what is its logical foundation? Confucius said that "there is one thread that runs through my doctrines." [43] This one thread is generally accepted to mean "none other than conscientiousness and altruism." [44] If this interpretation is correct, then we are forced to conclude that the foundation of the Confucian system lies in the moral realm, that is, in human experience itself. The thread is also generally taken to be identical with the Confucian doctrine of central harmony (*chung yung*, Golden Mean). Indeed, this doctrine is of supreme importance in Chinese philosophy; it is not only the backbone of Confucianism, both ancient and modern, but also of Chinese philosophy as a whole. Confucius said that "to be central (*chung*) [in our moral being] and to be harmonious (*yung*) [with all]" is the supreme attainment in our moral life.[45] This seems to suggest that Confucius had as the basis of his ethics something psychological or metaphysical. This was not developed, however, until two centuries later. For Confucius, *chung yung* definitely meant the Golden Mean, as indicated by the saying, "To go too far is the same as not to go far enough." [46] The psychological foundation is to be provided by Mencius and Hsün Tzu, and the metaphysical by the book known as the *Chung yung* (*The Doctrine of the Mean*).

Confucius was interested mainly in a practical world, and therefore taught us how to do good without going into the problem of why we should do good. To Mencius, however, we do good, not only because we *should*, but because we *must*, for "man's nature is naturally good just as water naturally flows downward." [47] "If men do evil, that is not the fault of their natural endowment." [48] All men originally have the feeling of commiseration, the feeling of shame and dislike, the feeling of respect and reverence and dislike, and the feeling of right and wrong, and these are what we call the "four beginnings" of humanity, righteousness, propriety, and wisdom.[49] This moral consciousness is rooted in the heart of all men,[50] which can be demonstrated by the facts that children all know how to love their parents,[51] and that, when men suddenly see a child about to fall into a well, a sense of mercy and alarm is inevitably aroused in their hearts.[52]

This native feeling for the good is "innate ability," which we possess without the necessity of learning, and is also "innate knowledge," which we possess without the necessity of deliberation.[53] Thus, "all things are already complete in oneself. There is no greater joy than to examine oneself and be sincere."[54] For "sincerity is the way of Heaven, whereas to think how to be sincere is the way of man."[55] The guiding principle of human conduct is therefore "the full exercise of one's mind." "To exercise our minds fully is to know our nature, and to know our nature is to know Heaven. To preserve our minds and to nourish our nature is the way to serve Heaven. To maintain singleness of mind whether we suffer premature death or enjoy long life, and to cultivate our personal character and wait for [Heaven's Mandate to take its own course] is the way to fulfill our destiny."[56] Thus the prerequisites of a harmonious moral order are all complete in us. Instead of looking to Nature in order to know ourselves, we look within ourselves in order to know Nature. We do not even have to look to the sage, because we "and the sage are the same in kind."[57] The clue to the centrality and harmony of the universe as well as ourselves is therefore not far to seek. It lies within our nature. To develop out nature is to realize the virtues intrinsic in it, which Mencius first reduced to the "four beginnings," and further to humanity, which is "man's mind," and righteousness, which is "man's path."[58] The former is the ethical basis of society, while the latter is the foundation of politics. The term "humanity" (*jen*) must be understood in its more fundamental meaning of true manhood, for "*jen* is [the distinguishing character] of man. When embodied in man's conduct, it is the Way."[59] The man of humanity does nothing which is not according to humanity.[60] In fact, he loves all men.[61] The most natural demonstration of humanity is loyalty to parents, which to Mencius was the greatest of all virtues.[62] "Of all which a filial son can attain to, there is nothing greater than honoring his parents."[63] Filial piety, then, is the foundation of the five human relationships. "Between father and son there should be affection; between ruler and minister, righteousness; between husband and wife, attention to their separate functions; between old and young, a proper order; and between friends, good faith." [64] When these are demonstrated, a harmonious social order will prevail.

This attempt to provide a psychological foundation for humanism is a significant development in the Confucian school, not only because it marks a great advance, but also because it exerted tremendous influence upon the whole school of Neo-Confucianism, especially from the fourteenth century to the present day.

The psychological development in Hsün Tzu, however, took almost the opposite direction. Not that the humanistic spirit is any weaker in him; on the contrary, it is much stronger. The Way (Tao) is "not the Way of Heaven, nor the way of Earth, but the way followed by man, the way followed by the superior man," [65] and, more specifically, "Tao is the way to rule a state," or, in other words, "to organize the people." [66] Consequently, he vigorously advocated the control of Nature:

> You glorify Nature and meditate on her:
> Why not domesticate her and regulate her?
> You obey Nature and sing her praise:
> Why not control her course and use it?
> You look on the seasons with reverence and await them:
> Why not respond to them by seasonal activities?
> You depend on things and marvel at them:
> Why not unfold your own ability and transform them?
> You meditate on what makes a thing a thing:
> Why not so order things that you may not waste them?
> You vainly seek the cause of things:
> Why not appropriate and enjoy what they produce?
> Therefore, I say, "To neglect man and speculate about Nature
> Is to misunderstand the facts of the universe." [67]

Hsün Tzu believed the control of Nature to be necessary because he found that human nature is sharply different from what Mencius pictured it to be. To Hsün Tzu, "The nature of man is evil; his goodness is the result of activity." [68] The motive here is obviously to emphasize education, an emphasis that made him the outstanding philosopher of education in ancient China. As the original nature of man is evil, he needs "the civilizing influence of teachers and laws." [69] Thus, virtue is not inborn, but is to be "accumulated," just as mountains are formed by accumulation of earth.[70] The guiding principle of accumulation for the individual is *li*, propriety; [71] that for society is the "rectification of names"; [72] and that for the government is "modeling after the latter-day Sage-Kings." [73] When virtue is "accumulated" to a sufficient degree, man then can "form a triad" with Heaven and Earth.[74]

By the end of the fourth century B.C., Confucianism took another step forward. There was an attempt to provide a metaphysical foundation for its humanism, as we can see from *The Doctrine of the Mean (Chung yung)*.[75] According to this book, *chung* (equilibrium, or moral being) is conceived to be "the great foundation of the world" and *yung* (harmony, or moral order) is "the universal path." "When equilibrium and harmony are realized to the highest degree, Heaven and Earth will attain their proper order and all things will flourish." [76] Thus, "the superior man [exemplifies] the *chung yung*." [77]

The Doctrine of the Mean further states that sincerity (*ch'eng*) is "the Way of Heaven," and "to think how to be sincere" is "the way of man." [78] Absolute sincerity is "eternal," "self-existent," "infinite," "vast and deep," "transcendental and intelligent." [79] It contains and embraces all existence; it fulfills and perfects all existence. "Such being its nature, it becomes prominent without any display, produces changes without motion, and accomplishes its end without action." [80] Only those who are "absolutely sincere can fully develop their nature. If they can fully develop their nature, they can then fully develop the nature of others. If they can fully develop the nature of others, they can then fully develop the nature of things . . . they can then assist in the transforming and nourishing process of Heaven and Earth . . . and can thus form a trinity with Heaven and Earth." [81] How original this metaphysical tendency was in Confucius is uncertain, but it became an extremely significant factor in later Confucianism, particularly in the Neo-Confucianism of the eleventh and fifteenth centuries.

Early Taoism: Yang Chu and Lao Tzu

While this movement of Confucian humanism was progressing, naturalistic Taoism developed in parallel, with different ways but similar aims of life. As the goal of Confucianism is the fully developed life, that of Taoism is simple and harmonious life. Although the term "Taoism" was not used until the first century B.C., in the *Shih chi* (Records of the Historian) by Ssu-ma Ch'ien (145–86?

B.C.), the Taoist movement must have been going on for some centuries. But whether Yang Chu or Lao Tzu was the first leader of the movement is a controversial matter.[82] In the case of Yang Chu (*ca. 440–ca. 366* B.C.), the spirit is certainly that of simplicity and harmony. He was not a hedonist who urged all men to "enjoy life" and to be satisfied with "a comfortable house, fine clothes, good food, and pretty women," as the spurious *Lieh Tzu* of the third century A.D. represents him,[83] or an egotist "who would not have plucked out one single hair though he might have benefited the whole world by doing so," as Mencius purposely made him appear to be.[84] He was, rather, a follower of Nature who was mainly interested in "preserving life and keeping the essence of our being intact, and not injuring our material existence with things," [85] "a man who would not enter an endangered city, join the army, or even exchange a single hair for the profits of the entire world." [86] Even in the chapter entitled "Yang Chu" in the *Lieh Tzu*, the main emphasis is to "let life run its course freely," [87] and to ignore, not only riches and fame, but also life and death. It was this naturalistic emphasis that made him the representative Taoist of his time.

In the case of Lao Tzu, the keynote of his *Tao-te ching* (Classic of the Way and Its Virtue) is "simplicity," a central idea by which other apparently strange concepts must be understood. A "simple" life is a life of plainness, in which profit is discarded, cleverness abandoned, selfishness minimized, and desires reduced.[88] It is the life of "perfection which seems to be incomplete" of "fullness which seems to be empty," of "absolute straightness which seems to be crooked," of "skill which seems to be clumsy," and of "eloquence which seems to stutter." It is the life of "producing and rearing things without taking possession of them," and of "leading things but not dominating them." [89] It is the life which is "as pointed as a square but does not pierce, as acute as a knife but does not cut, as straight as an unbent line but does not extend, and as bright as light but does not dazzle." [90]

Other fantastic ideas of Taoism have developed and died, but this is the living factor that has made Taoism a strong fiber of Chinese ethics even today. It is the point of agreement with the most powerful intellectual system of China, namely, Confucianism.

It is true that Lao Tzu was extremely critical of the existing order, even to the point of crying that "when the Great Way (*Tao*) declined, the doctrine of humanity and righteousness arose. When knowledge and wisdom appeared, there emerged great hypocrisy." [91] But he denounced civilization in the same spirit as he attacked war, taxation, and punishment,[92] essentially because of their excessive and destructive character. Lao Tzu was no deserter of civilization. According to authentic historical records, he was a minor governmental official. Hu Shih suggests that he and Confucius were both *ju*, literati of the priest-teacher type, who bore the torch of civilization; that Lao Tzu was an orthodox *ju*, a "*ju* of the meek," who clung to the culture of the conquered people of Yin, which was characterized by non-resistance, contentment, etc., whereas Confucius, in spite of the fact that he was a descendant of Yin, was a *ju* of a new type, a "*ju* of the strong," who advocated the replacement of the degenerating Yin culture by the growing culture of the ruling people of Chou.[93] Thus, we must look at Lao Tzu as a teacher of simple living rather than as a forsaker of life.

It is also true that Lao Tzu taught the strange doctrine of *wu-wei*, generally interpreted as "inaction." But it is a mistake to think of *wu-wei* as anything suggesting complete inactivity, renunciation, or the cult of unconsciousness. It is, rather, a peculiar way, or, more exactly, the natural way, of behavior. "The sage manages affairs without action, and spreads doctrines without words." [94] The natural way is to "support all things in their natural state" and thus allow them to "transform spontaneously." [95] In this manner, "The Way invariably takes no action, and yet there is nothing left undone." [96] "The sage-ruler acts without action, and thus all things will be in order." [97] From this it is quite clear that the way of *wu-wei* is the way of spontaneity, to be contrasted with the artificial way, the way of cleverness and superficial morality. It was the life of artificiality that drew Lao Tzu's vigorous attack and led him to glorify the reality of the non-existent, the utility of the useless, and the strength of the weak.[98]

This represents no effort to replace being with non-being, or the strong with the weak. It is, rather, an affirmation of the importance of both. "Eternal non-being" and "eternal being" are "the same" but "have different names." [99] The truly weak is identical with the truly strong. As Lao Tzu said, "What is most perfect seems to be incomplete," and "What is most full seems to be empty." [100] In these utterances, Lao Tzu was even a step nearer to the Golden Mean. On the surface, he seems to be the champion of the female as the fundamental principle of life, and of infancy as the ideal state of being.[101] He also seems to advocate emptiness and quietude.[102] At bottom, however, his ethical position comes much nearer to the center than to the extreme. Since "much talk will, of course, come to a dead end, it is better to keep to the center." [103]

The main difference between Lao Tzu and Confucius lies in the fact that, while with Confucius the measure of all things is man, with Lao Tzu it is Nature. Simplicity, *wu-wei*, and other ethical ideas are all moral lessons drawn from Nature, which is the standard for Heaven and Earth as well as for man.[104] It is the Way, *Tao*, the universal principle of existence. It is "the origin of Heaven and Earth" and "the mother of all things." [105] It is eternal, one, all-pervasive, and absolute.[106] Above all, it is natural.[107]

As reality is natural, so must our life be. To be natural is to live like water, which is "similar to the highest good" and so "near to *Tao*." [108] Water "dwells in places which people detest," but "it benefits all things and does not compete with them." [109] "There is nothing softer and weaker than water, and yet there is nothing better for attacking hard and strong things." [110] The idealization of infancy is nothing more than the idealization of the natural state. It is not the state of ignorance and incapability. It is, rather, a state of quietude, harmony, and insight. Above all, it is the state of life.

"*Tao* produced the One. The One produced the two. The two produced the three. And the three produced the ten thousand things. The ten thousand things carry *yin* [the passive or female principle] and embrace *yang* [the active or male principle], and through the blending of the vital force (*ch'i*) produces harmony." [111] To know this harmony is called "the Eternal," and to know the Eternal is called "enlightenment." [112] Lao Tzu said:

Attain complete vacuity.
Maintain steadfast quietude.
All things come into being, and I see thereby their return.
All things flourish, but each one returns to its root.
This return to its root means tranquillity;
It is called returning to its destiny.
To return to destiny is called the Eternal.
To know the Eternal is called enlightenment.
Not to know the Eternal is to act blindly, to result in disaster.
He who knows the Eternal is all-embracing
Being all-embracing, he is impartial.
Being impartial, he is kingly (universal).
Being kingly, he is one with Nature.
Being one with Nature, he is in accord with Tao.
Being in accord with Tao, *he is everlasting,*
And is free from danger throughout his lifetime.[113]

This is perhaps the most comprehensive passage in the *Tao-te ching*. We must note that the climax of the whole procedure is to be "free from danger throughout one's lifetime." Here we have the humanistic flavor of naturalism. Life is not to be abandoned but to be made secure and valuable. The greatness of *Tao* is perfect primarily because it never considers itself great.[114] "He who is contented suffers no disgrace. He who knows when to stop is free from danger. Therefore he can long endure."[115] It is "only those who are not seeking after life that excel in making life valuable."[116] In short, the philosophy of Lao Tzu can be summed up by his phrase "the way of long life and everlasting vision."[117]

When this emphasis on a simple and harmonious life in Taoism is understood, we are in a position to see why this naturalistic and atheistic philosophy should have been made the foundation of a superstitious religion in medieval China, which was notorious for its practice of alchemy and belief in immortals. The simple reason is that the primary motive of the corrupt Taoist religion was to search for longevity. The effect of the movement was that man took more and more to a negative philosophy, losing confidence in himself as well as in a progressive social order. Such an attitude was diametrically opposed not only by Confucianism but by Moism as well.

Moism, The Logicians, and Neo-Moism

As in Confucianism, the main interest of Moism is man. Instead of the general and vague "humanity," however, Mo Tzu (468–376? B.C.) advocated the welfare of men. "Promote general welfare and remove evil" became the motto of the whole Moist movement.[118] Mo Tzu was so much opposed to the Confucian empty talk of "rituals and music" that he entirely rejected them in favor of "benefits" in terms of population and wealth. "Ancient kings, dukes and great officials," he said, "in the administration of their states all aimed at wealth for the country and a great population."[119] Consequently, he insisted that "men should marry at twenty and women at fifteen,"[120] and it was on the ground of population that he denounced war. Military expeditions, he said, break up family life and result in the decrease of population.[121] He strongly advocated economy of expenditure.[122] He attacked elaborate funerals and music, not on the basis of morality or decorum, as Confucius would, but on a strictly utilitarian basis. "The practice of elaborate funerals and extended mourning inevitably results in poverty for the nation, in reduction of population, and in disorder of government." [123] By the same token, music enjoyed by the rulers leads to heavy taxes, interferes with farming and other productive enterprises by taking musicians away from their occupations, and wastes the time of government officials.[124]

Our practical philosopher arrived at this utilitarian humanism, not merely as a reaction against the formalistic tendency of Confucius, but also as a result of his scientific method. "For any doctrine," he said, "some standard must be established. . . . Therefore, for any doctrine there must be three standards. . . . There must be a basis or foundation; there must be an examination; and there must be practical application. How find the basis? Find it in the experiences of the ancient Sage-Kings above. How is it to be examined? By inquiring into the actual experience of the eyes and ears of the people below. How apply it? Put it into law and governmental measures and see if they bring about benefits to the state and the people." [125]

Instead of attempting to direct and regulate experience by a central principle such as the "central harmony" of Confucius or the *Tao* of Lao Tzu, this utilitarian philosopher chose to arrive at a general principle through a comprehensive survey of actual experience. Whether there is fate or not, for example, must be determined by the actual experience of the eyes and ears of the people. "If people have seen or heard it, I shall say that there is fate. If none has seen or heard it, I shall say that there is no fate." [126] Although this positivism sounds crude, the practical and objective character of Mo Tzu's philosophy is unmistakable.

This practical character carries with it a pragmatic flavor, because utility and choice are held to be the guiding principles for value and conduct and even for truth. "The reason why Mo Tzu censures music is not because the sound of bells, drums, harps, and flutes is unpleasant . . . but because it does not contribute to the promotion of general welfare and the removal of evil." [127] By the same token, "All activities that are beneficial to Heaven, the spirits, and men" are to be fostered as "heavenly virtues," whereas "all words and deeds that are harmful to them" are to be looked upon as an "enemy." [128] There can be nothing that is good but not useful.[129] The value of such virtues as loyalty and filial piety is their "great benefit" to all people.[130]

Thus, value in Moism is limited to "benefits," and every value is to be appraised in terms of its ability to "promote welfare and remove evil." A good life and a well-ordered society depend primarily on a right choice of such values. "A blind man cannot distinguish black and white, not because he is ignorant of their definitions, but because he cannot choose between them." Similarly, "the superior men of the world do not know what humanity really is, not because they do not know its definition, but because of their failure to choose." [131]

To test the utility of a value, it must be put to application to see whether it actually contributes to the "promotion of welfare and removal of evil." The fundamental principle of this application is the famous Moist doctrine of universal love, which aims at the greatest amount of happiness for the greatest number of people through people's "loving one another and benefiting one another." [132] "This is," Mo Tzu declared, "the principle of the ancient Sage-Kings and of the general welfare of men." [133] Lack of it is the cause of social disorder.[134] So, let everyone "treat other countries as his own, treat other families as his own, and treat other people as he treats himself." [135] It is interesting to note that even this principle is not free from utilitarian flavor, for at least one of the reasons for this benevolent doctrine is a utilitarian one, namely, "Those who love others will be loved." [136]

It is obvious that the foundation of such a utilitarian philosophy cannot be sought in any internal sanction. Instead, it is to be sought in "the experience of the wisest men of the past." This reverence for the past in no way undermines the practical spirit of the Moist philosophy. Rather, it enhances it, for, according to Mo Tzu, "The governmental measures of the ancient Sage-Kings were designed to revere Heaven, to serve the spirits, and to love men." [137]

Another sanction, the religious one, also sounds the note of practical interests. "If everybody believes in the power of the spirits to bless the good and condemn evil, there will be no disorder." [138] This belief, when applied to the state and the people, "becomes a principle of restoring order to the state and promoting the welfare of the people." [139] It was because of this practical efficacy of religion that Mo Tzu became its chief defender in ancient China, more so even than Confucius. One may not accept the theory that Mo Tzu founded a religion, and that his followers organized a religious order of some sort. One cannot deny, however, that Mo Tzu went further than Confucius in the attempt to preserve a religious system. While Lao Tzu definitely tended toward the left and Confucius adhered to the "Golden Mean" in the belief in the supernatural, Mo Tzu unmistakably represented the right. We may safely say, however, that the criterion of the Moist religious belief was again human interest, for Mo Tzu said, "I do whatever Heaven wishes me to do; and Heaven does whatever I wish Him to do." [140]

Just how the Moist school developed after Mo Tzu is still a matter of controversy. There is some evidence that it became a religious order. But another aspect of its development, its logical tendency, known as Neo-Moism, is of more interest to us. The Neo-Moists, who flourished in the fourth and third centuries B.C., sought to establish their practical philosophy on a logical foundation, and, in doing so, they found it necessary to refute the sophistry of Hui Shih (380-305? B.C.), Kung-sun Lung (b. 380? B.C.), and other Logicians. The former expressed his ideas in such paradoxes as: "The greatest has nothing beyond itself: it is called the Great Unit. The smallest has nothing within itself: it is called the Little Unit." "The sun begins to set at noon; a thing begins to die at birth." "I go to Yüeh today and arrived there yesterday." [141] Hui Shih and his group were even more sophistical, and claimed: "The egg has feathers." "A fowl has three legs." "Wheels never touch the ground." "The shadow of a flying bird never moves." "A swiftly fleeting arrow sometimes does not move and sometimes does not rest." "A brown horse and a dark ox make three." "If a rod one foot in length is cut short every day by one half of its length, it can never be exhausted even after ten thousand generations." [142] Kung-sun Lung further asserted: "A white horse is not a horse," because "the word 'horse' denotes the term and the word 'white' denotes the color." "A horse is not conditioned by any color, and therefore both a yellow horse and a black one may answer. A white horse, however, is conditioned by color. . . ." [143] He propounded the theory that all things are "marks," designations or predicates,[144] and that the qualities of solidity and whiteness are independent of the substance of the stone.[145] The main interest of the Logicians lay in such concepts as space and time, potentiality and actuality, motion and rest, the general and the particular, and substance and quality. In short, the whole movement of the Logicians represented an interest in knowledge for its own sake, an interest not at all in harmony with the keen interest in life of Taoism, Confucianism, and Moism alike. It is no wonder that the Logicians became the target of attack by all of them.[146]

But the Neo-Moists, in order to maintain their practical interest in the face of the intellectualism of the Logicians, had to make their own logical system strong enough to defend their utilitarian philosophy. Consequently, they wrote the Neo-Moist Canon in the form of definitions, propositions, notes, and proofs, now incorporated in the *Mo Tzu*.[147] They developed seven methods of argumentation: "possibility," "hypothesis," "imitation," "comparison," "parallel," "analogy," and "induction." [148] They classified names into three classes, "general, generic, and private." [149] They discovered the "method of agreement," which includes "identity, generic relationship, co-existence, and partial resemblance"; the "method of difference," which includes "duality, absence of generic relationship, separateness, and dissimilarity"; and the "joint method of differences and similarities." [150] "Identity means that two substances have one name, while generic relationship means inclusion in the same whole. Both being in the same room is a case of co-existence, whereas partial resemblance means having some points of resemblance. . . . Duality means that two things necessarily differ. Absence of generic relationship means to have no connection. Separateness means that things do not occupy the same space. Dissimilarity means having nothing in common." [151] They defined a model as "That according to which something becomes," [152] and explained that "the concept of a circle, the compass, and the actual circle . . . all may be used as a model." [153] They rejected the theory of the Logicians that solidity and whiteness and stone are three. On the contrary, they maintained that solidity and whiteness are in the stone,[154] and that the two qualities are not mutually exclusive.[155]

While it is significant that the Neo-Moists refused to tolerate distinctions such as that of quality and substance, an equally important point is that knowledge is power. To the Neo-Moists, knowing means "to meet." [156] Whether it takes the form of "understanding," [157] "learning," "inference," or "searching," [158] its end is conduct.[159] The function of knowledge is to guide man in his behavior, especially in the intelligent "choice" between pleasure and pain. "If a man wants to cut off his finger, and his knowing faculty is not aware of its harmful consequences, it is the fault of his knowing faculty. If he knows the harmful consequences and is careful about it, he will not be injured. But, if he still wants to cut off his finger, then he will suffer." [160] But, "when one cuts off a finger to preserve the hand, that is to choose the greater benefit and to choose the lesser harm." [161] By such intelligent "choice," the Moist "promotion of general welfare and removal of evil" may be carried out.

It is unfortunate that this logical movement died almost in its infancy, and thus deprived China of a disinterested, analytical, and scientific system of logic on which metaphysics and epistemology might have been built. However, the overwhelming interest in human affairs was not the only factor that prevented the growth of intellectualism. There was a strong anti-intellectual movement in China in the fourth century B.C., the best representative of which was Chuang Tzu.

Chuang Tzu and the Yin-Yang School

In both the moralistic humanism of the Confucian school and the utilitarian humanism of the Moists, the intellect enjoyed a rightful place. It is true that Lao Tzu condemned knowledge in no uncertain terms, but "enlightenment" in the *Tao-te ching* is contrasted with cleverness and deceit. By the time of Chuang Tzu (b. 369? B.C.) it was developed to the point of almost complete unconsciousness. In Chuang Tzu's own language, true knowledge is "great knowledge," and great knowledge is "all-embracing and extensive." [162] By this he meant that the intelligent "knows how to identify all things as one. Therefore he does not use [his own judgment] but abides in the common [principle]." [163]

The underlying principle for this doctrine of pure unity is that *Tao* produced all things,[164] is the ground for all things,[165] and is in all things, even in such lowly things as the ant, the tare, the potsherd, and ordure.[166] From the point of view of *Tao*, therefore, "all things are equal," a theme to which the entire second chapter of the *Chuang Tzu* is devoted. "Take the large beam and the small pillar, or take an ugly woman and Hsi-shih (a famous beauty), or take generosity, strangeness, deceit, and abnormality. *Tao* identifies them all as one. What is division [to others] and what is production [to others] is destruction [to some].[167] Generally speaking, "the 'this' is also the 'that,' and the 'that' is also the 'this.' " [168] From the standpoint of "mutual production," the " 'that' is produced by the 'this', and the 'this' is caused by the 'that.' " [169] This is to say that "when there is life, there is death, and when there is death, there is life. When there is possibility, there is impossibility, and when there is impossibility, there is possibility. Because of the right, there is the wrong, and because of the wrong, there is the right." [170] By the standard of *Tao*, too, "There is nothing in the world greater than the tip of a hair that grows in the autumn, while Mount T'ai is small." [171]

This doctrine of "equality of things" cannot be pushed any further. Its glorification of unity, identity, and synthesis may be regarded as a virtue, but its condemnation of the particular, the concrete, and the specific must be viewed as a defect. If absolutely no distinction could be made, not only logic, but morality also, would be impossible. Indeed, in the eyes of Chuang Tzu, civilization is not a blessing, but a curse. "The sage, therefore, . . . considers knowledge as a curse. . . . He needs no virtue . . . he is nourished by Nature. To be nourished by Nature is to be fed by Nature. Since he is fed by Nature, what is the use of man's effort?" [172] All benevolence and righteousness, rites and music, must be "forgotten." [173]

This is primitivism to the last degree. Nowhere else in Chinese philosophy do we find such extreme primitivism. Chuang Tzu's naturalistic philosophy of life exerted tremendous influence on the fatalistic libertines of the fourth and fifth centuries, while his naturalistic metaphysical doctrines became points of contact between Taoism and Buddhism. His emphasis on incessant, spontaneous transformation and the "equality of things" has affected almost all Chinese philosophers in the last fifteen centuries. As a glorifier of Nature, he still is today, as he has been for the last fifteen centuries, the main fountain of inspiration and imagination to Chinese artists, particularly landscape painters.

The greatness and importance of Chuang Tzu lie primarily in his exaltation of Nature. Humanism to him lost all meaning, because man in the world is nothing more than "the tip of a hair upon a horse's skin." [174] This being the case, "those inwardly upright" want to be "companions of Nature" [175] and "followers of Nature." [176] They do not want to "assist Heaven with man." [177] That is to say, as long as "horses and oxen have four feet," do not "put a halter on a horse's head or a string through a bullock's nose." [178] Not to assist Heaven with man is Chuang Tzu's version of *wu-wei*, in which alone can happiness be found. "Perfect happiness and preservation of life are to be achieved through taking no unnatural action." [179] "Do not be the possesser of fame. Do not be the storehouse of schemes. Do not take over the function of things. Do not be the master of knowledge [to manipulate things]. Personally realize the infinite to the highest degree and travel in the realm of which there is no sign. Exercise fully what you have received from Nature without any subjective viewpoint. In a word, be absolutely vacuous." [180]

When one reaches this state, one becomes a "true man," "one who knew neither to love life nor to hate death. He did not rejoice in birth, nor did he resist death. Without any concern he came, and without any concern he went, that was all. He did not forget his beginning nor seek his end. He accepted [his body] with pleasure, and, forgetting [life and death], he returned to [the natural state]. He did not violate *Tao* with his mind, and he did not assist Nature with man. . . . Such being the true man, his mind is perfectly at ease. . . . He is in accord with all things, and no one knows the limit thereof." [181]

To achieve this end, we must "have no self," "have no achievement," and "have no fame." [182] We must "let our mind be at ease in abiding with the nature of things. Cultivate our spirit by following what is necessary and inevitable." "For our external life, there is nothing better than adaptation and conformation. For our internal life, there is nothing better than peace and harmony." [183] Here we have primitivism, mysticism, quietism, fatalism, and pessimism in a nutshell.

The tone of fatalism and pessimism was made intense by the fact that both reality and the life of men are ever changing. "The life of a thing passes by like a galloping horse. With no activity is it not changing, and at no time is it not moving? What shall we do? What shall we not do? The thing to do is to leave it to self-transformation." [184] Existence is transitory, the life of man being just as momentary as that of things. "Things are born and die, and their completion cannot be taken for granted. They are now empty and now full, and their physical form is not fixed in one place. The years cannot be retained. Time cannot be arrested. The succession of decline, growth, fullness, and emptiness go in a cycle, each end becoming a new beginning." [185] In this fleeting universe, the only way for man to have peace is to let Nature take its own course. He should not question whether there is "some mechanical arrangement so that heavenly bodies cannot help moving" or if "they keep revolving and cannot stop themselves." [186] Perhaps there is an Overlord of all, but, if "it seems there is a True Lord, there is no indication of his existence." [187] The only thing we are sure of is that "all things spring from germs and become germs again." "All species come from germs. Certain germs, falling upon water, become duckweed . . . become lichen . . . become the dog-tooth violet . . . produce the horse, which produces man. When man gets old, he becomes germs again." [188] In passages like these we cannot help being attracted by Chuang Tzu's poetic imagination and his evolutionary thought. But we are also impressed with the inevitable "spontaneous transformation" and transitory existence. In the face of these irreducible facts, the true man "harmonizes all things in the functioning of Nature and leaves them in the process of infinite evolution. This is the way to complete our lifetime. . . . We forget the passage of time [life and death] and the distinction of right and wrong. We relax in the realm of the infinite and thus abide there." [189]

We should not forget, of course, that, in spite of the idea of escape in Chuang Tzu, his main interest was still the "preservation of life." He devoted an entire chapter to "the fundamentals for the cultivation of life." [190] In this he joined the chorus of the "Hundred Schools" that flourished in the fourth and third centuries B.C. in China. They were all seekers after a good life, each having a unique doctrine of its own. In no other period in Chinese history, or in the history of any country, was there more freedom of thought and more profuse intellectual development.

Running through this multiple development was one strong intellectual current the origin of which can be traced to the remote past, when divination was the only form of intellectual activity. This is the theory of *yin* and *yang*, the passive or female and active or male universal forces, respectively, which, according to the *Tao-te ching*, made the harmony of the world possible. In the Confucian classic, *The Book of Changes* [191] (*I ching*); we read: "In the systems of change, there is the Great Ultimate (*T'ai-chi*), which generates the Two Modes [*yin* and *yang*]. The Two Modes generate the Four Forms [major and minor *yin* and *yang*.] The Four Forms generate the Eight Elements. The Eight Trigrams determine good and evil fortunes. And good and evil fortunes produce the great business of life." The date of *The Book of Changes* is still surrounded by an atmosphere of uncertainty, but the fundamental ideas, that the universe is a dynamic system of incessant change from the simple to the complex and that the Two Modes are the agents of the change must have antedated the compilation of the book by centuries.

No student of Chinese history should underestimate this idea of *yin* and *yang*, not only because it largely conditioned the Chinese outlook toward reality, but also because it provided the common ground for the intermingling of the divergent philosophical schools. The movement was so strong that by the fourth century B.C. it became an independent school. Eventually, it identified itself in the second century B.C. with the common and powerful movement under the name of Huang-ti as well as the prevailing philosophy of Lao Tzu, and assumed the name "Huang-Lao." At the same time, the *yin-yang* idea of *The Book of Changes* became the most important aspect of Confucianism. Indeed, the note of *yin-yang* is the dominant note in the second movement of China's intellectual symphony, namely, medieval Chinese philosophy.

Earlier Medieval Philosophy

It was around the doctrine of *yin-yang* that earlier medieval Chinese philosophy developed, in various directions. In both Huai-nan Tzu the Taoist and Tung Chung-shu the Confucianist, it led to a microcosm-macrocosm philosophy, while in Wang Ch'ung it led to naturalism in direct opposition to the correspondence theory. Huai-nan Tzu (d. 122 B.C.) attempted to develop a more rational cosmology than his predecessors. He suggested that "there was a beginning," a "beginning of an anteriority to this beginning," and a "beginning of an anteriority even before the beginning of this anteriority," [192] and that the great beginning produced in succession space, the universe, the material forces, the *yin* and *yang*, and, finally, the material form.[193] But these are merely the unfolding of *Tao*.[194] Furthermore, although insects, fish, birds, and animals "differ in their nature and destiny," "they all come from the same great beginning," "with reference to which the pure man makes no distinction." [195] So far, Huai-nan Tzu does not depart from ancient Chinese philosophy. But the *yin-yang* idea in him adds a new note to Taoism. "Heaven has the four seasons and the Five Agents or Elements. . . . These find correspondence in man's four limbs and five viscera . . ." [196] for they are merely different manifestations of the same principles of *yin* and *yang*.

The spirit of correspondence assumes an even more important aspect in Tung Chung-shu (176–104 B.C.), who was instrumental in making Confucianism a state ideology. To him, "All things have their complements of *yin* and *yang*. . . . The underlying principles of prince and minister, father and son, husband and wife, are all derived from the way of *yin* and *yang*. The prince is *yang*, and the minister is *yin*. The father is *yang* and the son is *yin*. The husband is *yang*, and the wife is *yin*." [197] In short, everything conceivable can be reduced to these two universal principles. These two principles express themselves through the medium of the Five Agents, with which all things in the world correspond. The Five Agents have their correspondence in the five tones, five tastes, five colors, the various directions, the seasons, and the moral virtues.[198]

This scheme of correspondence must have had unusual fascination for the medieval Chinese, for it dominated Chinese thought for no less than five centuries. Both Taoists and Confucianists found it congenial because it was a systematized expression of the idea of harmony, an idea close to their hearts. But the real spirit of harmony, whether the central harmony of Confucianism or the inner harmony of the Taoists, or the harmony between man and Nature as taught by both schools, was lost. The movement of correspondence became a matter of intellectual sport, a game of puzzles, and, finally, a superstition. Volume after volume of "apocryphal treatises" were written to aid the interpretation of *The Book of Changes*. This body of literature became so huge and so influential that many important state policies were decided upon by strange confirmations from these superstition-infested books. Chinese philosophy had entered upon a dark age, an age in which Confucianism developed into a state ideology rather than a rational philosophy, and Taoism degenerated and identified itself with the lowest forms of religious worship. It was natural that there should arise strong reaction against such a state of affairs. Gradually the critical spirit made itself felt, until it reached such a high pitch from the third to the fifth century that it gave rise to a strong movement of textual criticism and an equally strong movement of free political thought.

The outstanding representative of this critical spirit was Wang Ch'ung (27–*ca.* 100?). Perhaps no other Chinese philosopher could rival him in rational thinking and critical spirit. He attacked all kinds of erroneous beliefs, beliefs in ghosts,[199] in thunder as the sound of Heaven's growling,[200] in calamities as visitations of Heaven,[201] in the past as superior to the present,[202] and many other false beliefs. He held that "all things are produced spontaneously by the fusion of the vital forces of Heaven and Earth [*yin* and *yang*]." [203] These spontaneous creations are not for the sake of man, because the opinion that Heaven produces grain for the purpose of feeding mankind is tantamount to making Heaven the farmer of man.[204] Furthermore, "If Heaven had produced its creatures on purpose, it ought to have taught them to love each other and not to prey upon and destroy one another." [205] We have here the most thoroughgoing naturalism in Chinese philosophy.

Later Medieval Philosophy

Wang Ch'ung was fighting to reinstate naturalism on a rational ground by appealing to reason and experience. Had Chinese philosophy developed along this line, its story would have been different. Unfortunately, Taoism as a philosophy hardly developed, except in the case of the book called the *Lieh Tzu* (*ca.* 300), in which the idea of *Tao* is carried to the point of fatalistic mechanism,[206] and in the philosopher Ko Hung (Pao-p'u Tzu, 284–363) alone was the true spirit of Taoism revived. He restored and developed the Taoist doctrines of naturalism and spontaneous transformation to a position of dignity.

In Confucianism, the only notable development was in Han Yü (768–824), the success of whose theory of three grades of human nature and whose defense of Confucianism were due more to his beautiful literary style than to his reasoning. The really constructive phase of Chinese philosophy in the period was the introduction and development of Buddhist philosophy.

Buddhism

All the Buddhist schools were introduced, preserved, and developed in China, but only those consonant with the Chinese temper lasted. Neither the Theravāda school of being, the realistic Abhidharmakośa school (Chü-she, *ca.* 600–*ca.* 800), which held that "all exists," nor the Theravāda school of non-being, the nihilistic Satyasiddhi school (Ch'eng-shih, 412–*ca.* 700), which insisted that "neither the self nor the *dharmas* (elements of existence) are real," had a long history in China. Also, neither the Mahāyāna school of being, the idealistic Vijñaptimātratā school (Yogācāra, Fa-hsiang, Wei-shih, *ca.* 600–1100), which asserted that "all is mere ideation," nor the Mahāyāna school of non-being, the negativistic or, rather, absolutistic Mādhyamika school (San-lun, *ca.* 500–1100), which regarded reality as "void," flourished in China for long.

Clinging to either the being or the non-being position, they existed in China as essentially Indian systems, without being assimilated into Chinese thought. Those Buddhist schools that combined tendencies of both being and non-being, however, continue to live up to this day.

The tendency to combine different and even opposing elements into a synthetic whole is characteristic of Chinese thought. We will recall that, with Lao Tzu, *Tao* is conceived as both "is" and "is not," a point further developed by Chuang Tzu, to become his famous theory of the equality of things. We will also recall that Confucius held the Mean to be the highest ideal, to the rejection of anything one-sided or extreme. We will recall, too, that in Neo-Moism the distinction of substance and predicates, of the universal and the particular, etc., was severely criticized. The Yin-Yang tradition was, through and through, a tradition of synthesis of opposites. The whole movement of medieval Chinese philosophy was not only a continuation of the central emphasis on synthesis of the ancient schools, but was itself a synthesis of the opposing philosophies of Confucianism and Taoism. This synthetic tendency, which affected practically all indigenous Chinese philosophies, also affected Buddhism in China.

Roughly speaking, just as the Abhidharmakośa, Satyasiddhi, Vijñaptimātratā, and Mādhyamika were hardly more than Indian Buddhism on Chinese soil, the five Buddhist schools which are the most prominent in China today, whether in amount of influence or in length of time, are typically Chinese. They are typically Chinese, not only because they still exist in China, but also because of their synthetic character. They all discarded their original extreme position of being or non-being in favor of a synthetic position of the "Middle Doctrine." The Hua-yen school (Avataṁsaka, *ca.* 600) started with the theory of causation by mere ideation, developed the theory of "universal causation of *Dharma-dhātu*," or universal causation of Elements of the Principle, and culminated in what Professor Takakusu calls "Totalism." It originated the "Ten Metaphysical Propositions" to the effect that all elements are perfect and real, that the elements reflect one another, and that all of them are at the same time simple and complex, one and many, exoteric and esoteric, pure and varied, etc., so that the universe is a "grand harmony without any obstacle." Thus we see that this school, originating in India but chiefly developed in China, represents a culmination of the "both-and" spirit of Buddhism.

The other school which shifted from the position of being to the position of both-being-and-non-being is the Mystical school (True Word, Mantra, Chen-yen, *ca.* 300), which is a mystical religion rather than a philosophical system. Yet, even here, the synthetic mode of thought is evident. It is an Indian religion baptized and transformed by Chinese ethical ideals. This school treats the universe as the spiritual body, or the Body of Law, of the Buddha, which manifests itself as the "Realm of Diamond Element," that is, the static world, and the "Realm of Matrix Repository," that is, the dynamic world. These two phases, however, are but different manifestations of the same Buddha: "They are two and yet not two."

The same shift from an extreme position to the "Middle Doctrine" is even more evident in the other three schools which were formed in China and are therefore typically Chinese. While both the Avataṁsaka and the Mystical schools started from the position of being, the T'ien-t'ai (*ca.* 580) started from the position of non-being. Beginning with the negativistic doctrine of the Void, this school finally arrived at the "Perfectly Harmonious Triple Truth" of the Void (things have no reality), Temporariness (but they have temporary existence), and the Mean (they are at the same time the True State). These three are identical, and Suchness, or the True State, involves both phenomenon and noumenon. Consequently, it calls itself the "Round Doctrine." This synthetic spirit must strongly appeal to the imagination of the Chinese, for T'ien-t'ai is still the strong Buddhist sect in China today.

As to the Meditation (Ch'an, *ca.* 450) and the Pure Land (Ching-t'u, *ca.* 300) schools, they are essentially Chinese creations, although certain sources can be traced to India. The Pure Land sect is a creed of faith, the least philosophical of all the schools we have mentioned. Its fundamental beliefs, however, such as salvation for all and the salvation by faith, are based on the idea of "one in all and all in one." It accepts the idea that *Nirvāna* has neither space nor time, neither life nor death. But it intreprets this as nothing other than the land of the Buddha of Infinite Light and Infinite Life, that is, the Pure Land.

The most significant of all the Buddhist schools, so far as Chinese thought is concerned, is Ch'an (Zen, in Japanese). Ch'an is basically a method, not a method of writing or words, which the school rejects, but a method of "direct intuition into the heart to find *buddha*-nature." Nevertheless, this method is based, on the one hand, on the assumption of the eightfold negation of production and extinction, annihilation and permanence, unity and diversity, and coming and departing, and, on the other hand, on the affirmation of the reality of *buddha*-nature in all things. The Ch'an method of "direct intuition," together with its "sudden enlightenment," gave the Chinese mind a way of ready and complete release, and for this reason had a peculiar charm. Above all, its sole reliance on meditation imposed on the Chinese mind a severe mental and spiritual discipline which was invigorating and quickened the Chinese imagination which the glorious poetry and landscape painting of the T'ang Dynasty (618–907) had already awakened.

But such quietism was fundamentally out of harmony with the practical and humanistic Chinese. The zenith of Ch'an was soon reached, and its decline began. With this, Chinese medieval philosophy came to a close. Thus the second movement of the intellectual symphony of China concluded with a song without words. There was harmony, but harmony in silence.

Neo-Confucianism

Ever since the advent of Buddhism in China, Chinese philosophers had been very critical of it. The fatal attack was delivered by the Neo-Confucianists. They felt that there was nothing "substantial" in Buddhism, and that the Buddhists' fear of birth and death was motivated by selfish interest.[207] They considered the Buddhist theory of renunciation untenable because they insisted that, even though a man might desert his family, he could never escape from society so long as he sets his feet on earth.[208] They believed that things were always in the process of transformation, and, consequently, the Buddhist doctrine of formation, duration, deterioration, and extinction was unsound.[209] They criticized the Buddhists for mistaking concrete reality for emptiness, because the Buddhists regarded all things, including clothing and food, as void, and yet they lived on those things every day.[210] They found that the Buddhist Void was really founded on the failure to understand the principle of things.[211] They showed that even the Buddhists could not get away from human relationships, because, while they severed their kinship with their parents, they organized themselves in a society of masters and pupils.[212] They condemned the Buddhists as unjust and cowardly, because they worked for their own interest and avoided social responsibility.[213]

From these criticisms we can see the spirit of Neo-Confucianism. The story of Neo-Confucianism is virtually the story of modern Chinese philosophy. It has not only dominated Chinese thought for the last eight hundred years but has also dominated Japanese thought for many centuries. In China, it developed in three phases, namely, the School of Principle in the Sung period (960–1279), the School of Mind in the Ming period (1368–1644), and the Empirical school in the Ch'ing period (1644–1911). In Japan, it was represented by the Shushi school (Chu Hsi) and the Ōyōmei school (Wang Yang-ming).[214]

THE SCHOOL OF PRINCIPLE:
THE CH'ENG BROTHERS AND CHU HSI

The central idea of the movement is focused on the Great Ultimate (T'ai-chi). "The Great Ultimate through movement generates yang. When its activity reaches its limit, it becomes tranquil. Through tranquillity the Great Ultimate generates yin. When tranquillity reaches its limit, activity begins again. So, movement and tranquillity alternate and become the root of each other, giving rise to the distinction of yin and yang, and the two modes are thus established. By the transformation of yang and its union with yin, the Five Agents of water, fire, wood, metal, and earth arise. When these five material forces (ch'i) are distributed in harmonious order, the four seasons run their course." [215] "These Five Agents are the basis of their differentiation, while the two material forces constitute their actuality. The two forces are fundamentally one. Consequently, the many are [ultimately] one, and the one is differentiated in the many. The one and the many each has its own correct state of being. The great and the small each has its definite function." [216] A vivid example of the one-in-many and many-in-one relationship is that of the moon. "Fundamentally there is only one Great Ultimate, yet each of the myriad things have been endowed with it and each in itself possesses the Great Ultimate in its entirety. This is similar to the fact that there is only one moon in the sky, but when its light is scattered upon rivers and lakes, it can be seen everywhere. It cannot be said that the moon has been split." [217]

Thus, reality is a progressively evolved and a well-co-ordinated system. But it is not the only coherent order. Everything is a unified system, a Great Ultimate in itself. "With respect to Heaven and Earth, there is the Great Ultimate in them. With respect to the myriad things, there is the Great Ultimate in each and every one of them." [218] For instance, "Heaven and Earth are one great system of *yin* and *yang*. The year, the month, and the day, all have their own systems of *yin* and *yang*." [219]

This philosophy of one-in-all and all-in-one was a direct product of the Confucian metaphysics of change. But it is quite probable that its development was inspired by the totalistic philosophy of Buddhism. If that is so, we have here a fundamental distinction between the two systems. While Buddhist philosophy was based on the Void, which is the denial of the particular, the Neo-Confucian philosophy was based on principle, which is an affirmation of it. Principle (*li*, order) is the keynote of the Neo-Confucian system. In the words of the Ch'eng brothers (Ch'eng I, 1033–1107, and Ch'eng Hao, 1032–1085), "We say that all things form one body because all things have the same principle in them." [220] They all have principle because things "must have their principles of being." [221] As principle is the universal law, "The principle of a thing is one with the principle of all things." [222]

This principle needs an agency through which to operate and also needs to be embodied. It must be supplemented, therefore, by a substantiating and particularizing principle. This is *ch'i*, or material force, which, working through its own avenues of the Five Agents and in the forms of *yin* and *yang*, differentiates the one into the many so that each of the many has its own "definite function." "When *yin* and *yang* are equal, form and substance are present. When these two original principles are not equal, the dormant nature and manifest nature of things are differentiated." [223] Material force is indispensable to reality, because "without material force, principle would have nothing to attach itself to," [224] and would degenerate into the state of the Buddhist Void. To the Neo-Confucianists, the Buddhist Void, to be valid at all, must be substantiated with material force. "The Great Vacuity has no physical form. It is the original substance of material force. Its integration and disintegration are but objectification caused by change. . . . Vacuity, the Void, is nothing but the material force." [225]

While principle and material force function differently, it was never the intention of the Neo-Confucianists to contrast them sharply. Basically, there is no distinction between them, because "there is no principle outside of material force, and there is no material force outside of principle." [226] "The Great Ultimate is principle, whereas activity and tranquillity are the material force. As the material force operates, principle also operates. The two are mutually dependent and are never separated. The Great Ultimate may be compared to a man, and activity and tranquillity may be compared to a horse. The horse carries the man, and the man rides the horse. As the horse comes and goes, so does the man." [227] The main difference between them is that "principle is above form." From the point of view of its formlessness, therefore, we may say that principle is prior to material force.[228] This distinction is made, however, merely from "a certain point of view." They are really two phases of the same thing, each working for the realization of the other.

It is this co-operative functioning of principle and material force that makes the universe a cosmos and the fullest realization of "central harmony." "The universal principles of *yin* and *yang* and the Five Agents manifest themselves in all directions and in all degrees, but there is perfect order in them." [229] This order is demonstrated in the production and co-existence of things. "The sequence of creation is the sequence of being. The co-existence of the great and small, and the high and low, is the order of being. There is a sequence in the production of things, and there is an order in their existence." [230] Thus, the universe, with all its myriad things, is a harmonious system. "Centrality is the order of the universe, and harmony is its unalterable law." [231] Consequently, the cosmos is a moral order. This is the main reason why the greatest of the Neo-Confucianists, Chu Hsi, said that "the Great Ultimate is nothing but the principle of ultimate goodness." [232]

A moral order means a social order. Therefore, just as man is a social being, so is a thing a social entity. The Neo-Confucianists stressed emphatically the fact that no thing can be isolated from others. "According to principle, nothing exists alone. Unless there are similarity and difference, contraction and expansion, and beginning and end among things to make the thing stand out, it is not really a thing although it seems to be." [233] That is to say, unless there is community, there cannot be individuality.

This leads to a new and interesting emphasis in Neo-Confucianism, namely, that everything has its opposite. "According to the Principle of Heaven and Earth and all things, nothing exists in isolation, but everything necessarily has its opposite." [234] "As there are forms, there are their opposites." [235] This is true because the underlying principles of being cannot stand by themselves. "*Yang* cannot exist by itself; it can exist only when it is allied with *yin*. Similarly, *yin* cannot alone manifest itself; it can manifest itself only when accompanied by *yang*.[236] Consequently, "No two of the productions of creation are alike." [237]

This being the case, Chuang Tzu's doctrine of the "equality of things" and the Buddhist denial of birth and extinction must be totally rejected. "It is the nature of things to be unequal," [238] the Neo-Confucianists reiterated. "Although there is nothing in the world which is purely *yin* or purely *yang*, and *yin* and *yang* always interact, yet the distinction between rising and falling, and between birth and extinction, should not be ignored." [239] "In the operation of *yin* and *yang*, and Heaven and Earth, there is not a single moment of rest in their rise and fall, and in their zenith and nadir. . . . These two tendencies cause the differences of things and an infinite number of transformations take place. This is why it is said that it is the nature of things to be unequal." [240]

The constant succession of zenith and nadir may suggest that "appearance and disappearance follow a cycle." [241] But this cycle does not mean a cycle in the Buddhist sense. Things do not return to their origin, as the Buddhists and Taoists claim, because, "when a thing disintegrates, its material force is forthwith exhausted. There is no such thing as material force returning to its source. The universe is like a vast furnace. Even living things will be burned to the last and no more. How can material force that is already disintegrated still exist? Furthermore, what is the need of such a disintegrated material force in the creative process of the universe? It goes without saying that the force used in creation is vital and fresh." [242] Every creation is therefore a new creation, and the universe is perpetually new.

All these characteristics of the universe are but its principle. It is the duty of man to comprehend this principle in order to appreciate fully the meaning of his existence. We must "investigate things to the utmost." As the Ch'eng brothers said, "A thing is an event. A perfect understanding of an event can be obtained by investigating to the utmost the principle underlying it." [243] This does not mean "to investigate the principle of all things to the utmost or to investigate the principle of only one thing to the utmost. As one investigates more and more, one will come to understand principle." [244] We do not even have to go far for such investigation, for principle . . . lies before our very eyes." [245] It makes no difference whether the investigation is directed to the nature of fire and water or the relationship between father and son, nor does it make any difference whether it is done by reading about and discussing truth and principles or by handling affairs and dealing with people in the proper way. [246] When sufficient effort is made, understanding naturally comes. When this takes place, our nature will be realized and our destiny will be fulfilled, because "the complete realization of the principle of things, the full development of one's nature, and the establishment of destiny are simultaneous." [247]

This is inevitable because, if we investigate things thoroughly and understand their principle, we will find that "all people are my brothers and sisters, and all things are my companions," [248] since all men have the same principle in them. Consequently, we should not entertain any distinction between things and oneself. [249] We must love universally. It is only in fully developing the nature of other people and things that one's own nature can be developed. [250] This is the foundation of Neo-Confucian ethics, the ethics of *jen*, humanity, true manhood, or love. Thus ethics has a firm basis in metaphysics, because love is "the source of all laws," and "the foundation of all phenomena." [251] The fact of universal production is a concrete evidence of *jen*. [252]

To achieve the end of full understanding of principle and a life of *jen*, the human mind must go through severe discipline. The mind must be sincere (*ch'eng*) and serious (*ching*). As Chu Hsi defined them, "Seriousness is apprehension, as if there were something feared. Sincerity is truth and the utter absence of anything false." [253] They are the "Way of Heaven" and the "essence of human affairs." [254] Specifically, sincerity means "to have no depraved thought," and seriousness means "to maintain unity of mind, that is, absolute equanimity and absolute steadfastness." [255]

The emphasis on seriousness, especially in the Ch'eng brothers and Chu Hsi, soon assumed almost religious significance. Some of their followers frankly explained it in terms of Buddhist meditation. As a matter of fact, the dual formula of the Neo-Confucianists of the School of Principle, that is, extension of knowledge and the practice of seriousness, might have some correspondence with the *dhyāna* and *prajñā*, or meditation and insight, of Meditation Buddhism. [256] The Neo-Confucianist movement became an inward movement, the mind gradually assuming importance. With the ascendancy of the role of the mind, Neo-Confucianism passed on from its first phase to its second, from the School of Principle to the School of Mind.

THE SCHOOL OF MIND:
LU HSIANG-SHAN AND WANG YANG-MING

The philosophy of the School of Mind already had definite form in Lu Hsiang-shan (1139–1193), who said that "the universe is my mind, and my mind is the universe." [257] This is because both the mind and the universe are conceived as expressions of the Way. "There is no Way beyond events, and there are no events beyond the Way." [258] But "the affairs in the universe are my own affairs, and my own affairs are affairs of the universe." [259] There is no suggestion of solipsism in these utterances, for "my mind, my friend's mind, the mind of the sages generations ago, and the mind of the sages of generations to come are all one." [260]

This idealistic tendency developed until it reached its climax in Wang Yang-ming (1472–1529), to whom the mind and principle are one and the same thing. "The mind is principle. Is there any affair in the world," he asked, "outside of the mind?" [261] Take, for example, the matter of filial piety. The principle of filial piety lies, not in one's parents, but in one's own mind. "If the principle of filial piety is to be sought in parents, then is it acutally in my own mind or is it in the person of my parents? If it is actually in the person of my parents, is it true that as soon as the parents pass away the mind will lack the principle of filial piety? . . . What is true here is true of all things and events." [262] "The master of the body is the mind. What emanates from the mind is the will. The original substance of the will is knowledge, and wherever the will is directed is a thing. For example, when the will is directed toward serving one's parents, then serving one's parents is a 'thing.' . . . Therefore I say that there are neither principle nor things outside the mind." [263] If we say that Heaven and Earth and things exist, it is due to our consciousness of them. "Separated from my clear intelligence, there will be no Heaven, Earth, spiritual beings, or myriad things, and, separated from these, there will not be my clear intelligence." [264] As to the relationship between the mind and external objects, Wang Yang-ming argued that these objects are really not external to the mind. We see flowers blossom and drop on the high mountains seemingly without connection with the mind. But, as our philosopher observed, "Before you look at these flowers, they and your mind are in the state of silent vacancy. As you come to look at them, their colors at once show up clearly. From this you can know that these flowers are not external to your mind." [265]

Since the mind is the embodiment of principle, it follows that, if one would truly comprehend principle, he must discover it from his own mind. He must "fully exercise his mind." "Man's nature is, of course, good. . . . It becomes evil only because of deviation from the mean." [266] The emergence of evil is, therefore, to be explained by a disturbed condition of the mind which is originally good. "The mind is like a mirror. The mind of the sage is like a clear mirror, whereas the mind of the ordinary person is like a dull mirror. . . . The effort is to be directed toward the [active] role of polishing. When the mirror is clear, it does not cease to reflect." [267] In short, evil is due to the loss of the "original substance" of the mind.[268]

To return to the original nature of the mind, any disturbance must be avoided. The mind must be left in a state of "tranquil repose," in which alone is the highest good attained.[269] When the mind is clear as the result of tranquil repose, it will naturally know what is true and what is good. In other words, knowledge of the good is innate in us. "The mind is naturally able to know. When it perceives the parents, it naturally knows that one should be filial. . . . And when it perceives a child fall into a well, it naturally knows that one should be commiserative. This is innate knowledge of the good and need not be sought outside." [270]

Not only is knowledge of the good inborn, but practicing the good is also native, because knowledge and conduct are identical. This theory of the unity of knowledge and conduct is characteristic of Wang Yang-ming, although Neo-Confucianists of the School of Principle had suggested it. If man fails to treat his parents with filial piety or his elder brother with respect, it is due to obstruction by "selfish desires and is no longer knowledge and action in their original substance. There have never been people who know but do not act. . . . Seeing beautiful colors appertains to knowledge, while loving beautiful colors appertains to action. However, as soon as one sees that beautiful color, he has already loved it." [271]

Since man is born with the capacity to know and practice the good, the chief duty of man is to "manifest the clear character." "Manifesting the clear character consists in loving the people. . . .

The nature endowed in us by Heaven is pure and perfect. The fact that it is intelligent, clear, and not beclouded is evidence of the emanation and revelation of the highest good. It is the original substance of the clear character which is called innate knowledge of the good. . . . As the highest good emanates and reveals itself, we will consider right as right and wrong as wrong." [272]

Manifesting the clear character consists in humanity (*jen*) because the mind of man and the mind of things have a common structure.[273] This is to say that "Heaven and Earth and I form one body." [274] An ideal man "considers Heaven, Earth, and the myriad things as one body." Consequently, he "views the world as one family and his country as one man." [275] His love is extended even to plants and animals, because, when he hears the pitiful cry and sees the frightened appearance of a bird or an animal that is about to be slaughtered, a sense of commiseration instinctively arises in his mind.

In a metaphysical and ethical system such as this, the importance of the mind is supreme. Although Wang Yang-ming based his idealistic philosophy on the doctrine of the "rectification of the mind" of *The Great Learning* and the doctrine of the "preservation of the mind" of Mencius, one can easily detect the influence of Ch'an. The emphasis on tranquil repose definitely proves such influence. At any rate, no Confucianist, whether in medieval or modern times, had ever gone to such an extreme position and thereby departed from the Golden Mean of Confucius.

THE EMPIRICAL SCHOOL: TAI CHEN

Reaction against such extreme idealism, even in the camp of Neo-Confucianism itself, was inevitable. The third phase of Neo-Confucianism, that of the Ch'ing period (1644–1911), may be said to be such a reaction. In rejecting the philosophy of the School of Mind in favor of an empirical philosophy, however, the last stage of Neo-Confucianism was more than merely a reaction. It represented an effort to retain all that is good in ancient, medieval, and modern Confucianism, and to return to the central harmony of Confucius and Mencius.

Thus, to say that the Neo-Confucianism of the Empirical school was really an anticlimax of the Neo-Confucianism of the schools of Principle and Mind will do the Neo-Confucianists of the Ch'ing Dynasty great injustice. There were no names in this period so

great as those in the Sung (960–1279) and Ming (1368–1644)
dynasties, to be sure. Neither were there so many novel theories.
But if Tai Chen (1723–1777), the greatest philosopher of the
Empirical school, can be taken as representative, there was an
earnest attempt to re-establish Confucianism on a more balanced
basis. The Neo-Confucianists of the School of Principle had contrasted principle and material force, considering the former above
corporeity, pure, refined, and universal, and the latter corporeal,
mixed, crude, and particular. Tai Chen vigorously criticized this
bifurcation of reality. To him, "The distinction of what is corporeal
and what is above corporeity refers to the operation of material
force. . . . What is corporeal is that which has taken a definite
form, and what is above corporeity is that which has not taken a
definite form. . . . Thus corporeity means the transfiguration of
things and not the material force." [276] Material force, together with
its Five Agents and the two universal forces of activity and pas-
sivity, is not inferior to principle. To Chu Hsi and his circle, principle is the Way which is above material force. To Tai Chen, on
the other hand, the Way means nothing but the operation of material force. There is no distinction, then, between principle and the
Way, on the one hand, and material force, on the other. Both
principle and material force are the Way.

   The Way refers to the incessant transformation . . . whereas principle refers to the complete fullness of the Way. . . . That which
produces and reproduces is the source of transformation, and that which
produces and reproduces in a systematic order is the flow of transformation. . . . As there is growth, there is repose, and, as there is
repose, there is growth. This is how the universe keeps on forming and
transforming. That which produces and reproduces is called *jen,* and that
which is responsible for the orderliness of life is called propriety (*li*) and
righteousness(*i*)." [277]

   Thus the Way finds expression in constant and orderly transformation, the realization of which is principle. This name can apply to all that is in harmony with the characteristics of the universe.
"With reference to its naturalness, it is called harmony. With reference to its necessity, it is called constancy." [278] Consequently, only
"those who can comprehend the harmony of the universe are
qualified to discuss the Way." [279]
   With harmony as the keynote, the philosophers of the Empirical school advocated the harmony of human nature, which they,

following most of the Confucianists before them, held to be good. In the discussion of principle from the eleventh to the sixteenth century, the general opinion had been that good action proceeds from principle, whereas evil action proceeds from desire, thus sharply contrasting principle and desire. To later Neo-Confucianists such as Tai Chen, however, this opinion was erroneous, because "men and creatures all have desires, and desires are the functions of their nature. Men and creatures all have feelings, and feelings are the operations of their nature." [280] Since they are inborn, they "should not be violated." [281] The problem is, therefore, not how to suppress desires and feeling, but how to harmonize them with principle. If their functionings "do not err," they are in harmony with Heaven and Earth.[282] The general formula seems to be that "we should not be without desires, but that we should have few desires." [283]

Modern Neo-Confucianists came to the defense of desires and feelings, not only because they are inborn, but also because desire and principle are inseparable. "Desire is a fact, whereas principle is its specific law of beings." [284] "A thing is an event. In speaking of an event, we cannot go beyond daily matters such as drinking and eating. To neglect these daily matters and talk about principle is not what the ancient sages recognized principle to be." [285] Furthermore, feeling, which engenders desires, does not violate principle. On the contrary, "Principle never obtains where feeling does not. . . . When feeling is expressed neither too much nor too little, it is called principle." [286] When we harmonize feeling and desires with principle, we then come into harmony with the universe. When all men and things are in harmony with the universe, there will be the fulfillment of the Way.

In emphasizing the harmony of principle and "daily events," the Neo-Confucianists of the last three hundred years have been demanding a return from the speculative to the empirical, from the universal to the particular, from the abstract metaphysics of Chu Hsi and Wang Yang-ming to the socio-political interest of Confucius and Mencius. In short, they insisted on "practical application." This practical emphasis ultimately culminated in K'ang Yu-wei (1858–1927) and T'an Ssu-t'ung (1865–1898), who made *jen* the basis of their doctrine of "practical application" and political reform. For the guidance of social and political reform, however, modern China found her traditional philosophies inadequate. She looked to the West for the solution of her problems.

Stimulated by the Renaissance led by Hu Shih (1891–1962), Western philosophies became dominant in twentieth-century China. Western pragmatism, materialism, neo-realism, vitalism, and new idealism almost dealt indigenous philosophies a fatal blow. Nevertheless, Chinese philosophies have survived, because their ideals are still the ideals of China.[287]

These ideals have been examined throughout Chinese history and have been found valuable, and no philosophical system that hopes to enjoy a permanent place in China is likely to reject them. We refer particularly to the ideals of central harmony, or cordial relationship between Nature and man, of the "both-and" attitude, of the Golden Mean, of humanism, of the preservation of one's life and the full realization of one's nature, of mental tranquillity, of incessant transformation and spontaneous creation, of the interaction of the active and passive universal principles, of the harmony of the one and the many, and of the goodness of human nature. Because of the impact of Western philosophies, a change of tone is already noticeable in Chinese philosophy.[288] There can be no doubt that Chinese philosophy will be baptized by Western science, logic, and epistemology. In the next movement of the philosophical symphony of China, therefore, there will be new notes and new chords, combining those of traditional China into a new harmony.

Notes

1. Shanghai: The New China Book Co., 1922.
2. Derk Bodde, trans. 2 vols. (Princeton: Princeton University Press, 1952, 1953).
3. Confucius, *Lun yü* (*Analects*) XV.28: James Legge, trans., *The Analects*. The Chinese Classics, Vol. I (Oxford: Clarendon Press, 1893; London, 1861–1897, Vol. I, 1872). Also in *The Four Books* (Honan, 1871; new ed., Shanghai: The Chinese Book Co., 1932); also by W. E. Soothill, *The Analects of Confucius* (Yokohama, 1910; new ed., Oxford: Oxford University Press, 1937); and by Arthur Waley, *The Analects of Confucius* (London: George Allen & Unwin Ltd., 1938). Translations in this chapter, unless otherwise noted, are mine.
4. *Analects* (*Lun yü*), VII.7.
5. *Ibid.*, XV.38.
6. Literally, "the Way." The same word is used by both Confucianists and Taoists, but with radically different meanings.

7. *Analects,* VII.1.
8. *Ibid.,* III.14; XVII.5; VII.5.
9. *Ibid.,* XVI.8.
10. *Ibid.,* XIV.38.
11. *Ibid.,* III.12.
12. *Ibid.,* V.12.
13. *Ibid.,* VII.20.
14. *Ibid.,* XI.11.
15. *The Great Learning (Ta hsüeh),* Introduction; cf. translation by Lin Yutang, in his *The Wisdom of Confucius,* (New York: The Modern Library, 1938), pp. 139–140.
16. *Analects,* IX.1.
17. *Ibid.,* XII.1.
18. *Ibid.,* XIII.19.
19. *Ibid.,* XIII.27.
20. *Ibid.,* XVII.6.
21. *Ibid.,* VI.28.
22. *Ibid.,* XII.22.
23. *Ibid.,* XIV.30.
24. *Ibid.,* XV.17.
25. *Ibid.,* XVI.7.
26. *Ibid.,* XVI.10.
27. *Ibid.,* XII.1.
28. *Ibid.,* IV.24.
29. *Ibid.,* IV.16.
30. *Ibid.,* XVI.5.
31. *Ibid.,* IV.5.
32. *Ibid.,* XV.23.
33. *Ibid.,* XIV.36.
34. *Ibid.,* II.5.
35. *Ibid.,* I.2.
36. *Ibid.,* II.1, 3; XI.25; XII.17, 19; XIII.4.
37. *Ibid.,* XIII.9; XVI.1.
38. *Ibid.,* XII.22.
39. *Ibid.,* XIX.7.
40. *Ibid.,* XVII.9.
41. *Ibid.,* XVII.11.
42. *Ibid.,* XII.11.
43. *Ibid.,* IV.15.
44. *Ibid.,* IV.15.
45. *Ibid.,* VI.27.
46. *Ibid.,* XI.15.
47. *The Book of Mencius (Meng Tzu),* VIA.2. James Legge, trans., *The Works of Mencius.* The Chinese Classics, Vol. II (Oxford: Clarendon Press, 1895); also in *The Four Books, op. cit.*

48. *Ibid.*, VIA.6.
49. *Ibid.*, VIA.6; IIA.6.
50. *Ibid.*, VIIA.21; VIIB.24.
51. *Ibid.*, VIIA.15.
52. *Ibid.*, IIA.6.
53. *Ibid.*, VIIA.15.
54. *Ibid.*, VIIA.4.
55. *Ibid.*, IVA.12.
56. *Ibid.*, VIIA.1.
57. *Ibid.*, VIA.7.
58. *Ibid.*, VIA.11.
59. *Ibid.*, VIIB.16.
60. *Ibid.*, IVB.28; VIA.10.
61. *Ibid.*, IVB.28.
62. *Ibid.*, IVA.27.
63. *Ibid.*, VA.4.
64. *Ibid.*, IIIA.4.
65. *Hsün Tzu,* VIII; cf. H. H. Dubs, trans., *The Works of Hsüntze* (London: Arthur Probsthain, 1928), p. 96.
66. *Ibid.*, XII.
67. *Ibid.*, XVII (translation by Hu Shih, in his *The Development of the Logical Method in Ancient China* [Shanghai: The Oriental Book Company, 1928], p. 152).
68. *Ibid.*, XXIII. See trans. by Wing-tsit Chan, *A Source Book in Chinese Philosophy* (hereafter *Source Book*) (Princeton: Princeton University Press, 1963), p. 128.
69. *Ibid.*
70. VIII (cf. Dubs, p. 115).
71. *Ibid.*, XIX (cf. Dubs, p. 213).
72. *Ibid.*, XXII (cf. Chan, *Source Book,* pp. 124 ff.; Dubs, p. 284).
73. *Ibid.*, XXI (Dubs, p. 277).
74. *Ibid.*, XVII (cf. Chan, *Source Book,* p. 117; Dubs, p. 174).
75. Traditionally ascribed to Tzu-ssu (492–431 B.C.), grandson of Confucius. It is a chapter of the *Li chi, The Book of Rites.* For an English translation, see Ku Hung-ming, *The Conduct of Life.* The Wisdom of the East Series (London: John Murray, 1906), revised by Lin Yutang, *The Wisdom of Confucius,* pp. 104–134, and in his *The Wisdom of China and India* (New York: Random House, 1942), pp. 843–864; the translations here are by Chan, *Source Book,* chap. 5.
76. *Ibid.*, I.
77. *Ibid.*, II.
78. *Ibid.*, XX.
79. *Ibid.*, XXVI.
80. *Ibid.*

81. *Ibid.,* XXII.

82. Lao Tzu is traditionally dated at *ca.* 570 B.C. In the last two decades, the theory of Wang Ch'ung (1744–1794) that Lao Tzu and the *Tao-te ching* belonged to the fourth century B.C. has been revived and accepted by many Chinese and Western scholars. The former include Liang Ch'i-ch'ao, Ku Chieh-kang, Fung Yu-lan (*A History of Chinese Philosophy* [Peiping: H. Vetch, 1937], Derk Bodde's trans., Vol. I, pp. 170 ff.), Ch'ien Mu, etc. The latter include Arthur Waley, *The Way and Its Power* (London: George Allen & Unwin Ltd., 1934), pp. 101–108; Homer H. Dubs, "The Date and Circumstances of the Philosopher Lao-dz," *Journal of the American Oriental Society,* LXI, No. 4 (December, 1941), 215–221; also Dubs, "The Identification of the Lao-Dz," *ibid.,* LXII, No. 4 (December, 1942), 300–304; etc. Although Hu Shih does not rule out the possibility of this theory, he feels that evidences are insufficient to justify it. "A Criticism of Some Recent Methods Used in Dating Lao Tzŭ, 1933, translation in *Harvard Journal of Asiatic Studies,* II, Nos. 3 and 4 (December, 1937). For a detailed discussion on Lao Tzu, the man, and the *Lao Tzu* (*Tao-te ching*), the book, see Wing-tsit Chan, trans., *The Way of Lao Tzu,* (Indianapolis: Bobbs-Merrill, 1963).

83. *Lieh Tzu,* VII. See below, p. 53.

84. *The Book of Mencius,* VIIA.26.

85. *Huai-nan Tzu,* XIII. Cf. E. Morgan, *Tao, the Great Luminant* (Shanghai: Kelly and Walsh, 1933), p. 155.

86. *The Works of Han Fei Tzu,* L. Cf. W. K. Liao, trans., *The Complete Works of Han Fei Tzu,* Vol. II (London: Arthur Probsthain, 1938), p. 301.

87. *Lieh Tzu,* VII. See English translation of the chapter by A. C. Graham, *The Book of Lieh Tzu* (London: John Murray, 1960).

88. *Tao-te ching,* XIX, XII. A well-known translation of the *Tao-te ching* is by Arthur Waley, *The Way and Its Power* (London: George Allen & Unwin Ltd., 1934). Lin Yutang's translation, "The Book of Tao," in his *The Wisdom of China and India* (1st ed., New York: Random House, 1942) is good. See also translation by Chan, *The Way of Lao Tzu.*

89. *Ibid.,* XLV, X, LI, XII, XXIV.

90. *Ibid.,* LVIII.

91. *Ibid.,* XVIII, II, XII, XIX, XXXVIII.

92. *Ibid.,* XXX, XXXI, LXVIII, LXXIII, LIII, LXXV, LVII, LXXIV, LXXV.

93. Hu Shih, *Shuo-ju* (On the Literati), 1934, now included in *Hu Shih lun-hsüeh chin-chu* (Recent Essays on Learned Subjects by Hu Shih) (First Series, Shanghai: Commercial Press, 1935), pp. 3–81.

94. *Tao-te ching*, II.
95. *Ibid.*, LXIV, XXXVII.
96. *Ibid.*, XXXVII.
97. *Ibid.*, III, LVII.
98. *Ibid.*, XL, XI, LXXVIII, XLIII, LXXVI.
99. *Ibid.*, I.
100. *Ibid.*, XLV.
101. *Ibid.*, VI, XX, XXVIII, LXI, X, XLIX, LV.
102. *Ibid.*, XLV.
103. *Ibid.*, V.
104. *Ibid.*, XXV.
105. *Ibid.*, I, IV, XXV.
106. *Ibid.*, I, XIV, XLII, XXV, XXXIV, XXI.
107. *Ibid.*, XXV.
108. *Ibid.*, VIII.
109. *Ibid.*, VIII.
110. *Ibid.*, LXXVIII.
111. *Ibid.*, XLII.
112. *Ibid.*, LV.
113. *Ibid.*, XVI.
114. *Ibid.*, XXXIV.
115. *Ibid.*, XLIV.
116. *Ibid.*, LXXV.
117. *Ibid.*, LIX.
118. *Mo Tzu*, XVI. Cf. Yi-pao Mei, trans., *The Ethical and Political Works of Motse* (London: Arthur Probsthain, 1929), p. 87.
119. *Ibid.*, XXXV (cf. Mei, p. 182).
120. *Ibid.*, XX (cf. Mei, p. 118).
121. *Ibid.*, XX (cf. Mei, p. 119).
122. *Ibid.*, XX, XXI (cf. Mei, p. 119).
123. *Ibid.*, XXV (cf. Mei, p. 127).
124. *Ibid.*, XXXII (cf. Mei, pp. 175–180).
125. *Ibid.*, XXXV (cf. Chan, *Source Book*, p. 222; also Mei, pp. 182–183).
126. *Ibid.*, XXXVI (cf. Mei, p. 189).
127. *Ibid.*, XXXII (cf. Mei, pp. 175–177).
128. *Ibid.*, XXVIII (cf. Mei, p. 155).
129. *Ibid.*, XVI (cf. Mei, p. 89).
130. *Ibid.*, XVI (cf. Mei, p. 97).
131. *Ibid.*, XLVII (cf. Mei, p. 225).
132. *Ibid.*, XV (cf. Mei, p. 83).
133. *Ibid.* (cf. Mei, p. 97).
134. *Ibid.*, XIV (cf. Mei, p. 78).
135. *Ibid.*, XV (cf. Mei, p. 82).
136. *Ibid.*, XV (cf. Mei, p. 83).

137. *Ibid.*, XXVII (cf. Mei, p. 138).

138. *Ibid.*, XXXI (cf. Mei, p. 160).

139. *Ibid.*, XXXI (cf. Mei, p. 170).

140. *Ibid.*, XXVI (cf. Mei, p. 136).

141. *Chuang Tzu*, XXXIII.

142. *Ibid.*

143. *Kung-sun Lung Tzu*, II. See Chan, *Source Book*, chap. 10; also English translation by A. Forke, "The Chinese Sophists," *Journal of the North China Branch of the Royal Asiatic Society*, XXXIV (1901–1902), 61–82.

144. *Ibid.*, III.

145. *Ibid.*, V.

146. *Chuang Tzu*, II; *Hsün Tzu*, XXI.

147. *Mo Tzu*, XL–XLV.

148. *Ibid.*, XLV.

149. *Ibid.*, XL.

150. *Ibid.*, XL.

151. *Ibid.*, XLII.

152. *Ibid.*, XL.

153. *Ibid.*, XLII.

154. *Ibid.*, XLIII.

155. *Ibid.*, XL, XLII.

156. *Ibid.*, XL.

157. *Ibid.*

158. *Ibid.*

159. *Ibid.*

160. *Ibid.*, XLII.

161. *Ibid.*, XLIV.

162. *Chuang Tzu*, II. Cf. Chan, *Source Book*, chap. 8; also English translations by Fung Yu-lan, *Chuang Tzu* (I–VII) (Shanghai: Commercial Press, 1931), p. 45; and by H. A. Giles, *Chuang Tzŭ: Mystic, Moralist, and Social Reformer* (Shanghai: Kelly & Walsh, 1926), p. 14.

163. *Ibid.*, II (cf. Chan, *Source Book*, p. 184; also Fung, p. 52).

164. *Ibid.*, VI (cf. Fung, p. 117).

165. *Ibid.*, VI (cf. Fung, p. 118).

166. *Ibid.*, XXII (cf. Giles, pp. 285–286).

167. *Ibid.*, II (cf. Chan, *Source Book*, p. 184; also Fung, p. 52).

168. *Ibid.*, II (Fung, p. 50).

169. *Ibid.*

170. *Ibid.* (cf. Chan, p. 183).

171. *Ibid.*, II (cf. Fung, p. 56).

172. *Ibid.*, V (cf. Fung, p. 106).

173. *Ibid.*, VI (cf. Fung, pp. 128–129).

174. *Ibid.*, XVI (cf. Giles, p. 202).

175. *Ibid.,* IV (cf. Fung, p. 78).
176. *Ibid.,* VI (cf. Fung, p. 115).
177. *Ibid.,* VI (cf. Fung, p. 113).
178. *Ibid.,* XVII (cf. Giles, p. 211).
179. *Ibid.,* XVIII (cf. Giles, p. 222).
180. *Ibid.,* VII (cf. Chan, *Source Book,* p. 207; also Fung, p. 141).
181. *Ibid.,* VI (cf. Chan, *Source Book,* p. 192; also Fung, pp. 112, 113).
182. *Ibid.,* I (cf. Fung, p. 34).
183. *Ibid.,* IV (cf. Fung, pp. 85–86).
184. *Ibid.,* XVII (cf. Chan, *Source Book,* p. 206; also Giles, p. 209).
185. *Ibid.*
186. *Ibid.,* XIV (cf. Chan, *Source Book,* p. 203; also Giles, p. 173).
187. *Ibid.,* II (cf. Chan, *Source Book,* p. 181; also Fung, p. 46).
188. *Ibid.,* XVII (cf. Giles, p. 228).
189. *Ibid.,* II (cf. Chan, *Source Book,* p. 190; also Fung, p. 63).
190. *Ibid.,* III.
191. *I ching* (*The Book of Changes*), "Hsi-tz'u", Pt. I, XI.
192. *Huai-nan Tzu,* II. Cf. English translation by E. Morgan, trans., *Tao, the Great Luminant,* p. 31.
193. *Ibid.,* III (cf. Morgan, p. 58).
194. *Ibid.,* VII (cf. Morgan, p. 59).
195. *Ibid.,* XIV, VIII, XIX.
196. *Ibid.,* VII (cf. Morgan, p. 60).
197. Tung Chung-shu, *Ch'un-ch'iu fan-lu* (Luxuriant Gems of the Spring and Autumn Annals), LIII. See E. R. Hughes, *Chinese Philosophy in Classical Times* (London: J. M. Dent & Sons, Ltd., 1942), pp. 293–308.
198. *Ibid.,* XXXVIII, XLII.
199. Wang Ch'ung, *Lun heng* (Balanced Inquiries), XX. Cf. A. Forke's translation in *Mittelungen des Seminars für orientalische Sprachen,* IX, (1907–1911), 371–376.
200. *Ibid.,* VI (*Mittelungen,* X, 66–76).
201. *Ibid.,* XIV (*Mittelungen,* IX, 299–300).
202. *Ibid.,* XVIII (*Mittelungen,* XI, 84–85).
203. *Ibid.,* XVIII (*Mittelungen,* IX, 272).
204. *Ibid.,* XVIII (*Mittelungen,* IX, 272).
205. *Ibid.,* III (*Mittelungen,* IX, 284).
206. *Lieh Tzu,* English translation by A. C. Graham, *The Book of Lieh Tzu.*
207. *Ch'eng-shih i-shu* (Surviving Works of the Ch'eng Brothers), XIII, XV.
208. *Ibid.,* XVIII.
209. *Ibid.,* XVIII.
210. Chu Hsi, *Chu Tzu yü-lei* (Classified Conversations of Master Chu), CXXVI.

211. *Ibid.*
212. *Ibid.*
213. Wang Yang-ming, *Ch'uan-hsi Lu.* English translation by Wing-tsit Chan, *Instructions for Practical Living and Other Neo-Confucian Writings by Wang Yang-ming* (New York: Columbia University Press, 1963). Also *Ch'eng-shih i-shu*, XIII.
214. The term "Neo-Confucianism" is used in the West to designate the Confucian philosophy of the Sung, Ming, and Ch'ing dynasties (960–1911). For the sake of convenience, I am using it in this sense. However, the term is not a direct translation of any Chinese appellation. In Chinese the general term is *Li-hsüeh* (School of Principle), *Hsing-li-hsüeh* (Philosophy of Nature and Principle), or *Tao-hsüeh* (Philosophy of the Way), because principle, Nature, and the Way were the basic concepts of the time. Sometimes the school of the Sung period (960–1279) is called *Li-hsüeh* (Philosophy of Principle), while that of the Ming period (1368–1644) is called *Hsin-hsüeh* (Philosophy of Mind), because the outstanding philosophy of the period was idealism, although rationalism continued to exist. The philosophy of the Ch'ing period (1644–1911) has no general name since there were many philosophical currents, including rationalism and idealism. The predominating philosophy, however, was an empiricism which developed as a reaction against both of them. The Chinese call this empirical system *P'u-hsüeh* (Concrete Philosophy) and *Han-hsüeh* (Philosophy Based on the Han [206 B.C.–A.D. 220] Criticism of Ancient Texts). I use "Empirical school" for this system because it is more descriptive than the two Chinese terms.
215. Chou Tun-i, *T'ai-chi t'u shuo* (Explanation of the Diagram of the Great Ultimate) (Chan, *Source Book*, p. 463).
216. Chou Tun-i, *T'ung shu* (Penetrating *The Book of Changes*), XXII (Chan, *Source Book*, p. 474).
217. Chu Hsi, *Chu Tzu yü-lei*, XCIV (Chan, *Source Book*, p. 638).
218. Chu Hsi, *ibid.* (Chan, *Source Book*, p. 638).
219. *Ibid.*
220. *Ch'eng-shih i-shu*, II.
221. *Ibid.*, XVIII (Chan, *Source Book*, p. 532).
222. *Ibid.*, II (Chan, *Source Book*, p. 551).
223. Shao Yung, *Huang-chi ching-shih* (Supreme Principles Governing the World).
224. Chu Hsi, *Chu Tzu yü-lei*, I (Chan, *Source Book*, p. 635).
225. *Chang Heng-ch'ü hsien-sheng ch'üan-chi* (Complete Works of Chang Tsai), II.1 (Chan, *Source Book*, pp. 501–502).
226. Chu Hsi, *Chu Tzu yü-lei*, I (Chan, *Source Book*, p. 634).
227. *Ibid.*, CXIV.
228. *Ibid.*, I.

229. *Ibid.*, I.
230. Chang, II.5.
231. Ch'eng, VII.
232. Chu Hsi, *Chu Tzu yü-lei*, CVIV.
233. Chang, II.5 (Chan, *Source Book*, p. 515).
234. Ch'eng, XI (Chan, *Source Book*, p. 539).
235. Chang, II.1.
236. Shao, *op. cit.*
237. Chang, II.1.
238. *The Book of Mencius*, IIIA.4.
239. Ch'eng, II.
240. Ch'eng, *Ts'ui-yen* (Pure Words).
241. Chang, II.1.
242. Ch'eng, XV (Chan, *Source Book*, p. 558).
243. Ch'eng, XV.
244. Ch'eng, XV.
245. Chu Hsi, *Chu Tzu yü-lei* XCIV.
246. Ch'eng, XIX, XVIII.
247. Ch'eng, II (Chan, *Source Book*, p. 531).
248. Chang, I.
249. Shao, *op. cit.*
250. Chang, II.6.
251. Chu Hsi, *Chu Tzu ch'üan-shu* (The Complete Works of Master Chu), LXVII. English translation by J. P. Bruce, *The Philosophy of Human Nature by Chu Hsi* (London: Arthur Probsthain, 1922), p. 317.
252. Chou, XI.
253. Chu Hsi, *Chu Tzu ch'üan-shu*, XLVIII.
254. Ch'eng, XI.
255. Ch'eng, *Ts'ui-yen*.
256. Hu Shih, "Religion and Philosophy in Chinese History," in Sophia Zen, ed., *Symposium on Chinese Culture* (Shanghai: China Institute of Pacific Relations, 1931), p. 57.
257. *Lu Hsiang-shan ch'üan-chi* (Complete Works of Lu Hsiang-shan), XXII (Chan, *Source Book*, p. 579).
258. *Ibid.*, XV.
259. *Ibid.*, XXII (Chan, *Source Book*, p. 580).
260. *Ibid.*, XXV.
261. *Wang Yang-ming ch'üan-chi* (Complete Works of Wang Yang-ming), I. See Chan, trans., *Instructions for Practical Living*, p. 7.
262. *Ibid.*, II (Chan, *Instructions*, p. 99).
263. *Ibid.*, I (Chan, *Instructions*, p. 14).
264. *Ibid.*, III (Chan, *Instructions*, p. 257).
265. *Ibid.*, III (Chan, *Instructions*, p. 222).
266. *Ibid.*, III (Chan, *Instructions*, p. 203).

267. *Ibid.*, I (Chan, *Instructions*, p. 45).
268. *Ibid.*, I (Chan, *Instructions*, p. 33).
269. *Ibid.*, XXVI.
270. *Ibid.*, I (Chan, *Instructions*, p. 15).
271. *Ibid.*, I (Chan, *Instructions*, p. 10).
272. *Ibid.*, XXVI (Chan, *Instructions*, pp. 273–274).
273. *Ibid.*, III (Chan, *Instructions*, p. 257).
274. *Ibid.*, III, *ibid.*
275. *Ibid.*, XXVI (Chan, *Instructions*, p. 272).
276. Tai Chen, *Meng Tzu tzu-i shu-cheng* (Commentary on the Meaning of Terms in *The Book of Mencius*), Pt. II, No. 17.
277. Tai Chen, *Yüan-shan* (An Inquiry on Goodness), I.
278. Tai Chen, *Tu I Hsi-tz'u lun-hsing* (On the Discussions of Human Nature in the Appended Remarks of *The Book of Changes*).
279. *Ibid.*
280. *Ibid.*
281. *Yüan-shan,* I.
282. *Tu i,* etc.
283. *Meng Tzu tzu-i shu-cheng,* Pt. I, No. 10 (Chan, *Source Book,* p. 713).
284. *Ibid.*
285. *Ibid.*, Pt. I, No. 3 (Chan, *Source Book,* p. 713).
286. *Ibid.*, Pt. I, Nos. 1, 3 (Chan, *Source Book,* pp. 711, 713).
287. For a summary of philosophy in contemporary China, see my chapter, "Trends in Contemporary Philosophy," in Farley Farnsworth MacNair, ed., *China* (Berkeley: University of California Press, 1946), pp. 312–330. For a further bibliography on contemporary Chinese philosophy, see Wing-tsit Chan, *An Outline and An Annotated Bibliography of Chinese Philosophy* (New Haven: Far Eastern Publications, Yale University, 1959, supplements 1961 and 1965).
288. Fung Yu-lan's "New Rational Philosophy," for example, is the rationalism of the Ch'eng brothers and Chu Hsi modified by Western objectivism. See McNair, ed., *China,* pp. 561–567.

E. R. HUGHES *Epistemological Methods in*
Chinese Philosophy

I

NO ONE WHO has read Mr. Suzuki's paper could have failed
to be impressed by the scrupulous accuracy and integrity with
which he defined his position. From the point of view of an out-
sider, Suzuki's train of thought was comparable to the feat of
tight-rope walking. He preserved an assured balance, although
every new paradox that he enunciated seemed bound to bring
him crashing to the ground. To some, it might seem that there was
no rope at all for him to walk on. Yet, the fact remained that he
went on walking, preserving his precision of balance. Speaking for
myself, Suzuki brought home to me with new force what is to me a
plain fact of history, that man cannot dispense with philosophy,
and philosophy's first concern is criticism, criticism of appearance,
criticism of thought, criticism of language; and, that being so, the
philosopher from first to last is dealing with paradoxes, some of
which may be humanly irresolvable. But the final paradox is that
the philosopher is also a man, a man amongst men. He goes on
living, eating and drinking, wearing his clothes, performing his
daily duties. There, if I may venture a criticism which is not a
criticism since that side of Zen Buddhism was outside the subject of
his paper, Suzuki did not make the situation quite clear. Zen Buddhists from the very beginning of Zen Buddhism have always been
paradoxically engaged in ordinary living, the less deliberatively
the better. That, for them, was a necessary concomitant to enlight-

enment. They have maintained that there is no other way of arriving at enlightenment.

I make this preface to my paper on Chinese epistemology because Ch'anism and Zenism are, I submit, highly significant Chinese and Japanese reactions to Indian and Western Asian Buddhism. The Chinese Ch'an movement started with a simple unlearned monk who revolted against all the deliberate refinements and elaborations of thought, ritual, *yoga*, and the like which he saw in his fellow monks. He discovered that enlightenment was the one thing he needed, and that it was the one thing he could not get for himself: the more he tried to achieve it, the more sophisticated he became, and the less possible it was for him to be enlightened. Therefore, he went on living as a man on the simplest possible basis of living. There the Taoist and to a certain extent the Confucianist spoke in him.

If knowing in the fullest sense be considered dependent on living in the simplest sense, the natural inference is that a man with that kind of outlook will not be likely to evolve a very elaborate system of epistemology. True! I doubt whether the Chinese indigenous tradition, along its own line of conscious reasoning, achieved anything so intrinsically subtle and elaborate as the Indian tradition achieved. Thus, the material presented here may be disappointing because of its simplicity. On the other hand, it should be borne in mind that of all paradoxical writing in Chinese literature—and there is a good deal—the most paradoxical is that of the Ch'an Buddhist; and, when I say "paradoxical," I mean consciously and deliberately paradoxical, even with the intention of causing laughter, to make evident the incongruities in the human situation. In this respect a Chinese critic is never so philosophically Chinese as when he appears "dumb." So, in regard to epistemological theorizing, the facts may appear simple, but they are by no means as simple as they seem.

For instance, examine the writings of Chinese thinkers from the late fourth century B.C. (the first date of really consecutive dialectical composition) down to the eleventh century A.D. (the time when the Ch'eng-Chu Neo-Confucianist epistemology emerged): one constant recurrent characteristic is an appeal to history. In other words, one indispensable method of achieving reliable knowledge was the historical method. It was as if a man's contemporaries said to him, "Speculate, theorize, as much as you like, but check up on your speculations by finding out what has happened in the past." Now, such an attitude may easily reveal intellectual naïveté. As we know so well today, anybody can quote history to suit any theory he wants to put across. True, but, although in the earlier days the appeal to history was made in very simple unreflecting fashion, as time went on the citation of history became one of the severe tests of a scholar's integrity of mind and breadth of learning. He was expected to cite groups of relevant facts which shed light on each other. In other words, there came to be an empirical critique of history, one built on a fine sense of historical perspective: a division of the past into *shang ku, chung ku, hsia ku* (high antiquity, middle antiquity, low, i.e., later, antiquity), *chin shih* (recent times), this last being split up into Western Han (206 B.C.–A.D. 8), Eastern Han (A.D. 25–220), Three Kingdoms period, and so on. Each epoch stood in its own right on its own ground, had its high spots and low spots. Woe betide the scholar who had a confused perspective. According to this approach, the object of knowledge was not abstract and changeless, not a logical entity. It was shot through and through with a sense of the particular.

On the other hand, it would be disastrously erroneous to assume, for those same centuries in which the "Great Tradition" of the Chinese people was being slowly smelted and forged, that those thinkers were not interested in metaphysical problems and were incapable of realizing the questions which emerge in relation to categorical knowledge. As I shall show, they went on from crude experiments in reasoning to more and more refined and systematic inquiries. But the point I have to emphasize at the outset is that, as they refined their sense of reason in these abstract fields, they become more and more conscious that thought is conditioned by language and that language as communication fails unless it be disciplined and controlled. They were intrigued by the nature of thought and its relation to emotion. They were highly conscious of that mysterious monitor of the mind, reason (*li*); but to them the chief factor in the two-way traffic between thought, language, and logic was language.[1] So simple as that, and yet so curiously profound! R. G. Collingwood described philosophy as "thought of the second degree, thought about thought." [2] The distinctively Chinese epistemological reply to that would be to say, "Yes, more or less, but we do not know what your thinking is until it is expressed in language." From this angle, philosophy becomes (a) a critique of language, of communicated meaning, and (b) a checking of this critique by a critique of history.

This is the basic approach to Chinese epistemology. For this reason, I would urge that in our study of these matters we should learn to walk before we try to run. If we do not, as we run from Confucianism to Taoism, from Taoism to the Chin (Tsin) (265–420) transcendentalists, and from them to Chu Hsi and Wang Yang-ming, and try to appraise this system as against that, we are ignoring the prime factor in the situation, the thinking man and the language in which he got his thought, the language which was for him the molder of his thoughts, the language which objectified that essentially subjective thing, thinking.

The Distinction Between 500 B.C. and A.D. 500

The first of these dates stands for Confucius' lifetime, the second for the first collection of literary masterpieces, poetry, prose, state papers, dialectical essays, letters, inscriptions, etc., all put together under the one all-embracing title of *wen*, ordered artistic composition, writings which conveyed meaning in ordered fashion, in clear-cut patterned sentences and clear-cut patterned paragraphs. We have no term in English which covers the meaning of *wen*. It is significant that in this collection 98 per cent of the selected compositions are taken from writers not earlier than the second century B.C. The man who made the collection was Hsiao T'ung (d. A.D. 531), son of Emperor Wu of the Liang Dynasty (502–557). From this foreword we learn that the invention of writing was to him the most momentous invention of all history, and that in the development of literary composition he found evidence of both evolution and revolution. To give as nearly a first-hand impression as is possible of a very typical double approach to knowledge, I have translated the first two paragraphs of the foreword, marking by a special use of colons the coupling of the sentences, and so elucidating the actual movement of the author's mind.

PARAGRAPH 1

Let us make observation of primordial beginnings, strain our eyes to penetrate the cloud of [primitive] custom.

In the days when men lived in caves in the winter and [slept] perched

on trees in the summer, when they ate their meat uncooked and drank the blood:
that era was one of raw material (*ch'i*); its people were simple-minded; and this literature (*wen*) of ours had not been invented.
Coming down to the time of Fu Hsi's ruling over our world of men, he was the first to trace out the Eight Trigrams and invent the written language:
this he did with a view to their being a substitute for government by string knots.
From this came the birth of books.
In *The Book of Changes* it is written:
"We make observation of the patterns (*wen*) in the heavens with a view to understanding the seasonal changes:
We make observation of man's patterns (*wen*) with a view to transforming and completing the society of man." [3]
How far back the historical significance of pattern (*wen?* literature? pattern) goes!

PARAGRAPH 2
With regard to the [primitive] hammered-out wheel being the beginning of the imperial carriage, the imperial carriage actually has the raw material (*ch'i*) of the primitive wheel:
With regard to a block of ice being the product of a quantity of water: the water does not have the iciness of the ice.
How about this? (How do I make this out?)
It would appear [in the one case] that with the toe-and-heel succession of events there comes the accretion of ornamentation:
[in the other case] with the subversal of the original condition there comes the addition of whet-stone hardness.
Since ordinary material objects have this [double tendency], it is [logically] right that literature also should have it.
[And since] the movement of time ever brings revolution and evolution, it is practically impossible to identify changes in full detail.

PARAGRAPH 3
I make the experiment of discussing this as follows . . .

In Paragraph 1 the appeal to history appears—an appeal, I might add, couched in conventional language, assuming the factual truth that the first Sage-Emperor was the inventor of the trigrams and the script. In Paragraph 2 the following points should be noted: (1) Hsiao T'ung selects two relevant data from his field of empirical observation. (2) Although the imperial carriage is a man-made thing and ice is what we call the result of natural process, the two phenomena are treated as on the same level. That, to the

Chinese, is logical. The idea of natural process for them applies equally to man-made products. (3) Process led to two directly opposite results; thus the author draws two separate conclusions. (4) From those he goes on to urge that what applies to carriages and blocks of ice applies to that infinitely multiform and ever-changing product of the human mind, *wen.* (5) His final reflection, in a vein common since the Taoist fathers, is that our knowledge cannot but be limited, since every process in Nature consists of an infinite number of steps, so minute that no one can discern them. All we can do is to mark such effects as are discernible to our limited powers of observation.

To these five points should be added the following three in relation to the presentation, the manner, and the style of the argument. (1) Discursive thought is packed into pairs of sentences related to each other, sentences of equal length so that contrasted meaning may stand out clearly. (2) The two trains of thought are presented in paragraphs of equal length. (3) The author does not dogmatize. He uses the form of words which we find in thinker after thinker in that and later ages: "Let us make observation," "It would appear that," "How about that?" and "I make the experiment of discussing this."

It would be interesting to know what your several reactions are to this kind of reasoning. I suggest that it is epistemologically simple in certain respects, e.g., accepting sense-data at their face value, and arguing from analogy; and yet as a continuous piece of ratiocination it is highly impressive, pointing to premeditation, a drastic discipline of the mind, involving also a language structure of considerable syntactical refinement. This leads me to make a comparison with the Confucius whom we find in *The Analects,* not the Confucius of Han State Confucianism four hundred years after his death—a very different person, or, rather, set of persons, produced by the hagiographical instinct. The real Confucius, as far as we can envisage him, had a much simpler and ruder language as the tool for cutting out his thoughts. Also, in his day no one had ever thought of taking a stylus and a set of bamboo slips and scratching down a consecutive account of his personal ideas. Nor did it occur to Confucius. The written documents he read could have been little more than various collections of folk songs, elegiac laments, and congratulatory and sacrificial odes; and, in addition to these, at most, the annals of his home state and those of one or two others, some notes on ritual procedure by liturgists, and maybe some records in the archives at the Chou capital and some lists of divining oracles. I am not trying to "debunk" Confucius or sow any suspicion as to his essential greatness. On the contrary, the more historical criticism deals with his story, the more truly great he appears. But he was not a philosopher, except in the most rudimentary sense, namely, asking probing but disconnected questions about accepted ideas and accepted institutions, and then discovering the individual in society and making his great affirmation that a man is a man in the full sense only if he treats his fellow man as equally a man. From that affirmation sprang the Confucian logic of human relationship and the categorical imperative. Confucius himself clearly was no metaphysician, no logician. It is not until Mencius' time, 150 years later, that we get clear evidence of the language of hypothesis and conclusion, and get also such basic revelation of a philosophic consciousness as *"yu-tz'u kuan-chih"* (looking at the matter from this angle) and *"wu t'a"* (for no other reason than).

It is well known what Plato and Aristotle did to the Greek language, carrying it, for example, from the simple *eníai* (to be) to that exquisite abstraction *tò ón* (being), and from that to *tò rì ēn eínai* (that which makes being what it is, the nature of being). In this connection I would draw your serious attention to Dr. Richard Robinson in his *Plato's Earlier Dialectic:* "It often takes more than a lifetime for humanity to advance from the more concrete 'A rose cannot be both red and not red' to the more abstract 'X cannot be both Y and not Y,' and it may take as many years again to get from the latter to some established label such as the phrase 'The Law of Contradiction.'"[4] I think Robinson is a little on the short side when he says "one lifetime" and "as many years again." It may take several lifetimes. Thus, it would appear that Confucius first made the suggestion that names should correspond to facts in the moral realm, but it was not until some four lifetimes later that a new group of "name specialists" began to ask searching questions on that and kindred matters. These men, Teng Hsi, Hui Shih, and Kung-sun Lung, threw out the logician's challenge on accepted notions about classification, about the relation of sense impressions, about similarity and dissimilarity, and about universals; but they strained current language to the breaking point to convey their meaning. Chuang Tzu (Chuang Chou), the Neo-Moists, and Hsün

Tzu (Hsün Ch'ing) took up the challenge from various angles. But then the impulse went dead for four hundred years,[5] until Wang Pi and his fellow transcendentalists set the logical ball rolling again. This they could do more effectively, for the language was by then refined to the pitch of expressing these recondite notions.

Further, there was no real consciousness of empirical reasoning as such until there was a canon of sacred writings, a bible to which the ordinary man could appeal for an authoritative statement on what was true and what was false. When did that time come in China? Not in Confucius' time: there was no *ching* then. The character *ching* meant in that age the warp set up on a loom. But after Confucius' time there came the practice of recording a teacher's noteworthy dicta, and these records came to be called *ching*, i.e., warp teaching on which disciples could weave the woof of their amplifications. Finally, in mid-Han times (second century B.C.), came the establishment of State Confucianism and with it the colleges for expounding the Five Classics (*wu ching*).[6] Unless we understand this movement in history and its effect on thought and language, we cannot understand the emergence of higher levels of consciousness in regard to knowledge. In the beginning, when Confucius urged his disciples to study and get knowledge, he meant knowledge of the ancestral *Tao*, the ways of their fathers. When a good Eastern Han conservative, in the first and second centuries A.D., urged the duty of study, he meant knowledge as found in the sacred canon; and there is no lack of evidence of that dogmatic attitude toward the objects of knowledge. But that is not the whole of the matter. The Han mind was by no means all of one pattern. There were the *po shih,* on the one hand, the exegetes, authoritarians, bibliolaters. There were the *wen shih,* on the other hand, the literateurs, critics of popular beliefs, satirists, men with an eye for paradox: the men whom Hsiao T'ung commemorated in his ever-famous collection, and whose language and empirical attitude toward knowledge his foreword so admirably exemplifies. A *wen shih* could be as much of a sycophant of the court as a *po shih,* but when the Han Confucianist (so-called) State collapsed in shame and confusion and long years of civil disorder ensued, it was the *wen shih* empirical mind which alone was sufficiently resilient to face facts. It was their influence which enabled thinking men to look beyond the accepted Confucianist and Taoist ideas of knowledge, and search afresh for a system of abstract categories.

Chinese Thinking in Terms of Abstract Categories

I want here to ask a very simple, even seemingly stupid, historical question. As I have said, let us learn to walk before we try to run. Is there any known case of a culture which entered on the self-conscious philosophizing stage and yet failed to proceed, on the ruins of its old animistic myth-abstractions, to erect new and more essentially abstract categories for the mind? If it is true that there is no such case, we can move confidently on to a generalization, namely, that the envisaging of such categories is more than a strait-jacketing of the mind. To men playing with the newly discovered tool of individual self-conscious reasoning these apparently restrictive concepts actually have a liberating effect, at any rate temporarily. They constitute acts of imagination, an envisagement of order, of pattern, in the universe.

In regard to China it is advisable to make this cautious approach, for it looks as if the development of systematic categorical thinking came a little slowly and was hampered by the Confucianists' tendency toward authoritarianism and by the Taoists' tendency toward a denial that any categorical statement can be more than relatively true. Nonetheless, the search for abstract categories began, and continued, and even in Confucius, the first of the individual thinkers, instinctive as the temper of his mind was, we can find evidence of this. In its beginnings the movement was along simple enough lines, one of reason coping with a three-dimensional universe and using the idea of exact measurement for things of the mind. Also, men followed Mo Ti's (Mo Tzu's) lead in tracing the nexus of cause and effect. Also, they developed a sense of the relativity of the large and the small, and so arrived at the abstractions, infinity at one end of the scale and nothingness at the other end. There was much daring exploration, particularly as the fourth century B.C. went over into the third century: the discovery of metaphysical abstractions as well as cosmological. Then, in the second century B.C., with the coming of the syncretism, which we speak of as "State Confucianism," the attempt was made to be inclusive with results that were not coherently systematic.[7] Thus, we do not find in Han philosophy anything comparable to Aristotle's analysis of the Greek language and its underlying categorical abstractions, nor do we find a parallel to the syllogistic logic which he built on his categories.

On the other hand, if we compare the categories within the

four walls of which the third- and fourth-century transcendental logicians (*Hsüan hsüeh chia*) carried out their speculations, we find that they go further. For example, compare Kant's categories of quantity, categories of quality, categories of relation, and categories of modality. We find clear evidence of a consciousness of all these categories in the Chinese mind at that time. That, however, is not all that has to be said on this score. There was, in addition, from mid-Han times on, the category of the *yin* and *yang*, and alongside it, more or less dovetailed into it, the five *hsing*, i.e., the five physical forces operating in the universe. As if that were not enough, a school of so-called Confucianist thought took the diviners' cabalistic figures of divided and undivided lines and linked them by a sort of science of symbolism to the *yin* and the *yang* and the five *hsing*. For many minds this symbolism was the key to the march of history. For others it was an epistemological method, a sure guide to all possible forms of knowledge. The correlation of these abstract categories with the other more universally recognized abstractions was never, as far as I have been able to discover, successfully made. Today they are, rightly or wrongly, despised by the intelligentsia as having had a crippling influence on Chinese philosophy.[8]

Nevertheless, when all is said on this point and all due weight given to certain Sung (960–1279) philosophers and their mathematical schematizations of the hexagrams and the five *hsing* and the *yin* and the *yang*, I have still to be convinced that this line of abstraction had only a crippling influence on Chinese powers of ratiocination. The significant thing is that these symbols, i.e., the lines in the hexagrams and the trigrams, were regarded as centers of energy continually acting and reacting on each other according to their relative positions. We find, also, the correlative notions of *t'i* (substance) and *yung* (function) used in connection with them; but the impression I get is that greater importance was attached to the functional side. The center of interest lay there, so that the logic at work in these thinkers' minds led them to concentrate more on categories of relationship than on categories of substance. That fact is worthy of serious consideration. So also, although to a lesser degree, is the fact that the idea of a macrocosm's being paralleled by a microcosm in the human body[9] was worked out in a kind of precise scientific spirit. Clearly, however, the main attraction of this line of systematic thinking lay for the Chinese in the direct clue it gave to the dualistic nature of the universe with its correlation of phenomena in the heavens and phenomena on earth, e.g., in connection with the farmer's year, cycles of prosperity and disaster, etc. In this way, also, a satisfactory explanation was found for the fact of male and female, and of life and death; and this explanation was on the basis that no entity in the universe could be static or self-contained. One triumph of the system was what can only be called its ecological good sense. The plumage of birds and the pigmentation of animals' skins were guessed at as deriving from the nature of the terrain in which the birds and animals lived.[10]

In the light of the above, it would appear that the cogency of late classical and early medieval philosophy did not in the final upshot suffer from a failure to appreciate the necessity for abstract categories, but from the promulgation of too many such categories. No amount of fitting them together could produce a coherent system. Here, however, we have to beware of assuming that every thinker accepted these categories equally at their face value. That would manifestly be an unwarranted assumption, although a tendency in that direction is traceable in foreign circles through the influence of Alfred Forke's excellently informative but highly generalized work, *The World Conception of the Chinese*.[11] In this connection it must always be borne in mind that the Chinese way, apart from a few exceptions such as the iconoclast Wang Ch'ung (A.D. 27–ca. 100), was for writers just to leave out of their philosophic pictures those categories about which they had their doubts. They would not denounce unless there were some very compelling reason. We have, therefore, to use the argument from silence more often than we are naturally predisposed to do. Thus, in the notable case of Yang Hsiung (53 B.C.–A.D. 18), we find a thinker much given to speculation on the nature of knowledge but having a profound sense of the inscrutability of the natural order. It is to be taken as significant that he produced two books, one the *T'ai Hsüan* (The Supreme Mystery), the other the *Fa Yen* (Regulatory Measures), two books which bear very little, indeed no obvious, relation to each other. Since the author was silent on this, we can only assume that he was content that the two sides of his mind should so appear, each for what it was worth, no more and no less.

I submit that the above is evidence of an empirical mind at work in these writers, an empirical mind applied in the field of abstract categories as well as in the field of historical attestation. From that we must go on to envisage a continual process of promotion and de-motion in thinkers' attitudes toward generalizations, on the one hand, and abstract categories, on the other: a process which can be found in other cultures as well as the Chinese. Thus, thinkers in the third and fourth centuries A.D., men like Kuo Hsiang and Ko Hung, subjected the generally accepted absolutes to fresh scrutiny and by no means accepted them all as being as certain as the stars in their courses. The point is that they did not discard these absolutes outright but relegated them to the lower position of being tentative generalizations.

The empirical mind, once it has discovered itself and has been enshrined in cogent literary form, can never be denied its right of way. Yet, that same mind cannot work without categories, and therefore makes choice of such as it finds best suited to its purposes. This may be a dangerous philosophical path to tread, but even philosophers have to think, perhaps not perfectly, but as best they can. That this kind of thing happened in China may be taken as part of the abiding influence of the greatest of the Taoist thinkers, Chuang Chou. He sowed in Chinese thinkers' minds the unceasing suspicion that all categorical thinking, by very reason of its being categorical, was in the very nature of a tentative experiment into the mysterious hinterland of knowledge. What is true today may easily be untrue tomorrow.

The Evidence for Controlled Experiment in Language in Eastern Han Times and Thereafter

I have given in the quotation from Hsiao T'ung's foreword a typical instance of what is sometimes called parallelistic prose, but to which the Ch'ing (1644–1912) scholars gave the title "double-harness writing." This designation seems to me more illuminating. The word "*p'ien*," which they used, meant originally driving horses in double harness. The importance of this style of writing lies in the fact that it came into existence when the language was first pulled together after the unification (*ca.* 220 B.C.), and that it remained in one form and another as a continual influence right down to the twentieth century. Epistemologically, it is significant because it presupposes that all clear thinking moves forward in pairs of complementary propositions, one pair releasing the mind for the next pair. Further, it was definitely laid down by the expositors of this style that the only sound approach to inward experience, or alternatively to any object of outward attention, was from a double angle of vision, and that these two angles must be strictly correlated in the syntactical structure of the sentences. We are reminded of Aristotle's sweating over the problem of getting the bare bones of syl-logizing clear, and in consequence setting up two propositions, relating them, and getting a third: in other words, making a constructional language experiment, and doing so with a strong sense of the importance of grammar; not worrying over concepts so much, but getting down to the living molecule of thought, the sentence. It is commonly supposed that the Chinese failed to do anything commensurate along this line. That idea is not true. Not only was there the great experiment of double-harness writing; there was also in Eastern Han times (first and second centuries A.D.) and for some centuries afterward the prac-tice among scholars of making what they called "linked pearls." [12] Since these are the nearest Chinese approach to the Aristotelian syl-logism, I will deal with them before treating the major experi-ment in detail.

A "linked pearl" consisted, first, of two general propositions introduced by the words, "Your servant has heard." These proposi-tions expressed matters of common knowledge or common, accepted principles. A third and final proposition was then enunci-ated, introduced by the logical connective "therefore" (*shih i*), in the logical sense, not the factual. That, plainly, is a conclusion, so that here we have an alternative method of syl-logizing. The interesting thing is that conclusions in many cases were statements which did not correspond to hard facts. One is driven to suspect that the author's intention was to indicate the wide difference there is between theory and fact. The conclusion, therefore, was not in the nature of a new item of assured knowledge, but a *point d'appui* from which the auditors of the "linked pearl" were expected to be driven on to reconsider the nexus of the two initial propositions and the conclusions from them. In a word, here in these "linked pearls" is a methodological device for stirring criticism of accepted knowledge. In that respect their objective is fundamentally differ-ent from that of the Aristotelian syllogism, or at any rate the objec-tive as discerned in the European traditional use of it.[13] Thus, by comparing the two ways of syl-logizing, it is arguable that the Westerner gets new light on his ancestral mode of formal reasoning. To me it becomes clear that the conclusion of a syl-logism is not final in any sound epistemological sense but is merely a concrete hypothesis, clear-cut and evidential in its own way but requiring examination in the light of all the other available evidence. In other words, the proper use of the syllogism is in connection with empirical reasoning, and there its value lies in its being an experiment in which the language is under strict control.

I go on to the problems connected with empirical reasoning. We speak a great deal about empiricism, empiricism here, empiricism there, empiricism everywhere; but, in the last analysis, empirical reasoning does not produce results unless the mind is driven to make some form or other of controlled experiment. This is quite clear from the history of the natural sciences down to the present day. This seems to me the gist of what the logical positivists have been trying to emphasize, namely, that a reliable philosophical method of empirical reason requires controlled experiments in language. Now, the particular ways in which some of these neo-logicians deal with their theses may be obnoxious to some, but the main contention as I have ventured to describe it is surely incontestable. It is in that connection that the Chinese attempts at controlled language experiment are worth consideration, the more so because they have been couched in a language which at first sight is so alien to the Indo-European languages.[14]

The nature of double-harness rational discourse is especially exemplified in Hsiao T'ung's two empirical observations as expressed in the opening words of paragraph 2 of his foreword. What we have to realize is that the correlation of the imperial-chariot-*cum*-primitive-wheel observation with the block-of-ice-*cum*-quantity-of-water observation is effected by an exact parallelism in the syntactical structure of the sentences. Thus, "with regard to the [primitive] hammered-out wheel's being the beginning of the imperial carriage," in the Chinese the clause consists of seven words. So, also, does the phrase "with regard to a block of ice's being the product of a quantity of water." The same principle operates in regard to the other two clauses: "the imperial carriage has the raw material of the primitive wheel" and "the water has not got the iciness of the ice"—each clause is eight words long. What you will certainly have noticed is that these two statements are in contrast, the one being positively affirmative, the other negatively affirmative. What you should also have noticed is that in the two introductory clauses you have two complementary approaches to the two subjects of discourse: the one approach from the angle of the beginning, the other approach from the angle of the final product. Thus the two sets of observations are brought into exactly comparable form so that the mind can deal with them. The result is immediately apparent. First, the two contrasted data provoke the question, "How about this?" Second, the mind is impelled to comparative analysis of the two situations (or should I call them "events"?). "It would appear" (*kai*) introduces these two analyses, and after "*kai*" we find two six-word sentences of exactly parallel syntactical structure, which the translation faithfully reproduces. The final stage in the argument consists of two couplets of four-word sentences. Here the syntactical structure is not precisely parallel, but the relation of the two sets of meanings is sufficiently obvious.

I have chosen this passage by Hsiao T'ung partly for the reason that, although the insistence on parallelism in grammatical structure was a strong insistence, it was not carried to insane lengths. The exact comparison of meaning was the object, and, so long as that was obtained, variations in syntax were permissible. These variations were more common in the simple four-word sentences, less common in the more complicated, longer sentences.

In regard to paragraph 1, it is more a piece of historical description than a piece of dialectical reasoning, so that the parallelism is not quite so close at all points. Yet, the first parts of the description are conducted in three consecutive couplets, respectively, 4+4, 6+6, 4+4. In the second half of the description there appear to be two complementary final statements separated from each other: (a) "From this came the birth of patterned books," and (b) "How far back the historical significance of *wen* goes."

The final emphasis with regard to this double-harness thinking and writing is to be laid on the consciousness which lies behind it, of wandering, discursive thinking being necessarily disciplined by language into clearly comparable meanings. From the impact of one meaning on its fellow meaning, the mind is impelled along a straight course of comparable meanings until the author arrives at what he regards as a conclusion, or a complementary pair of conclusions. This is ratiocination, disciplined, directed, formalized, yet embodying the basic freedom of empirical investigation.

The question for the Indian and Western minds is whether this is reasoning in the strict sense of the term. As I see it, it is; but, then, I must confess my heretical predilection for regarding poets as conducting controlled experiments in language through the medium of prosodic form. I would also maintain that a painter, particularly a landscape painter, conducts an experiment controlled by the size of the canvas or piece of silk within the compass of which he tries out an idea. Moreover, I suspect that a physicist, a biologist, or a behavioristic psychologist, does something which is basically of the same sort. Imagination comes into every one of these experiments, but imagination which is subjected to control. So, also, with regard to philosophy and the latest experiments in logic: I venture to suggest that such a book as Professor Ayer's *The Foundations of Empirical Knowledge* [15] is distinguished above all by the acuteness of his imaginative powers and the pertinacity with which he works to control language.

Desiderata

Finally, I offer a brief survey of desiderata, outlining work needing to be done before Chinese epistemology can be in a fit state to make its contribution to the new science of comparative epistemology.

1. That the various critically historical studies of Chinese key philosophical terms should be evaluated in the light of modern semantic techniques, and that, after that evaluation, further studies should be undertaken with a view to clarifying the blurred meanings which now so hamper the advancement of scientific knowledge in the field of epistemology. (The work must be done by a group of scholars, Chinese and Western, and, if at the same time the Hellenists and Latinists would put their learning into better and more systematic semantic shape, we should really be able to compare.)

2. That the epistemological significance of "double-harness" writing generally and "double-harness" dialectic in particular should be made the subject of intensive study.

3. That the influence of "double-harness" thinking and writing on Chu Hsi's mind should be carefully explored; e.g., *li* (organic principle) and *ch'i* (constitutive ethers) are obviously complementary abstractions.

4. That the interplay of the scholar-mind and the artist-mind should be made the subject of exhaustive study, particularly for the Six Dynasties when the idea of graded perspective in landscape painting began to emerge, and that this should be followed by similar studies in the minds of men like Su Shih in the Sung era (960–1279).

5. That the texts of the *Kung-sun Lung* dialogues and the Neo-Moist chapters in the *Mo Tzu* should be subjected to severe critical examination.

6. That much more intensive study of the Chinese particles should be made, especially the logical connectives, and this by scholars with good philosophical training.

II

Strategic Reasons for the Above Specialized Approach to the Study of Chinese Epistemology and Methodology

The foregoing approach to Chinese epistemology and methodology may cause surprise since it refers only incidentally to the great age of Sung and centers attention on what has been generally regarded as an off-time in Chinese philosophical history. Since the Sung era produced among its various methodologies one clear and, along its own line, cogent methodology, namely, that of the Ch'eng-Chu school,[16] and, since this became dominant and remained so for some seven centuries, why this one-sided treatment? There are a number of reasons, three of them of strategic force in relation to this Conference in which distinguished Western and Indian philosophers are anxious to take Chinese philosophy into due account, no more and no less. That being so, in the first place, the Ch'eng-Chu synthesis, for all the signs of Buddhist influence on the minds of its makers, was nonetheless a great token of revulsion against the Buddhist thesis of a higher knowledge, which stood in complete contrast to the knowledge of this world. Chu Hsi went back to the ancient Confucian tradition, as did most of the Sung philosophers; and there they found this element and that which expressed for them the truth about the universe and man and about the way to achieve knowledge which is truth. It is arguable, therefore, that the Ch'eng-Chu synthesis was only a rehash of the old dogmas, and, since the doctrines of the school became the pattern of orthodoxy, the inference stares the foreign student in the face that we have here the final culminating evidence of a damning Chinese proclivity for bibliolatry and its attendant epistemological authoritarianism. The question is whether such an inference can stand, and the answer in my considered opinion is that it is only very partially true; and, when I say that, I am keenly aware that Chu Hsi's emphasis on *ko wu* (examination of things, i.e., objects of attention) became sidetracked, as the modern scientist would allege, first by Chu Hsi himself to the examination of the *li* (something akin to the Platonic ideal pattern) of things, and afterward by the Ming (1368–1644) and Ch'ing (1644–1912) devotees of the school to what they could find in the authoritative books about things and their *li*. The evidence against the truth of the accusation of authoritarianism lies, first of all, in the kind of empirical and categorical thinking the growth of which has been pictured in Part I, and, last of all, in the fact that, when modern Western mathematics and science came to the attention of the sons of the *li* doctrine devotees, some of them took to the new learning like ducks to water. Moreover, in the writings of Han Yü and Li Ao (T'ang Dynasty, 618–907), whom Dr. Fung calls the forerunners of the Ch'eng brothers and Chu Hsi, the studied language and ideation are double-harness throughout, and this in spite of the fact that these two writers revolted against the euphuistic excesses of the double-harness art in their day.

In the second place, it is as well that foreign students of Chinese cultural history should understand a recent trend in historical research in China, namely, the realization of the intrinsic importance of the Six Dynasties (third to sixth century A.D.). [17] Thus, now that the fury of the revulsion against the past and all its works, which characterized the period following the 1911 Revolution, has had time to subside, the new driving force in critical historical studies is showing itself in (a) a more impartial appreciation of Chinese Buddhism, and (b) in discovering that *"ex nihilo nihil fit"* applies to the great flowering ages of T'ang and Sung. Had it not been for the "smelting and forging" of the language done by the later Han and Six Dynasties scholars, had it not been for the close scrutiny of abstract thinking conducted by the transcendental logicians, how could T'ang poetry and Sung philosophy have come into being?

In the third place, we cannot but take into serious consideration the main thesis of F. S. C. Northrop's *The Meeting of East and West*. It is undoubtedly the main contribution which has come from the East-West movement in comparative philosophy, and we are all indebted to Northrop for his trenchant defining of problems in this particularly blurred field. His distinctions of "concepts by intuition" and "concepts by postulation" will be with us for some time to come. Yet—to confine myself to the Chinese side—there has been an unfavorable reaction amongst some Chinese scholars and most Sinologists to the lumping of China and India and Japan all in the same philosophical boat. Speaking personally, the more I have examined this matter from Northrop's angle of approach, the more I have appreciated his challenge to certain well-intrenched ways of thinking, and the more I have come to doubt whether his over-all classification of the "Oriental" traditions and their methodologies is in line with the historical facts. For that reason, therefore, as well as the other two, it became my business to draw attention to those, methodologically speaking, highly formative centuries between the collapse of Chou (third century B.C.) and the rise of T'ang and Sung, the centuries in which empirical thinking became associated with controlled language experimentation, the centuries in which the categories necessary to deductive reasoning were explored consciously and deliberately.

With Regard to Concepts by Intuition and Concepts by Postulation

"The clarification of the distinction between 'mathematicals' and 'ideas' must await the further development, in the sequel, of our technical terminology of comparative philosophy, and in particular the clarification of the different possible types of concepts by postulation." [18] The crux lies there: what kinds of concepts by postulation are we to allow as valid? Are only those which are expressed in mathematical and physical terms valid for "deductively formulated theories," and, if so, are cosmogonical as well as cosmological hypotheses of the same logical genus or not? Further, if—as seems legitimate and necessary—we are to allow valid postulation in relation to the fields of biology and physiology, of psychology and social science, is there not also a case to be made for valid postulates concerning ethical values?

I do not want to whittle at Northrop's distinctions. Obviously his emphasis on Plato the mathematician is extremely important, and the Greek consciousness of "incommensurable magnitude" did put mathematics on a very different footing from that on which it is for the man who is conscious of it only as the rule of thumb $2+2$ and 2×2. So, then, I do not minimize the fact that the ancient Greeks got as far as that and that the Chinese of classical China did not get so far. On the other hand, as I note that "concepts by postulation" were first introduced into Western philosophy because of the need for them in Greek physics and mathematics, so I note also that Aristotle, for two reasons, one of them his concern for biology, was forced to reject all postulated scientific objects, such as the physical atoms of Democritus. The interesting thing is that Epicurus a few years later went back to the Democritean atom but changed the postulate to one in which the deductive movement of his mind seems to have been that men are of the same basic stuff as the atoms in Nature, that some freedom of movement is characteristic of men, that therefore some freedom of movement is characteristic of atoms (cf., Leibniz on his monads). Now, it is not required of a concept by postulation that it should be true but that it should give birth to a deductively formulated theory and should not spring from one or more direct sense-apprehensions. But does the use of analogy come into the postulatory picture, for Epicurus plainly intuited (or postulated) an intrinsic affinity between the basic stuff of man and the basic stuff of Nature?

The significance of these questions is, of course, in relation to China, where there came to be a vivid and even subtle conscious-ness of the biological-*cum*-physiological side of Nature, and where a basic affinity was assumed between men and things. [19] The level of mathematical interest seems to have remained low, although in the Neo-Moist books (third century B.C.?) a number of geometrical definitions are given. A sort of Pythagorean playing with numbers is found in the Hsi tz'u (sometime between the third century B.C. and the first century A.D.) and elsewhere, but it is not until early Sung times that we can find such high-level calculations as produce an abstract theory of numbers. [20] At first sight, therefore, the whole range of scientific thinking seems to be at the natural-history stage, sometimes a little childishly so, but also often enough maturely so. E.g., as early as the third century B.C. we find one Ho Kuan Tzu, a Taoist-minded philosophizer, noting that between an object and its shadow there is no interstice of space, but between a sound and its echo there is an interval of time. What is more, he noted that the direct unbroken connection is necessary if the shadow is to be there at all, and assumes, infers, postulates (?) that the interval of time is necessary if the echo is to come. There, however, he stopped. He was not driven, as were William Derham and the French Acad-emy in the eighteenth century, to image the existence of sound waves and to experiment accordingly.

Thus, in China there was controlled experimentation all the time, but, apart from alchemy, it was in the direction of control of the language of discourse, of the language of poetry, as of the language of prose. The line of demarcation which the West has come to draw between the two ways of thinking and writing does not work out the same way in China. Most of China's philosophical history is to be found in essays and not in ponderous treatises, and in those essays there is generally attention to form as well as to matter. This at first sight would seem to give Northrop all that he claims, namely, a highly developed sense of art and a poorly developed sense of logic, the employment of the artistic genius militating against the employment of the scientific: minds working by intuitive imagination and not by the cold light of reason. To a certain extent I agree. I am the first person to acknowledge that he has some justification for his theories in relation to China. Nonetheless, I do not agree when he rules out concepts by postulation and deductively formed theories. It is not a case of "either-or" in the China field but of "both-and." And this "both-and" state of affairs surely applies to Western philosophy as well as to Chinese. The only thing is that in the Chinese philosophizing tradition there is probably rather more of the artistic power of discourse than there is in the Western philosophizing tradition.

If Northrop can grant me, as certain utterances of his lead me to suppose he can, that not all valid postulations are directly connected with physics and mathematics, then I think we can start getting a little further in our common explorations. In order to define the comparative situation, I submit, by way of example, that the two concepts *jen* and *yin-yang*, concepts which have exercised so profound an influence on Chinese ways of thinking, are concepts by postulation, not concepts by intuition in Northrop's sense. In the one case, in very early days, when, as Hsiao T'ung might have said, philosophical thinking was in the stage of primitive simplicity, one Confucius made a practical syl-logism: man can live well only in society: we men of Lu State and its neighbors are men: therefore, we must be socially minded, i.e., man-to-man-ly (*jen*). In this way, by postulation, he revolutionized the current meaning of *jen* and gave the Chinese a deductively formulated theory which the disciples of Confucius have been trying to prove experimentally ever since. In the second case, at a time when philosophical thinking as such was beginning to take shape in Chinese minds, by direct apprehension some thinkers saw the heavens and the earth, two different entities sharply distinguishable yet self-evidently related, since life on the earth depended on the regular day-and-night, spring-summer-autumn-winter, rain-and-sunshine cycle of movement in the skies. They analyzed this cosmic situation in their minds, and—I would say—arrived at a hypothesis that there were two theoretic forces behind this range of phenomena viewed as a whole: a constructive force and a destructive force working in conjunction, the one the logical antithesis of the other, but the two working as one indivisible existential process. They then proceeded to try out this hypothesis in relation to the various departments of life in Nature and life in man. In the light of this *yin-yang* postulation (as I would call it) they discovered all sorts of relationships, some of them ludicrous from Wang Ch'ung's point of view in the second century A.D., others unsound from Chu Hsi's point of view in the twelfth century, and still others merely naïvely common-sensical and not true to fact from our scientific point of view today.

Yet, its main presuppositions, that the positive must entail the negative, that movement must entail stillness, that what we see as life must entail death (although, as Chuang Tzu maintained, we do not know what death is), stand today. Along with these, yet sanely enough not differentiated as *yin,* on the one hand, and *yang,* on the other, went the two presuppositions that the idea of limited space carries with it its complement, unlimited space, as also the idea of time carries with it the idea of eternity. These, surely, were not intuitions or hunches but inferences. And now we come to Chu Hsi again, with his concepts by postulation (as I would say), *li* and *ch'i,* the one metaphysical, the other physical, or perhaps paraphysical, together constituting the current coin of later methodological theorizing, and in their basic complementality furnishing an incontrovertible instance of the double-harness mind at work, since by their means Chu Hsi made observation of all phenomena. We have to bear in mind: (a) that the Sung scholars had inherited a strong sense of the importance of history, and to them we owe those massive tomes, the *Tzu-chih t'ung-chien* and the *T'ai-p'ing yü-lan,*[21] both of them monuments of historical discrimination, and the latter documenting every citation it makes under its fifty-five main headings, while Chu Hsi himself set his disciples to work on making a shortened version of the former; and (b) that, although later ages read and revised these vast works with painstaking care, yet the actual tendency inherent in Chu Hsi's line of reasoning was to view things *sub specie aeternitatis* rather than *sub specie temporis.* That being so, the practical moral for both Northrop and me is that the historian's sense of impartiality demands that we should do justice, no more and no less, to China's epistemological devil and saint, "Chu Wen Kung" (prince of *wen*, patterned thinking), China's arch-deductive theorist, Chu Hsi.

Conclusion

Since our main desideratum here must be a more denotative examination of epistemological method, may I plead for the exercise not only of more studied care but also of a more imaginative mind in comparing East and West on a historical basis. For instance, no illumination of the comparative field can be gained by treating *The Analects* of Confucius and the *Metaphysics* of Aristotle *pari passu* as typical examples of the methodological approach to knowledge in the respective cultures. The one book came into existence before there was any conscious, much less consecutive, philosophical thinking, and was not written by Confucius, while Aristotle was stimulated by a Plato and had the philosophical reflections of two centuries on which to draw. The more legitimate comparison is with the ordered and more competent literary mind of Hsün Ch'ing, two centuries after Confucius. And even then the comparison cannot have much weight unless we are able to preface it with a comparison of the relative philosophical maturity of the Greek and Chinese languages at those two particular times. This procedure would come nearer to the basic principle of comparison, namely, comparing like with like.

A second instance may be cited in relation to the era of the Six Dynasties. Because the collapse of Rome and the overrunning of the Mediterranean world by barbarians brought a period commonly known as the "Dark Ages," it is rather generally taken for granted that the collapse of the Han order in the third century, followed by the barbarian rule of North China in the fourth to sixth centuries, produced a very similar dark age. The history of civilization is by no means as tidy as that. A comparison of Lu Chi, the literary critic, who died in A.D. 303, with Longinus, who died in A.D. 273, and a comparison of the respective achievements in the writing of history and the creation of new art motifs would show how different the two eras were. Not that they should not be compared, for they should. The rise of the Holy Roman Empire and the rise of the T'ang Dynasty are essentially comparable historical phenomena, and our task of comparing philosophies goes haltingly until competent work has been done in this matter. This reflection is closely linked with another reflection, namely, one in connection with the growing practice of using the European historians' terminology, such as "Early Medieval" and "Late Medieval." I do not see how this is to be avoided in Western learned circles, but it is obviously attended by great dangers. The crux of the problem lies in the unconscious assumption by Western students that the uneven levels of intellectual acumen to be found in the Western Middle Ages are roughly a criterion as to what Chinese learning and philosophy could have achieved, i.e., presumably did actually achieve, in their Middle Ages. That does not follow in the least. The attainments of new levels of rational consciousness do not come *pari passu* in the different cultures, just as the Mediterranean time-schedule of advance and pause is not necessarily that of other cultures. Thus, for example, the Chinese had their major attack of religious utilitarianism followed (may we say, inevitably?) by non-religious utilitarianism twenty-one to twenty-three centuries back, while Europe got its major attack and aftermath one to three centuries ago. On the other hand, Greek mathematics was what it was—and later was forgotten for several hundred years—while even eleventh-century Chinese mathematics did not produce a Euclid or a Democritus. Here are pitfalls for the unwary philosopher in the new field of culture comparison.

In this connection note should also be taken of Fung Yu-lan's pithy statement that all post-classical Chinese philosophy is in the medieval stage. We know what he means by that and we need not quarrel with it, until we come to consider what is called "The Renaissance" in textbooks of European culture. It is then apt to be assumed that not only did "The Renaissance" take place in Europe, but that no renaissance could have taken place in China in the twelfth century. No true historian, of course, would soil his historian's tongue with so gross a *non sequitur*. That stands. On the other hand, there have been these four last centuries of the advance of natural science in the West and not in China. What are we to assume? That the Chinese intelligentsia are incurably artistic and unscientific? We cannot do that when before our eyes stands the evidence of the nineteenth-century mathematicians, Li Shan-lan and Hua Heng-fang, of the brilliant geodecist of this generation, Li Ssu-kuang, and many others, including the younger men working in the Princeton Institute of Advanced Studies after gaining mathematical doctorates at Oxford. Can we assume a time lag of a few negligible centuries which the Chinese will quickly overtake? No one can know for a generation or two.

Meanwhile, there is the little matter of the historical imagination, that indispensable tool of the historian's science and art, which is even more needed in intercultural comparison. There would be great virtue in learned experiments in the imaginative depicting by Chinese scholars of various key periods transplanted by a magic carpet into some American or European *mise en scène:* Yang Hsiung dining with Seneca or Marcus Aurelius, Han Yü in the Rome of Gregory the Great, and Chu Hsi coming into the England of James I and Donne and Milton. What would these critics of the thought of their times have made of the philosophic foundations of the culture they saw in process of evolving? My impression is that the Sung visitor to England would have felt that the Protestant reform in England had produced but a rehash of the old classics and that both the new Protestant and the Trentine Catholic were sunk in authoritarianism. But then he could have met Francis Bacon or read his *Novum Organum* and said, "Ah, yes, that is what I was thinking of when I said *ke wu* (investigating things), but he does not realize the necessity of having a *kang chi* (over-all binding principle)." But, then, if Chu Hsi had seen Shakespeare played and had mastered Shakespeare's *Hamlet* with its immortal picture of filial piety torn two ways, if he had gone over to Holland and studied the Dutch painters, being a little too early to talk with Benedict Spinoza, he might, yes, he might have said to himself, "How muddled and inconclusive the philosophy of this people is, and how great their poetry and art." And then he would have gone back to China muttering something about the aesthetic, intuitive approach to the problems of the universe and man and would have thanked Heaven that his China knew how to combine the scientific [22] and the artistic approach and make sense of it all. How wrong he would have been, and yet how excusably wrong, how even illuminatingly wrong!

Notes

1. Cf., e.g., *Wen hsüan* (*chüan* 15), the long prose poem on "Ssu hsüan" (Thought the Transcender) by Chang Heng (A.D. 78–139). Cf. also the chapter by Liu Hsieh (sixth century) on the same subject in his famous book *Wen-hsin tiao-lung* (The Literary Mind and the Carving of Dragons).
2. R. G. Collingwood, *The Idea of History* (Oxford: The Clarendon Press, 1946), p. 1.
3. See the "Hsi tz'u Amplification" of the *I ching*, early in Part II; cf. English version, Sacred Books of the East, Vol. XVI, p. 382. That is the main reference, but Hsiao T'ung's quotation includes phrases from other parts of the *I ching*.
4. Richard Robinson, *Plato's Earlier Dialectic* (Ithaca: Cornell University Press, 1941), p. 2.
5. Authoritarian-minded Confucianists of the Han era regarded these speculations as casuistical and morally subversive. Nevertheless, the *Kung-sun Lung* dialogues and the Neo-Moist texts (the *Ching shuo* and *Ch'u*) survived and are extant today.
6. The number of works recognized as canonical was gradually extended until in Sung times the total was thirteen.
7. Cf. Tung Chung-shu, *Ch'un-ch'iu fan-lu*. Cf. also Edward VI's and Queen Elizabeth's efforts to find a middle way of agreement for the English religious mind of the sixteenth century.
8. Cf. Ku Chieh-kang, "Wu-Te chung shih shuo-hsia te Cheng-chih li-ho shih" (The Studies of Politics and History under the [influence] of the [study of the] Five Virtues) *Tsing-hua Learned Journal*, VI (June, 1930).
9. Chinese speculation along this line definitely started with Nature as the type to which men on the smaller scale must surely conform. In this respect thinking started from the opposite end to what it did in some Greek thinking.
10. Cf. Part II, *init.*, of the "Hsi tz'u" of the *I ching* (dating probably from Former Han times). A popular name for the "Hsi tz'u" is "Ta chuan." This is used by Richard Wilhelm in *The I Ching* by R. Wilhelm and C. F. Baynes, Bollingen Series, XIX (New York: Pantheon Books, Inc., 1950). Wilhelm also uses the "Hsi tz'u" name, which, with its meaning of "Appended Judgments," is in my judgment preferable. The reference to birds and beasts is *op. cit.*, Vol. I, p. 353.
11. London: Arthur Probsthain, 1925.
12. I strongly suspect satirical intention in this naming of them. The evidence points to the practice being a form of court amusement.
13. In recent years the "hypothetical syllogism" has, of course, been the subject of close study.

14. A loose-grammared language in contrast to Greek and Latin. But, then, the English language is also loose grammared.
15. A. J. Ayer, *The Foundations of Empirical Knowledge* (London: Macmillan and Company, 1947).
16. That epistemology was personal illumination following on a long period of arduous study plus commensurate ethical practice plus concentrated meditation.
17. Ch'en (Tschen) Yin-ko, T'ang Yung-t'ung, Fung Yu-lan, and Lo Ken-tse are the men behind this, four of the best critical historians in China today.
18. F. S. C. Northrop, "The Complementary Emphases of Eastern Intuitive and Western Scientific Philosophy," in Charles A. Moore, ed., *Philosophy—East and West* (Princeton: Princeton University Press, 1944), p. 179, esp. p. 175; reprinted in *The Logic of the Sciences and the Humanities* (New York: The Macmillan Company, 1947), p. 89.
19. The term *"wu"* (commonly translated "things") was accepted by Han times, if not before, to denote the animate and the inanimate. Within the scope of the term distinctions were drawn between birds, beasts and fishes, and insects, between plants and trees (though not very clearly), between rocks, metals, and soils, between rivers and dry land, mountains, valleys, and marshes. *Wan wu*, literally, "myriad things," was the generic term for the discrete in Nature.
20. Cf. Chu Ch'ien-chih, *Chung-kuo ssu-hsiang tui-yü Ou-chou wen-hua chih ying-hsiang* (The Influence of Chinese Thought on European Culture) (Shanghai: Commercial Press, 1940). The author gives a number of diagrams in connection with the theory of numbers. His view is that Leibniz was stimulated by receiving these Sung diagrams and the explanation of them from his Jesuit friends in Peking.
21. For notes on these two works, see Alex Wylie, *Notes on Chinese Literature* (Shanghai: Presbyterian Mission Press, 1922), pp. 25, 183. The latter work is not strictly a historical work at all and is rightly listed as the "cyclopaedia"; yet, its contents from the point of view of later ages are all historical data. Quotations are made in it from 1,690 works of different ages.
22. For him "science" (*scientia*) would mean primarily the applied sciences of government and of behavior in the family and the community. Chu Hsi wrote a book on family behavior, the *Chia li.*

HU SHIH   *The Scientific Spirit and Method*

in Chinese Philosophy

I

IN THE COURSE of the past work in East-West philosophy, the
question has been raised as to whether there was science in the
East, and why the East developed little or no science.

To the first question, some of the answers seem definitely in
the negative. "So the West generated the natural sciences, as the
East did not," said Professor Wilmon Henry Sheldon.[1] And Professor
Filmer S. C. Northrop said, "There is very little science [in the
East] beyond the most obvious and elementary information of the
natural history type."[2]

To the second question as to why there was very little or no
science in the East, the answers vary. But the most challenging
and provocative answer has come from Northrop, who declares,
"A culture which admits only concepts by intuition is automatically prevented from developing science of the Western type
beyond the most elementary, inductive, natural history stage."[3] As
defined by Northrop, concepts by intuition are those "which denote,
and the complete meaning of which is given by, something which
is immediately apprehended."[4] This is Northrop's theory:

> Formal reasoning and deductive science are not necessary if only
> concepts by intuition are used in a given culture. If what science and
> philosophy attempt to designate is immediately apprehended, then
> obviously all that one has to do in order to know it is to observe and
> contemplate it. The methods of intuition and contemplation become the

sole trustworthy modes of inquiry. It is precisely this which the East affirms and precisely why its science has never progressed for long beyond the initial natural history stage of development to which concepts by intuition restrict one.[5]

This theory is concisely expressed in these words ". . . the East used doctrine built out of concepts by intuition, whereas Western doctrine has tended to be constructed out of concepts by postulation." [6]

I have no intention to go into the details of this Northropean theory, which must have been familiar to us who have followed our philosopher-friend all these 20 years.

I only wish to point out that this theory of bifurcation of East and West is unhistorical and untrue as far as the intellectual history of the East is concerned.

In the first place, there is no race or culture "which admits only concepts by intuition." Indeed, there is no man who "admits only concepts by intuition." Man is by nature a thinking animal, whose daily practical needs compel him to make inferences for better or for worse, and he often learns to make better and surer inferences. It has been truly said that inference is the business man never ceases to engage in. And, in making inferences, man must make use of all his powers of perception, observation, imagination, generalization and postulation, induction, and deduction. In that way, man develops his common sense, his stock of empirical knowledge, his wisdom, his civilization and culture. And, in the few centers of continuous intellectual and cultural tradition, man, of the East and of the West, in the course of time, has developed his science, religion, and philosophy. I repeat, there is no culture "which admits only (the so-called) concepts by intuition," and which "is automatically prevented from developing science of the Western type."

In the second place, I wish to point out that, in attempting to understand the East and the West, what is needed is a historical approach, a historical attitude of mind, rather than a "technical terminology for comparative philosophy." Northrop includes among his examples of "concepts by postulation" these items: Centaurs,[7] the opening sentence of the Fourth Gospel, the concept of God the Father, the Christianity of St. Paul, of St. Augustine, and St. Thomas Aquinas,[8] as well as the atoms of Democritus, the atomic models of Bohr's and Rutherford's classical atomic physics,[9] and the space-time continuum of Einstein's physics.[10] Surely, one can find a thousand imaginary concepts in the mythological and religious literature of India and China that can compare with the Greek concept of "Centaurs." And, surely, one can point to many scores of religious ideas in India and China that can compare with the concept of God contained in the first sentence of the Fourth Gospel.[11] Are we not justified in calling a halt to such "bifurcating" terminology that tends to emphasize a difference between East and West which historically does not exist?

I would like very much, therefore, to present here what I mean by the historical approach to the comparative study of philosophy. Briefly, the historical approach means that all past differences in the intellectual, philosophical, and religious activities of man, East and West, have been *historical* differences, produced, conditioned, shaped, grooved, and often seemingly perpetuated by geographical, climatic, economic, social and political, and even individual or biographical factors, all of which are capable of being studied and understood historically, rationally, and intelligently. Through this historical approach, patient and fruitful studies and researches can then be conducted, always seeking to be understood, never merely to laugh, or to cry, or to despair. It may be that, through this historical approach, we may find that, after all, there are more similarities than differences in the philosophies and religions of East and West; and that whatever striking differences have existed are no more than differences in the degree of emphasis brought about by a peculiar combination of historical factors. It may be that, through this historical approach, we may better understand the rise and rapid development of what has been called "science of the Western type"—not as an isolated or exclusive creation of any chosen people, but only as the natural product of an unusually happy combination of many historical forces. It may be that, as a result of patient historical researches, we may better understand that none of those historical forces, nor a combination of them, will ever "automatically prevent" or permanently incapacitate any race or culture from learning, adopting, developing —and even excelling in—the intellectual activities historically initiated and developed by any other race.

To say that any culture "is automatically prevented from developing science of the Western type" is to despair prematurely. But to seek to understand what historical forces have conspired to give the nations of Europe the glory of leading the entire world by at least fully four hundred years in the development of modern science, and, on the other hand, what other historical forces or what combinations of such forces have been largely responsible for retarding or even crushing such scientific development by any race or culture throughout historic times, not excepting the Graeco-Roman-Christian culture throughout the Middle Ages—that would be a legitimate ambition not unworthy of such a learned assembly of philosophers and historians of philosophy.

II

It is in the direction of suggesting some such historical approach to comparative philosophy that I have prepared this paper with the rather immodest title: "The Scientific Spirit and Method in Chinese Philosophy."

I have deliberately left out the scientific *content* of Chinese philosophy, not merely for the obvious reason that that content seems so insignificant compared with the achievement of Western science in the last four centuries, but also because I am of the opinion that, in the historical development of science, the scientific spirit or attitude of mind and the scientific method are of far more importance than any practical or empirical results of the astronomer, the calendar-reformer, the alchemist, the physician, or the horticulturist.

This point of view has been eloquently presented by Dr. James B. Conant, former President of Harvard University, and a first-rank scientist in his own right, in his Lectures, *On Understanding Science*. Let me, therefore, quote him:

Who were the precursors of those early investigators who in the sixteenth and seventeenth centuries set the standards for exact and impartial inquiries? Who were the spiritual ancestors of Copernicus, Galileo and Vesalius? Not the casual experimenter or the artful contrivers of new mechanical devices who gradually increased our empirical knowledge of physics and chemistry during the Middle Ages. These men passed on to subsequent generations many facts and valuable methods of attaining practical ends but not the spirit of scientific inquiry.

For the burst of new ardor in disciplined intellectual injuiry we must turn to a few minds steeped in the Socratic tradition, and to those early scholars who first recaptured the culture of Greece and Rome by primitive methods of archaeology. In the first period of the Renaissance, the love of dispassionate search for the truth was carried forward by those who were concerned with man and his works rather than with inanimate or animate nature. During the Middle Ages, interest in attempts to use the human reason critically and without prejudice, to probe deeply without fear and favor, was kept alive by those who wrote about human problems. In the early days of the Revival of Learning, it was the humanist's exploration of antiquity that came nearest to exemplifying our modern ideas of impartial inquiry. . . .

Petrarch, Boccaccio, Machiavelli, and Erasmus, far more than the alchemists, must be considered the precursors of the modern scientific investigator. Likewise, Rabelais and Montaigne who carried forward the critical philosophic spirit must be counted, it seems to me, among the forerunners of the modern scientists.[12]

I believe that the position taken by President Conant is essentially correct. It is interesting to note that he gave his lectures a subtitle: "An Historical Approach."

From this historical standpoint, "the love of dispassionate search for the truth," the "interest in attempts to use the human reason critically and without prejudice, to probe deeply without fear and favor," "the ardor in disciplined intellectual inquiry," "the setting of standards for exact and impartial inquiry"—these are characteristics of the spirit and method of scientific inquiry. It is these aspects of the scientific spirit and method, as they are found in the intellectual and philosophical history of China, that will form the main body of my paper.

III

To begin with, there was undoubtedly a "Socratic tradition" in the intellectual heritage of classical China. The tradition of free question and answer, of free discussion, independent thinking, and doubting, and of eager and dispassionate search for knowledge was maintained in the school of Confucius (551–479 B.C.). Confucius often described himself as one who "learns without satiety and teaches without being wearied," and as one who "loves antiquity and is earnest in seeking to know it." * On one occasion, he spoke of himself as one "who is so eager to know that he forgets to eat, whose cares are lost in moments of rapturous triumph, unmindful of the coming of old age."

That was the man who founded and molded the orthodoxy of the Chinese intellectual life of the past twenty-five centuries. There

* Editor's note: Because of serious illness and death of Dr. Hu it has been impossible to provide complete references for some of his quotations from classical texts.

was much in Confucius that reminds us of Socrates. Like Socrates, Confucius always professed that he was not a "wise man" but a man who loved knowledge. He said: "He who knows does not rank with him who loves knowledge; and he who loves knowledge does not rank with him who really delights in it."

An interesting feature in the Confucian tradition is a deliberate encouragement of independent thinking and doubt. Thus Confucius spoke of his most gifted student, Yen Hui, "Hui is no help to me: he is always satisfied with what I say." But he also said, "I often talk to Hui for a whole day, and he, like a dullard, never raises an objection. But when he is gone and I examine his private life, I find him fully capable of developing [my ideas]. Hui is no dullard." Confucius apparently wanted no docile disciples who would feel pleased with everything he said. He wanted to encourage them to doubt and raise objections. This spirit of doubt and questioning was best shown in Mencius, who openly declared that to accept the whole *Book of History* as trustworthy is worse than to have no *Book of History* at all, and that, of the essay "Wu-ch'eng" (a section of *The Book of History*), he would accept no more than two or three (bamboo) pages. Mencius also suggested a free and independent attitude of mind as a necessary prerequisite to the understanding of *The Book of Odes* (*Shih ching*).

The best-known Confucian dictum is: "Learning without thinking is labor lost; thinking without learning is perilous." He himself, however, seemed to be always inclined to the side of learning. He said of himself: "I have often spent a whole day without food and a whole night without sleep—to think. But it was of no use. It is better to study." "Study as if life were too short and you were on the point of missing it." "He who learns the truth in the morning may die in the evening without regret." That was China's Socratic tradition.

Intellectual honesty was an important part of this tradition. "Yu," said Confucius to one of his students, "shall I tell you what knowledge is? To hold that you know a thing when you know it, and to hold that you do not know when you really do not know: that is knowledge." When on another occasion the same student asked Confucius how to serve the spirits and the gods, Confucius said, "We have not yet learned to serve men, how can we serve the spirits?" The questioner then asked about death, and the Master said, "We do not yet know life, how do we know death?" This was not evading the questions; it was an injunction to be intellectually honest about things one does not really know. Such an agnostic position about death and the gods and spirits has had lasting influence on Chinese thought in subsequent ages. That, too, was China's Socratic tradition.

In recent decades, doubt has been raised about the historicity of the man Lao Tzu (or Lao Tan) and about the authenticity and the dating of the ancient book known as *The Book of Lao Tzu.* But I, for one, still believe that Confucius was at one time a student of and an apprentice to the older philosopher, Lao Tzu, whose influence in the direction of a naturalistic conception of the universe and of a laissez-faire (*wu-wei*) philosophy of government can be observed in the thinking of Confucius himself.

To have postulated a naturalistic view of the universe at so early a date (the sixth century B.C.) was truly revolutionary. The ancient Chinese notion of *T'ien* (Heaven) or *Ti* (Supreme God), as represented in the songs and hymns of *The Book of Odes,* was that of a knowing, feeling, loving, and hating supreme ruler of men and the universe. And the fate of men was also supposed to be in the hands of all kinds of gods and spirits. In place of such an anthropomorphic deity or deities, an entirely new philosophic concept was proposed.

> *There is something of indeterminate origin,*
> *And born before Heaven and Earth.*
> *Without voice and without body,*
> *It stands alone and does not change;*
> *It moves everywhere but is never exhausted.*
> *It may be regarded as the mother of the universe.*
> *I do not know its name:*
> *I call it "the Way"* (Tao),
> *And perforce designate it "the Great"* (ta).

So, the new principle was postulated as the Way (*Tao*), that is, a process, an all-pervading and everlasting process. The Way becomes so of itself (*tzu jan*), and all things become so of themselves.

"The Way (*Tao*) does nothing, yet it leaves nothing undone." That is the central idea of this naturalistic conception of the universe. It became the cornerstone of a political theory of non-activity, non-interference, laissez faire (*wu-wei*). "The best ruler is one whose existence is scarcely noticed by the people." And the same idea was developed into a moral philosophy of humility, of non-resistance to evil and violence. "The supreme good is likened to water which benefits all things and resists none." "The weak and yielding always wins over the hard and strong." "There is always the Great Executioner that executes. [That is the great Way, which does nothing but leaves nothing undone.] To do the executing for the Great Executioner is like doing the chopping for the master carpenter. He who does the chopping for the master carpenter rarely escapes injuring his own hand."

Such was the naturalistic tradition formed by Lao Tzu, the teacher of Confucius. But there was a fundamental difference between the teacher and his student. Confucius was a historically minded scholar and a great teacher and educator, whereas Lao Tzu was a nihilist in his conception of knowledge and civilization. The ideal utopia of Lao Tzu was a small state with a small population, where all the inventions of civilization, such as ships and carriages "which multiplied human power by ten times and a hundred times are not to be put in use; and where the people would restore the use of knotted cords instead of writing!" "Always let the people have no knowledge, and therefore no desires." How different is this intellectual nihilism from Confucius' democratic philosophy of education, which says, "With education there will be no classes!"

But the naturalistic conception of the universe, as it was germinated in *The Book of Lao Tzu* and more fully developed in subsequent centuries, has been a most important philosophical heritage from the Classical Age. Naturalism itself best exemplifies the spirit of courageous doubt and constructive postulation. Its historical importance fully equals that of the humanist heritage left by Confucius. Whenever China has sunk deep into irrationality, superstition, and otherworldliness, as she has done several times in her long history, it was always the naturalism of Lao Tzu and the philosophical Taoists, or the humanism of Confucius, or a combination of the two, that would arise and try to rescue her from her sluggish slumbers.

The first great movement "to use the human reason critically and to probe deeply without fear and favor" in the face of the State Religion of the Han empire was such a combination of the naturalistic philosophy of Taoism and the spirit of doubt and intellectual honesty that was the most valuable heritage handed down from Confucius and Mencius. The greatest representative of that movement of criticism was Wang Ch'ung (A.D. 27–*ca.* 100), author of a book of 85 essays called the *Lun heng* (Essays in Criticism).

Wang Ch'ung spoke of his own essays in these words, "One sentence sums up my essays: I hate falsehood." "Right is made to appear wrong, and falsehood is regarded as truth. How can I remain silent! . . . When I read current books of this kind, when I see truth overshadowed by falsehood, my heart beats violently, and my brush trembles in my hand. How can I be silent! When I criticize them, I examine them in my reasoning power, check them against facts, and show up their falsehood by setting up proofs." [13]

He was criticizing the superstitions and falsehoods of his age, of which the greatest and most powerful were the central doctrines of catastrophes (*tsai*) and anomalies (*i*), which the state religion of the Han empire, under the name of Confucianism, interpreted as warnings sent by a benevolent and all-seeing God (or Heaven) (*T'ien*) to terrify the rulers and governments so that they might repent and reform their acts of misrule. This religion of Han Confucianism had been formulated by a number of philosopher-statesmen of the second and first centuries B.C. who were justifiably worried by the real problem of how to deal with the unlimited power of the absolute monarchy in a vast unified empire, and who, consciously or semiconsciously, had hit upon the religious weapon and had worked out an elaborate theology of "reciprocal relationship between Heaven (*T'ien*) and the rulers of men" which seemed to have been able to hold the absolute sovereigns in awe throughout the several centuries of the Han dynasties.

This theology of the state religion of catastrophes and anomalies was best expressed by Tung Chung-shu (*ca.* 179–*ca.* 104 B.C.), who spoke like a prophet and with authority: "The action of man, when it reaches the highest level of good and evil [that is, when it becomes government action affecting vast numbers], will flow into the course of Heaven and Earth and cause reciprocal reverberations in their manifestations." "When a state is on the verge of ruin, Heaven will cause catastrophes [such as floods, famines, great fires] to befall earth as warnings to the ruler. When these are not hearkened to, Heaven will cause strange anomalies [such as sun eclipses, comets, unusual movements of planets] to appear to terrify the ruler into repentance. But, when even these anomalies fail to check his misrule, then ruin will come. All this shows that Heaven is always kind to the ruler and anxious to protect him from destruction." This theology of intimate reciprocal reverberations between Heaven and the rulers of men was supposedly based on an elaborate interpretation of the pre-Confucian *Book of History* and the Confucian *Ch'un ch'iu Annals* (*Spring and Autumn Annals,* which recorded numerous unusual events on earth and in the heavens, including thirty-six eclipses of the sun and five earthquakes between 722 and 481 B.C.). But the canonical Classics of established Confucianism were not enough for the support of this fanatic and fantastic theology, which had to be reinforced by an ever-increasing crop of apocryphal works known as the *wei* (woofs or interweaving aids to the Canon) and the *ch'an* (prophecies), which are collections of bits of empirical knowledge intermixed with hundreds of astrological fantasies.

It is a historical fact that this state religion of pseudo-Confucianism, at the height of its glory, was taken so seriously that many a prime minister was dismissed, and one was forced by the Emperor to commit suicide, all because of the belief in Heaven's warning in the form of catastrophes and abnormalities. One of the three great medieval religions was in full sway over the empire.

It was against the basic idea of a reciprocal responsive relationship between a teleological God and the rulers of men that Wang Ch'ung was directing his main criticism. He was criticizing the theology of the established religion of the empire. The world view with which he set out to attack the current theology was the naturalistic philosophy of Lao Tzu and the Taoists. He said:

The Way (*Tao*) of Heaven is that it does nothing and all things become so by themselves. If Heaven were to give warnings to men or mete out punishments, that would be "doing" things and not things "becoming so of themselves." . . . Those who hold that catastrophic and abnormal occurrences were purposeful warnings from Heaven are in reality degrading the dignity of the great Heaven by interpreting natural phenomena in terms of human action. They are therefore not convincing at all.[14]

For, he pointed out,

Heaven is most exalted, and man is tiny. Man's place between Heaven and Earth is like that of a flea inside one's clothes, or that of an ant in an anthill. . . . Surely it is absolutely impossible for man with his tiny body of seven feet to hope to bring about any response from the vast atmosphere of the great firmament.[15]

That is why Wang Ch'ung said that the doctrine of reciprocal response between Heaven and man was in reality "degrading the dignity of the great Heaven."

And he offered to prove that man and all things in the universe were never purposefully (*ku*) produced by Heaven and Earth, but were accidentally (*yu*) so, of themselves:

It is wrong to hold that man is born of Heaven and Earth purposely. Certain fluids are combined, and man is born accidentally. . . . All things are formed of fluid (*ch'i*), and each species reproduces itself. . . . If it were true that Heaven purposely produced all living things in the world, then Heaven should make them all love each other and not allow them to injure or prey on each other. . . . But there are tigers and wolves, poisonous snakes and insects, which prey on man. Can we say that it is the purpose of Heaven to create man for the use of those ferocious and poisonous animals? [16]

The first century of the Christian era was a period of calendar reform under the Han empire. And Wang Ch'ung made full use of the astronomical knowledge of his age to expose the folly of the current theological doctrine of catastrophes and anomalies as warnings from Heaven against the evil acts or policies of the rulers of the empire. He said:

There is one eclipse of the sun in about forty-one or forty-two months, and there is one eclipse of the moon in about six months. Solar and lunar eclipses are regular occurrences which have nothing to do with government policies. And this is true of the hundreds of anomalies and thousands of calamities, none of which is necessarily caused by the action of the rulers of men.[17]

But Wang Ch'ung more frequently cited facts of everyday experience as proofs or evidences in his numerous criticisms of the superstitions or falsehoods of his age. He offered five "tests" (*nien*) to prove that thunder was not the wrath of Heaven but only a kind of fire generated by the friction of the *yin* and *yang* fluids in the air. And he produced many a proof to support his thesis that there were no ghosts or spirits. One of those proofs is most ingenious and so far irrefutable: "If a ghost is the spirit of the dead man, then the ghost should be seen only in naked form and could not be seen with clothes on his body. For surely the cloth or silk can have no soul or spirit to survive destruction. How can it be explained that ghosts have never been seen in naked form, but always with clothes on?" [18]

So much for my favorite philosopher, Wang Ch'ung. I have told his story to show how the spirit of courageous doubt and intellectual honesty of the Classical Age of Chinese philosophy could survive centuries of oblivion and would arise to carry on the fight of human reason against ignorance and falsehood, of creative doubt and constructive criticism against superstition and blind authority. To dare to doubt and question without fear and favor is the spirit of science. "To check falsehoods against facts and to expose them by setting up proofs" constitute the procedure of science.

IV

The rest of my paper will be devoted to a brief interpretative report on a great movement in the history of Chinese thought which started out with the ambitious slogan of "investigation of the reason of all things and extension of human knowledge to the utmost" but which ended in improving and perfecting a critical method of historical research and thereby opening up a new age of revival of classical learning.

That great movement has been called the Neo-Confucian movement, because it was a conscious movement to revive the thought and culture of pre-Buddhist China, to go back directly to the humanist teaching of Confucius and his school, in order to overthrow and replace the much Indianized, and therefore un-Chinese, thought and culture of medieval China. It was essentially a Confucian movement, but it must be noted that the Neo-Confucian philosophers frankly accepted a naturalistic cosmology which was at least partially of Taoist origin and which was preferred probably because it was considered to be more acceptable than the theological and teleological cosmology of the "Confucian" religion since the Han Dynasty (206 B.C.–A.D. 220). Here was another case of a combination of the naturalism of Lao Tzu and the philosophical Taoists and the humanism of Confucius once more rising in protest and rebellion against what were considered as the un-Chinese otherworldly religions of medieval China.

This new Confucian movement needed a new logical method, a *"novum organum,"* which it found in a little essay of post-Confucian origin entitled *The Great Learning*, an essay of about 1,700 Chinese characters. From that little essay, the founders of Neo-Confucianism picked out one statement which they understood to mean that "the extension of knowledge lies in the investigation of things." That soon became one of the central doctrines in the philosophy of the school of the Ch'eng brothers (Ch'eng Hao, also called Ch'eng Ming-tao, 1032–1085, and Ch'eng I, also called

Ch'eng I-ch'uan, 1033–1107), especially as that philosophy was interpreted and reorganized by the great Chu Hsi (1130–1200). The investigation of things was further interpreted to mean "seeking exhaustively to investigate the reason (*li*) in all things."

What are "things"? According to the Ch'eng-Chu school, the scope of "things" was as extensive as Nature itself, including "every grass and every shrub" as well as "the height of the heavens and the thickness of the earth." But such a conception of the "things" to be investigated was beyond the capability of the philosophers, who were men of affairs and politicians as well as thinkers and teachers of men. They were more vitally interested in the moral and political problems of men than in the investigation of the reason or law in every grass or shrub. So Ch'eng I himself began to narrow down the scope of "things" to three categories: the study of books, the study of men of the past and the present, and the study of what is right in dealing with practical affairs. "Always begin with what is nearest to you," he said. And Chu Hsi, the greatest of the Sung (960–1279) philosophers and the most eloquent and untiring exponent of the philosophy of the investigation of the reason in all things, devoted his whole life to the study and exposition of the Classics of Confucianism. His Commentary on *The Four Books* (the "New Testament" of Neo-Confucianism) and his Commentaries on *The Book of Odes* and *The Book of Changes* were accepted as the standard texts for seven centuries. The philosophy of the investigation of the reason in all things was now definitely applied to the limited field of classical studies.

Truly inspired by the "Socratic tradition" of Confucius, Chu Hsi worked out a set of principles on the spirit, the method, and the procedure of investigation and research. He said, "Investigate with an open mind. Try to see the reason (*li*) with an open mind. And with an open mind follow reason wherever it leads you." What is an open mind? Chu Hsi said, "Retreat one step back, and think it over: that is the open mind." "Do not press your own opinion too much forward. Suppose you put your own opinion aside for a while, and try to see what the other side has to say. Just as in hearing a case of litigation, the mind is sometimes prejudiced in favor of A, and you are inclined to seek evidences against his opponent B, or vice versa. It is better to step aside and calmly and slowly study what both sides have to say. Only when you can step aside can you see things more clearly. The Master Chang Tsai (also called Chang Heng-ch'ü, 1020–1077) said, 'Wash away your old ideas to let new ideas come in.' If you do not put aside your pre-conceived notions, where and how can you get new ideas?"

The Neo-Confucians of the eleventh century often stressed the importance of doubt in thinking. Chang Tsai had said, "The student must first learn to be able to doubt. If he can find doubt where no doubt was found before, then he is making progress." As an experienced worker in textual and semantic researches, Chu Hsi was able to develop a more practical and constructive methodology out of the idea of doubt. He realized that doubt did not arise of itself, but would come only when a situation of perplexity or diffi-culty was present. He said: "I used to tell students to think and to seek points of doubt. But I have come to understand that it is not fruitful to start out with the intention of finding things to doubt. Just study with an open mind. After working hard at a text, there will be places which block your path and cause you per-plexity. That's where doubts naturally come up for you to compare, to weigh, to ponder over." "The student [as it has been said] should learn to find doubt where no doubt had previously existed, but he should also learn to resolve the doubt after it has arisen. Then he is making real progress."

Doubt would arise in a situation in which conflicting theories simultaneously claimed credulity and acceptance. Chu Hsi told of his early doubts when he found that "the same passage in *The Analects* had been given widely different explanations by various commentators." "That," said he, "led me to doubt." How is doubt to be resolved? "By keeping one's mind open," he said. "You may have your own view, but it may not be the correct view. Do not hold it dogmatically. Put it aside for a while, and search for more and more instances to be placed side by side, so that they may be compared. Then you may see through and understand." In one of his letters to his friend and philosophical opponent, Lu Chiu-yüan (also called Lu Hsiang-shan, 1139–1193), he again used the example of the judge trying a case of litigation: "Just like the judge trying a difficult case, one should keep his mind open and impartial, and must not let his own inclination or disinclination influence his thinking. He can then carefully listen to the pleading of both sides, seek evidences for cross-checking, and arrive at a correct judgment of right and wrong."

What Chu Hsi was saying amounts to a method of resolving doubt by first suggesting a hypothetical view and then searching for more instances or evidences for comparison and for checking the hypothesis "which may not be correct" and which Chu Hsi sometimes described as "a temporarily formed doubting thesis" (*ch'üan-li i-i*). In short, the method of doubt and resolution of doubt was the method of hypothesis and verification by evidence.

Chu Hsi told his students: "The trouble with you is that you are not capable of doubting; that's why you do not make progress. As for myself, I have my doubt even in the least significant matters. As soon as one begins to doubt, one has to go on [thinking] until the doubt is completely resolved."

It was because of this inner urge to resolve doubts that Chu Hsi often confessed that, from his younger years on, he was fond of making investigations based on evidences (*k'ao-cheng*). He was one of the most brilliant minds in human history, yet he was never tired of hard work and patient research.

His great achievement lies in two directions. In the first place, he was never tired of preaching the importance of doubt in thinking and investigation—doubt in the sense of a "tentatively formed doubting thesis," doubt, not as an end in itself, but as a perplexity to be overcome, as a puzzling problem to be solved, as a challenge to be satisfactorily met. In the second place, he had the courage to apply this technique of doubt and resolution of doubt to the major Classics of the Confucian Canon, thereby opening up a new era of classical scholarship which did not attain its full development until many centuries after his death.

He did not produce a commentary on *The Book of History,* but he made epoch-making contributions to the study of that classic by his great courage to doubt the authenticity of its so-called "ancient-script" portion consisting of 25 books which were apparently unknown to the classical scholars of the Han Dynasty, but which seemed first to appear in the fourth century A.D., and came to be accepted as an integral part of *The Book of History* after the seventh century. The 28 (actually 29) books that were officially recognized in the Doctors' College of the Han empire had been transmitted orally through an old scholar, Fu (who survived the book-burning of 213 B.C.), and had been transcribed in the "modern script" of the second century B.C.

Chu Hsi started out with a great doubt: "There are two distinct languages in these books—some of them are difficult to read and understand, others can be read and understood quite easily. It is very strange that the books which were transmitted from memory by the old scholar Fu are all hard to read, whereas the other books, which made their appearance much later, should all turn out to be quite easy to understand. How can we explain the strange fact that the old scholar Fu could memorize only those most difficult texts but could not transmit those that are so easy to read?"

In his *Chu Tzu yü-lei* (Classified Sayings), he kept repeating this great doubt to every student who asked him about *The Book of History*.[19] "All the books easy to understand are the 'ancient-script' texts; all those most difficult to read are the 'modern-script' texts." Chu Hsi did not openly say that the former group of texts were later forgeries. He merely wanted to impress upon his students this most puzzling linguistic distinction. Sometimes he suggested a very mild explanation to the effect that those books most difficult to read probably represented the language actually spoken to the people in those public proclamations, whereas the books easy to read were the work of official historians who probably did some revising or even rewriting.

Naturally such a mild theory did not explain away the doubt which, once raised, has persisted for many centuries to plague classical scholars.

A century later, under the Mongol (Yüan) Dynasty (1279–1368), Wu Ch'eng (1247–1331) took up Chu Hsi's challenge and drew the logical conclusion that the so-called "ancient-script" books were not genuine parts of *The Book of History*, but were forgeries of a much later age. So, Wu Ch'eng, in writing a Commentary on that classic, accepted only 28 "modern-script" books, and excluded the 25 "ancient-script" books.

In the sixteenth century, another scholar, Mei Tsu, also took up the question, and published in 1543 a book to prove that the "ancient-script" portion of *The Book of History* was a forgery by a fourth-century writer who apparently based his forgeries on the numerous passages found in ancient works wherein specific titles of "lost" books were mentioned as sources of the quotations. And Mei Tsu took the trouble to check the sources of those quotations which formed the kernel of the forged books.

But it took another and greater scholar of the seventeenth century, Yen Jo-ch'ü (1636–1704), to put a finishing touch to the task of resolving the doubt raised by Chu Hsi in the twelfth century about the "ancient-script" portion of *The Book of History*. Yen devoted thirty years to the writing of a great book entitled "Inquiry into the Authenticity of the Ancient-Script Portion of *The Book of History*." With his wonderful memory and great learning, Yen proved these books to be deliberate forgeries by tracing almost every sentence in them to its source and by showing how the forger had misquoted or misunderstood the meaning of the original passages. Altogether, Yen offered over a hundred proofs to expose the forgery. Although his views were vehemently attacked by conservative scholars of his day, it is now considered that Yen Jo-ch'ü's book has convincingly rendered a final verdict, and that nearly one-half of a major book of the Confucian Canon, which had been accepted as sacred scripture for a thousand years, must be recognized as a proven forgery.

And for this intellectual revolution of no small magnitude credit must be given to our philosopher Chu Hsi, who in the twelfth century expressed a courageous doubt and proposed a meaningful question which he himself was not yet fully prepared to answer.

Chu Hsi's treatment of the *I ching* (*The Book of Changes*), another of the "sacred scriptures," was even more daring, so daring indeed that it was never accepted and developed during the last seven centuries.

He published a Commentary on the *I ching* and a little book entitled "A Primer on the Study of the *I ching*." And he left a number of letters and discussions on that classic.[20]

His most daring thesis about the *I ching* was that that book, which had always been regarded as a sacred book of profound philosophical truth, was originally devised as a text of divination and fortune-telling, and could be understood only if it were studied as a book of divination and no more than a book of divination. "The sentences or judgments for every *kua* (hexagram), of which there were 64, and every line (of which there were 384) were meant to be used as answers to people who wanted to know whether it was propitious to do such-and-such a thing or not. Some answers were for sacrifices, others for hunting, others for traveling, or for war, or emigration. If the sages had intended to talk about philosophy, why should they not simply write a philosophy book; why should they talk always in terms of fortune-telling?" "If the book is studied merely as a text for the diviner, then so many passages which had been wrongly explained as mysterious and profound wisdom immediately become quite plain, simple, and intelligible."

This common-sense theory was the most courageous doubt ever uttered about that strange book. But it was rejected by his friends as an "oversimplification." But Chu Hsi replied: "It is just like this big lantern. Every strip of bamboo added to the lantern frame simply takes away that much of the light. If we could only get rid of all those light-covering devices, how much more light there would be, and how much better it would be for all of us!"

That was a truly revolutionary theory which illustrates one of his great remarks, that "the simplest theory is usually the true theory." But Chu Hsi realized that his view of the *I ching* as nothing more than a text for divination was too radical for his time. He sadly said, "It is difficult to talk to people about this theory. They would not believe it. Many distinguished people have argued so vehemently against me, and I have spent so much energy to explain and analyze my view to them. As I now look back, it is better to say nothing more. I shall leave it here, regardless of whether people believe it or not. I shall waste no more strength arguing for it."

Chu Hsi was justly proud of his *Commentary* on *The Book of Odes* (1177), which was to remain a standard text for many centuries after him. Two features of this work have been fruitful in leading to future developments in research. One was his courageous discarding of the traditional interpretation as represented in the so-called "Prefaces to the Poems" and his insistence that the songs and poems should be read with an open mind and independent judgment. The other feature was his recognition of the "ancient pronunciation" of the end-rhymes, a recognition that was at least indirectly responsible for the future development of a more exact study of the entire field of ancient pronunciation, leading to the beginnings of a science of Chinese phonology.

When *The Book of Odes* became a major Classic of the Confucian Canon under the Han empire, there were four different schools of textual reading and interpretation. After the first two centuries of the Christian era, only one school, the Mao school, was in the ascendency, overshadowing all the other schools. This Mao school claimed to have based its interpretation of the poems on the authority of the "Prefaces," which were supposedly handed down from Tzu-hsia, a great disciple of Confucius, but which were probably the work of some Han scholar who had taken the trouble to assign each poem to some historical occasion or event, or even to some historic personage as its author. Some of the historical assignments were taken from the *Tso chuan,* one of the three commentaries of the Confucian *Ch'un ch'iu Annals*, in which the origin of a few "Poems" was specifically mentioned. This display of historical erudition was quite impressive and probably accounted for the success of the Mao school in gradually winning general acceptance and official recognition. The "Prefaces to the Poems," therefore, were regarded as having sacrosanct authority throughout more than a millennium before the time of Chu Hsi.

Chu Hsi's senior contemporary, Cheng Ch'iao (1104–1162), the learned author of the encyclopedic *T'ung chih*, published a little book with the title, "An Examination of the Absurdities about *The Book of Odes*," in which he strongly attacked the "Prefaces" as absurd interpretations by vulgar and ignorant persons with no sense of literary and poetic appreciation. Cheng Ch'iao's vehemence of language at first shocked our philosopher Chu Hsi, but, he confessed, "After reading several of his criticisms and checking them with historical works, I soon came to the conclusion that the 'Prefaces' of those poems were really not reliable. When I went on to compare some other poems with their Prefaces, I found the content and meaning of the poems did not tally at all with their Prefaces. I was finally convinced that most of the 'Prefaces' were not trustworthy."

Here was a good illustration of conflicting ideas leading to doubt, and also of an open mind being receptive to new ideas and successful in resolving the doubt by evidence. Chu Hsi told how he had tried unsuccessfully to persuade his life-long friend and philosophical comrade, Lü Tsu-ch'ien (1137–1181), to reject the Prefaces. He pointed out to Lü that only a few Prefaces were confirmed by clear references in the *Tso chuan*, but most of them were grounded on no evidences. "But my friend said: 'How can one expect to find so many documentary evidences!' I said: 'In that case, we shall have to leave out all those Prefaces not based on evidences. We cannot use the Prefaces as evidences for the interpretation of the poems.' 'But,' said my friend Lü, 'the Prefaces themselves *are* evidences!' From our discussion, I realized that many people prefer to explain each poem by its Preface, and refuse to seek understanding by reading the poem itself."

In his courageous fight to overthrow the authority of the Prefaces and seek to understand the meaning of the poems by reading each poem with an open mind, Chu Hsi was only partially successful, both in his own new commentary and in leading future workers to go farther in the same direction. The weight of tradition was still too great for Chu Hsi himself and for future generations. But the great and creative doubt of Cheng Ch'iao and Chu Hsi will always be remembered whenever modern and unprejudiced scholarship undertakes to work on *The Book of Odes* with new tools and in an entirely free spirit.

For the second new feature of Chu Hsi's work on *The Book of Odes,* namely, the aspect of the ancient pronunciation of the rhymes, he was inspired and aided by the work of another learned contemporary of his, Wu Yü, who died in 1153 or 1154. Wu Yü was the real pioneer in the study of Chinese phonology in working out an inductive method of comparing rhymed lines in that ancient Classic among themselves and with other ancient and medieval rhymed poetry. He wrote quite a few books, including "A Supplement on the Rhymes of *The Book of Odes,*" "Explaining the Rhymes in the *Ch'u t'zu,*" and "A Supplement to the Standard Rhyme-Book" (*Yün pu*). Only the last-named has survived to this day, through reprints.

There is no doubt that Wu Yü had discovered that those many end-rhymes in *The Book of Odes* which did not seem to rhyme according to "modern" pronunciation were natural rhymes in ancient times and were to be read according to their "ancient pronunciation." He therefore carefully listed all the end-rhymes in the 300-odd poems of *The Book of Odes* and worked out their ancient pronunciation with the aid of ancient and medieval dictionaries and rhyme-books. A preface written by Hsü Ch'an, a friend and distant relative of his, clearly described his patient method of collecting and comparing the vast number of instances. "The word now pronounced '*fu*' appears 16 times in *The Book of Odes,* all, without exception, pronounced '*bek*' [or '*b'iuk,*' according to Bernard Karlgren]. The word now pronounced '*yu*' appears 11 times in *The Book of Odes,* all, without exception, rhymed with words ending -*i.*"

This strict methodology impressed Chu Hsi so much that he decided to accept Wu Yü's system of "ancient pronunciation" throughout his own Commentary. Probably with a view to the avoidance of unnecessary controversy, Chu Hsi did not call it "ancient pronunciation" but "rhyming pronunciation"—that is to say, a certain word should be pronounced in such a way as to rhyme with the other end-rhymes the pronunciation of which had apparently remained unchanged.

But, in his conversation with his students, he frankly said that he had followed Wu Yü in most cases, making additions or modifications in only a few instances; and that the rhyming pronunciations were the natural pronunciations of the ancient poets, who, "like us in modern times, composed their songs in natural rhymes." That is to say, the rhyming pronunciations were ancient pronunciations.

When asked whether there was any ground for the rhyming pronunciation, Chu Hsi answered: "Mr. Wu produced proofs for all his pronunciations. His books can be found in Ch'üan-chou. For one word he sometimes quoted as many as over ten proofs, but at least two or three proofs. He said that he originally had even more evidences, but had to leave out many [in order to reduce the cost of copying and printing]." And in those cases in which Chu Hsi found it necessary to differ with Wu, he also cited examples for comparison in his "Classified Sayings" and in the *Ch'u-t'zu chi-chu* (An Annotated Edition of the *Ch'u t'zu*).

But because Chu Hsi used the expression "rhyming pronunciation" throughout his Commentary on *The Book of Odes* without ever referring to the expression "ancient pronunciation," and because Wu Yü's books were long lost or inaccessible, a discussion was started early in the sixteenth century in the form of a severe criticism of Chu Hsi's improper use of the expression "rhyming pronunciation." In 1580, Chiao Hung (1541–1620), a great scholar and philosopher, published in his "Notes" (*Pi-ch'eng*) a brief statement of a theory (probably his friend Ch'en Ti's [1541–1617] theory) that those end-rhymes in ancient songs and poems that did not fit into modern schemes of rhyming were all natural rhymes whose pronunciations happened to have changed in the course of time. He cited a number of instances to show that the words would rhyme perfectly if pronounced as the ancients sang them.

It was Chiao Hung's friend Ch'en Ti who undertook many years of patient research and published a series of books on the ancient pronunciation of hundreds of rhyming words in many ancient books of rhymed poetry. The first of these works was published in 1616 under the title: *Mao-shih ku-yin k'ao* (An Inquiry into the Ancient Pronunciation of *The Book of Odes*), with a preface by Chiao Hung.

In his own preface, Ch'en Ti proclaimed his main thesis that the end-rhymes in *The Book of Odes* were naturally rhymed in their original pronunciation, and that it was only the natural change of pronunciation which made some of them appear not to rhyme at all. What had been suggested by Chu Hsi as "rhyming pronunciations," said Ch'en Ti, were in most cases the ancient or original pronunciations.

"I have done some evidential investigation (*k'ao-chü*)," he said, "and have grouped the evidences into two classes: internal evidences (*pen-cheng*) and collateral evidences (*p'ang-cheng*). Internal evidences are taken from *The Book of Odes* itself. Collateral evidences are taken from other ancient rhymed works of approximately the same age."

To show how the word "*fu*" was invariably rhymed in its original archaic pronunciation (*bek*, or *b'iuk*), he listed 14 internal evidences and 10 collateral evidences, a total of 24. The same inductive method was applied to the study of ancient pronunciation in other rhymed literature of ancient China. To prove the ancient pronunciation of the word "*hsing*," he cited 44 instances from the rhymed sections of *The Book of Changes*, all rhyming with words ending in -*ang*. For the word "*ming*," he cited 17 evidences from the same book.

Nearly half a century later, the patriot-scholar Ku Yen-wu (1614–1682) completed his *Yin-hsüeh wu-shu* (Five Books of Phonology). One of them was on "The Original Pronunciation of *The Book of Odes*"; another on "The Pronunciation of *The Book of Changes*"; and another on "The Rhyming Groups of the T'ang Period," which is an attempt to compare the ancient pronunciation with that of the Middle Ages. Ku acknowledged his indebtedness to Ch'en Ti and adopted his method in classifying his proofs into internal and collateral evidences.

Let us again use the word "*fu*" as an example. In his "Original Pronunciations of *The Book of Odes*," Ku Yen-wu cited 17 internal evidences and 15 collateral evidences, a total of 32. In his larger work on the rhyming groups of the T'ang Dynasty (618–907), he listed a total of 162 evidences from available ancient rhymed literature to show how that word was rhymed and pronounced in ancient times.

Such patient collecting and counting of instances was intended to serve a twofold purpose. In the first place, that was the only way to ascertain the ancient pronunciation of the words and also to find possible exceptions which may challenge the rule and demand explanation. Ku Yen-wu acknowledged that some exceptions could be explained by the possibility of local and dialectal deviations in pronunciation.

But the most valuable use of this vast statistical material was to form a basis for systematic reconstruction of the actual groupings of ancient sounds. On the basis of his study of the rhymed literature of ancient China, Ku Yen-wu concluded that ancient pronunciations could be analyzed into ten general rhyming groups (*yün p'u*).

Thus was begun the deductive and constructive part of Chinese phonetics, namely, the continuous attempts, first, to understand the ancient "finals" (rhyming groups), and, in a later period, to understand the nature of the ancient initial consonants.

Ku Yen-wu proposed ten general rhyming groups in 1667. In the following century, a number of scholars continued to work on the same problem and by the same inductive and deductive methods of evidential research. Chiang Yung (1681–1762) suggested 13 rhyming groups. Tuan Yü-ts'ai (1735–1815) increased the number to 17. His teacher and friend, Tai Chen (1724–1777), further increased it to 19. Wang Nien-sun (1744–1832) and Chiang Yu-kao (died in 1851), working independently, arrived at a more or less similar system of 21 rhyming groups.

Ch'ien Ta-hsin (1728–1804), one of the most scientifically minded men of the eighteenth century, published in 1799 his "Notes," which includes two papers on the results of his studies of ancient initial labials and dentals. These two papers are outstanding examples of the method of evidential investigation at its best. He collected over 60 groups of instances for the labials, and about the same number for the dentals. In the identifying of the ancient sound of the words in each group, each step was a skillful combination of induction and deduction, of generalization from particulars and application of general rules to particular instances. The final outcome was the formulation of two general laws of phonological change regarding labials and dentals.

It is important for us to remind ourselves that those Chinese scholars working in the field of Chinese phonetics were so greatly handicapped that they seemed almost from the outset to be doomed to failure. They were without the minimum aid of an alphabet for the Chinese language. They had no benefit of the comparative study of the various dialects, especially of the older dialects in southern, southeastern, and southwestern China. Nor had they any knowledge of such neighboring languages as Korean, Vietnamese, and Japanese. Without any of these useful tools, those Chinese scholars, seeking to understand the phonetic changes of their language, were actually faced with an almost impossible task. Their successes or failures, therefore, must be evaluated in the light of their numerous and important disadvantages.

The only dependable tool of those great men was their strict method of patiently collecting, comparing, and classifying what they recognized as facts or evidences, and an equally strict method of applying formulated generalizations to test the particular instances within the classified groups. It was indeed very largely this meticulous application of a rigorous method that enabled Wu Yü and Chu Hsi in the twelfth century, Ch'en Ti and Ku Yen-wu in the seventeenth century, and their successors in the eighteenth and nineteenth centuries to carry on their systematic study of Chinese phonetic problems and to develop it into something of a science—into a body of knowledge answering to the rigorous canons of evidence, exactitude, and logical systematization.

I have sketched here what I have conceived as the story of the development of the scientific spirit and method in the Chinese thought of the past eight centuries. It began in the eleventh century with the ambitious ideal of extending human knowledge to the utmost by investigating the reason or law in all things of the universe. That grandiose ideal was by necessity narrowed down to the investigation of books—to the patient and courageous study of the few great books which formed the "sacred scripture" of the Chinese classical tradition. History saw the gradual development of a new spirit and a new method based on doubt and the resolution of doubt. The spirit was the moral courage to doubt even on questions touching sacred matters, and the insistence on the importance of an open mind and impartial and dispassionate search for truth. The method was the method of evidential thinking and evidential investigation (k'ao-chü and k'ao-cheng).

I have cited some examples of this spirit and method at work, notably in the development of a "Higher Criticism" in the form of investigations of the authenticity and dating of a part of the classical texts and in the development of a scientific study of the problems of Chinese phonology. But, as a matter of history, this method was fruitfully and effectually applied to many other fields of historical and humanistic research, such as textual criticism, semantics (i.e., the study of the historical changes of the meaning of words), history, historical geography, and archeology.

The method of evidential investigation was made fully conscious by such men as Ch'en Ti and Ku Yen-wu in the seventeenth century, who first used the expressions "internal evidences" and "collateral evidences." The efficacy of the method was so clearly demonstrated in the scientific works of the two great masters of the seventeenth century, Ku Yen-wu and Yen Jo-ch'ü, that by the eighteenth and nineteenth centuries practically all first-class minds in intellectual China were attracted to it and were devoting their lives to its application to all fields of classical and humanistic study. The result was a new age of Revival of Learning which has also been called the Age of Evidential Investigation.

Even the most violent critics of this new learning had to admit the scientific nature of its rigorous and effective method. One such violent critic was Fang Tung-shu (1772–1851), who in 1826 published a book which was a vehement criticism and condemnation of the whole movement. Even Fang had to pay high tribute to the rigorous method as it was used by two of his contemporaries, Wang Nien-sun and his son, Wang Yin-chih (1766–1834). Fang said, "As a linguistic approach to the classics, there is nothing that surpasses the *Ching-i shu-wen* (Notes on the Classics As I Have Heard from My Father) of the Wangs of Kao-yu. That work could actually make the great Cheng Hsüan (d. 200) and Chu Hsi bow their heads (in humble acknowledgment of their errors). Ever since the Han Dynasty (206 B.C.–A.D. 220), there has never been anything that could compare with it." Such a tribute from a violent critic of the whole movement is the best proof that the meticulous application of a scientific method of research is the most effective means to disarm opposition, to undermine authority and conservatism, and to win recognition and credence for the new scholarship.

What was the historical significance of this spirit and method of "exact and impartial inquiry"?

A brief but factual answer must be: It succeeded in replacing an age of subjective, idealistic, and moralizing philosophy (from the eleventh to the sixteenth century) by making it seem outmoded, "empty," unfruitful, and no longer attractive to the best minds of the age. It succeeded in creating a new age of Revival of Learning (1600–1900) based on disciplined and dispassionate research. But it did not produce an age of natural science. The spirit of exact and impartial inquiry, as exemplified in Ku Yen-wu,

Tai Chen, Ch'ien Ta-hsin, and Wang Nien-sun, did not lead to an age of Galileo, Vesalius, and Newton in China.

Why? Why did this scientific spirit and method not result in producing natural science?

Some time ago, I tried to offer a historical explanation by making a comparative chronology of the works of the intellectual leaders of China and of Europe in the seventeenth century. I said:

If we make a comparative chronology of the leaders of Chinese and European learning during the seventeenth century—the formative period both for the new science in modern Europe and the new learning in China—we shall see that four years before Ku Yen-wu was born (1613), Galileo had invented his telescope and was using it to revolutionize the science of astronomy, and Kepler was publishing his revolutionary studies of Mars and his new laws of the movements of the planets. When Ku Yen-wu worked on his philological studies and reconstructed the archaic pronunciations, Harvey had published his great work on the circulation of blood [1628], and Galileo his two great works on astronomy and the new science [1630]. Eleven years before Yen Jo-ch'ü began his critical study of the *Book of History*, Torricelli had completed his great experiment on the pressure of air [1644]. Shortly after, Boyle announced the results of his experiments in Chemistry, and formulated the law that bears his name [1660–1661]. The year before Ku Yen-wu completed his epoch-making *Five Books* on philological studies [1667] Newton had worked out his calculus and his analysis of white light. In 1680, Ku wrote his preface to the final texts of his philological works; in 1687, Newton published his *Principia*.

The striking similarity in the scientific spirit and method of these great leaders of the age of new learning in their respective countries makes the fundamental difference between their fields of work all the more conspicuous. Galileo, Kepler, Boyle, Harvey, and Newton worked with the objects of nature, with stars, balls, inclining planes, telescopes, microscopes, prisms, chemicals, and numbers and astronomical tables. And their Chinese contemporaries worked with books, words, and documentary evidences. The latter created three hundred years of scientific book learning; the former created a new science and a new world.[22]

That was a historical explanation, but was a little unfair to those great Chinese scholars of the seventeenth century. It was not enough to say, as I did, that "the purely literary training of the intellectual class in China has tended to limit its activities to the field of books and documents." It should be pointed out that the books they worked on were books of tremendous importance to the moral, religious, and philosophical life of the entire nation. Those great men considered it their sacred duty to find out what each and every one of those ancient books actually meant. As Robert Browning sang of the Grammarian:

"What's in the scroll," quoth he, "thou keepest furled?
"Show me their shaping,
"Theirs who most studied man, the bard and sage,—
*   "Give!"—So, he gowned him,*
Straight got by heart that book to its last page. . . .
. . . .
"Let me know all! . . .
. . . .
"Even to the crumbs I'd fain eat up the feast." . . .
. . . .
". . . What's time? Leave Now for dogs and apes!
"Man has Forever." . . .[23]

Browning's tribute to the spirit of the humanist age was: "This man decided not to Live but Know."

The same spirit was expressed by Confucius: "Study as if life were too short and you were on the point of missing it." "He who learns the truth in the morning may die in the evening without regret." The same spirit was expressed by Chu Hsi in his age. There is no end to knowledge. I can only devote my whole energy to study: death alone will end my toil."

But Chu Hsi went further: "My friends, you are not making progress, because you have not learned to doubt. As soon as you begin to doubt, you will never stop until your doubt is resolved at last." And his true successors, the founders and workers of the new age of Revival of Learning, were men who had learned to doubt— to doubt with an open mind and to seek ways and means to re- solve the doubt, to dare to doubt even when they were dealing with the great books of the Sacred Canon. And, precisely because they were all their lives dealing with the great books of the Sacred Canon, they were forced always to stand on solid ground: they had to learn to doubt with evidence and to resolve doubt with evidence. That, I think, is the historical explanation of the remark- able fact that those great men working with only "books, words, and documents" have actually succeeded in leaving to posterity a scientific tradition of dispassionate and disciplined inquiry, of rigorous evidential thinking and investigation, of boldness in doubt and hypotheses coupled with meticulous care in seeking verification —a great heritage of scientific spirit and method which makes us, sons and daughters of present-day China, feel not entirely at sea, but rather at home, in the new age of modern science.

Notes

1. "Main Contrasts Between Eastern and Western Philosophy," in Charles A. Moore, ed., *Essays in East-West Philosophy* (Honolulu: University of Hawaii Press, 1951), p. 291.
2. "The Complementary Emphases of Eastern Intuitive and Western Scientific Philosophy," in Charles A. Moore, ed., *Philosophy—East and West* (Princeton: Princeton University Press, 1944), p. 212.
3. *Ibid.*
4. *Ibid.,* p. 173.
5. *Ibid.,* p. 223.
6. F. S. C. Northrop, *The Meeting of East and West* (New York: The Macmillan Co., 1946), p. 448.
7. *Philosophy—East and West,* p. 183.
8. *Ibid.,* p. 216.
9. *Ibid.,* p. 183.
10. *Ibid.,* p. 185.
11. Northrop may be interested to know that the *"Logos"* in the opening sentence of the Fourth Gospel has been translated *"Tao"*—the same *Tao* as appears in the first sentence of the *Lao Tzu (Tao-te ching).* A scholar trained in modern linguistics will probably translate *"Logos"* as *"ming"* (the Word)—the same *"ming"* which appears in the second sentence of the *Lao Tzu* and which is erroneously translated as "the name," as quoted by Northrop. *Ibid.,* p. 204.
12. James B. Conant, *On Understanding Science* (New York: Mentor Books, 1951), pp. 23–24. See also, Conant, *Science and Common Sense* (New Haven: Yale University Press, 1951), pp. 10–13.
13. *Lun heng,* chap. 24.
14. *Ibid.,* chap. 42.
15. *Ibid.,* chap. 43.
16. *Ibid.,* chap. 14.
17. *Ibid.,* chap. 53.
18. *Ibid.,* chap. 62.
19. Chap. 78.
20. *Ibid.,* chaps. 66–67.
21. *Ibid.,* chap. 80, pp. 15–17; also *Ch'u-t'zu chi-chu,* III, p. 21.
22. *The Chinese Renaissance* (Chicago: University of Chicago Press, 1934), pp. 70–71.
23. "A Grammarian's Funeral," in Augustine Birrell, ed., *The Poetical Works of Robert Browning* (London: John Murray, 1951), Vol. I, pp. 424–426.

WING-TSIT CHAN   *Syntheses in*

Chinese Metaphysics

CHINESE PHILOSOPHERS, both ancient and modern, have been interested primarily in ethical, social, and political problems. Metaphysics developed only after Buddhism from India had presented a strong challenge to Confucianism. Even then, basic metaphysical problems, such as God, universals, space and time, matter and spirit, were either not discussed, except in Buddhism, or discussed only occasionally, and then always for the sake of ethics. Discussions have been unsystematic, seldom based on hypothesis and logical analysis, for Chinese philosophers have always shunned abstraction and generalities and have always been interested more in a good life and a good society than in organized knowledge. If in our search for a world perspective in philosophy we rely chiefly on theoretical foundations and logical subtlety, Chinese philosophy has little to offer.

But if we are interested in a synthesis of philosophies, it will be worth while to look into what has taken place in Chinese philosophy, for one of the outstanding facts in the history of Chinese philosophy has been its tendency and ability to synthesize. The history of Chinese philosophy is usually divided into four periods, and each period ended in some sort of synthesis.

In the Han Dynasty (206 B.C.–A.D. 220), even before Confucianism was made a State cult and became supreme, the metaphysical doctrines of Taoism, of the Yin-Yang school, and of the *Chung yung* (*The Doctrine of the Mean*) were in the process of merger. The result was the philosophy of change, accepted by

Confucianism, Taoism, and all other schools. The Taoist ideal of the Great Unit, the Yin-Yang theory of the interaction of the positive and negative cosmic principles, and the Confucian philosophy of *ch'eng*, or truth, in *The Doctrine of the Mean* were synthesized into one philosophy that was to dominate Chinese thought for centuries and form a firm basis for Neo-Confucianism.

The second synthesis took place within the sphere of Buddhism. The significant thing is that in metaphysics the various Buddhist schools of nihilism, realism, idealism, and negativism were synthesized into the philosophy of Hua-yen totalism (Avataṁsaka, Kegon), which was distinctly Chinese in spirit. In this philosophy, the "Realm of Principles" and the "Realm of Facts" are so harmonized that the theoretical and the practical, the one and the many, and noumenon and phenomenon are interwoven, so that all things "arise simultaneously," co-exist, are complementary, mutually penetrating, mutually identifying, and involve and reflect one another.

The third synthesis took place in Neo-Confucianism, in which Buddhism and Taoism were assimilated into traditional Confucianism, as we shall see.

The fourth synthesis is going on in our own day. Modern Chinese philosophy is still in its infancy. The few philosophers who are building up systems of their own are all attempting to combine Western philosophy with traditional Chinese thought.

I shall not go into the various historical factors in these four stages of synthesis. What interests us more is the synthesis of ideas. This will be discussed briefly under six topics which represent the most important problems in Chinese metaphysics.

Being and Non-Being

The first is the problem of being and non-being, on which Confucianism, Buddhism, and Taoism radically disagreed. Being and non-being were both denied in Buddhism; they were reduced to non-being in Taoism; and were synthesized in Neo-Confucianism.

According to Buddhism, to *be* is impossible, because, in order to *be*, a thing has to be produced. But, in order to be produced, a thing has to come either from itself or from another, both of which are absurd. Furthermore, to *be* means to have self-nature. But a thing is nothing but an aggregate and as such has no self-nature. Consequently, being is an illusion. By the same token, non-being is also an illusion. Both may be granted "dependent reality" and "secondary truth," but the Void transcends them all. It is true that Buddhist philosophers such as Seng-chao (384–414) interpreted the Void as "not true Void," since everything involves the entire universe. In the middle of the first millennium, Buddhist schools north of the Yangtze, such as Hua-yen, exhibited realistic tendencies and were called "Schools of Being." But those south of the river, especially the Meditation school (Ch'an, Zen), were labeled "Schools of Non-being." They were so called because they insisted on the "highest truth," that "all matter and form are identical with the Void, and the Void is identical with all matter and form." [1] In the end, both being and non-being are negated in the Void.

Instead of denying both being and non-being, Taoism reduced all to non-being, wu: "Heaven and Earth and all things come from being," says the Tao-te ching, "and being comes from non-being." [2] Early Taoists understood wu to mean "having no name," that is, that Tao cannot be described. Later Taoists, especially Kuo Hsiang (d. ca. 312), went a step further and definitely identified wu with nothingness. They argued that Tao is nowhere and has no activity. To say that a thing comes from Tao is merely to say that it comes from nowhere or from nothing. In truth, it comes from itself.

It should be noted that Taoists were not arguing for nihilism. Rather, they were arguing for the doctrine of "self-transformation," that a thing comes from itself. This is Tao. Nevertheless, the negativistic character is unmistakable. After all, the emphasis is on non-being, and Taoism, whether in ethics or government, has been the champion of the negative spirit.

Neo-Confucianists did not deny being or non-being, but affirmed both. To them the nature of a thing or man consists in production. It is interesting to note that the Chinese word for the nature of things or man, "hsing," has the word "sheng," birth, life, or production, as its chief component. And production is the very essence of change.

It has been pointed out that the philosophy of change laid the foundation for Neo-Confucianism. In a nutshell, its metaphysics is stated in these words:

In the system of change there is the Great Ultimate (T'ai-chi). It generates the Two Modes (yin and yang). The Two Modes generate the Four Forms [major and minor yin and yang]. The Four Forms generate the Eight Trigrams. The Eight Trigrams determine good and evil fortunes. And good and evil fortunes produce the great business [of life]. [3]

Thus, reality is a continuous process of production and repro-duction. This is possible only because there is the interplay of in-activity, decrease, etc., which constitute *yin*, and activity, increase, etc., which constitute *yang*. Now, *yang* is being, and *yin* is non-being. Reality, then, is possible only because of the interaction of being and non-being. In other words, in the fact of change, being and non-being are synthesized.

Several consequences follow this synthesis. In the first place, of the three systems, Confucianism alone accepts change, not only as natural but also as desirable. Not that Buddhism and Taoism are blind to the fact. The Buddhists look upon the universe as a "sea of waves"; the Taoists, as "a great transformation"; and Con-fucianists, as "a great current." On the fact of change they agree. Their attitudes toward the changing universe, however, differ vastly. Buddhists devote all their effort to crossing the sea of waves to arrive at the "Other Shore" where the perpetual becoming will cease. Taoists, comparing the universe to a "galloping horse," view the drama fatalistically, often with a sense of humor, always in the spirit of indifference. Confucianists, on the contrary, intend to take a leading role in the drama and to like it. This is the meaning of the little incident, much cited by Neo-Confucianists—when a Confucian pupil, Tseng Tien, declared that it was his ambition to go with a group of grown-ups and children, bathe in the river, enjoy the breeze, and come home singing, Confucius said, "You are after my own heart." [4] For, to Confucianists, change is good. Sig-nificantly, all the Confucian terms for reality have the meanings of both process and good. In *The Doctrine of the Mean,* reality is *ch'eng*, or truth, meaning, on the one hand, sincerity, and, on the other, "the end and the beginning of things," which "leads to activ-ity . . . change . . . and transformation." [5] In the philosophy of the Great Ultimate, "The successive movement of *yin* and *yang* constitutes the Way. What issues from the Way is good." [6] In Neo-Confucianism, the Great Ultimate is equated with *li* (principle), which means both a principle and what is proper.

Another consequence of the Neo-Confucian synthesis of being and non-being is that Confucianism alone looks upon time as travel-ing forward. Absolute time was hardly touched upon in Chinese philosophy. With Chinese philosophers, time has always been as-sociated with events. In Buddhism, since events are illusory, time is illusory. As such it moves on but will come to an end in *Nirvāṇa.* In Taoism, time travels in a circle, since a thing comes from non-being and returns to non-being. In the Confucian process of production and reproduction, however, time never comes to an end or repeats itself. Every production has an element of novelty, since it requires a new relationship of *yin* and *yang*. When Confucius urged people to "renovate oneself every day,"[7] he meant a daily development of personality. Neo-Confucianists, however, gave the phrase a metaphysical flavor, that everything is new.

There is another consequence which is quite serious. The synthesis of being and non-being, in making change possible, also makes it natural. The Great Ultimate, reality (*ch'eng*), change, and principle (*li*) are not caused. In this respect, Taoism fully agrees, for the very concept of *Tao* as the Way of self-transformation precludes any possibility of a creator or a supernatural director. It is true that Lao Tzu spoke of *Ti* the Lord, and Chuang Tzu mentioned the "maker of things" (*tsao-wu-che*). But, if there is any idea of God, it is completely overshadowed by the cardinal Taoist doctrine of "self-transformation." Heaven in ancient Confucianism did have an anthropomorphic character, but Hsün Tzu (313–238? B.C.) clearly equated it with Nature, and Neo-Confucianists identified it with *li*. The *kuei-shen* in Neo-Confucianism are no longer the heavenly and earthly spirits of popular religion that interfere with human events, but are "traces of the operation of *yin* and *yang*," and Shang-ti, instead of being the personal God that Bruce supposed it to be,[8] is but the "greatest mystery in the process of production and reproduction."

The great difference between Confucianism and Taoism is that the latter allows no room for teleology, unless it is the ultimate realization of *Tao*. Although Taoism is not mechanistic, it is difficult to conceive the Taoist universe as a moral one. "Heaven and Earth are not humane [not man-like]," declares the *Tao-te ching*.[9]

To Confucianists, what proceeds from production is good. This conviction runs through the entire Confucian tradition. In a more rational frame of mind, Neo-Confucianists argued that the universe is good because it is a process of production and reproduction, and production and reproduction are the greatest acts of love. Furthermore, in the oscillation of *yin* and *yang* there is harmony, and harmony is good. Thirdly, the universe embraces all, and what moral act can be greater than identification with all? Finally, in the production and reproduction of things, Mother Nature is impartial to all. God is just, as we say.

Li *and* Ch'i

We now pass on to the second problem, that of *li* and *ch'i*. In synthesizing being and non-being, early Neo-Confucianists created a dichotomy of their own, namely, the bifurcation of *li* and *ch'i*. The concept of *li* was borrowed from Hua-yen Buddhism. In borrowing it, Neo-Confucianists also borrowed the Hua-yen bifurcation of the realm of principles (*li*) and the realm of facts.

Briefly stated, *li* is the universal principle underlying all things, the universal law governing all things, the reason behind all things. It is at once the cause, the form, the essence, the sufficient reason for being, the highest standard of all things, that is, their Great Ultimate, or *T'ai-chi*. It is self-caused, indestructible, eternal. There is nothing without it. It combines all things as one. It is manifest everywhere. It is fully embodied in the mind. *Ch'i*, on the other hand, is the material, particularizing principle, the concretion, expression, and operation of *li*. It provides the conditions for the production, evolution, and destruction of things. It gives them substantiality and individuality. It differentiates them.

Such being the characteristics of *ch'i*, obviously it is inadequate to translate it as matter. The concept of *ch'i* goes back to ancient times and was shared by practically all schools, but was promoted by Taoists, who inspired the Neo-Confucianists in this regard. It has always meant force, energy, breath, power. When Chu Hsi (1130–1200) considered it as matter and described it as corporeal, he was unorthodox indeed.

Neo-Confucianists differed greatly in their interpretation of *li* and *ch'i*. The two Ch'eng brothers (Ch'eng Hao, 1032–1086; Ch'eng I, 1033–1107), for example, did not see eye to eye with respect to *li*. The former looked upon it as merely the natural tendency in things, whereas the latter considered it as transcendental. For convenience, we may summarize the three main Neo-Confucian movements in propositions. As the representatives of the philosophy of the Sung period (960–1279), philosophers Ch'eng I and Chu Hsi postulated that:

(1) All things have *li*.
(2) *Li*, in contrast to *ch'i*, is a priori, incorporeal, and transcendental.
(3) Existence is not necessary to *li* but is necessary to *ch'i*.
(4) Actually there is no *li* without *ch'i*, "for, without *ch'i*, *li* would have nothing to adhere to."

(5) The mind embraces all *li*.

(6) *Li* can be, but need not be, known.

(7) Knowledge consists in "extending" the mind to all things. Hence all things must be "investigated." (Here Ch'eng and Chu differed, the former emphasizing intensive study of one thing, Chu advocating the extensive study of all things.)

The Ch'eng-Chu philosophy aroused opposition in the Sung Dynasty itself, especially by Lu Hsiang-shan (1139–1193). But the opposition did not reach its height until the Ming Dynasty (1368–1644), in the person of Wang Yang-ming (1472–1529). The Lu-Wang philosophy may be summed up in these propositions:

(1) Mind is *li*.

(2) The universe is my mind, and my mind is the universe.

(3) Every person has this mind, and every mind has *li*.

(4) To understand the mind is to understand *li*.

The main effort of this school was to remove the bifurcation of *li* and *ch'i* in the Ch'eng-Chu philosophy by identifying *li* and mind. But, in doing so, the Ming philosophers went to the extreme of idealism. To this, philosophers of the Ch'ing Dynasty (1644–1911) were vigorously opposed. Roughly, the metaphysical views of the outstanding Ch'ing philosophers, notably Yen Yüan (1635–1704) and Tai Chen (1723–1777), are:

(1) *Li* is the principle of a thing, and *ch'i* its substance.

(2) Wherever there is *li*, there is *ch'i*; wherever there is no *ch'i*, there can be no *li*.

(3) *Li* is immanent in things.

(4) To know *li*, it is necessary to observe and analyze things.

It is important to note that, while the three schools held different views on *li* and *ch'i*, none held that only one of them was real. Ming philosophers seldom talked about *ch'i*. But to them *ch'i* was the operation or function of *li* and as such it was fully real. While Chu Hsi claimed that *li* was prior to and independent of *ch'i*, he quickly added that in fact no *li* exists apart from *ch'i*. Ch'ing philosophers denied that *li* was a priori or transcendental, but they did not go so far as to say that *li* was only an abstraction. One is justified in saying that the general Chinese position is that *li* and *ch'i* exist in each other. Once more, the Chinese tendency to synthesize asserts itself.

The One and the Many

Such a mutual relationship between *li* and *ch'i* rules out the contrast between the one and the many. Historically, the problem of the one and the many was first and most thoroughly discussed in Buddhism. The most famous treatise on this question is the essay "The Golden Lion," by Fa-tsang (643–712). According to him, in the golden lion the gold and the lion are inseparable. The gold penetrates every part of the lion, and the lion penetrates every part of the gold. Furthermore, since every part of the lion penetrates the gold and since the gold penetrates the whole lion, every part of the lion penetrates the whole lion. In short, the one is the many, and the many are the one.

On the surface, the one and the many are synthesized. But Buddhists still insisted that the one was the True Norm or the True Mind. If everything is a manifestation of the entire universe, it is the entirety that is important. In Taoism, too, there has always been emphasis on the Great One, or Great Unit. These emphases have resulted in the Buddhist doctrine of non-discrimination and the Taoist doctrine of the equality of things. In ethics, these doctrines have promoted such virtues as tolerance, love, unselfishness. But in metaphysics they raise the serious question as to whether a thing has any specific character, determinate nature, independence, or individuality at all.

Neo-Confucianists would have no quarrel with Buddhists and Taoists on the view that reality is one. Incidentally, it is interesting to note that no Chinese philosopher has rejected the one in favor of the many. Pluralism has been conspicuously absent in Chinese metaphysics. Even dualism has been weak. The dualism of Chu Hsi is not complete, since the *T'ai-chi* includes both *li* and *ch'i*.

This does not mean, however, that Chinese metaphysics has tended toward monism. Here the Neo-Confucian synthesis is that both the one and the many are real. "The many and the one are each rectified," said philosopher Chou Tun-i (1017–1073). "The one and the many each has its own correct state of being. The great and the small each has its definite function."[10] As Chang Tsai (1021–1077) put it, the pervasiveness of *ch'i* makes the universe an infinite harmony. At the same time, since the effect of *ch'i* on everything is different, no two things are alike.[11] In fact, since *ch'i* operates through concentration and dissipation and through increase and decrease, and since increase in one thing means decrease in another, everything necessarily has its opposite. This does not mean, however, that a thing can stand in isolation, for all things are combined as one in the infinite harmony. Or, as other Neo-Confucianists would say, all things are combined as one by *li*. Thus, the one and the many co-exist. As has been suggested, this idea was borrowed from Hua-yen Buddhism. The important difference is that in Buddhism the harmony is achieved by the non-discrimination or even the denial of the one and the many, whereas in Neo-Confucianism the harmony is achieved by affirming both. Furthermore, in Buddhism the harmony is to be achieved in a transcendental world, whereas in Neo-Confucianism the harmony is to be achieved here and now.

Man and the Universe

From the foregoing, the position of man as an individual in relation to the universe is clear. While every man, as an individual, has his place, he can also be identified with the universe. This idea of the unity of man and the universe runs through virtually the entire history of Chinese philosophy. In Taoism, identification with Nature has always been held as an ideal. Both Taoist and Confucian philosophers of the Han period (202 B.C.–A.D. 220) saw man and the universe in a microcosm-macrocosm-relationship. In both *The Book of Mencius* and *The Doctrine of the Mean*, the theory is propounded that, since the nature of man and that of the universe are the same, one who fully develops his nature will develop the nature of others, that one who develops the nature of others will develop the nature of things, and that one who develops the nature of things will develop the nature of the whole universe.[12] This is the basis of the Neo-Confucian theory. To this central point of the common nature of man and the universe they added that, since the mind is the full embodiment of *li*, a fully developed mind will embrace all *li*, which amounts to saying that it will embrace the whole universe. Also, one who is *jen* (humanity, true manhood, love) "will form one body with Heaven and Earth."

Good and Evil

It follows that, since man is one with the universe, and, since the universe is good, man by nature must be good. This has been an unflinching conviction among the Chinese ever since Mencius. But opinions have not been unanimous on this question. Before the Han Dynasty, theories fell into five groups: (1) that human nature is good; (2) that human nature is evil; (3) that human nature is both good and evil; (4) that human nature is neither good nor evil; and (5) that some people are born good and others evil.

This problem has been the most important one in Chinese metaphysics. It was the earliest metaphysical question to be debated, and it has been most extensively discussed. It has engaged the attention of practically every Chinese philosopher worthy of the name. Taoists discussed it because they were keenly interested in nourishing, preserving, and restoring the original nature of man. Confucianists discussed it because it formed the logical basis for their entire social and ethical philosophy. In Buddhism, it even created a crisis, which eventually led to a radical transformation of Buddhism from Hīnayāna to Mahāyāna.

In the first part of the *Mahā-parinirvāṇa-sūtra,* there is the idea that a class of people called *icchantikas* were so depraved as to be beyond the hope of salvation. Such a concept was repulsive to the monk Tao-sheng (d. 434). Evidently influenced by the traditional doctrine that human nature was originally good, he argued that, since *buddha*-nature is all-pervasive, even the most depraved has *buddha*-nature in him and therefore can be saved. He was first excommunicated by conservative Buddhists, but later reinstated when the entire *Mahā-parinirvāṇa-sūtra,* which confirmed his theory, was introduced from India. The result was the doctrine of universal salvation, which turned Buddhism into Mahāyāna, or the great vehicle for the salvation of all.

As has been indicated, the main argument for the original goodness of human nature is that man is part of the universe, which is morally good. If so, how is evil, at least moral evil, to be explained? Opinions differ as to its emergence. Buddhism ascribes it to ignorance. Taoism ascribes it to desire. Among Neo-Confucianists such as Chu Hsi, there was a strong tendency to hold desire responsible. Chu Hsi even contrasted *li* as the source of good and *ch'i* as the source of evil, although he by no means implied that *ch'i* is by nature evil. In him the climax of the controversy over the contrast between the *li* of Heaven and the desire of man was reached. This question had been debated for centuries and continued for a long time after Chu Hsi. As time went on, more and more Neo-Confucianists held that desires are good simply because they are a part of nature. In the end, whatever the theory of the origin of evil, evil means deviation from the Golden Mean. This is not just moderation or compromise. It means the harmony of *li* and *ch'i*, or the harmony of reason and desire. The fall of man is due to selfish desires, external influence, lack of education, lack of self-control, failure to develop one's moral capacity, wrong judgment, etc. Thus, evil is unnatural, incidental, and temporary, due primarily to one's own defects. Salvation obviously lies in fully developing one's originally good nature. In so doing, one "fulfills" and "establishes" one's own fate. This being the case, one must work out his own salvation. Since his nature is originally good, this is not only possible but imperative. Furthermore, since everyone shares to the fullest extent the goodness of the universe, everyone can become a sage.

Knowledge and Conduct

Developing one's nature requires education, and education involves both conduct and knowledge. These topics, as such, lie beyond the province of our discussion. However, we must not bypass the important fact that knowledge and conduct were identified by most Chinese philosophers. Actually, in this respect, there has been a series of syntheses.

First of all, there is the identification of the knower and the known. Influenced by the Buddhist distinction between the "higher truth" and the "lower truth," and by the Taoist distinction between "great knowledge" and "small knowledge," Neo-Confucianists distinguished between "knowledge through information" and "knowledge through one's moral nature." The difference between Buddhism and Taoism, on the one hand, and Neo-Confucianism, on the other, is that, whereas in Buddhism and Taoism the "lower truth" and "small knowledge" are considered untrustworthy, in Neo-Confucianism "knowledge through information" is acceptable. It is, however, "knowledge through moral nature" that leads to the true understanding of *li* and to the fulfillment of one's nature. The emphasis throughout the last eight hundred years has been on this type of knowledge. Philosophers refused to direct the effort of knowledge to a transcendental Absolute or to a self which dissolves itself into nothingness, as in Taoism and Buddhism, respectively. The only worth-while knowledge is that of *li*. Now, the *li* of a thing is the same as the *li* of the universe. Therefore, to know a thing, the mind must first of all be its true self, that is, realize its own *li*, and then extend it to the *li* of things. This "extension" is possible because *li* is one. By virtue of this common nature of the knower and the known, the two can establish rapport. In other words, to know a thing truly, the knower must approach it with "sympathetic intelligence" and a feeling of unity. To make this possible, not only must the mind be clear, calm, concentrated, and unselfish, but the entire personality must be morally sound.

Similarly, knowledge requires both intellectual activity and actual practice, as is indicated by the term *"ko-chih."* The term really defies definition. One writer listed sixty-two different interpretations, ranging from "the extending of the mind to things," through "investigating things to the limit," "finding out the form of things," etc., to "studying the causes of peace and chaos in history" and "handling human affairs." The Lu-Wang school advocated "the extension of inborn (or intuitive) knowledge" by manifesting the good nature of one's own mind. Rebelling against this doctrine, Yen Yüan and other Ch'ing philosophers demanded actual practice, declaring that the only way to learn to play a musical instrument, for instance, is to play it and not just to read the musical score. The most generally accepted interpretation of *ko-chih,* however, is that of the Ch'eng-Chu school, which combines the intuitive, rational, and empirical methods. Chu Hsi said:

> The meaning of the expression, "The perfecting of knowledge depends on the investigation of things," is this: If we wish to extend our knowledge to the utmost, we must investigate the *li* of all things we come in contact with, for the intelligent mind of man is certainly formed to know, and there is not a single thing in which *li* does not inhere. It is only because all *li* are not investigated that man's knowledge is incomplete. For this reason . . . [man should], in regard to all things in the world, proceed from what knowledge he has of their *li*, and pursue his investigation of them until he reaches the limit. After exerting himself in this way for a long time, he will suddenly find himself possessed of wide and far-reaching penetration. Then the qualities of things, whether external or internal, subtle or coarse, will all be apprehended, and the mind in its entire substance and its great functioning will be perfectly intelligent.[13]

This "wide and far-reaching penetration" has often been interpreted as intuition. If so, it is different from the Buddhist variety,
for here intuition is rationally arrived at, and there is no leap and
no necessity for meditation. In fact, Chu Hsi condemned meditation as based upon the fallacious assumption that reality reveals
itself only when thought is cut off. He even condemned introspection, for, according to him, that would mean splitting the mind in
two, one to observe and one to be observed. The "extension of
inborn or intuitive knowledge" in the Lu-Wang school is not self-
introspection or meditation, but, rather, the extension of one's mind
to embrace the whole universe. This is the true meaning of Lu
Hsiang-shan's dictum, "The universe is my mind and my mind is
the universe." [14] It is true that many Neo-Confucianists of the
Sung and Ming dynasties practiced quiet sitting, but they adopted
meditation only as an aid to mental hygiene, not as a way of
knowledge.

Two important things are to be stressed in this method of discovering *li*. First, both the deductive and the inductive methods are
employed. One may study a thing intensively or study many things
extensively, one by one and day by day, or one may do both. The
result will be the same. This is not to suggest that Neo-Confucianists
knew the scientific method. Although most of them were learned in
astronomy, phonetics, mineralogy, etc., they never dreamed of the
spirit or the technique of experiment. One must remember, however, that the nature of *li* is rational, and there is no reason why the
scientific method cannot be fully applied to it.

The second point to stress is that knowledge must be obtained
by oneself. The extension of the mind cannot be accomplished
through an agent. Incidentally, I have not found a single case in
which a philosopher asserted that reading the classics is the only
or chief way of obtaining knowledge or that a thing is true simply
because the classics say so. Knowledge is always one's own adven-
ture. This is not to deny the heavy weight of authoritarianism in the
Chinese tradition. But authority is found in other quarters, not in
knowledge. Yen Yüan said that knowledge consisted in practice,
and by practice he meant the Six Arts, that is, the arts of government, social intercourse, etc., as laid down in the classics. Still he
insisted that one must make his own discovery of truth. This is why
revelation has had no place in Chinese philosophy, including Buddhism and Taoism. This is also why dreams have been regarded by

Buddhists as illusory and by Confucianists as obstructions to clear thinking, although Taoists see in them a large measure of truth.

From the foregoing, the relationship between knowledge and conduct can be appreciated. Next to the question of human nature, the question of the relationship between knowledge and conduct has been most persistent in Chinese philosophy. Philosophers have differed greatly as to whether knowledge or action comes first, and as to which is more difficult. But most of them have agreed that, in essence, knowledge and conduct form a unity. Some philosophers, such as Wang Yang-ming, confined their discussions to certain types of knowledge, such as tasting, perception of color, the practice of filial piety, etc. Others included all types of knowledge. The general argument is that, unless coupled with action, the full value of knowledge cannot be realized, and, unless coupled with true knowledge, no action can be really intelligent or correct.

The whole matter of the understanding of *li* is summed up in the Chinese term *"t'i-yen,"* which, roughly, means personally testing, or *"t'i-jen,"* that is, personally understanding. The word *"t'i"* also means the body, thus emphasizing active personal experience. This experience involves, first of all, one's identification with the object of knowledge, secondly, moral preparation and social action, and, thirdly, both the rational and the intuitive methods. In a word, it combines metaphysics, epistemology, and ethics into one harmonious whole. Many contemporary Chinese philosophers believe that this *t'i-yen* or *t'i-jen* may be an important contribution China can make to the world. Even if the claim is exaggerated, there can be no mistake as to where the Chinese emphasis lies.

I have stressed the tendency in Chinese philosophy to synthesize. Not all syntheses have been successful. For example, the macrocosm-microcosm relationship is not supported by the evidence of science. The concept of the identity of knowledge and conduct needs to be more critically analyzed. The moral for us, however, is that apparently contrary concepts may not be incompatible after all. Of course, there can be no compromise between good and evil. To define clearly what is good and what is evil has occupied much attention of Chinese philosophers throughout the ages. But, significantly enough, in Chinese metaphysics even the relationship between good and evil in man has not been placed in such an impossible position as to require either the denial of evil or the grace of God for its removal.

Observations

As a footnote to this paper, let me make a few observations.

1. Chinese metaphysics is simple, unsystematic, and in some instances superficial. Chinese philosophers have debated metaphysical questions in conversations, letters, and commentaries on the classics, and have debated them primarily as theoretical foundations for ethics.

2. Western philosophy developed from metaphysics to social and moral philosophy, whereas Chinese philosophy developed the other way.

3. Since Chinese philosophy has been devoted chiefly to the good life, those metaphysical questions which have been discussed were those closest to the moral life, and the conclusions have made Chinese metaphysics very earthly and practical.

4. There has been a curious absence of any deduction of categories.

5. There has also been a conspicuous absence of materialism. It is definitely wrong to label Hsün Tzu a materialist. All he did was to describe Heaven in naturalistic terms, but nowhere did he ever reduce the mind to matter or to a quantity. Even Wang Ch'ung (A.D. 27–ca. 100), often called a materialist in the West, did not go that far. He merely elaborated the Taoist doctrine that all things are "self-transformations," and denied the existence of spirits. This shows that Western terms need to be applied to Chinese philosophy with great care. For example, Chu Hsi has been called both a rationalist and an empiricist. Some say he was an empiricist because he insisted on moral preparation for knowledge and on rapport with the object, and because he demanded not only self-evident premises but also a finer degree of receptivity to the realities operating in the given world. Others say he was a rationalist because he insisted that observation must be attended by thought, and that, since the nature of *li* is rational, the only correct method of knowing *li* was the rational one. What was Chu Hsi, then, a rationalist or an empiricist? The answer is a typically Chinese one: he was both.

6. The word "mysticism" has not been mentioned in this paper. One can detect a mystical element in Mencius, Chu Hsi, and Wang Yang-ming. But after the decline of Buddhism and Taoism in the eleventh century, mysticism ceased to have any appreciable place in Chinese philosophy. In this paper, less space has been given to

Taoism and Buddhism than to Neo-Confucianism, partly because they have been assimilated into Neo-Confucianism and partly because Neo-Confucianism has been *the* Chinese philosophy for the last eight hundred years.

7. If the history of Chinese philosophy proves anything, it shows that materialism and extreme forms of mysticism, or indeed any extreme philosophy, will not find China fertile soil. In the last two decades there has been a revival of Buddhist idealism and Buddhist mysticism. But, very significantly, they soon reached their climax and rapidly declined. No one should be so dogmatic as to say that Buddhism and Taoism will remain dormant in the next eight hundred years as they have in the last eight centuries. Besides, Buddhism has tremendous possibilities. But the fact remains that the most influential philosophers today are those who are trying to reconstruct Neo-Confucianism in the light of Western philosophy or combine it with Western objectivism.

8. Any future Chinese metaphysics will have to be fortified by science and logic. Fortunately there is nothing in the nature of Chinese metaphysics to prevent the introduction of these two.

9. The synthesis that is going on today and will likely continue for years to come will be easier than the task of the early Neo-Confucianists, for in the eleventh century the three systems that were finally synthesized had incompatible features, whereas today the currents that meet reinforce each other.

10. Finally, most contemporary Chinese philosophers I have talked to feel that, while in ethics China will probably have something to offer the world, in metaphysics she is on the receiving end. Personally, I feel that when different streams come together, all of them, no matter how large or small, will affect the river. Ideas travel in strange ways. If Buddhism influenced Schopenhauer, as indeed it did, and if Chu Hsi impressed Leibniz, as certainly he did,[15] who can foretell with certainty that Mencius or Tai Chen will not influence a future Spinoza who may be in our midst?

Notes

1. *Prajñā-pāramitā-hṛdaya-sūtra,* in E. B. Cowell, trans., *Buddhist Mahāyāna Texts,* Part II, *Buddha-Karita of Aśvaghosha.* Sacred Books of the East, Vol. XLIX (London: Oxford University Press, Humphrey Milford, 1894, 1927), p. 153.
2. *Tao-te ching.* See Wing-tsit Chan, trans., *The Way of Lao Tzu* (Indianapolis: Bobbs-Merrill, 1963), chap. 40.
3. *The Book of Changes (I ching),* Appendix I ("Hsi tz'u"), Pt. I, sec. 11.
4. *The Analects (Lun yü),* XI. 25. See James Legge, trans., *The Four Books* (Shanghai: The Chinese Book Company, n.d.), p. 153; also Arthur Waley, trans., *The Analects of Confucius* (London: George Allen & Unwin Ltd., 1938).
5. *The Doctrine of the Mean (Chung yung),* XXIII, XXV. See *The Doctrine of the Mean* in *The Four Books,* pp. 400–402; also Ku Hung-ming, trans., *Central Harmony,* in Lin Yutang, *The Wisdom of Confucius* (New York: Random House, 1942), pp. 123–124; also E. R. Hughes, trans., *The Great Learning and the Mean-in-Action* (New York: E. P. Dutton & Co., 1943), pp. 128, 131; also Wing-tsit Chan, *A Source Book in Chinese Philosophy* (Princeton: Princeton University Press, 1963), chap. 5.
6. *The Book of Changes,* Appendix I, Pt. I, sec. 4.
7. *The Great Learning (Ta hsüeh),* II. See James Legge, *The Four Books,* p. 316; also Hughes, *op. cit.,* p. 150; also Wing-tsit Chan, *A Source Book in Chinese Philosophy,* chap. 4.
8. J. P. Bruce, *Chu Hsi and His Masters* (London: Arthur Probsthain, 1923), XII.
9. *Tao-te ching,* 5.
10. *T'ung shu* (Penetrating *The Book of Changes*), XXII.
11. *Cheng-meng* (Correcting Youthful Ignorance), II.
12. *The Doctrine of the Mean,* XXII; *The Book of Mencius,* VIIA.1.
13. *The Great Learning,* V.
14. *Lu Hsiang-shan ch'üan-chi (The Complete Works of Lu Hsiang-shan)* (Shanghai: The Commercial Press, 1919–1922), XXXIII.
15. Henri Bernard, "Chu Hsi and Leibniz," *T'ien Hsia Monthly,* V (August, 1937), 9–18.

Y. P. MEI   *The Basis of Social, Ethical, and*

Spiritual Values in Chinese Philosophy

THE FIELD OF SOCIAL, ethical, and spiritual values in Chinese philosophy is so wide and the content so rich that the paper here presented will have to be highly selective in scope. It is proposed to limit the treatment to the following sub-topics:

    I. Some general characters and the problem of Chinese phi-
       losophy
   II. Values in Confucianism—as expounded by Confucius
  III. Values in Confucianism—as developed by Mencius
   IV. Values in alternative systems: (a) Moism, and (b) Taoism
       of Lao Tzu and Chuang Tzu
    V. Values restated in Neo-Confucianism

The discussion of values in the several systems will be concentrated on their respective search after the highest good, as the other virtues and standards are usually found subsumed thereunder. It is hoped that such a plan of treatment will afford the best perspective for a general view of the basis of values in Chinese philosophy, without permitting ourselves to get involved in the many features that might sidetrack us from the central issue.

I

Insofar as one may speak of Chinese philosophy and not of Chinese philosophies, he may suggest that Chinese philosophy is predominantly a system of ethical realism. The major tenets of this philosophy may be outlined as follows:

METAPHYSICS

(1) Both the universe and man's life are real.
(2) The nature of reality is dynamic and not static, relational and not absolute.
(3) All forms of change may be regarded as expressions of the interaction of two forces, the *yin* and the *yang*, between which there can be equilibrium and harmony, as well as conflict and opposition.
(4) Change takes place in the form of supplementation and alternation and usually in the form of cycles or spirals, but never extremes.
(5) The universe is a macrocosm and man is a microcosm.

ETHICS

(1) Running through life and the universe is one all-pervading principle, rational and ethical in nature.
(2) Man's duty is to follow this principle, which brings him into harmony with society and in tune with the universe.
(3) Evil results when there is deviation from this path.
(4) Every mortal has in him the capacity to become a sage.
(5) The sage is one who "assists the transforming and nourishing powers of Heaven and Earth, and so with Heaven and Earth forms a ternion." [1]

These tenets are most fundamental in Chinese thought. In fact, they are as much the contents of a credo of the Chinese race as the doctrines of Chinese philosophy. Such a faith about man and his universe antedates all philosophical systems, on the one hand, and is still the basis of Chinese life and conduct, on the other. Philosophy only performed the useful service, a very useful service to be sure, of midwifery to the embryonic ideas in the ancient culture and of outlining more clearly defined precepts for later ages. The feeling of kinship between man and the universe is so strong that it is sometimes difficult to know where ethics ends and where metaphysics begins.

Assuming a common root for man and the universe, Chinese philosophy is grounded in man and his life. Man is the center of all things, and it is his nature, his relations, and the development of his personality that are of absorbing interest. And how, in the end, is man able to achieve perfection and to identify himself with the universe—a synthesis of this world, which man affirms and does not relinquish, and a world beyond—this is the final problem of Chinese philosophy and particularly of Chinese ethics.

If man gives rise to the problem, life itself is considered adequate to provide the basis and standard for all values. Transcendental and supernatural considerations have as little place here as do methods of abstraction and objectification. The world beyond is beyond in the ontological and moral, but not the temporal, sense. Of course, agricultural people are children of Nature living among vegetation and growth and moving in the intimate circle of the family. Everything goes on in the experience of the immediate, and understanding depends upon appreciation rather than analysis and calculation. Plato's problem of abstract justice, for instance, has hardly ever been discussed in China. Knowledge means wisdom, as it did in Greek before Aristotle distinguished between *sophía* (philosophic wisdom) and *phrónēsis* (practical wisdom), and wisdom is virtue. It is something direct and personal, something like what is called a "realizing sense." Philosophy is therefore decidedly a way of life, just as the Orphic communities in ancient Greece claimed they were. And ethical inquiry is always conducted in the same spirit as that of Aristotle when he said, "We are inquiring not in order to know what virtue is, but in order to become good, since otherwise an inquiry would have been of no use." [2] Thus, there is a large aesthetic element in morality, whereas an ethics based on abstraction leaves life in want of the saving grace of art that is developed independently and provided as an addition. It might be significant to realize that the component Chinese character for ethics, *lun*, comes under the *jen* (meaning "man") radical, and that an ancient form of the character for morality is *te*, which comes under the *hsin* (meaning "heart") radical, whereas the Western terms "ethics" and "morality" have their origins either in the nature of gods or in social customs.

II

Confucius (551–479 B.C.) may or may not have been the keenest thinker among the Chinese, but for two and a half millenniums he surely has been the chief molder of China. The Confucian way of life remains the key to a study of values in Chinese philosophy.

Confucius repeatedly spoke of his "one unifying principle," which is also rendered as "an all-pervading unity."[3] This unifying principle is generally assumed to be *shu,* reciprocity, which Confucius once said was the one word that might guide one's conduct throughout life.[4] Reciprocity was stated to be "what you would not have others do unto you, do not unto them,"[5] and this formula has usually been referred to as the Chinese Golden Rule. But, when Confucius tried to make clear to a disciple what *jen* meant, the explanation consisted of exactly the same Golden Rule.[6] *Jen* is, of course, the cornerstone of Confucianism, and it may be assumed that reciprocity, or the Golden Rule, is an expression of *jen,* and that it is just as proper to regard *jen* as the one unifying principle of all of Confucius' teachings. Historically, *jen* is a distinct Confucian concept, a concept that was little used before his time.[7]

Now, *jen* has been variously translated as "magnanimity," "benevolence," "perfect virtue" (James Legge), "moral life," "moral character" (Ku Hung-ming), "true manhood," "compassion" (Lin Yutang), "human-heartedness" (Derk Bodde), "man-to-manness" (E. R. Hughes), etc. Evidently there is no term in the English language that corresponds exactly to this fundamental Confucian concept. It is probably just as profitable if we do not try to adopt some one translation but use the transliteration *"jen"* in these paragraphs.

While not one of the list of translated terms seems entirely satisfactory, the whole list together should afford some notion as to what *jen* means. Confucius' own brief answer, when a disciple asked about *jen,* was, "Love men."[8] Han Fei Tzu (d. 233 B.C.) elaborated this idea and said, "*Jen* is to love men joyously and from the inmost of one's heart."[9] In *The Doctrine of the Mean* (*Chung yung*) there is the pun, *"jen* is *jen"* or *"jen* is manhood."[10] One of the earliest and most influential commentaries [11] on the Confucian *Analects* (*Lun yü*) pointed out that *"jen* denotes what is common in two men," which is right in line with the etymological origin of the character. (An older form of the character is made up of the two components which separately mean "thousand" and "hearts.")[12] When Mencius inquired what it was that distinguished man from the birds and beasts, the answer was also *jen.*[13] Thus, *jen* is the common denominator of humanity on the one hand, and the mark which distinguishes man from animal on the other. It is both the

innermost nature and the highest ideal of true manhood, the beginning and the end of the way of life. The man of *jen* has no anxieties [14] and is free from evil,[15] and it is only he who knows how to
love men or to hate men.[16] All virtues, like love, reciprocity, loyalty,
courage, trustworthiness, etc., may be regarded as expressions of
jen, and *jen* is thus, like Socratic justice, the super-virtue of virtues.
A superior man is said not to act contrary to *jen,* but to hold himself
true to it under all circumstances.[17] The Master's highest praise for
his favorite disciple was that his heart did not deviate from *jen* for
as long as three months.[18] And, when necessary, the virtuous man
would rather give up life than permit the *jen* in him to be injured.[19]

One arrives at *jen* not so much by way of intellect or emotion
as by intuition. *Jen* is inborn in us all, and we all have the "feel"
for it. He whose intuition is more sensitive than others' has a better
apprehension of *jen* and attains it to a higher degree. Even today,
Chinese medical language speaks of paralysis as "absence or lack of
jen." Confucius said, "Is *jen* something remote? If I want *jen,* behold,
jen has arrived." [20] And, "The attainment of *jen* depends upon oneself. What does it have to do with others?" [21] Borrowing Professor
F. S. C. Northrop's immensely suggestive term, without subscribing
to all the uses he has put it to, however, one might say that *jen* was
to Confucius "an immediately apprehended aesthetic continuum
or manifold." [22]

In spite of several frequently employed quotations from *The
Analects* which seem to point to the contrary, Confucius was truly
a religious man. Confucius had a deep sense of affirmation of life
and was ever ready to offer his praise. He had something of the
feeling that "God's in his heaven: all's right with the world." He
prayed,[23] he fasted,[24] he attended sacrifices,[25] and once he even
swore by Heaven.[26] In his disappointments, he trusted that Heaven
knew him.[27] His sense of a heavenly mission grew upon him only
with the years. He observed, "Does Heaven speak? The four seasons run their course and all things grow. Does Heaven speak?" [28]
This observation might partly account for his own reticence in such
matters. Confucius was not a preacher of an institutional religion,
but he was a God-filled man.

One of the marks of the superior man that Confucius emphasized was that he was always composed and contented, whereas
the inferior man was always worried and full of distress.[29] A record
in *The Analects* says Confucius' manners were easy and his looks
very cheerful.[30] There was an occasion when four disciples were in

attendance. Of the four, Tseng Hsi was the last to speak his mind and said:

We will suppose now that we are in the latter days of spring, when the new, light garments are ready. I would then take with me five or six grown-ups and six or seven boys. We will go and bathe in the I River, after which we will air and cool ourselves on top of that ancient terrace; and then we will loiter back home, singing on our way.

Confucius, who had kept his silence as he listened to the others speaking their minds, which invariably consisted of some political ambition or plan, thereupon spoke up and said, "Ah, you are a man after my own heart!" [31] In describing his own spiritual development, Confucius said that at fifty he knew the will of Heaven, at sixty he was obedient to it, and at seventy he could follow his heart's desire without transgressing the moral law.[32] Confucius thus achieved an ease and serenity within himself and attained a harmony and identity with the universe. He was at once a perfect citizen of society and of the universe, and in him was a synthesis of this world and the world beyond. Confucius knew that such a state of mind was neither reducible to conceptual analysis nor subject to systematic teaching. But his personal example has stood like a beacon light to all seekers after truth. Worthily indeed has Confucius been revered during these long centuries by the Chinese as their Supreme Sage and Foremost Teacher.

Although *jen* is inborn in us all, Confucius understood very well that it was only the few who would reach the final stage in the pilgrim's progress of the soul. For the benefit of the many, and to pave the way leading to their attainment, he discoursed constantly on the various virtues and the proper relations of men in their several stations in life. Subsequently Confucian followers developed out of these the code of the five social relations and the codes of filial piety and ancestor worship, which have had an important influence on Chinese life. Confucius' reiteration of the Golden Mean, an idea dating from antiquity, gave rise to *The Doctrine of the Mean*, and it has since in turn become a central doctrine in all philosophical thinking. Confucius made much of the rites of propriety and music. The manner in which an act is performed is of as much importance as the motive that prompts it. If *jen* is the spirit of conduct, propriety and music are to be its form and to give it the finishing touch. When the natural qualities and good manners are well blended in a person we have a superior man.[33] In politics, Confucius was the champion of the idea of government by virtue, a novel idea at a time when absolute powers were vested in a hereditary aristocracy. Elevation of the citizen's character becomes the purpose and procedure of such a government, and moral life and education are one with political activity and process. The liberating and democratic tendencies of such a political ideal are evident, but it was left to Mencius to give these tendencies a clear and definite formulation.

III

Mencius (372–289 B.C.) had the greatest admiration for Confucius. He accepted all the tenets of Confucius and devoted himself to their clarification and to giving them a more intelligible formulation. In the process, he made his own very significant contributions. The Confucian idea of government by virtue was at the hands of Mencius directly turned into government by *jen*.[34] Government by *jen* is actually the easiest thing in the world. All that a ruler has to do is to let his innate *jen* impulse have its natural play and give it a wide extension toward all people.[35] Of course, special attention should be given to the needs of the people, material and spiritual. Mencius went into great detail about what may be called his economic planning. He was very insistent about it, and in *The Book of Mencius* reiterated this plan several times.[36] When, finally, there is plenty in the country, the rulers are to share all the good things of life with the people and then provide them with proper education. Government by *jen* is the political norm. In case of disharmony between the ruler and the people, usually due to the degeneracy of the ruler, he should be emphatically reminded that the people rank the highest, the spirits of the land and grain next, and the sovereign the lowest.[37] And Mencius quoted with emphasis from the *Shu ching* (*The Book of History*), "Heaven sees as my people see; Heaven hears as my people hear." [38] If a wayward ruler should turn a deaf ear to such warnings and admonitions, then, not only would his forceful removal be permitted, but he by whose hands this act is done would be regarded as a vessel of God as well as a savior of men.[39]

Here we have the most articulate expression of the democratic ideal in Chinese political thought. The right of the sovereign rests on a trust, a divine trust if you wish, but God exercises his vigilant powers through the people. In such a system revolution becomes part and parcel of the scheme and poses no problem for political theory. The exaltation of the individual resolves itself in providing for his needs as much as in calling attention to his worth. Mencius' maxim is to "live and let live," and thus the formalism of Confucius' political thought is here given a realistic content. At the bottom of it all, we shall find that Mencius' enthusiasm for political democracy comes from his deep-seated faith in moral democracy. Such enthusiasm and such faith are indeed remarkable when we realize that at that time the individual common man was just emerging out of the tenant slavery of feudalistic society and had hardly shaken off all its vestiges.

Confucius simply posited the concept of *jen*. Mencius explicitly maintained that *jen*, with its accompanying virtues of righteousness, propriety, and wisdom, arose from the inner springs of the human heart. His doctrine of the goodness of human nature [40] is well known, and his illustration of the poor "child about to fall into the well" [41] has been used until it is in tatters. What it says, in a nutshell, is that the expressions of the four cardinal virtues are universal and come naturally, just as taste for food and hearing for music and sight for beauty come naturally.[42] Therefore, if it is guided by its innate feelings, our nature will be good. Evil and misbehavior are due to pressure and influence, the source of which is external. We all have the seeds of the four virtues in us,[43] sparks of divinity in terms of some theology, and our business is to give them the opportunity of full extension and development. Self-cultivation is a task that requires constant attention, but one must not overexert oneself trying to be good. That would be like the foolish man of the State of Sung who tried to help his crop grow by pulling up the young sprouts just a little.[44]

Mencius has thus given a theory of the origin of the all-important Confucian concept of *jen* and outlined a procedure for its development. Both are important supplements to the Confucian doctrine. The theory of the goodness of human nature has since stimulated much discussion and is one of the major problems in Chinese philosophy.

Mencius' ideal of personal cultivation stops at nothing short of the true sage. When he was asked wherein did he excel, he replied that he knew well how to feed his boundless spirit. As to the meaning of this boundless spirit, Mencius said:

It is rather difficult to describe. The spirit is infinitely vast and powerful. When properly cultivated and carefully preserved, it will fill up all between Heaven and Earth. It is in accord with both virtue and reason. Without the spirit, man is but an empty shell. It is the sum total of all righteous deeds, and not the result of incidental acts of righteousness.[45]

There is a strong element of mysticism in Mencius. And his sagehood constitutes a power permeating man and the universe and Heaven and Earth,[46] again "an immediately apprehended aesthetic continuum or manifold." It would be futile to try to describe this feeling on his part except in his own words. But we have to limit ourselves to the briefest of his remarks:

All the ten thousand living things are found within us. There is no greater joy than to look into our life and find this true. To have strong feelings for others and follow them is the nearest road to *jen*.[47]

He that goes to the bottom of his heart knows his own nature; and knowing his own nature he knows Heaven. By keeping his heart and feeding his nature he serves Héaven. Long life and early death are as one to him. By mending his life whilst he waits, he carries out the bidding.[48]

And yet, the truly great man is he who is able to preserve his heart like that of a new-born babe.[49]

Although such a state may appear too lofty and unattainable for the ordinary man, Mencius exhorted him to take heart. When Mencius was asked if it was true that every man could become like Yao and Shun (the great ancient Sage-Kings), he exclaimed, "Certainly!" [50] And he put into the mouth of Yen Yüan, the favorite disciple of Confucius, the following expression of confidence: "Who was Shun? Who am I? To do our all is to be like him." [51] If Mencius departed from the traditional anthropomorphic God, he laid his faith in a new realization of the true worth of man. For traditional religion he substituted a vital ethical mysticism. Mencius was confident that not only he himself but everyone else as well could attain the identity of man with the universe. Everyone has potential sagehood in him. It all depends on how well he can extend and develop those inborn beginnings of the virtues. To a more profound moral democracy than this no man can profess.

IV

(A) Mo Tzu (470–391 B.C.) had a vivid sense of a personal God and was an outspoken champion of orthodox religion. He considered Confucius' reticence about religious matters indicative of a lack of faith and his skepticism a danger to morals. Religion is to be revitalized and new content put in, to be sure, but it must be God and not man who is to be the center of things. Confucius' spontaneous quality of *jen* suffers from the lack of a solid foundation, and in practice it works for gradation and partiality, the root evil of all the chaotic conditions of the day. Universal love (*chien-ai*) becomes, therefore, the well-known ethical doctrine of Mo Tzu, with emphasis placed on the quality of universality.[52] Mo Tzu's political teachings consist of establishing a hierarchy of rulers chosen on the basis of virtue and talent, and then carrying through a process of identification with the superior.[53] This process reaches its climax through the emperor, the "Son of Heaven," in Heaven itself, just as the concept of universal love finds its origin in the content of the Will of Heaven.[54] Both ethics and politics thus receive their sanction from religion. At the same time, Mo Tzu was an outspoken utilitarian. The phrase "universal love and mutual profit," which he used repeatedly,[55] did not seem to embarrass him in the least, and, in fact, seemed to him to be the only possible expression that would make the idea meaningful and intelligible. For the same reason, Mo Tzu found Confucius' idea that *jen* was derived from the direct intuitive sense unintelligible. For instance, he was greatly annoyed when a Confucianist announced, "We make music for music's sake." To Mo Tzu this was sheer nonsense, the same as telling people we build houses for houses' sake. What one ought to have said is that a house is built so as to keep off the cold in winter and the heat in summer, and to separate the men from the women properly.[56] His own doctrine of universal love was proposed because it would result in mutual benefit and eventually the greatest good to the greatest number.

Mencius' doctrine of the goodness of human nature may be regarded as an answer to Mo Tzu's criticism regarding the origin of Confucius' concept of *jen*. Confucianism insists on grounding morality and value in man himself. No external standard, though it be from God, will be acceptable. Self-conscious, self-critical, and self-realizing manhood is the center of all goodness and the origin of all virtues. Therefrom Mencius went on to condemn Mo Tzu's principle of universal love. Universal love, contrasted to love as *jen* in action—call it graded love if you must—is not at all a higher level of moral sentiment but simply an arbitrary and artificial notion about human relationships. What could be more ideal than to let the well-spring of the human heart issue forth freely in its natural course and to its natural degree? To say that one loves or should love the man on the street as much as one's parents violates every sense of rationality. As to proposing love for profit, well, the Sage Mencius could do without any such sacrilege. When Mencius compared Mo Tzu to birds and beasts,[57] he meant that Mo Tzu altogether overlooked the all-important *jen* in himself and in others, which was to Mencius the line of demarcation between man and animal.

His twofold religious and utilitarian motive enabled Mo Tzu to develop a way of life characterized by asceticism, obedience, and self-denial. Mo Tzu had a considerable following for several generations after his death, and these followers organized themselves into a community that can very properly be called a church under the undisputed authority of a grand master. Members were men of strict discipline, and the community had a stern sort of order.[58] But the strength of this discipline and of this order was of the brittle kind, and the movement lasted for about two centuries and then dwindled into oblivion. The teachings of Mo Tzu left their marks on Chinese life, and it would be difficult to find a more self-sacrificing person than Mo Tzu himself. But to lead a man to inner peace with himself and happy relationship with his fellow men, as well as harmony with the universe, Mo Tzu's way would hardly suffice.[59]

(B) Lao Tzu (fifth century B.C.) and Chuang Tzu (369–286 B.C.) had no use for the anthropomorphic God that Mo Tzu tried so desperately to salvage for the orthodox tradition. To Mo Tzu, God was the absolute standard and the final reality. To the Taoists, God was neither. Heaven was said to be unkind and to treat the creation like the straw-dogs we use at sacrifices.[60] And Lao Tzu spoke of the *Tao* as "an image of that which existed *before* God." [61] On the other hand, the Taoists could not see anything in the *jen* of Confucius or the *i* (righteousness) of Mencius. *Jen* and *i* are, at best, of secondary significance: after *Tao* is lost then arises the doctrine of *jen*; after *jen* is lost then arises the doctrine of *i*.[62] And people are told to abandon their saintliness and put away their wisdom, to abandon their *jen* and put away their *i*.[63]

The highest good and at the same time the most fundamental reality is *Tao*. It is difficult to talk about *Tao* because it is nameless and unnamable,[64] elusive, and evasive.[65] If one must call it something, one may call it great.[66] Out of *Tao* the created universe is born; [67] *Tao* is the mother of all things.[68] Yet *Tao* does nothing.[69] In fact, the things of this world come from being, and being comes from non-being.[70] *Tao* transcends time and space and causality and knowledge, and is beyond good and evil, truth and falsehood, life and death. *Tao* is the prime mover, and underlies man, God, and the universe.

While in Lao Tzu there is still room for a life of humility and quietude in society, in Chuang Tzu the one aim in life for man comes to consist in apprehending the *Tao*. He who attains the *Tao* becomes the true man, the ultimate man (*chih-jen*), the spiritual man (*shen-jen*). The stages in the pilgrim's progress of the mind are marked by forgetfulness of the world, of the manifold, and of life itself.[71] Positively, there is enlightenment, then a sense of the wholeness of things, then the merging of the present and the past, and, finally, the oneness of death and life.[72] What may be called the Taoist beatific vision may be described as an equilibrium in which all differences and distinctions—those between the ego and the non-ego, between man and the universe, as well as between life and death—disappear and are melted into a sea of identity. The true man is therefore conditioned by nothing and is free in the absolute sense.[73] Taoist religion later readily turned him into a fairy spirit, practicing alchemy and teaching the secrets of longevity. Worst blasphemy and irony can hardly be imagined. Actually, what we have here is again an "immediately apprehended aesthetic continuum," and the term is used in Northrop's sense, this time with less reservation. Chuang Tzu, of course, employed to the full his power of literary imagery in inducing an appreciation of the *Tao*, and at times he achieved poetic heights of fantasy.

In relation to the all-important attainment of the *Tao*, all else becomes secondary. A naturalistic pantheism is all, if there is anything, that is left of religion; ethical values become relative or insignificant; and the political ideal is found in the primitivity of small rural communities where the voices of cocks and dogs would be within hearing and yet the people might grow old and die before they visited one another.[74] Both the ethical realism of Confucianism and the naturalistic mysticism of Taoism are interested in the final perfection of man or his identification with the universe, but there is a difference. Whereas to Confucius this attainment is the crowning glory of a process of cultivation in which each step is a positive good contributing to the upbuilding of the personality of the individual and the welfare of his society, to the Taoists the towering height of the one all-engrossing goal dwarfs all other values to the level of insignificance. This contrast between Taoism and Confucianism may be grasped in another way. Lao Tzu and Mencius were equally fond of speaking of the new-born babe. But Lao Tzu was attracted by its freedom from the fetters and burdens of life, whereas Mencius was impressed by its vitality and promise and potentialities. Maybe here is a key to the proper approach to, and understanding of, the two systems.

V

For nearly a millennium, roughly speaking from the time of Christ, Confucianism was overshadowed by Taoism and, more fundamentally, by Buddhism. The teachings of Buddhism brought from India proved to be refreshingly interesting to the Chinese mind. It is no exaggeration to say that for the greater part of the millennium the best thinkers in China were all Buddhist thinkers. The Ch'an school, or Zen, with its charm of simplicity and yet its depth of profundity, for instance, is one of the fruits of Buddhism flowering in the Chinese mind. The story of Buddhism's arriving in China as a foreign doctrine both geographically and intellectually, coming there to its fruition, and, finally, ingraining itself in the very fiber of the Chinese mentality, is an intellectual epic to which a conference devoted to a synthesis of the philosophies of the East and the West would do well to pay some attention.

Stimulating as the Buddha's teachings may be, they go against the grain of the Chinese outlook on life and have always been regarded by the orthodox Confucianists with suspicion. Voices have recurrently been raised against this foreign system, and large-scale persecution has occurred more than once in history. But the Neo-Confucianism of the Sung and Ming dynasties was the first revival movement that succeeded in directing the Chinese mind from Buddhism to the indigenous Chinese heritage. The Neo-Confucianists had to state their philosophy with the challenge of Buddhism very much in mind. In their formulation, they leaned heavily on such sources of Confucianism as *The Book of Changes* (*I ching*), *The Doctrine of the Mean*, *The Great Learning* (*Ta hsüeh*) and the mystical phase in Mencius. Although they claimed to be stating their views from the purely Confucian position, they were actually influenced by Buddhism and occasionally they even made use of certain Taoist ideas. Synthesis does seem to come easily to the Chinese temper of mind.

By the time of the Neo-Confucianists, the time-honored feeling of kinship between man and the universe had grown even stronger.[75] Chang Tsai (A.D. 1020–1077) bluntly announced, "Heaven is my father and Earth is my mother. . . . What fills the universe is my body, and what commands the universe is my nature. All men are my brothers; all things are my relatives." And the essay known as "The Western Inscription," from which the preceding quotation is taken, is a classic in Confucian ethics.[76] This twofold aspect must be borne in mind in following the discussion of this period of either the cosmos or of man's being. According to Ch'eng Hao (1032–1085), the older of the two Ch'eng brothers, the man who has jen in him identifies himself with all things without discrimination,[77] and the superior man is in a position "to extend his affection to all and to respond spontaneously to any occurrence." [78]

Chu Hsi (A.D. 1130–1200) was, of course, the most comprehensive scholar of the period. His metaphysics is built on the basic notions of li (rational principle) and ch'i (material principle). Every object is an embodiment of these two components. Human beings in common derive their essential nature from the li, whereas individual characteristics are accounted for by the ch'i. Evil is due to the coarse grade of ch'i that a person embodies in his make-up. Chu Hsi used this explanantion to buttress Mencius' doctrine of the goodness of human nature and at the same time to account for the phenomenon of original evil. The Supreme Ultimate, which is like a super li embracing all the individual li, is, at the same time, the supreme good, and there is a sharp contrast of human passion over against heavenly reason (li). Final unity can be achieved only by way of jen, which to Chu Hsi is the life-giving vitality in the universe as much as it is the heart-warming sentiment of love in man.[79]

Chu Hsi's keenest critic was his contemporary Lu Chiu-yüan (Lu Hsiang-shan, 1139–1193). Lu found the dualism of li and ch'i in Chu untenable and unnecessary, and he discovered the true being completely in the rationality of his own mind. Against the authoritarian background of Chinese thought, he was prompted to declare that there was no use in writing commentaries on the

Six Classics, as the Six Classics were but commentaries on his mind. And his saying, "The cosmos is in my mind; my mind is in the cosmos," has since become celebrated. Man's attainment comes, therefore, entirely through an inner process. In this way Lu represented a synthesis of Confucianism and the teachings of Ch'an Buddhism, although he was very wary of being called a Buddhist.[80] And Lu's great contribution lies in his having been the source of inspiration to Wang Shou-jen (1472–1529), more popularly and respectfully known by his appellation Yang-ming. The first mention of the idea of intuitive knowledge (liang-chih) occurred in The Book of Mencius.[81] Wang Shou-jen expounded the doctrines of the extension of intuitive knowledge and the unity of knowledge and conduct. Thus knowledge contains in itself the factor of action, and action has an intelligible reference. Wang's Dialogue on the Great Learning is an elaboration of his doctrine of intuition as it bears on the concept of jen. Jen is an all-inclusive whole, and in the ordinary life of man this natural feeling of jen becomes the categorical imperative of conduct.[82]

These teachers of the Sung and Ming dynasties reaffirmed Confucius' way of jen. To them, the views on life of both the Taoists and the Buddhists of their time were unacceptable. The Taoists suffered from too much attachment to life and hence their cultivation of magic and alchemy in the hope of discovering the elixir of longevity. The Buddhist suffered from too much negation of life and hence their search for release and freedom from the perpetual wheel. In common, they suffered from a mistaken view. Life is here: it is to be lived. Man is to be of this world and, at the same time, of the world beyond. To achieve this ideal is possible only when the individual has apprehended the jen that is the final unity or continuum.

It is remarkable that out of an intervening intellectual heterogeneity and richness that lasted for centuries the eventual sanction of the Chinese mind went back to Confucianism. And to this day the way of jen is the accepted way among the Chinese masses, and in it some few Chinese seers have, with the sages and teachers across the ages, found joy and satisfaction and a peace that passes understanding. The catholicity of jen breeds tolerance. May I conclude this paper with the suggestion that the system of jen will be found, by those who will try, to synthesize easily and well with any system of values the world over that has an element of true worth?

Notes

1. *Chung yung* (*The Doctrine of the Mean*), XXII, in James Legge, trans., The Chinese Classics, Vol. I (Oxford: Clarendon Press, 1893), p. 416.
2. Aristotle, *Ethica Nicomachea*, 1103.
3. *Analects*, IV.15; XV.2.
4. *Ibid.*, XV.23.
5. *Ibid.*, XV.23.
6. *Ibid.*, XII.2.
7. The character "*jen*" is not found once in all the ancient bronze or oracle-bone inscriptions.
8. *Analects*, XII.22.
9. *Han Fei Tzu*, XX. See W. K. Liao, trans. (London: Arthur Probsthain, 1939), p. 171.
10. *The Doctrine of the Mean*, XX.
11. Commentary by Cheng Hsüan (127–200).
12. An older form of the character is one with the combination of the character for "thousand" and the character for "hearts."
13. *The Book of Mencius*, IVB.19.
14. *Analects*, IX.28.
15. *Ibid.*, IV.4.
16. *Ibid.*, IV.3.
17. *Ibid.*, IV.5.
18. *Ibid.*, VI.5.
19. *Ibid.*, XV.8.
20. *Ibid.*, VII.29.
21. *Ibid.*, XII.1.
22. F. S. C. Northrop, *The Meeting of East and West* (New York: The Macmillan Company, 1946), p. 332.
23. *Analects*, VII.34.
24. *Ibid.*, X.7.
25. *Ibid.*, III.12; X.8.
26. *Ibid.*, VI.26.
27. *Ibid.*, XIV.37.
28. *Ibid.*, XVII.19.
29. *Ibid.*, VII.36.
30. *Ibid.*, VII.4.
31. *Ibid.*, XI.25.
32. *Ibid.*, II.4.
33. *Ibid.*, VI.16.
34. *The Book of Mencius*, IVA.1,3.
35. *Ibid.*, IA.7; IIA.6.
36. *Ibid.*, IA.3; IA.7; VIIA.22.

37. *Ibid.*, VIIB.14.
38. *Ibid.*, VA.5.
39. *Ibid.*, IB.3, and other passages.
40. Mencius' doctrine of the goodness of human nature is discussed in several passages in *The Book of Mencius*. VIA is probably the most important and should be read in its entirety.
41. *The Book of Mencius*, IIA.6.
42. *Ibid.*, VIA.7.
43. *Ibid.*, IIA.6.
44. *Ibid.*, IIA.2.
45. *Ibid.*, IIA.2.
46. *Ibid.*, VIIB.25.
47. *Ibid.*, VIIA.4.
48. *Ibid.*, VIIA.1.
49. *Ibid.*, IVB.12.
50. *Ibid.*, VIB.2.
51. *Ibid.*, IIIA.1.
52. *The Works of Mo Tzu*, 14–16. See Yi-pao Mei, trans., *The Ethical and Political Works of Motse* (London: Arthur Probsthain, 1929), pp. 78–97.
53. *Ibid.*, 8–13; Mei, pp. 30–77.
54. *Ibid.*, 26–28; Mei, pp. 135–159.
55. See Note 52.
56. *The Works of Mo Tzu*, 48; Mei, p. 237.
57. *The Book of Mencius*, IIIB.9.
58. Y. P. Mei, *Motse the Neglected Rival of Confucius* (London: Arthur Probsthain, 1934), pp. 170–173.
59. Cf. *Chuang Tzu*, XXXIII.
60. *Tao-te ching*, V.
61. *Ibid.*, IV.
62. *Ibid.*, XXXVIII.
63. *Ibid.*, XIX.
64. *Ibid.*, I, XXXII.
65. *Ibid.*, XXI.
66. *Ibid.*, XXV.
67. *Ibid.*, XLII.
68. *Ibid.*, XXV.
69. *Ibid.*, XXXVII.
70. *Ibid.*, XL.
71. *Chuang Tzu*, 6; Fung Yu-lan, trans. (Shanghai: Commercial Press, 1931), pp. 119, 128–129.
72. *Ibid.*, 6; Fung, pp. 119–120.
73. *Ibid.*, 1; Fung, p. 33.
74. *Tao-te ching*, LXXX.

75. J. P. Bruce, in his study of Neo-Confucianism, found it relevant to give the following warning to his fellow students of Chinese philosophy:

"It is very important that the reader of Chinese works on philosophy should keep this twofold aspect continually in mind. When reading of Law and Matter, for example, or of the Supreme Ultimate, we must remember that the writer is treating of these from the point of view of human nature; and perhaps in some passage where it is least expected, he is referring to them as inherent in man, and as explaining the constitution of man's being. And, vice versa, when reading of man's nature or mind, we must keep before us the wide cosmic outlook if we are to keep in touch with the writer's thought. Only thus can we obtain a true perspective for the study of Chinese Philosophy." J. P. Bruce, *Chu Hsi and His Masters* (London: Arthur Probsthain, 1923), p. 4.

76. Chang Tsai, "The Western Inscription," in P. C. Hsü, trans., *Ethical Realism in Neo-Confucian Thought* (Columbia University Thesis, 1931), Appendix, p. xi.

77. Ch'eng Hao, "Essay on the Nature of *Jen*," in Hsü, trans., *op. cit.*, pp. xii–xiii.

78. Ch'eng Hao, "Essay on the Stabilization of the Self," in Hsü, trans., *ibid.*, pp. xiii–xv.

79. Cf. J. P. Bruce, trans., *The Philosophy of Human Nature* (London: Arthur Probsthain, 1922).

80. Cf. Huang Siu-chi, *Lu Hsiang-shan—A Twelfth Century Chinese Idealist Philosopher* (New Haven: American Oriental Society, 1944).

81. *The Book of Mencius*, VIIA.15.

82. Cf. F. G. Henke, trans., *The Philosophy of Wang Yang-ming* (London, Chicago: The Open Court Publishing Co., 1916).

Filial Piety and Chinese Society

THIS PAPER WILL discuss the practicality of Chinese ethics and explain the doctrine of filial piety (*hsiao*) and its place in the Chinese ethical realm. We shall then discuss the far-reaching influence of this doctrine in Chinese society, including family life, religious worship, social activities, and political affairs generally. Finally, this paper will shed some light upon what the doctrine of filial piety may contribute to the peace and welfare of the world.

Since the Confucian teaching of filial piety has held for four thousand years the most important place in Chinese ethics, I have selected it as the leading Chinese moral principle. In terms of this teaching, I shall explain the characteristics of Chinese society in the light of the relationship between these principles and the realistic life of the Chinese people.

I

The Great Learning, as the words of Confucius (551–479 B.C.) taken down by his disciple Tseng Tzu, has this leading passage: "What *The Great Learning* teaches is: to demonstrate illustrious virtue; to renovate the people; and to rest in the highest excellence attainable." [1] This sentence forms the central thought of Chinese philosophy. What most ancient Chinese philosophers strived for generally was put under these three items: "demonstrating illustrious virtue," "renovating the people," and "resting in the highest excellence." These three objectives form the focus of most classical

Chinese philosophers. It starts with the cultivating of one's personal virtues, progresses in stabilizing the social order, and culminates in the perfection of one's personality. Hence, Liang Ch'i-ch'ao (1873–1929), a renowned Chinese scholar, remarked that:

. . . most Chinese learning has been the study of human behavior rather than theoretical knowledge. The pursuit of theoretical knowledge is neither the starting point nor the final goal. The literal translation of Chinese academic thought as philosophy is rather misleading. If we borrow the term it should be qualified as "philosophy of life." Chinese philosophy took for its starting point the study of human beings, in which the most important subject was how to behave as a man, how one can truly be called a man, and what kind of relationships exist among men.[2]

Even though I cannot agree with Liang Ch'i-ch'ao in treating Chinese philosophy merely as a philosophy of life or ethics, it is still correct to say that the main theme of Chinese philosophy has centered around ethics, which also formed its starting point. The Chinese philosophical domain includes metaphysics and epistemology, but these were shaped on the basis of ethics. They derived their source from ethical principles, and were systematized through ethical interpretation. Starting from the standpoint of "demonstrating illustrious virtue," the philosopher advances to the study of human nature, in which the virtue of benevolence (*jen*) is inherent; by this the philosopher tries to reveal the "Mind of Heaven" and the "natural laws" by deduction in order to "assist the transforming and nourishing powers of Heaven and Earth." As *The Doctrine of the Mean* has said:

It is only he who possesses the most complete sincerity that can exist under Heaven and who can give full development to his nature. Able to give full development to his own nature, one can do the same to the nature of other men. Able to give full development to the nature of other men, he can give full development to the natures of animals and things. Able to give full development to the natures of creatures and things, he can assist in the transforming and nourishing powers of Heaven and Earth. Able to perform this latest feat, he may with Heaven and Earth form a trinity.[3]

If man can thoroughly understand physical laws and heavenly matters and even join himself with Heaven and Earth as in a trinity only by developing his own nature to the utmost, does this metaphysical theory not proceed from Chinese ethics?

Classical Chinese philosophers had also discussed ways and

means for the "perfecting of knowledge through the investigation of things," which in turn was conducive to "making one's thoughts sincere" and "rectifying the mind" in everyday living conditions. As the aim of investigating the nature of things was primarily "making thoughts sincere" and "rectifying the mind," this theory dwells upon the necessity for action after the acquiring of knowledge. Any and all knowledge is worth while only when it is applicable in action in daily life with goodness as its result. The ancient savants then pursued epistemological discussion of the relationship of knowledge and practice. Hence, Wang Yang-ming (Wang Shou-jen, 1474–1529) urged the "unity of knowledge and action," whereas Dr. Sun Yat-sen advocated the theory that "knowledge-acquiring is hard, but practice may be easy." These two views were set forth in epistemological studies on an ethical basis.

Hence, in the eyes of Chinese philosophers, the establishment of ethics rested, not in its theoretical system, nor in mere language or words, but in energetic striving for practice. That is one distinctive point by which Oriental ethics is to be differentiated from the Western pattern. The latter more or less concentrates its discussion especially on the question as to what constitutes "right" or "good." Most Western philosophers treat ethics in a sense as a science or a line of thought rather than a way of life or as a kind of conduct; they separate ethical thinking from the actual practice of the thinker. Hence, some authors of ethical works who may be highly learned in the scientific expounding of what is good in morality may actually be ignorant as to how to bring about goodness in daily life, and their own behavior may also have gone astray, because they treat ethics merely as one aspect of thought and possibly as having nothing to do with conduct. Such a concept or attitude is not acceptable to the orthodox Chinese philosopher.

Mencius (371–289? B.C.) said, "Why should I be fond of disputing? I am compelled to do it!" [4] Such an attitude of speaking with reluctance and only when it is absolutely necessary has been a tradition handed down by Confucius to the Sung-Ming (960–1644) Neo-Confucian scholars.

II

As Chinese ethics stresses the practicality of moral teachings, its central idea is benevolence, on the one hand, and filial piety, on the other. They are correlated, the latter serving as the basic requirement of the former. As Confucius' disciple Yu Tzu said, in the Confucian *Analects*, "Filial piety and fraternal submission!— are they not the root of all benevolent actions?" [5]

Why should benevolence and filial piety be joined? And why should the latter serve as the foundation of all benevolent actions? This point may be generally overlooked or misunderstood, not only by Western Sinologists, but also by many Chinese students. Some intellectuals in the New Cultural Movement in the early years of the Chinese Republic went so far as to vow against filial piety. Such a radical campaign demonstrated that in modern China there are many literati who are ignorant of the meaning of this traditional virtue. In fact, the tenet of filial piety has always held the most important place in Chinese ethics and also in the Chinese cultural tradition as a whole.

The Confucian scholar often linked filial piety with benevolence, and did not regard it as an incidental expediency. There are two weighty reasons for this. First, benevolence as a paramount and comprehensive Chinese virtue must have its roots. And, second, benevolence must have its application in human society.

Where may we find any root of benevolence? As Mencius put it, "Every human being is endowed with the sense of commiseration." [6] And he added, "The feeling of commiseration is the starting point of benevolence." [7] As everyone possesses an inherent feeling of commiseration, this is the evidence that everyone is endowed with the virtue of benevolence. Mencius also said, "The ability possessed by men without having been acquired by learning is their 'intuitive ability,' and the knowledge possessed by them without the exercise of thought is their 'intuitive knowledge.' Children carried in arms all know to love their parents, and, when they are grown up, they all know to respect their elder brothers." [8] This is to emphasize that human love toward one's own parents is innate, as in the case of little children, without any need of being acquired through study. This inherent love-and-respect toward parents is the feeling of filial piety. And this is the fountainhead of benevolence. It is the germination or starting point of the gradually expanding virtue, the universal love of mankind.

However, the seed of benevolence as sown in filial piety still needs timely cultivation, without which it tends to wither away or completely disappear, and then the great virtue of benevolence, even though it may have been developing in other directions, will be rootless, whereas it should have been a foundation. Or, the drifting virtue of benevolence may soon dry up like a tree without a root or a stream without a source. In order to keep benevolence durable and expanding, cultivation of the feeling of filial piety as its fountainhead is indispensable. This is one essential reason explaining why Confucians had all along championed the correlation between benevolence and filial piety.

Another reason lies in the fact that benevolence needs realization through actual practice. But then how should men practice benevolence? The Confucian *Analects* related, "Fan Ch'ih asked about benevolence. The Master said, 'It is to love all human beings.'" [9] And Mencius also asserted, "The benevolent man loves others." [10] Then, whom should everyone love? Theoretically, he should love all others throughout the world as a matter of course. In such a great love, how should one start and whom should he love first of all? Is it not correct to say that he should love his parents to start with? As everyone has an inherent love toward his parents, is it not right that this filial piety should be observed as the starting point of one's practice of benevolence?

To all such questions, the answers of Confucian scholars were in the affirmative. They agreed unanimously that the realization of benevolence must begin with the love of children toward their parents. This means that, in the complicated relations among men, filial piety forms the primary and most fundamental unit of mutual connection between two or more persons, in which the practice of benevolence must first be fulfilled. By inference, all other relations among human beings should emanate from this basic virtue as their source; otherwise, they may not stay on the right course of benevolence for the attainment of peace and prosperity.

Meanwhile, it is possible that, if one ignores his duty of showing love to his own parents, he will also be apt to neglect the practice of benevolence toward other people. Hence, the Confucian tenet "The benevolent man loves others" must be interpreted in the light of filial piety to the effect that "The benevolent man loves others, with his own parents as the starting point." This is a sound postulate because of its factual basis and indisputable reasoning.

It is a universal fact that every human being loves his parents from the beginning. If one should love others instead of his own parents, this would be a treacherous act. *The Classic of Filial Piety* thus set the warning: "Therefore to be without love of parents and to love other men [in their place] means to be a 'rebel against virtue'; to be without reverence for parents and to rever- ence other men means to be a 'rebel against sacred custom.'" [11] Actually, such moral rebels are rare in any civilized country. And eventually those who do not love their own parents will also have no love toward others; those who do not respect their own parents will not respect others in the proper way. Therefore, even though fraternal love may be prevalent, any biased practice of benevolence is vacillating and void if it is not rooted in the prime sense of filial piety. As Mencius pointed out, "The substantiation of benevo- lence begins with service to one's parents." [12] This, again, means that the observance of filial piety is one phase of the practice of benevolence, if not its starting point. This is another reason why the Confucian so closely related these two virtues.

Accordingly, the doctrine of filial piety was recognized as primary among Chinese ethical principles, with the virtue thus shaped also taking the paramount position in Chinese morality. After the Han Dynasty (206 B.C.–A.D. 220), from the early part of third century B.C., in which *The Classic of Filial Piety* was sup- posed to have been "drastically revised by some Han filial pietist," this human virtue firmly established itself as the foundation of Chinese ethics. One can hardly understand Chinese ethics, and to some extent even Chinese political activities, if he cannot grasp the true import of this filial doctrine with is practical application in Chinese society.

Western philosophers generally appeal to reason, to con- science, to sympathy, or to the idealism of universal love of man- kind in order to discover or expound the source of morality. All these are important, of course, in the exploration of the ethical domain. And yet, without filial piety as their mainstay, all go adrift in confusion or are limited in their development and appli- cation. In other words, if one's love toward his parents withers away due to negligence of cultivation, where can he find better soil for developing reason, conscience, sympathy, and fraternal love? In this case, his conscience or sympathy may go astray or even die. His moral sense, then, is liable to become twisted into an abnormal state.

It is plain that the ideal development of good morality must derive from its true source, that is, filial piety in its enlightened and broad interpretation. This explains why classical Chinese phi- losophers emphasized the doctrine of filial piety as the fountain of all good conduct.

Nevertheless, the foregoing observations do not mean that filial piety is all-embracing as the exclusive virtue. It is merely the starting point, not the final goal, of moral practice. Most Confucian scholars well understood this basic principle. As *The Classic of Filial Piety* put it: "Filial piety at the outset consists in service to one's parents; in the middle of one's path, in service to his sovereign; and, in the end, in establishing himself as a mature man." [13] Mencius further extended this virtue, saying, "The superior man should love his parents and be lovingly disposed to people in general; and so he should also be kind to all living creatures." [14] He had previously pointed out, "Treat with reverence the elders in your own family, so that the elders in other families shall be similarly treated; treat with kindness the young in your own family, so that the young in other families shall be similarly treated." [15] All such passages show that filial duties toward one's parents must be expanded to the whole society. With the broad view in mind, the developing process may be pushed on, step by step. *The Doctrine of the Mean* points out: "The ways of the superior man may be compared to what takes place in traveling, when to go to a distance we must first traverse the space that is near; and, in ascending a height, we must begin from the lower ground." [16] This way marks out the general process which is to start with one's loving and serving his own parents. Otherwise, by following the roundabout and difficult way, there may be "too much putting of things in confusion, fear, and sorrow, which may result in a standstill." [17] For this reason, it is plain why Mo Tzu's (fifth century B.C.) "principle of all-embracing love" and Jesus' doctrine of universal love have not been readily acceptable to the Chinese masses.

The Chinese ethical principle is not opposed to the doctrine of universal love, however. In embracing the latter, the former insists on starting with the observance of filial piety. That is the easiest approach. And then, step by step, its expanding process might readily be directed toward the goal of universal love. The Confucian advocacy of this tenet definitely indicates the easy and practical way from filial service to moral practice in general.

All of the human virtues, therefore, should be born through observance of filial piety, which serves as the dynamic force of all other virtues. With genuine and comprehensive love toward one's own parents, in its developing process, one may naturally learn to be benevolent to all living creatures, affectionate toward mankind as a whole, loyal to his country and to the duties of a free citizen, faithful in keeping obligations, righteous in action, peaceful in behavior, and just in all dealings. All these eight virtues, together with many others, emanante from filial piety through its expansion. *The Classic of Filial Piety* says, "It is filial piety which forms the root of all virtues, and with it all enlightening studies come into existence." [18]

As the Confucian scholars always taught, in the learning of filial piety there should be concurrently the cultivation of other virtues for its supplementation. The main virtue must be endowed with benevolence and righteousness as well as loyalty to country and courage in justifiable actions. Hence, Tseng Tzu, the chief exponent of the Confucian doctrine of filial piety and one of the most learned disciples of the Sage, once said, "Those who lack propriety in private life, loyalty in serving the sovereign, seriousness in discharging official duties, faithfulness in treating friends, or bravery in waging war are all found wanting in filial piety." [19] Therefore, for the fulfillment of the paramount virtue of filial piety many more moral aptitudes are required as its necessary supplementation. And, in this sense, filial piety has been extended to embrace all virtues. Since all virtues derive from filial piety, they all are also contained within the full development of filial piety.

There was no independent treatise on benevolence among Chinese classical works, but there was the distinguished filial-piety Classic. By inference, it is unmistakable how important the feeling as well as the practice of filial piety was considered in Chinese ethics. It serves as both the fountainhead and the accomplished state of Chinese morality as a whole.

III

We are now in a position to appreciate the paramount virtue of filial piety in its relation to Chinese society as a whole.

What influence has the doctrine of filial piety had on Chinese society? During the past several thousand years, how has the Chinese world been affected by this moral concept as its basic virtue? And how was Chinese society built upon the doctrine of filial piety as the cornerstone of Chinese ethics?

Chinese society has always been thoroughly under the sway of the ethical concept of filial piety. In other words, it was built up on the basis of filial piety, which has penetrated into every corner of Chinese life and society, permeating all the activities of the Chinese people. Its influence has been all-prevailing. All traditional habits and customs of the people, collectively as well as individually, show the influence of the practice of this ethical principle. This observation may be verified through a careful survey of the family life, religious life, social life, and political life of the Chinese people.

First, with reference to family life, Chinese society, which has laid special emphasis on the integrity of household relations, treats the family as the foundation and the unit of society. Mencius held it to be true that "the root of the empire is in the state, and the root of the state is in the family." [20] *The Great Learning* advocated that "in order rightly to govern the state, it is necessary first to regulate the family; in order to put the empire in peace and prosperity, it is necessary first to regulate the state." [21]

Prior to the setting up of a community or a state, there must be the social unit called the family. Therefore, to put one's household in good order is the primary stage to demonstrate one's ability to hold a public office in such a way as to bring well-being to the state and peace to the empire. The primary stage, according to the Confucian view, was absolutely important as a prerequisite for the attainment of the latter. The logical reasoning was based on the premise: "What is meant by 'In order rightly to govern the state, it is necessary first to regulate the family,' is this: It is not possible for one to teach others if he cannot teach his own family." [22] As everyone's parents, and by inference also his ancestors, are the source of his life, this fundamental blood relationship legally as well as morally dictates the imperative rule that one owes certain unavoidable obligations to his parents. Taking for granted that he is endowed with the virtue of love, he must first show it toward his parents. Otherwise, how can he be expected to show kindness to society at large or to the country in which he lives? He must first be able to uphold his responsibility to his parents and his family as a social unit before he can shoulder his heavier, though more remote, responsibility toward society and the state. The logical conclusion of this reasoning on the importance of the family obviously revolves around the theme of filial piety.

Chinese society has therefore laid its emphasis upon the family system, in which the relationship between parents and children assumes the top priority, and filial respect and love toward one's elders are held to be urgently required even after their death. Mencius put it emphatically: "Of services, which is the greatest?

Service toward parents is the greatest. . . ." [23] Failing to perform this service, the root of all other services, one cannot be expected to do good to others.

But, how can one perform well the greatest service in one's life—to teach and to cultivate? This was what Chinese ethics and all other related learning, such as rituals and music, concentrated their efforts upon. From the emperor and his ranking officials down to the common people, such as peddlers and hirelings, all without exception were taught and urged to practice filial piety. The teaching of their tutors, the inspiration drawn from customs and illustrations, and praise by the literati all emphasized filial piety. As *The Classic of Filial Piety* has taught, "Filial piety is the unchanging truth of Heaven, the unfailing equity of Earth, the [universal] practice of man." [24] Before the dawning of the twentieth century, most Chinese had actually observed this text and translated it into practice, though deviations may be found, of course, in certain respects.

Later, during the past half-century, since Western culture seeped into Chinese society with some ill effects, the former Chinese large-family system was gradually dissolved and the virtue of filial piety was also gradually relegated to obscurity. Nevertheless, most Chinese families still maintain reverential service to their elders as the Heaven-ordained obligation of all children. In practically all Chinese households elderly parents are living with their married son or daughter in harmony. Such a condition may be found less often in the Western world. This characteristic of the Chinese family system unmistakably demonstrates the practice of filial piety, which prevails in Chinese society.

Next to the parent-son relationship is the marriage relation, which in ancient China was held to be inviolable except in the case of certain adequately prescribed conditions. Again, with the doctrine of filial piety as the nucleus of the family system, the Chinese nuptial relationship was evolved. For the purpose of continuing the blood line as one important phase of filial piety, one must first of all keep oneself in sound physical condition. It was taught by *The Classic of Filial Piety* that "the body with its limbs and hair and skin comes to a person from father and mother, and it is on no account to be spoiled or injured." [25] This precept reaffirmed the importance of one's life as handed down by his ancestors. Then, as a necessary tribute to his forefathers, it is one's duty to perpetuate the blood line by producing offspring through wedlock. Marriage was not an affair forged through instinctive desire alone but was based also on the higher concept of creating new life or lives so as to prolong those of one's ancestors, including one's parents. Therefore, the Chinese family system placed great importance on marriage, not only because of the husband and the wife themselves, but also because of their children.

It is plain that, on the premise of filial piety, there were at least three essential points governing traditional Chinese marriage. First, wedlock, once formed, was not to be dissolved without adequate reasons strictly prescribed. Second, the parents should see to it that their children were properly married, though not necessarily in terms of mutual love prior to the nuptial ceremony. And, third, the younger couple had the inherent obligation to produce offspring, and again bore of themselves the responsibility of getting their children married when they became of marriageable age. Consequently, many of the ancient Chinese families have been propagated for thousands of years down to the present era in innumerable descendants.

Love counts after the nuptial ceremony of a couple and seldom before it. Such an ancient custom in China might seem absurd and even ridiculous to Westerners. The principal mission of marriage, then, lay in the perpetuation of the family line. If the couple failed to produce a male descendant, it was permissible for the husband to divorce his wife, or, as an alternative, for the husband to take one or more concubines. Even though such a practice is, from the modern viewpoint, unreasonable or unjust to womanhood, the ancient custom might be understood better in terms of practicing filial piety in its historical sense.

Aside from the vertical line of lineage involved in the Chinese family system, there is also the horizontal, as represented by the brotherly relationship. Between father and son, filial piety was highly emphasized, while between the elder and the younger brothers mutual respect was the keynote. Chinese ethics urged the younger to respect his elder brother with submission, whereas the elder must love and take good care of the younger. Their connection was like that of hands and feet, with close co-operation as their reciprocal obligation.

Brotherly love in China may, nevertheless, be attributed to esteem for the source of their lives, which in turn had recourse to the filial-piety doctrine. As we highly esteem our parents, by inference we must also esteem their creatures. Hence, the fraternal duty was correlated with filial piety. As Mencius emphasized, "The great course in life of Yao and Shun [emperors of antiquity] was simply that of filial piety and fraternal love." [26] Those who can perform the former well would, of course, know how to perform the latter. In many old Chinese families, brothers persistently shared the same household, even though they had themselves married and raised a host of children. And they retained the same household as long as either one or both of their parents remained alive. Some Chinese took pride in sharing the same household with several generations of the same paternal line. The large-family system thus brought about was gradually abandoned, for there were various drawbacks. But, as the origin of this system is explained, it is seen to be derived from the practice of filial piety.

Aside from the Chinese family system, which was built upon the practice of filial piety, Chinese religious life also had much to do with the doctrine of filial duties.

Apparently most Confucian scholars seldom touched upon religious subjects. They seemed to have behaved complacently toward the issue of life and death. They also slighted such controversial topics as the existence of God and the immortality of the soul, which have been so extensively discussed by Western philosophers. The Confucian *Analects* took the following stand: "Chi-lu [a disciple of Confucius] asked about serving the spirits [of the dead]. The Master said, 'While you are not able to serve men, how can you serve their spirits?' Chi-lu added, 'I venture to ask about death?' He got the answer, 'While you do not know life, how can you know about death?'" [27] This attitude of avoiding the issue of the unknown world was later almost unanimously adopted by Confucian followers. Some even openly disparaged the prevalent Taoist and Buddhist religions. What is the reason for this? Was there no need for a Confucian to have some sort of religious belief?

It is to be noted that most Confucian followers, though not openly professing religious worship, actually had faith in some basic principle in place of religion. This substitute was the observance of filial piety. The Confucian religion was intrinsically involved with the doctrine of filial piety.

How can this doctrine take the place of religion? Or, how can the doctrine of filial piety be formulated as a doctrine of religious worship? These two questions can be answered only by considering the essential elements of religion and the religious value of filial piety. Definitions of religion are varied. The essentials of any religion should consist of at least the following three points: first, faith in a supernatural being or a supernatural force; second, the hope for salvation from extinction; and, third, consolation for sentimental cravings. Since no religion can lack these three elements, any emotional or intellectual belief abounding with them may be called a religion or a substitute for religion. The doctrine of filial piety therefore transformed itself into a kind of religious worship, with beliefs and practices, or at least a substitute for them, and with all their essentials provided for.

Filial piety involves paying due respect, not only to one's living parents, but also to the deceased and to remote ancestors. Therefore, ancestor worship took place as a natural sequence of paying tribute to one's parents. *The Classic of Filial Piety* states:

> In filial piety there is nothing so great as honoring the father. In doing this, there is no achievement so great as making him an "Associate of Heaven": and the Duke of Chou [d. 1094 B.C.] was the man who succeeded in this achievement. In ancient times Duke Chou offered sacrifice to his high ancestor Hou-chi in the suburbs as an "Associate of Heaven," and set up King Wen's [reigned, 1171–1122 B.C.] [his father's] tablet in the Ming-t'ang [the Illustrious Hall] as an "Associate of Shang-ti" [God-on-High]. The result was that from all the lands within the Four Seas came princes each with tribute to join in the sacrificial ceremony.[28]

Though some contemporary scholars, such as E. R. Hughes, doubt the interpretation given for these terms, "Associate of Heaven" and "Associate of Shang-ti," as being tinted with exaggeration, the quoted passage nevertheless portrays the sentiment of identifying the deceased father with a sort of superhuman force which deserved worship in the expanded expression of the feeling of filial piety. Hence, the Confucians laid particular emphasis on the solemnization of the rites in ancestral worship, including funeral rites for deceased parents.

Before offering sacrifice to one's ancestors, the most rigorous vigil was kept inwardly by the pious offspring, while outwardly he fasted and bathed for at least one or more days.

> On the day of the sacrifice when he enters the apartment [in the ancestral temple], he gasps: Surely there is a vision by the spirit tablet! After he has moved here and there [in making his sacrifice] and comes to the threshold, he is struck with awe: Surely he hears the particular tones of the deceased parents' voices! Then, as he hears and listens, he catches his breath: Surely he hears the sound of the deceased parents' sighing! [29]

All such descriptions show Chinese ancestral worship to be laden with so much care and awe that it might even have surpassed the similar attitudes and practices of Christians in their church service. As ancestral worship had provided all the essentials of a religion, though in certain respects it differed from most of the regular religious sects, its essential meaning or significance may still be identical with that of, say, Christianty.

The main sentiment of Chinese ancestor-worship lay in commemoration of one's origin—the fountain of his life—and in repaying the debt that he owes to his ancestors, yet without much praying for blessings. To a certain extent, however, the rituals of worship may involve praying for blessings. As Confucius once put it, "When I wage war I will win the victory, and when offering sacrifice I will gain blessings, because I have practiced the right way." [30] He also pointed out, "For offering sacrifice, there are many purposes: one for praying for blessings, another for paying obligations, and still another for purification from sin." [31] Hence, Confucian ancestral worship did not conceal the desire for blessings from some supernatural force or forces, on the one hand, and the desire to avoid calamity, on the other. When facing some critical moment— for example, prior to waging war or making important decisions on state affairs—ancient Chinese emperors or kings appealed to their ancestors for oracular revelations and blessings.

Later, the Chinese geomancy practiced by the common people in another form of ancestral worship laid even more emphasis upon the seeking of blessings from the supernatural power through the intermediary grace of ancestors, who, in certain respects, were looked upon as identical to Buddhist or Taoist deities.

Next, the doctrine of filial piety played even a greater role in the search for emotional consolation through ancestral worship. Human beings cannot avoid death. Practically all religions have been built upon the sentiment that even after passing into the unknown world the human soul will be taken care of by some supernatural force, with deserved reward or punishment awaiting it. However, if there is another way to dispose of the soul without the need of the help of such abstract faith, there is no need to seek help from any religious sect.

The Confucians had their own particular way of disposing of this problem. Their way hinged upon the doctrine of filial piety. Mencius said, "There are three things which are unfilial, and having no posterity is the greatest of them." [32] This utterance may seem enigmatic to many, especially Westerners. Why was it so important for one to have posterity? To Confucians, one's offspring are the continuation of his own and also of his ancestors' lives. With such continuation, his and his ancestors' lives are looked upon as being immortal. Therefore, anyone who has cut short the flow of his ancestors' lives would be condemned as having committed the gravest sin of being unfilial.

On the other hand, anyone who has generations of offspring to prolong his lineage—especially one who has "father-like sons" to continue and, better still, to develop his father's academic attainment or industrial enterprise or other honorable pursuit—might take great consolation and pride in that fact. He may also deem it to be the immortality of his own life in succession to those of his ancestors. In this respect, the filially pious son is always cautioned to take good care of his own body and his own mental and moral attainments. Thus, *The Classic of Filial Piety* says, "The body with its limbs and hair and skin comes to a person from father and mother, and it is on no account to be spoiled or injured." [33] The Confucian *Analects* also teaches, "If the son for three years does not alter from the way of his father, he may be called filial." [34]

As the continuous flow of one's life in his offspring, together with his trade or mental achievement, was looked upon by Confucians as the perpetuity of his own life, then the question concerning the continued existence of the soul (and where his soul will be) is unimportant. It was said, "When one has a son or sons, he will be satisfied with all in his life." [35] Professor T'ang Chün-i has said, "As the life of one's offspring comes from his, the survival of one's life in future generations proves directly that his own life will never . . . perish. . . . Hence, in the preponderant love of one's offspring there will be only slight desire for immortality of his own soul after death." [36] Such a view undoubtedly was derived from the doctrine of filial piety. So, Chinese religious life virtually consists in the practice of filial piety.

Regarding social life, the Chinese people essentially expanded or extended family life into a larger area. This was an expansion of the practice of filial piety. In the Chinese community, kinship was formed through the marriage relationship, clans were established through blood relationship, and villages were built up through the regional relationship in which one was born and brought up. One's ancestors, and, still further, tutors and friends, were linked together through academic pursuit or mutual attraction or other causes—all these revolved around the center of gravity of the practice of filial piety. In Confucian ethics, the position of the tutor was particularly respected, ranking next to the father's position in every household. In a series of worshipped, more or less personified, objects, as stated in a simple tablet in the family alcove, there were "Heaven, Earth, Sovereign, Father, and Tutor." It was then observed that, as the parents had given birth to the physical body of the son, it was the teacher who had much to do in formulating the pupil's spiritual and cultural life. By expanding the view that one must honor his physical-life giver, he must also honor his cultural-life giver. By the same reasoning, one treats his bosom friends with high respect, too. Confucius' disciple Tseng Tzu therefore said, "The superior man on grounds of culture meets with his friends, and by their friendship helps to establish his virtue." [37]

While the Chinese respect for the tutor was an extension of filial piety, the respect of friendship was, as an expansion of tutorship, also an extension of filial piety. The closely knit patterns of relatives, clansmen, fellow countrymen, and tutors, together with friends, were all interwoven around the filial axis in the Chinese community. Such a condition still prevails in some conservative groups of overseas Chinese residents.

Finally, in regard to the Chinese people's political life in its traditional form, it may be said that the Chinese seem to have shown little interest in politics as viewed in the West. The traditional political life of the Chinese was different from that of Westerners. It emphasized the principle of laissez faire, because in every community or every village and in every trade organization the local self-government, based on the social relationship as stated above, usually functioned instead of higher administrative regulation. From the filial viewpoint, everyone was exhorted to respect the elder in the family in the management of family affairs and in the settlement of intra-family disputes, if any serious dispute arose; and then, in case of inter-family controversies, the village chief was at hand to settle them as amicably as possible. *The Book of Rites* emphasized, "As the people are taught filial piety and brotherly love at home, with reverence toward the elder and diligent care for the aged in the community, they constitute the way of a great king; and it is along this line that states as well as families will become peaceful." [38]

In the traditional local government of China, the village elder took the place of the administrator and the judge, and the observance of the traditional rituals or ceremonies also considerably eliminated the function of legal provisions. It was said, "The power which the rituals have of transforming by instruction is not on the surface. They put a stop to evil before it takes form. They cause men day by day to travel toward the good and leave wrongdoing far behind." [39] Thereupon, Confucius remarked that there is no more excellent method than the rituals for making those in authority secure and the people well-ordered. If every village is kept in good order, the whole state will naturally be in good order. Confucius said, "By reviewing the local rule in the villages, I comprehend that the King's Way should be easy." [40] Even though the whole empire might collapse, with the ruling house changing hands sometimes frequently, yet the people might still take advantage of the local village rule which, as stated above, was an expansion of the practice of filial piety in every good household.

For several thousand years, the Chinese people thus enjoyed their family life, religious life, social life, and political life—all involving, directly or indirectly, the practice of filial piety. Chinese society is thus seen to have been under the sway of the doctrine of filial piety and to have been built virtually upon the basis of filial piety as its essential foundation.

IV

One of the outstanding characteristics which have marked the difference of social and cultural patterns between China and Western countries is, therefore, the Chinese emphasis upon filial piety.

Chinese society and its cultural flow have been based on the doctrine of filial piety, which was derived from the intrinsic love of human beings in its natural course of development. The working principle may be found in the theme of extending such virtue beyond the household into society at large, with pure, true, and durable love, devoid of any consideration of selfish profit. By the practice of such a virtue as filial piety, although still far from being perfect, Chinese society and its culture could therefore endure throughout the past several thousand years up to the present. The unity of every family, the solidarity of the community, and the unification of the whole nation all depend upon the strengthening of such love.

The problem which now demands careful consideration is

whether the present Chinese nation may still resort to the application of filial piety as one means to its rejuvenation and whether the ethical sense and practical value of filial piety still may hold its position in Chinese society. And, ultimately, from the synthetic or comparative point of view, whether the doctrine of filial piety still is worth being preserved and expanded in the cultural interflow between the East and the West in the light of philosophical examination and scrutiny. Before the paper is concluded, it is fitting that these questions should be answered, though only briefly.

Chinese society has been undergoing drastic change. The ancient large-family system is collapsing, while filial piety as a paramount virtue is also being ignored progressively and gradually by the younger generation. In the face of such a critical period, will the modern philosophers of China sail with the tide that seems formidable enough to sweep people off their feet, or will they put up a gallant stand against this trend?

As ethics must not bend itself to any evil force, what it should emphasize is not what the fact unwarrantedly dictates, but what the moral law discerns as the best for the world. There should be no expediency, submitting what ought to be to what society blindly prefers. Further, the Chinese ethics of today must take upon itself the responsibility of correcting the wrong and championing the right.

Therefore, the doctrine of filial piety must be propagated and put into practice in Chinese society and in other communities—though revision and modernization of certain phases of it are desirable. The intrinsic love which is inherent in the filial doctrine is most valuable to mankind.

Why should filial piety be preserved in the modern world? The import of this virtue is the affirmation of affection for human life and society, if not exactly love; and it is an essentially consolidating factor of society. As its starting point is the children's love of their parents, it is conceivable that the inherent nature of life must be good and of intrinsic value. Hence, the filially pious son should highly esteem the origin of his life, should carefully cherish his own life and the name of his family, and then create the next generation so as to maintain the flow of life without interruption. This is the full affirmation of the value of life. And this is the most fundamental attitude of the Chinese toward life, indicating that life is worth living.

By use of the filial doctrine to solidify human society, with the correlated virtues of mankind, such as benevolence, righteousness, justice, faithfulness, and the love of peace, together with bravery in fighting against the aggression of brutes, all brought up to the fullest possible extent, then and only then may the world achieve the blessings of durable peace.

In this regard, the fundamental premise to be definitely and universally recognized should be mutual love of all men in place of jealousy and hatred. Only through mutual love may human beings come together, with reciprocal co-ordination and co-operation of efforts for the common good. This is only common sense—for all mankind.

QUESTION: What is the relation of justice to filial piety? In case there is a conflict, how can you reconcile them? What about the story in Confucius' *Analects* in which the father stole the sheep and the son refused to appear as a witness in the court against him.

ANSWER: Such conflicts between virtues, especially between loyalty and filial piety, were frequently found in the history of the Chinese ethical thought. There is no simple solution to such conflicts, that is, no fixed general rule for settling them. The only solution is that you have to consider the situation in which you are. In other words, you have to consider what F. H. Bradley called "My Station and its Duties." For example, if you are an official, you will decide in favor of justice, but, if you are an ordinary person, then you will decide in favor of filial piety. In the case of the father who stole the sheep, the son should not appear as witness against his father. In not appearing as witness, the son is not violating justice. For, whether his father is guilty or not, the son is not in the position to judge. If you judged your own father, you would not feel right in your heart. Thus, the Confucian ethical point of view is that, in case of such conflicts, though there is no fixed rule, you should do what is proper in your heart, that is, what you will feel right about when you have done it.

QUESTION: Why should we love and respect our ancestors? The important thing for us to do is to educate the young.

ANSWER: If anyone does not like his ancestors, how can he like the man in the street? The doctrine of filial piety is aimed at the cultivation of love toward your parents, your ancestors, and then extending your love toward others. If you don't like your ancestors, there is the end of the matter. But my advice is that you should like your ancestors. That is all.

COMMENT BY T'ANG CHÜN-I

A parent's love of his child is strictly biological, whereas filial piety, love and respect for one's parents, is not biological but is moral, being based upon a sense of obligation or a debt of gratitude, and is therefore spiritual.

Notes

1. *Ta hsüeh* (*The Great Learning*), I.1.
2. Liang Ch'i-ch'ao, *Ju-chia che-hsüeh* (The Confucian Philosophy), Yin-ping shih ho-chi edition (Shanghai: Chung-hua Shu-chu, 1936), Vol. 34, p. 2.
3. *Chung yung*, (*The Doctrine of the Mean*), XXII.
4. *Meng Tzu* (*The Book of Mencius*), IIIB.9.
5. *Lun yü* (*The Analects*), I.2.
6. *Book of Mencius*, VIB.11.
7. *Ibid.*, IIA.6.
8. *Ibid.*, VIIA.15.
9. *Analects*, XII.22.
10. *Book of Mencius*, IV.28.
11. *Hsiao ching* (*The Book of Filial Piety* or *The Classic of Filial Piety*), IX.
12. *Book of Mencius*, IVA.27.
13. *Book of Filial Piety*, I.
14. *Book of Mencius*, VIIA.45.
15. *Ibid.*, IA.7.
16. *Doctrine of the Mean*, XV.
17. *Chuang Tzu* (*The Works of Chuang Tzu*), IV.
18. *Book of Filial Piety*, I.
19. *Li chi* (*The Book of Rites*), VIII.24.
20. *Book of Mencius*, IVA.5.
21. *Great Learning*, I.4.
22. *Ibid.*, IX.1.
23. *Book of Mencius*, IVA.19.
24. *Book of Filial Piety*, VII.
25. *Ibid.*, I.
26. *Book of Mencius*, VIB.2.
27. *Analects*, XI.11.

28. *Book of Filial Piety*, IX.
29. *Book of Rites*, VIII.24.
30. *Ibid.*, V.10.
31. *Ibid.*, V.11.
32. *Book of Mencius*, IVA.26.
33. *Book of Filial Piety*, I.
34. *Analects*, IV.20.
35. A common adage in ancient China.
36. T'ang Chün-i, *Chung-kuo wen-hua chih ching-shen chia-chih* (The Spiritual Worth of Chinese Culture), (Taipei: Cheng Chung Bookstore, 1953), p. 322.
37. *Analects*, XII.24.
38. *Book of Rites*, X.45.
39. *Ibid.*, II.
40. *Ibid.*, X.45.

T'ANG CHÜN-I   *The Development of Ideas*

of Spiritual Value in Chinese Philosophy

I. A Tentative Definition of Spiritual Value

Before I Talk about the ideas of spiritual value in Chinese philosophy, I will define what I call spiritual value.

By the word "spirit" I mean any self-conscious subject and its activities which are initiated by self-conscious ideas. Any value which has the following characteristics is called spiritual: (1) created or realized "by the spirit"; (2) presented or revealed to the spirit, that is, "for the spirit"; (3) self-consciously recognized as such in (1) and (2), and then the value can be predicated on the spirit, that is, "of the spirit."

According to (1), we can differentiate spiritual values from the values of outer natural objects and from the values of the satisfaction of our natural instincts. Outer natural objects usually have the value of utility, for they are instrumental in the realization or attainment of spiritual aims or purposes. Sometimes, outer natural objects may have some aesthetic values which are presented to our enjoying spirit, too. However, at least at the moment when we say these values are created or originated or manifested by outer Nature and belong to outer Nature they are not spiritual values. It is generally agreed, too, that, when our instinctive desires are satisfied in instinctive ways, there is the realization of natural values which need not be taken as spiritual.

According to (2), we can differentiate spiritual values from a certain kind of social values which come from the effects of a certain action (or actions) or a person (or persons) on other persons and the whole historical society. As the chain of effects of human action may stretch and extend to an indefinite number of persons, areas of society, and even ages in history, the social values of a human action cannot all be presented and known by any personal spiritual subject except God. These values are always realized outside the self-consciousness of the person who performs the action. Therefore, the existential status of these values should be said to be in the historical society as a whole and not within any particular personal spirit.

According to (3), we may differentiate a genuine spiritual value from a certain quasi-spiritual value, which is created by a certain spirit and then presented to that same spirit but is not self-consciously recognized as such. For example, the imagery of a dream may be merely symbols of a spiritual idea we have had before. Thus, it is created by our spirit and presented to our spirit. However, when we are dreaming, the aesthetic value of the imagery seems to belong to the imagery itself and is not self-consciously recognized as created "by the spirit," "for the spirit," and "of the spirit." This is therefore not a genuine spiritual value. So, any value of human activity, though originally created by the spirit and presented to the spirit, if its origin is forgotten and taken as belonging to the world outside the spirit, is only a quasi-spiritual value, which is alienated from the originating spirit itself.

From the above, we may say that the first kind of spiritual values consists of values of moral and religious activities. Generally, in moral and religious activities, one is self-consciously commanding himself how to act, to meditate, or to pray. All such activities are initiated, at least to some degree, by one's spiritual subject in the very beginning, and their values, such as goodness, peace of mind, holiness, and so on, are more or less taken as created or realized by the spiritual subject and presented for the spiritual subject, and can be taken as inhering in, and then predicated of, the same spiritual subject.

The second kind of spiritual values consists of those of the artistic and intellectual activities of man. It is doubtless that there are values of beauty and truth realized by, and presented to, the spiritual subject through one's spiritual activities, such as speculative thinking, experimental observation, and creative imagination. Yet, the truth-value or beauty-value is not only capable of describing the spiritual activities of man but also can be predicated of aesthetic objects or the objective realities as outside of the spirit of men. It is much more difficult to say that moral goodness and peace of mind exist in themselves outside the spirit or personality of man, even when we believe in a Platonic metaphysics of value. Thus, the spiritual values of artistic and intellectual activities are differentiated from the moral and religious values, and they may not have the same degree of spirituality.

The third kind of spiritual values consists of natural values and social values, defined above as non-spiritual, which are transformed into spiritual values. These transformations are achieved usually by highly exalted spiritual activities. For example, the utility or beauty of natural objects is generally taken as having originated from the objects themselves. If we, as some poets, religious men, and metaphysicians have done, take man and Nature as created by some absolute spirit, such as God or *Brahman,* or as the manifestation of some absolute spirit, then all the utilitarian aesthetic values of natural objects may be taken as having originated from the same spiritual substance of man, in which case the values of natural objects can be taken as transformed into spiritual values.

On the question as to how social value also can be transformed into spiritual value, the crucial point is that any social value of one's action which is taken as outside the personal spirit can also be taken as inside the spirit by the more fully developed moral consciousness of the subject. For example, a discovery in the theoretical study of a scientist may benefit mankind in the indefinite future and generate infinite social values which are beyond the expectation of the theoretical consciousness of the scientist. Yet, if the moral consciousness of the scientist is fully developed into infinite love of mankind, such as the love of Jesus or the *jen* (humanity, love, benevolence) of Confucius (551–479 B.C.), then he understands that all the social values generated from his inventive action are by principle such as can satisfy his love of mankind, although all the details of all the effects of his action could never be foretold by him. If the satisfaction of this love is purely spiritual and has spiritual value, then the actual realization of any social value of his present discovery any time in the future is at the same time a realization of the spiritual value of his present love of mankind. The realizations of these two kinds of values are co-extensive and equivalent in domain, at least in his present lofty moral consciousness. Therefore, for this consciousness, all social values which are not taken as external values become internalized, immanently present to the spiritual subject, and thus transformed into spiritual values. Needless to say, outside such a lofty moral consciousness, the social value is just a social value, just as, outside the consciousness of poets, religious men, and metaphysicians, as mentioned above, natural value is merely a natural value.

II. Spiritual Values in Confucian Moral Teachings and The Key Concept of "Searching in Oneself"

The Confucian school and the Taoist school are the main currents of thought of native Chinese philosophy. They and Buddhism have usually been mentioned together and called *"san-chiao,"* three teachings or three religions. Generally speaking, these three teachings all intend to deepen spiritual experience and cultivate the spiritual life of man, and have had much social-cultural influence on Chinese historical society. Hence, if we wish to know the main ideas of spiritual value in Chinese philosophy, we have to study them in the Confucian and Taoist and Buddhist philosophies.

It is held by some writers that there are no really spiritual values in Confucianism. It is said that in the body of Confucianism dealing with the virtues of men in definite relations only social values can be realized. Some contend that when Confucius talked about the importance of the cultivation of these virtues he always said this is a way for preserving the social solidarity of the nation or the peace of the world or for training the people to be contented with their circumstances and not to offend their superiors. These values are therefore alleged to be only socio-political and not spiritual values as defined above. Others contend that when Confucius talked about the values of the virtues he was considering the values as a means to the achieving of harmony and order in human relations, which were taken as a part of the harmony and order of the natural universe. But, the harmony and order of the natural universe may have a natural value only and not necessarily a spiritual value.[1]

The views which efface the ideas of spiritual value from the Confucian ethical system are not without some justification. Actually, many Confucians in the course of Chinese history, such as those of the Yung-k'ang school and Yung-chia school of the Sung Dynasty (960–1279), and Yen Yüan (1635–1704) and Tai Chen (1723–1777) of the Ch'ing Dynasty (1644–1912), emphasized the social utilitarian value of ethical actions. Many Confucians in the

Han Dynasty (206 B.C.–A.D. 220) emphasized the natural value of ethical action.

But the values of the virtues in Confucian ethics should be considered essentially spiritual values. The central idea of virtue peculiar to Confucius, Mencius (371–289? B.C.), and the Neo-Confucianism of the Sung-Ming period (960–1644) is to consider the virtues as the inner essence of one's personality, and their values as intrinsic to one's moral consciousness and tinged with a certain religious meaning, and thus as definitely spiritual values. The key concept in this interpretation is the concept of "searching in oneself," which is a teaching handed down from Confucius himself and developed by all later Confucians. I shall explain its meaning from three aspects.

(1) In the first aspect, "searching in oneself" means that in all ethical relations one has to do his duty to others, but not require others to do their duties to him, reciprocally, though the others should do their duties of their own accord. In order to explain this we have to know that there are three ways to develop one's spiritual life to the fullest extent, and all three may be called in a certain sense "backward" ways.

The first way is to get real freedom from all the instinctive and irrational desires in human life. The extreme of this is what Schopenhauer called the denial or mortification of the will. This way is practiced, more or less, by all ascetics and mystics, as a negative step in the very beginning of spiritual cultivation for higher positive spiritual development.

The second way searches for some kind of higher or highest Idea or Existence in the very beginning of spiritual cultivation which is supernatural and transcendent, such as the Idea of the Good in Plato and the self-existent God in the otherworldly religions. We may call this the way of leaving the mundane world behind, in our process of spiritual ascent.

The third way is to live in definite ethical relations with others in the actual world, practicing the morality of doing one's duty to others but not asking them to do their duties, reciprocally, as taught in Confucianism. This way of life may be called the way of thinking or acting morally just for oneself, which is opposite to the "forward way of asking others to do something morally for me," as in the common attitude of our daily life. It is a "backward" way of life and is as difficult to put into practice as the other two ways.

The difficulties of this third way arise from the fact that when one does his duty to others he naturally supposes that others are moral beings like himself. According to the universal principle of reason, man naturally expects others to do their duties in response to his action. Thus, he naturally thinks he has the right to demand that others do their duties. Actually, social justice and legislation are based upon the reciprocity of rights and duties. One who does his duty without asking others to do theirs is the same as one who has only duty-consciousness without rights-consciousness and lives beyond the idea of social justice. In duty-consciousness, one does what his conscience commands him to do, and never goes beyond his conscience to see what happens in other consciences, and so the value realized is completely internal to his conscience and is therefore a purely spiritual moral value. If I have this kind of duty-consciousness in full degree, then, the less others do their duty to me, the more I shall do my duty to others. That is to say, the more my expectation from others is disappointed, the more intensified is my self-expectation from myself. The value of social justice, which is offended and lost because others do not do their duty, is recompensed and satisfied by the moral values of my fulfillment, which is purely spiritual and belongs to my inward life. Yet, this kind of duty-consciousness is the most difficult for human beings, because we have to do to others more than they deserve. What we do to others is the same as the grace of deity conferred on man, though man may not be aware of it or respond to it with a sense of thanksgiving. It is significant that Christians translate the word "grace" with the Chinese word "en" in the term "en-i," which means that one does his duty without reciprocation, and so confers something which is absolutely beyond what others deserve. Therefore, we may say that in the first meaning of "searching in oneself" in Confucianism a deification of human life is implied and has religious and spiritual meanings.

(2) The second meaning of "searching in oneself" is that one ought to cultivate his virtues and abilities without asking praise from others. This is also very difficult to practice, due to the fact that men, motivated by the universal principle of reason, naturally want others to appreciate or approve what they themselves have appreciated or approved. This desire may not be morally bad, if it is accompanied by a moral feeling of respect when we request it from others and accompanied by our gratitude when we receive it from others. But, leaving the desire for praise itself alone and as unconditionally right, then we may simply take the praise of others

as personal gratification. When we are anxious to receive this kind of gratification, many modes of moral evils, such as ambition, or the will to power to control the will of others, or disloyalty to one's original ideals in flattering others and then receiving praise in return, can be generated in different circumstances. When I ask the praise of others, I am taking my virtues and abilities, and their expressions in actions and speech, as a means, and they then have only instrumental or utilitarian value, which is non-spiritual social value or quasi-spiritual value as defined in Section I, above.[2]

If our ordinary outward desire of gaining others' praise is diminished, we may live a life which is directed by our moral conscience itself. We can then eradicate the roots of our desire to control the will of others; we will never be disloyal to the moral ideal in order to please men, and, at the same time, never have any complaint or grudge against others or Heaven. This is the meaning of the Confucian saying: "There is no one that knows me. . . . I do not murmur against Heaven. I do not grumble against men. . . . But it is Heaven that knows me."[3] This is a kind of deified human life.

(3) The third meaning of "searching in oneself" is that all the moral principles, moral ideals, and moral values of our actions and intentions can be discovered by self-reflection. This is strongly implied in the teaching of Confucius, and is explicitly stated and elaborated in the teaching of Mencius and many later Confucians, as in the thesis that "human nature is good."

The thesis that "human nature is good" has had various interpretations in the various schools of Confucianism. In the teaching of Mencius, the first exponent of this thesis, the doctrine does not say that all actions or intentions of men are actually good enough. It says simply that there are good tendencies or good beginnings in human nature and, most important, that, when we have good intentions or do good actions, there is usually an accompanying feeling of self-satisfaction or self-joy or self-peace.[4] This may be said to be deep self-praise when I find my intention or action is really good. This deep self-praise is usually concealed when we are eager to ask for praise from others or when we lack deep self-reflection. Yet, when we withdraw the desire to ask others for praise and have deep reflection, then everybody can find the deep self-praise which accompanies all good intentions or good actions. However, this deep self-praise is a result of my deepest self-evaluation, which immediately follows my intention or action. This self-evaluation reveals to me what is good as good and what is not good as not good, and from the former I feel self-satisfaction, self-joy, and self-peace, but from the latter I feel disquieted, unjoyful, and dissatisfied. As my mind feels self-peace or self-joy or self-satisfaction in the good only, so my human nature is disclosed as essentially good. This is the orthodox doctrine of the thesis that "human nature is good," which was morally expounded in Mencius' teaching, was metaphysically explained by Chu Hsi's (1130–1200) theory of li (principle, reason, or law), and culminated in the teaching of liang-chih (almost the same as conscience) in Wang Shou-jen's (Wang Yang-ming, 1472–1529) philosophy.

If we take human nature as essentially good, moral ideals and moral principles are nothing other than the norms or standards awakened within or originating in the nature of our mind and immanently presented to our moral self-consciousness for self-evaluation. Consequently, our moral training and moral cultivation have no other purpose than to preserve and extend what is judged or evaluated as good, and all the achievements of moral life and the formation of a moral personality express no more than the desire to conform to these immanent norms or standards, to realize what originates from the nature of the mind, and to know and to fulfill to the maximum what is implicitly contained in the nature of the mind.

However, in the development of our moral life, any phase of our ordinary life which is taken by common sense as non-moral or immoral can be evaluated as either good or evil. So, every phase of our life has moral meaning, can be made moral by a certain cultivation, and then has moral value, which can be presented immediately to our self-reflection, as defined above, and become a purely internal value. It is not difficult to see that if we resolve to have all the phases of our life made moral then our self-evaluations and self-reflections may arise successfully and co-extensively with the extensions of all phases of life, including those phases of our life which are considered by common sense as merely directing to, or dealing with, the so-called external environment.

Hence, self-evaluation and self-reflection should not be taken as subjective and self-closed, but should also be taken as objective and self-open to all the other social and natural objects of the universe as our whole environment. Here the "investigation of things" as taught by Confucianism has not only intellectual value but also moral value, and then we may have the wisdom that all the objects in the universe can be taken as the occasions for the realization of spiritual moral values, and that all may be lighted and permeated by spiritual and moral values as well. This is the vision of the moral man, who realizes his good nature, develops his moral life to the fullest extent, attains unity of the inner world and the outer world, and achieves the grandeur and beauty of personality as expounded in *The Doctrine of the Mean* [5] and *The Book of Mencius.*

III. (1) *Human Nature As Good,* (2) *Heaven,* (3) *Mind,* and (4) *The Universal Attainability of Sagehood*

If we compare the thesis that human nature is good with the idea of original sin in Christianity or the *karma* theory and the *avidyā* theory of Buddhism, there are many pros and cons worthy of discussion. Yet, if we acknowledge the existence of original sin or impure *karma* in the depth of our mind, we may still believe that human nature is essentially good. We may hold that original sin and impure *karma* are not derived from real human nature, but that the feeling of unrest that arises when we are told we have original sin or impure *karma* originates from our real human nature. This nature, as revealed in unrest, is the same as the nature revealed in our unpeacefulness in our evils, and is absolutely good. In the feeling of unrest, of course, I may find at the same time that I am so weak as to try to set myself free from the bondage of original sin or impure *karma,* and I may pray to some transcendent being, such as God, *Brahman,* or Amida Buddha, to save me. In this type of religious consciousness, we think our nature is not good enough. Yet, the very confession of our weakness and our praying come from our nature, too. Our very confession may not be weak, and our praying must be good in itself. If it is objected that the very confession and words of prayer do not come from our human nature, but are the result of human nature as affected by a transcendent being or receiving grace from above, then we reply that our capacity for being (and our unconscious willingness to be) affected and receiving grace are additional evidences that human nature is essentially good. If we deny this, then how is it possible that men can be saved? The thesis that human nature is good does not fundamentally oppose the ultimate teachings of Christianity or Brāhmaṇism or Buddhism, which believe either that man is the image of God, or that man is *Brahman,* or that the Buddha is a sentient being awakened to the fullest extent. Therefore, the thesis that human nature is good cannot be denied, even if we concede the existence of original sin or impure *karma*, because we can reassert our nature as good again in the very self-reflection of our unrest or unpeacefulness in our evils and our very unwillingness to be bound by them. However, the Confucian thesis that human nature is good is still different from many religious points of view which take the evil origin of human actions much more seriously and believe that only a transcendent being can save man from evil. Men who hold the latter point of view always look at human nature as a mere potentiality and insist that the principle of its actuality resides in some transcendent being. Yet, from the thesis that human nature is good the principle of actualization is seen to be immanent in human nature.[6]

What we have said above does not imply that Confucian thought lacks the idea of a transcendent reality, such as God, the Mind of Heaven, or the Universal Mind. In fact, many Confucians have these ideas. The real difference between the Confucian point of view and the above religious point of view is that, in the latter, the idea of a transcendent being, such as God, *Brahman*, etc., is more easily brought to light by contrasting it with our sin or impure *karma* or bondage; while, in the former, the idea of the Mind of Heaven, the Universal Mind, God, or Heaven is usually brought to light by the positive development of our moral life to the fullest extent, with the knowledge that the transcendent being is at the same time immanent in our moral life. How is it possible to have these ideas brought to light by the positive development of our moral lives? The answer was suggested in the teaching of Mencius and culminated in the Neo-Confucians of the Sung-Ming period, who had a deep understanding of the thesis that human nature is good.

Briefly, the central theme of this trend of thought is that when we develop our moral life to the fullest extent, as a sage does, the essence of our good nature is wholly actualized in, presented to, and known by, our self-consciousness. The essence of our good nature may be said to be *jen*, which is love, beginning with filial piety, and flowing out as universal love to all the men with whom we have definite ethical relations, to all the people under Heaven, and to all natural things. So, the moral consciousness of *jen*, in its fullest extent, is all-embracing love, which pervades, permeates, and fills Heaven and Earth as a whole. So, Mencius said, "The virtuous man transforms all experiences he passes through and abides in holiness or deity-nature. His virtues are confluent with Heaven above and with Earth below." [7] Chang Tsai (Chang Heng-ch'ü, 1020–1077), Ch'eng Hao (Ch'eng Ming-tao, 1032–1085), Ch'eng I (Ch'eng I-ch'uan, 1033–1107), and Chu Hsi had the same idea namely, that the man who realizes *jen* considers Heaven, Earth, and the ten thousand things as one body. Lu Chiu-yüan (Lu Hsiang-shan, 1139–1193) said, "The universe is my mind and my mind is the universe." Wang Shou-jen said, "Pervading Heaven and Earth is just this spiritual light—my spiritual light—which is not separated by, or separated from, Heaven, Earth, deities, and the ten thousand things." [8] But is this mind only my own? In the mind which identifies itself with the universe, where is the dividing point between what is mine and what is not mine? When selfish ideas and motives are transformed into universal and all-pervading love, where is the borderline or the boundary between our mind and the universe? Why can I not take this type of mind as belonging to me and also to Heaven? Why can I not take this type of mind both as created and presented by myself and as revealed and descended to me from Heaven? Is its belonging-to-me incompatible with its belonging-to-Heaven? If I take this kind of mind as mine and not of Heaven, does this not simply contradict the very nature of this kind of mind, which has no borderline to differentiate itself from what is not itself and which is felt as a universal and all-pervading mind? Therefore, when I have this kind of mind and know its nature truly, I shall never take this mind merely as my own; I shall know that this kind of mind is conferred by Heaven as much as it is mine, and I shall know Heaven (which was originally synonymous with the word "God" in the Chinese Classics). As this kind of mind is the mind of one who develops his moral life to the fullest extent, and whose *jen* is wholly actualized as a sage, so the sage is said to be the same as Heaven, and human nature is therefore sometimes called Heaven-nature, and the human mind is called the mind of Heaven in some Confucian literature. So, Mencius said, "To have our mind preserved and Nature nourished is the way to serve Heaven" and "The man who has passed through the stage of completing his virtues and sheds forth his spiritual light brilliantly, and then can transform the world, is called a sage. The sage, unfathomable by intellect, is called holy or divine." [9]

Yet, the highest teaching of Confucianism is not merely the realization that the sage is the same as Heaven, but the realization of the universal attainability of sagehood for all men and what is implied by that. The universal attainability of sagehood is a logical consequence of the belief that human nature is good. The sage is the man who has fully realized his nature. If all men have the same good human nature, surely all can realize their nature and attain sagehood. Furthermore, the universal attainability of sagehood is itself an immanent belief of the mind of the sage. Since the mind of the sage is full of love and unselfishness to the fullest extent, he could not have any idea that he is the only sage, because this is selfish and contradictory to the very nature of his mind. He must love to see, expect, and hope that everyone else will be a sage. Therefore, the universal attainability of sagehood is a belief immanently involved in the mind of the sage. If I believe there is a sage, or if I can be a sage, then I have to think of the idea of the sage through the mind of the sage, and thus the universal attainability of sagehood is also involved in my idea. Yet, according to the thesis that human nature is good, I must believe there is a sage and that I can be one, because sagehood is nothing more than my own nature, *jen*, wholly realized. So, I must believe in the universal attainability of sagehood.[10]

According to the idea of the universal attainability of sagehood, an actual sage can be born at any time and any place in the world, and no one sage of any particular place or particular time has the privilege of being the only sage. As all sages have the same fundamental virtue, *jen*, or universal love, so all sages go in the same way, and are of the same spirit of mind, and live with the same principle or the same *Tao*.[11] This idea led the Chinese people to believe that there can be sages in different religions of different peoples.[12] This is one reason there were no religious wars or large-scale religious persecutions in Chinese history. So, this idea has its religious value.

Furthermore, when we know there is a single spirit, or a single mind, or a single principle, or a single *Tao* in the world of sages, we have to know one thing more. This is: "I can know all this in my here-and-now mind." This is to say that I can comprehend what is universal and all-pervading in the world of sages in my here-and-now mind. So, the world of sages is as much immanent in my here-and-now spiritual world as it is transcendent to my here-and-now actual existence. When I am awakened to this idea, then all that is remote, such as the highest ideals or holy virtues of sages, is nearest to my here-and-now mind, and all the values of the highest ideals and holy virtues belong to my mind as much as they do to the minds of sages themselves. This is perhaps the highest idea of human spiritual life expounded by the thinkers of the late Ming (1368–1644) after Wang Shou-jen. It is too subtle to explain all its meanings here.[13]

IV. Spiritual Values in Taoism

Taoist ideas about spiritual life were usually expounded as in contrast with the life of worldly man. Such names as "real man," "Heavenly man," "spirit-man" or "divine man," "perfect man," and "sage-man" were used by Taoist philosophers to differentiate their ideal man from the worldly man.

Taoist philosophers, who looked aloof at everything here, felt some fatigue in worldly affairs and sought spiritual quiescence and tranquillity, and then, withdrawing their minds from worldly things, were men who had a transcendent mentality. Taoist philosophers usually thought and spoke about their ideals of human life negatively, unlike the Confucians, who usually thought and spoke positively. Lao Tzu (sixth century B.C.) taught men to be weak, soft, quiet, and foolish, instead of strong, hard, active, and wise. Chuang Tzu (399–295? B.C.) taught man not to seek reputation, honor, or social success, to forget himself and be indifferent to worldly gain and loss, happiness and misery, and life and death. They taught people to live a way of life which is neither driven by instinctive desires nor motivated by calculation, forgetting worldly benefits. So, the value of their ideal life is quite beyond the category of the satisfaction of natural desires and utilitarian value as defined in Section I, above. But what is the spiritual value of this kind of life, which seems purely negative and from which we can derive nothing?

The answer is twofold. First, the Taoist ideal of life has its positive side. Second, this positive value of life can be realized by living in a negative way. I shall begin with the latter point.

The reason the positive value of life can be realized by living in a negative way is very simple. If our ordinary way of living is considered of no value or of disvalue, then not living in this way is a positive value. For example, if the toil of the whole day is considered to be disvalue, is not rest itself a positive value? The important thing is that the negating of disvalue should be presented to the spiritual subject. If the negating of disvalue is presented to a spiritual subject, the value of the negating itself is positively presented to the spiritual subject, immanently exists in the subject, and becomes positive spiritual value. So, when I am not seeking worldly wealth, reputation, and honor, which are considered to be of disvalue, the very quiescence and tranquillity in my non-seeking can be presented to my spiritual self as full of positive value (just as rest after a day of toil can be presented as of positive value).

If we understand this clearly, then we know there are as many kinds of values experienced by the men who want to transcend worldly things as by men who cling to worldly things. The sense of tranquillity and quiescence of the men who transcend worldly things successfully seems homogeneously extended. Yet, under this homogeneous extension, the heterogeneous worldly things are transcended co-extensively. So, the spiritual content of the life of the man who transcends worldly things is as full as the life of the worldly man, the difference being that all worldly things are transcended and superseded in his mind. From this point we may proceed to the reason many Eastern and Western mystics who see the transcendent world as Divine Nothing estimate the value of the Divine Nothing as higher than everything, full of everything that has been superseded, and as a Divine All-Being.

The problem of all mystics, who want to transcend worldly things, is that the deep quiescence or tranquillity of the spirit is not easily preserved, and the Divine Nothing is not easily revealed. So, it may be easily concluded that, without faith in a transcendent savior who descends from above to help us ascend to the transcendent world, we can never raise ourselves. However, in Oriental religious and metaphysical thought there is an idea which is most important: that it is not necessary for us to have faith in a transcendent savior to help us transcend the mundane world. Instead, we may have wisdom to see that worldly things are themselves sunk down and have no power to disturb our tranquillity and quiescence of mind and that the world is itself a place where something like the Divine Nothing reveals itself. This is the wisdom of Nothing in Taoist philosophy.

This wisdom is very simple in essence. It is the realization that any worldly thing begins in or comes from "where it is not," or "Nothing," through a process of transformation or change, and ends at or goes back to "where it is not." Then, "beginning and ending in Nothing" is the general nature of all things and the Great Way, or *Tao*, where all things pass through. This idea is based primarily on our everyday experience. Everybody agrees, at least from the point of view of phenomena, that the future is what has not "yet been" and is now nothing, and that the present, which was the future and becomes the past, may be said to come from Nothing and go to Nothing. If we know deeply that everything comes from Nothing and goes back to Nothing, then all things may be taken as involved in a Great Nothing,[14] or as floating out from the Great Nothing, only to sink into it again. Then not anything can really constitute bondage or disturb our spirit. When its very nature of "shall-be-sinking" is really presented to me in the immediate present, it is already nothing and has no effect as a disturbance or bondage for me even now.

The two great founders of Taoist philosophy, Lao Tzu and Chuang Tzu, both present the wisdom of Nothing in metaphysics as the theoretical basis for the development of the spiritual life of tranquillity and quiescence so as to achieve an actual transcendence over worldly things. This is the negative side of their teachings. On the positive side, there are differences in their teachings on the spiritual life.

When Lao Tzu thought about the relation of worldly things to the "Nothing," he usually thought that worldly things were involved and contained in the Nothing. The ideal spiritual life, corresponding to this metaphysical vision, is identified in our mind or spirit with the Nothing and is free from all the limitations of finite particular worldly things. Thus we can comprehend and embrace all things without partiality. When this kind of mind is used in political philosophy, it is the mind of a sage-king, which has no special reaction to any particular thing, but is glad to see all things and actions of all people well done, and embraces all people as his children. This kind of mind is mild, kind, soft, as broad as Heaven or the Void, always wishing for all things to go their own way, and tolerating them, following them, and never interfering with them. This is the first aspect of Lao Tzu's teaching, which has cultivated the virtue of tolerance and broad-mindedness in the Chinese people, and has provided Chinese government with the political ideals of non-interference with the people, concession to the will of the people, and so on.

In the second aspect of Lao Tzu's teaching, the mind, which is identified with Nothing and is as broad as Heaven or the Void, may simply contemplate the "coming and going," "birth and death," and "prosperity and decay" of all things without affection or mercy.

It is the mind of a spectator of the universe. It is neither morally bad nor morally good, and maintains ethical neutrality. The metaphysical truth is thus presented to this mind with a kind of intellectual value.

In the third aspect of Lao Tzu's teaching, the mind, which knows that what is prosperous shall decay, that what is strong shall become weak, and that what is born shall die, can generalize all these into a principle: Everything moves in a curve which represents the natural law of all things. According to this principle, when a thing reaches the top of the curve it is destined to fall. Therefore, if we do not want to be a victim of this natural law, the only way is never to progress to the top of the curve, or, when we approach the top, to go back to the beginning of the curve again, for then the top of the curve will always be in our purview, but we shall never arrive there, and so we shall never fall. So, Lao Tzu taught us to go backward, to learn the way of the child or the female, and to be humble and modest, in order to preserve our vitality and other powers to prevent falling down. This is the utilitarian aspect of Lao Tzu's philosophy, which is neither morally good nor morally bad and may not include any spiritual value to be realized by this kind of mind.

In contrast with Lao Tzu, when Chuang Tzu thought about the things of the world, he did not hold that all things are contained in the Great Nothing, but paid more attention to the great process of incessant change or transformation of all things in the Infinite Heaven. In this process, all definite forms and colors of things come into being and pass away. So, this process can also be taken as a great change or transformation of a great ether or air, which is itself formless and colorless, being combined with non-being. Since Chuang Tzu paid more attention to the process of transformation in the universe, his view of human life placed more emphasis on the spiritual transformation of human life itself. If one wants to be a real man or a man of Heaven, free from one's past habits or ordinary self, one ought to live a life of spiritual flight, or spiritual wandering, through the process of the infinite transformations in the universe. He should also take all things as equals when they are presented and enjoyed by one's spirit, yet without judging them as good or bad from one's partial, personal point of view. In its flight or wandering in the universe, one's spirit sees everything with empathy and takes the myriad forms as the forms of things which it encounters, yet without attachment to any one, and lets the forms successfully be taken and then left. When the form of anything is left, then nothing remains and nothing needs to be remembered. When the form of anything is being taken, it is absolutely new, just as the world which is present to the new-born child or new-born animal is preceded by nothing, and, as we may not expect anything from it, is followed by nothing. It is immediately presented and enjoyed, as if it were floating in an infinite Void or Heaven as its background. This is the way of life of the real man, the man of Heaven, or the spirit-man of Chuang Tzu. Therefore, the word "spirit" (*shen*), which originally meant an invisible spirit which existed objectively, was used by Chuang Tzu as the name of the spiritual mood or activity of the spirit-man which extends his spirit beyond the limitation of the universe. He used "*shen-yü*" (literally, spirit-meeting) as the term for the way of the ideal man when he encounters anything immediately with empathy for the moment, without attachment.[15]

From the above, we may conclude that the spirit of Chuang Tzu's way of life is more aesthetic than Lao Tzu's way of life, and therefore can appreciate with empathy the beauties of all things or the "beauty of Heaven and Earth," as he called it.[16] Yet, this kind of beauty does not consist simply in the forms of things. As every form exists in the process of "transformation of ether or air," so the most beautiful forms should never be clear-cut and should be permeated by the flow of ether and become ethereal forms. As the forms pass through the ether and return, they create rhythms. Ethereal rhythm (*ch'i-yün*) is a key term of Chinese aesthetics; it has the Infinite Void or Heaven as its background. It permeates the whole universe charged with life.[17]

V. Buddhist Ideas As a Supplement to Chinese Philosophy

From the Chinese point of view, the Buddhist theory of the non-permanence of everything is very similar to the Taoist idea that everything is in a process of change, as coming from Nothing and returning to Nothing. Yet, impermanence in Buddhism is based on the principle of *yüan-sheng*, sometimes translated as causal or dependent origination, meaning that everything is a combination of conditions. (It was never consciously posited by Lao Tzu or Chuang Tzu.) The meaning of *yüan-sheng* is simple in itself. It leads our thinking from the assertion that "a thing is generated by its conditions and has no 'self' concealed in it to sustain its existence" to the assertion that "the self-nature or self-essence of a thing is emptiness," that is, that there is no such self-nature.

To show that *śūnyatā* (emptiness) is the nature of everything, according to the theory of *yüan-sheng*, the Buddhists argue that, if we know a thing is generated by its conditions, then there is absolutely nothing which exists as such, before or after all conditions have met together. Since all the conditions which come together can be separated, nothing has any permanence, and what is existing can also be non-existing. Therefore, the existing thing has no self-nature or self-essence to sustain its existence, and the possibility of its non-existence is the very nature of its existence. (This is *śūnyatā*.) Yet, when we really know this starting point and other, further theories of *śūnyatā*, we have to see directly and intuitively the *śūnyatā* of all things. This requires strict training in spiritual concentration, spiritual quiescence, and spiritual wisdom. When we understand *śūnyatā*, then all things of the world become clear to us. Then all is enlightened by non-being, and non-being is enlightened by being. This is, of course, an awakening which is beyond the self-consciousness of the layman and the speculation of philosophers.

The idea of *yüan-sheng* in Buddhism, especially in the Mādhyamika school, never requires us to know merely the conditions of a thing. On the contrary, its main purpose is to direct our consciousness to depart negatively from the false idea of self-nature or self-essence, and to look to the conditions of a thing. As every existing condition has its various conditions, too, so the idea of *yüan-sheng* directs our consciousness to depart from the thing as a center, to extend its light to the conditions, to the conditions of conditions, and to go beyond the thing itself. Then the self-nature or self-essence of anything can be cancelled and the *śūnyatā* of all things may be revealed.

In the cultivation of spiritual life, the value of the teaching of *śūnyatā* is tremendous. Since all the bonds of our spiritual life and the infinite evils of human life come from clinging to the apparent realities of worldly things, these teachings remove the roots of all bonds and evils. Infinite merits can be achieved and infinite virtues or spiritual values can then be realized by us. This is the ideal of *buddha*hood.

Buddhist demonstrations of the *śūnyatā* of all things are based upon the conditional relations of things, which are acknowledged as actually existing in the intellect of common sense and science. Therefore, all these demonstrations can logically be carried out as in the Mādhyamika school of Buddhism.

Another point is the idea of the *ālaya* (storehouse) consciousness and its seeds as expounded by the Yogācāra school of Buddhism. These ideas come from our spiritual light reaching into the unconscious nether world. From the teachings of the Yogācāra school, we can understand the world of *ālaya* and its seeds through indirect and mediate reasoning only, though they can be consciously known directly and immediately by deep contemplation of the *bodhi-sattva* (one whose nature is perfect wisdom) or the Buddha. In the teachings of this school, many layers and aspects of the world of unconsciousness are elucidated and analyzed, and so are many ways of *yoga* for the self-transformation of the whole personality in order to attain the vision of the *bodhi-sattva* or the Buddha. These were all new teachings of spiritual cultivation for the Chinese people.

The ultimate purpose of Buddhism is to teach man to attain *buddha*hood and to see the *śūnyatā* of all things, which is super-intellectual. This is different from Taoist philosophy, which usually uses metaphorical symbolism or aesthetic imagination to attain the super-intellectual. The combination of the spirit of the teaching of Buddhism, mainly the Mādhyamika school, and the spirit of Taoist philosophers is the way of Ch'an (Zen), which may be taken as the free use of intellectual ideas to cancel other ideas and let the vision of *śūnyatā* of Ch'an experience be expressed by symbolic language and actions.

VI. New Orientation of Value-Consciousness in the Neo-Confucianism of the Sung-Ming Period

It is generally agreed that the Neo-Confucians of the Sung and Ming dynasties were men of an introvert type. They propounded the values of quiescence, serenity, reverence, self-reflection, and self-examination. They even adopted static sitting as a way to spiritual cultivation. All this seems quite different from the pre-Ch'in (220–206 B.C.) Confucians, who were more active in social, political, and cultural activities. So, the Confucians of the Ch'ing (1644–1912) criticized the Confucians of the Sung and Ming dynasties as Buddhists or Taoists in disguise. This is an exaggeration. Almost all the Confucians of the Sung and Ming dynasties most sincerely opposed many teachings of the Buddhists and Taoists. Their ideas of ethical relations and of sacrificial ceremonies for ancestors, sages, and worthies and their many other historical, cultural, political, and economic ideas are all of Confucian origin. So, we have to explain why they laid more emphasis on the self-reflective or quietistic way of spiritual cultivation through the influence of Buddhism and Taoism, plus the development of Confucianism itself.

Compared with the earlier Confucians, the Neo-Confucians were more conscientious about the inner obstructions to the development of spiritual life. These obstructions, such as the evil elements of *karma* and *ālaya*, had not been taken seriously by earlier Confucians. It is usually the case that the higher in spiritual life one wants to ascend, the more inner obstructions one finds. The more self-reflective one is, the more faults or potential inner motive of faults one finds deep in his mind. The Neo-Confucians called these inner obstructions insincere ideas, e.g., selfish desires, habitual materialistic tendencies, obstinate opinions, variegated temperaments, and the manipulative or calculating mind, which are all deeply rooted and always concealed in our minds. Only deep inner meditation or self-reflection can illuminate and reveal the way to eradicate the roots of these obstructions. In order to eradicate these ideas, which are all purely negative to the development of spiritual life, we have to avoid absolutely doing certain things and let the negative things be arrested, appeased, and transformed, and thus our spiritual life may be purified. In these cases, all our ways of life must be quiet and static, at least in appearance.

Secondly, the Neo-Confucians were more metaphysical and religious than the earlier Confucians, and consequently they usually had a sense of life, both moral and super-moral. The ideas of Heaven, God, the Reason of Heaven, and the Mind of Heaven, as mentioned before, were always discussed by them. They always talked of man from the point of view of Heaven and had a belief in the eternal *Tao*. These were somewhat similar to Taoist thought. Ch'eng Hao said that "the achievements of the Sage-Emperors, such as Yao and Shun, may be like a floating cloud in an infinite void," [18] since the eternal *Tao* of the universe has no addition by "the achievements of Yao or Shun, the Sage-Emperors," nor is there any loss by all the evils done by Chieh or Chou, the worst kings. When a pupil of Lu Chiu-yüan regretted that Chu Hsi (an opponent of his master) did not know the *Tao* rightly, Lu reproached his pupil and regretted that he had made no improvement, and said, "The *Tao* shall neither be added nor subtracted whether there are Lu Hsiang-shan (Lu Chiu-yüan) and Chu Yüan-hui (another name of Chu Hsi)." [19] All these sayings took the standpoint of Heaven and originated from a metaphysical and religious faith in the eternal existence of *Tao*, or a spiritual mood which is, at least in a sense, beyond the distinction of the good and evil of conduct and the right and wrong ideas of man. In the philosophy of Wang Shou-jen, *liang-chih* (conscience) is sometimes said to be beyond good and evil. This is based upon the fact that, in the practice of *liang-chih*, when evil is wholly undone, no evil is left, and, when good is done, no good is left. So, in the practice of *liang-chih* we can pass beyond good and evil, and the nature of *liang-chih* is neither good nor evil, and this is called the chief good of *liang-chih*. Here we find Wang's view to be moral thought combined with the super-moral idea, and this may be said to be a combination of the moral ideas of earlier Confucians and the super-moral ideas of the Buddhists and Taoists.

However, the Tao and the *liang-chih* of the Neo-Confucians are still essentially moral concepts. "To see man from the point of view of Heaven" is itself a phase of moral life, according to the Neo-Confucians. When Wang Shou-jen said that *"liang-chih* is neither good nor evil, and this is called the chief good," it is still beyond mere evil and ordinary good, but never beyond the chief good. So, the super-moral ideas of the Neo-Confucians should be taken as the expressions of their highest moral experience, though, in the profundity and depth of this moral experience, they may exceed all the earlier Confucians in certain respects.

VII. Spiritual, Social, and Natural Values During the Past Three Centuries

In the development of Chinese thought there has been a great change since the end of the Ming Dynasty. During this period, generally speaking, the trends of thought have moved from depth of thought to extent of thought, from inward reflection to comprehensive understanding, from meditation on the spiritual and moral life to a consideration of natural and social life, and from the gaining of material for thought from personal experience to the gaining of material for thought from historical documents and relics. At the end of the Ming Dynasty, great scholars, such as Wang Fu-chih (1619–1692), Ku Yen-wu (1613–1682), and Huang Tsung-hsi

(1610–1695), even though they were erudite and usually based their ideas upon documentary evidence, all held a lofty idea of culture and had high personal characters, to which their knowledge was subordinated, and the spiritual and moral values of all social, political, and cultural life was expounded by them. From the school of Yen Yüan and Li Kung (1659–1733), a new current of thought began to flourish which laid more emphasis on the social utilitarian values. Even the values of music and of the moral virtues were considered by them according to a utilitarian standard. From the middle of the Ch'ing Dynasty, in the thought of Tai Chen and Chiao Hsün (1768–1820), much attention was paid to the satisfaction of men's natural feelings and desires. The moral values of benevolence and social justice were interpreted to be the results of men's mutual consideration of the satisfaction of natural feelings and desires. So, the ideas of moral value, social utilitarian value, and natural values were combined into one homogeneous system. The most important current of thought late in the Ch'ing Dynasty was the thought of the Kung-yang school, which gradually laid more emphasis on the political and economic problems of the time (and found its justification in the Commentaries on the Classics). These currents of thought finally joined with the thoughts of social construction from the West and resulted in the thought of K'ang Yu-wei (1858–1927). In recent decades, the spirit of searching the documentary evidence of the scholars of the Ch'ing Dynasty has become gradually connected with the Western scientific spirit and transformed into the popular high estimation of all things of scientific value. The two watchwords of the so-called new cultural movement at the beginning of the Republic of China were democracy and science, which were taken to have a very high social utilitarian value and truth value. Other spiritual values were generally neglected. When Marxism attracted the minds of the young generation, a communist party was organized and now has gained political power on the mainland of China. The communists' sense of value has further narrowed down to the political and social sphere. Only the technical value of science has been emphasized by them.

From the above, it is clear that the direction of the development of Chinese thought from the end of the Ming Dynasty to recent years has gradually left the spirit of Neo-Confucianism, which paid more attention to the spiritual values of human life, and now pays more attention to the importance of the social, utilitarian, technical, and natural values of human life. Since the nineteenth century, the value-consciousness of Westerners has gradually concentrated on the social, utilitarian, and technical sphere and on the values of satisfaction of natural desire. Here is a meeting of the value-consciousnesses of East and West, which represents a *"Zeitgeist."* On its good side, this *"Zeitgeist"* may be taken as an extensive development of human value-consciousness for the preparation of the spiritual ground of the coming age, which should pay more intensive attention to the importance of spiritual values. But when and how the various kinds of natural values, social values, and spiritual values can be integrated into a great harmony in the new age is a complicated problem which is quite beyond the sphere of this essay.

QUESTION: You talk about spiritual life in Taoist philosophy, and you identify the wisdom of Lao Tzu with the wisdom of Nothing in metaphysics as the theoretical basis for the development of spiritual life. It seems to me that the *Tao* of Lao Tzu is a metaphysical being, the primordial mover of the universe or the Godhead. How can the wisdom of Lao Tzu be identified with the wisdom of Nothing?

ANSWER: The wisdom of Lao Tzu is not identified simply with the wisdom of Nothing. I did not use the word "identified." Surely, the *Tao* of Lao Tzu may be interpreted as a metaphysical being or primordial mover of the universe, perhaps something like the Godhead. However, in this paper, I had to stress the Nothingness side of Lao Tzu's *Tao*. One reason for this is that the *Tao* of Lao Tzu as a metaphysical being is said to be revealed to us through the transiency of natural things. The transiency of things is explained as their coming from Nothing and sinking into Nothing. The other reason is that meditation on *Tao* as metaphysical must begin with the thought of worldly things themselves as nothing. "Nothing" is a mediation between the thought of worldly things and meditation on *Tao*. When we want to ascend to *Tao*, we must transcend worldly things and encounter Nothing first, and the very transcending is itself a "nothing-ing" activity initiating from the *Tao*. This is explicitly stated in Lao Tzu's thought also. When we talk about Lao Tzu's idea of spiritual value as a higher value transcending worldly values, as my paper does, the wisdom of Nothing in Lao Tzu must be stressed.

Notes

1. Many writers, such as Ch'en Tu-hsiu (1879–1942) in the period of the New Culture movement at the beginning of the Republic of China, took the utilitarian point of view to interpret the ethical value of Confucian teachings, and some missionaries and naturalism-biased Chinese scholars usually interpret the ethical values of Confucian teachings as merely natural values in contrast with supernatural or spiritual values.

2. Cf. my essay, *Tsai ching-shen sheng-huo fa-chan chung chih hui-yü i-shih* (A Phenomenological Study of the Consciousness of Praise and Defamation in the Development of Spiritual Life), *Jen-sheng*, X, No. 1 (1954).

3. Cf. Legge's translation, *Confucian Analects*, XXXVII (Republished, Hong Kong: Hong Kong University Press, 1960).

4. The Chinese words are *"tzu-te"* for self-satisfaction, *"yüeh"* for self-joy, and *"an"* for self-peace.

5. Cf. *Chung yung* (*The Doctrine of the Mean*), XXV.

6. For example, in Aristotelian-Thomian metaphysical and religious thought, human nature is usually taken as a potentiality in contrast with God, which is pure actuality.

7. This is my own translation of *The Book of Mencius*, VIB.13.

8. Wang Shou-jen, *Ch'uan-hsi lu* (Records of Instructions for Practice), III.

9. My free translation of *The Book of Mencius*, VIIB.25, from 5 to 9, and condensed into two sentences.

10. Cf. on the spiritual aspect of forgiving, chap. 12, sec. 9, of my book: *Chung-kuo jen-wen ching-shen chih fa-chan* (The Development of the Chinese Humanistic Spirit) (Hong Kong: Yin-Sun Press, 1958).

11. About the universal attainability of sagehood, we may cite the sayings of Mencius and Lu Chiu-yüan. Mencius said, "Those regions [of Shun and King Wen, reigned 1171–1122 B.C.] were distant from one another more than a thousand *li* [about a third of a mile], and the age of one sage was later than that of the other by more than a thousand years. But . . . the principles of the earlier sage and the later sage are the same." (Legge's translation, *Book of Mencius*, IVA.1.) Lu Chiu-yüan said, "The universe is my mind, and my mind is the universe. If in the Eastern Sea there were to appear a sage, he would have this same mind and this principle (*li*). If in the Western Sea there were to appear a sage, he would have this same mind and same principle. If in the Southern or Northern Seas there were to appear sages, they, too, would have this same mind and this same principle. If a hundred or a thousand generations ago, or a hundred or a thousand generations hence, sages were to appear, they

[likewise] would have this same mind and this same principle." Fung Yu-lan, *A History of Chinese Philosophy*, Derk Bodde, trans. (Princeton: Princeton University Press, 1953), Vol. II, p. 537.

12. In the *Lieh Tzu*, supposedly written by a Taoist philosopher of the pre-Ch'in period, there is a paragraph about the sage of the West which was originally taken as an argument to convince Chinese people that the Buddha is a Western sage. Yet, when Jesuits came to China during the Ming Dynasty, this sentence was reinterpreted by Matteo Ricci in his book, *T'ien-chu shih-i*, as the prophecy of Jesus Christ as a Western sage.

13. The sayings of Wang Lung-ch'i (1498–1583), Lo Chin-ch'i (1515–1588), Lo Nien-an (1504–1564), and Liu Chi-shan, (1578–1645) are available in *Ming-jü hsüeh-an* (Writings of Ming Confucians), edited and written by Huang Tsung-hsi. (Republished, Shanghai: Chung Hua Co., 1930.)

14. Taoist philosophers used the word *"wu,"* which does not actually have the same meaning as "nothing." *"Wu"* means nothing or non-being in phenomena but may not mean nothing or non-being in reality. We use the phrase "Great Nothing" here as the translation of the word *"wu"* to indicate that it is like nothing in the phenomenal world, yet it may be something in reality.

15. The whole paragraph is my elaboration of Chuang Tzu's idea of spiritual life. It would require much space to cite all the documents concerned with comments which are omitted.

16. Cf. *Chuang Tzu*, XXII.

17. This is just a way of deducing an idea of Chinese aesthetics from the philosophy of Chuang Tzu. Historically speaking, the idea of Chinese aesthetics has its origin in the philosophy of Confucianism, too. But, as we know that almost all the later Chinese artists liked to read Chuang Tzu, we have more reason to suppose that the philosophy of Chuang Tzu strongly influenced the aesthetic ideas of later artists.

18. *Erh-Ch'eng ch'üan-shu* (*The Complete Works of the Ch'eng Brothers*), Vol. III, para. 35.

19. *Hsiang-shan ch'üan-chi* (*The Collected Works of Lu Hsiang-shan*), Vol. XXXIV, para. 17, of *Yen-sung Records*.

JOHN C. H. WU   *Chinese Legal*

and Political Philosophy

IT IS IMPOSSIBLE to cover the whole field of Chinese legal and political philosophy in a short discourse. I shall therefore confine myself to three basic questions: (1) the foundations of political authority, (2) the relations between law and ethics, and (3) the ultimate ideal of human society and the historical process of its realization.

I. Foundations of Political Authority

The sources of all political authority, according to the most ancient of Chinese documents, *The Book of History*,[1] are three: the Mandate of Heaven, the people's good will, and the ruler's virtue.

It goes without saying that the Mandate of Heaven is the real cornerstone. But it is worthy of note that the ancients did not think of the Mandate as fate. It is something that one must gain and maintain by constant virtue and effort. The ancients never tired of teaching that the Mandate of Heaven is not fixed once and for all in a single family and that it is subject to forfeiture should its incumbent prove unfaithful to the solemn trust.

It is further to be remembered that Heaven manifests its will in many ways. Natural calamities and other unusual phenomena were considered grave warnings of God to the reigning monarch. It is even more clearly revealed in the people's resentment against the abuses of power, particularly greed and injustice on the part of their rulers, and their spontaneous flocking to a newly arisen leader who knows their sufferings intimately. Besides possessing other qualities of leadership, this new leader must be unselfish and capable of judging justly the conflicts among his followers. He must use the faults of the dying dynasty as a mirror in order to cultivate the virtues that present a clear contrast to them.

In ancient China, revolution was not regarded as a right, but as a solemn duty that the new leaders of the people owed to Heaven to rectify the abuses or perversions of its Mandate, and to relieve the people from intolerable oppressions of the tyrant. As the great T'ang [2] declared, on starting a revolution, "The ruler of Hsia [2183–1752 B.C.] has committed innumerable crimes, and it is the will of Heaven to slay him. . . . As I fear God on high, I dare not refrain from rectifying the perversion." [3] Even after T'ang had succeeded in overthrowing the Hsia Dynasty, a spokesman of the new dynasty, fearing lest T'ang's action might be misunderstood by later generations and even cited as a justification for ordinary rebellions, explained its underlying philosophy in clear and emphatic terms: "It is always necessary to remember the beginnings in order to secure a happy end. By protecting the law-abiding people and overthrowing the lawless oppressor, by carefully observing the dictates of the Natural Law, the Mandate of Heaven will be perpetually kept intact. [4] The expeditionary forces of T'ang are said to have been welcomed by the people of the whole country, to such an extent that their only complaint was that he did not arrive earlier. In the graphic words of Mencius (371–289? B.C.), "The people were hoping for his coming as they would hope to see the cloud in a time of great drought." [5]

The Shang Dynasty (1751–1112 B.C.) lasted six centuries. In the twelfth century B.C., another revolution was necessary. In the Grand Oath of King Wu [6] (reigned 1121–1116 B.C.), he pointed out to the people that King Chou (reigned 1175–1121 B.C.) of Shang was even worse than King Chieh (reigned 1801–1752 B.C.) of Hsia. Just as the crimes of Chieh had moved Heaven to direct the great T'ang to deprive the Hsia of its Mandate, so it now fell upon King Wu to execute the sentence of Heaven upon Chou. In the same oath he announced a great principle which has been quoted through the ages: "Heaven sees as our people see and hears as our people hear." [7]

The Chinese philosophy of political authority may be summed up in a few words. Political authority is a trust conferred by the

Mandate of Heaven upon the government for the welfare of the people. The government is created for the people, not the people for the government. The whole philosophy finds its best exposition in the works of Mencius. I have dealt with it at some length elsewhere, but here I can only introduce a dialogue between Mencius and King Hsüan of Ch'i [8] (reigned 342–423 B.C.). "Suppose," he asked the king, "that one of Your Majesty's servants were to entrust his wife and children to the care of a friend, while he went to the State of Ch'u for a trip, and that, on his return, he should find that his friend had caused his wife and children to suffer cold and hunger. How is such a one to be dealt with?" "He should be cast off as a friend," the king replied. Mencius proceeded, "Suppose that the minister of justice could not regulate his officers, how should he be dealt with?" "Dismiss him," was the ready answer. Mencius pursued further, "If within the four borders of the kingdom there is no order and peace, what is to be done?" The king is reported to have "looked to the right and to the left, speaking of other matters."

The idea that the ruler is a steward of the common good, who must forget his own interests, including his physical safety, is clearly brought out by Lao Tzu (604–531 B.C.): "Only he who is willing to give his body for the sake of the world is fit to be entrusted with the world. Only he who can do it with love is worthy to be the steward of the world." [9] He even says, "To receive all the dirt of a country is to be the lord of its soil-shrines. To bear the calamities of a country is to be the king of the world." [10]

Thus, both Lao Tzu and the Confucians draw upon *The Book of History* as a common source of political wisdom. In spite of their differences on many points, they are in accord on some vital points. Both are emphatic on the ruler's virtue of humility toward the people. Take, for instance, the following song recorded in *The Book of History*:

> The people should be cherished,
> And should not be downtrodden.
> The people are the root of a country,
> And, if the root is firm, the country will be tranquil. [11]

This should bring to mind what Lao Tzu says:

> Truly, humility is the root from which greatness springs,
> And the high must be built upon the low.
> That is why the dukes and princes style themselves as

*"The Helpless One," "The Little One," and "The Worthless One."
Perhaps, they, too, realize their dependence upon the humble.*[12]

Even the doctrine of *wu-wei* (non-assertiveness) seems to have
its seed in the famous song of Kao Yao: [13]

> *When the head is enlightened,*
> *The arms and legs will function smoothly*
> *And the people's well-being ensured.*
> *But if the head is fussy and meddlesome,*
> *The arms and legs will become indolent,*
> *And all affairs fall into decay.*[14]

I need hardly point out that this is in entire consonance with
the spirit of Lao Tzu. But even Confucius (551–479 B.C.) has
praised the *wu-wei* of Emperor Shun of antiquity: "May not Shun
be said to have governed by non-assertiveness? For what assertion
was there? All that he did was to control himself with great care
and reign reverently with his face toward the south." [15] On another
occasion, he said, "Sublime were Shun and Yü [founders of the
Hsia Dynasty]! They possessed the whole world, but were not
possessed by it." [16] This is Confucius' notion of *wu-wei*, and it cannot
be very far from what Lao Tzu himself had in mind.

Confucius and Lao Tzu are in agreement in maintaining that
punishment must not be relied upon as a policy of government, that
the ruler must guard against luxury, against the lust of power,
against giving rein to his arbitrary will, against violence and extreme measures, especially against pride and self-complacency.
Both stress the necessity of self-denial, although there are some
differences in their ideas of self-denial.[17]

True enough, Confucius thinks of reality in terms of the Will
of Heaven, while Lao Tzu thinks of it in terms of the Way of Heaven
or the Way of Nature. But, for our present purposes, this makes
little or no difference, for in both cases the starting point is a Higher
Law, which should serve as the pattern for all human laws.[18] Both
of them would be opposed to the absolutism of the legalists.

A very interesting and significant conversation between Confucius and Duke Ting (reigned 509–495 B.C.) is recorded in *The
Analects*.[19] The Duke asked if there is a single saying by the adoption of which a country could be made to flourish. With his usual
candidness, Confucius replied, "No saying can really be of such
potency as that. However, there is the popular saying, 'It is hard to
be a prince, and not easy to be a minister.' Now, if the prince

realizes how hard it is to be a prince, is it not a good beginning toward the fulfillment of the saying?" The Duke again asked, "Is there a single saying which would ruin a country?" Confucius again pointed out that there really could not be a saying so potent as that. "But," he continued, "there is the common saying, 'I see no pleasure in being a prince except that no one would then dare to disobey my words.' Well, if one's words are always wise, it would be well for them to go uncontradicted. But, if they are foolish, and yet carried out without opposition, would that not be almost an instance of a saying that would ruin the country?"

This conversation, casual as it may appear, reveals some of the basic tenets of Confucius' political philosophy. In the first place, what makes it so hard to be a prince is that it is not merely a privilege but a grave responsibility. To realize the difficulty of the task is the beginning of political wisdom. As Lao Tzu says, "He who thinks everything easy will end by finding everything difficult. The sage alone begins by considering everything difficult and ends by having no difficulties." [20] Nothing is easier than to indulge one's self-will, nothing harder than to sacrifice it in favor of justice and the common good. How carefully the monarch should guard against his self-will finds a good illustration in what King Ch'eng said to Chün-ch'en, whom he had appointed magistrate of Hsia-tu, a colony for the people of the superseded Yin Dynasty (1384–1112 B.C.). "When any of the Yin people are under trial for a crime," said the King, "if I should tell you to convict, do not convict; and, if I should tell you to release, do not release. Justice is all." [21]

In the second place, the responsibility consists in taking care of the people. All governmental measures and policies must therefore be judged in the light of their effects upon the people's well-being. In answer to a disciple's inquiry as to how to achieve the proper administration of government, Confucius enumerated five good things to be pursued and four evils to be avoided.[22] The five good things are: "That the ruler be beneficent without expending the public revenue, that in exacting service he should take care not to arouse dissatisfaction, that his designs be free from personal greed, that he maintain a dignified ease without being proud, and that where it is necessary to assert his authority he should do it without violence."

Concerning the four evils to be avoided, he said: "Putting men to death without first teaching them their duty is cruelty. Expecting the completion of tasks without giving due warning is called oppression. To be remiss in issuing orders and at the same time demand instant performance is called extreme unreasonableness. Likewise, to show a grudging spirit in giving pay or rewards due to a man is called playing the petty functionary."

It is because Confucius and his followers had a clear view of the true foundations of political authority that they never lost sight of the well-being of the people. They never regarded political authority as an end, but only as a means to an end. The end is the development of the human personality and human civilization. This is why the saying, "I see no pleasure in being a prince except that no one would then dare to oppose my words," was picked out by Confucius as indicating the beginning of all troubles in the state, for this would imply that political authority was taken as an end in itself, and that the arbitrary will of the ruler rather than reason was considered as the essence of law. The fact is that it is the first duty of the prince to mortify his self-will in order to minister to the actual needs and legitimate desires of the people. In the words of *The Great Learning*, "When a prince loves what the people love, and loathes what the people loathe, then he truly deserves to be called the parent of the people." [23] The Confucians cherish profound respect for the people, who, with few exceptions, can be assumed to be good, honest commoners. For, as *The Book of Odes* has it:

> Heaven gives birth to the teeming people,
> Affixing a law to every relationship of man.
> Being endowed with a constant norm,
> They have a natural love for the beauty of virtue.[24]

Lao Tzu and Mo Tzu (fl. 479–438 B.C.), each in his own way, shared with the Confucians the same respect for the common people and the Way of Heaven or the Law of Nature.[25] Lao Tzu, for instance, says that the sage has no preconceived intentions, for he takes the heart of the common people for his own heart.[26] Further, he says, "The Way of Heaven is to diminish the superabundant and to supply the needy, while the way of man is to take from the needy to swell the superabundant." [27] Thus, a Higher Law than the positive laws of the state is recognized. The same is true of Mo Tzu, who wrote: "The emperor may not make the standard at will. There is Heaven to give him the standard. The gentlemen of the world all understand that the emperor gives the standard to the world but do not understand that Heaven gives the standard to the emperor." [28]

On the whole, it may be said that Chinese legal and political philosophy has the same starting point as that of Bracton, the Father of the Common Law, who wrote that the king is "under God and the law, for it is the law that makes the king," [29] and that only the power to do good is derived from God, while the power to do evil is from the devil and not from God. "So long, therefore, as the king administers justice, he is the vicar of the Eternal King, but he would be a servant of the devil if he turned aside to do injustice." [30]

II. Law and Ethics

The outstanding characteristic of the legal system of old China is that it is a system of duties rather than rights. Logically speaking, rights and duties are correlatives. If I have a duty, then the one to whom I owe the duty necessarily has the right to demand my performance of the duty. Similarly, if I have a right, then somebody else must owe me a duty corresponding to my right. Thus, rights and duties are inseparable. But here, as elsewhere in the field of moral sciences, emphasis makes the song; and there can be no question that in the Chinese legal system the emphasis is markedly on duties, so much so that the notion of rights was not as fully developed as in the Common Law and Roman Law. The emphasis being on duties, the law has never been freed from its dependence on morality. This forms a contrast to the legal systems of the West in modern times, especially in the heyday of individualism, when the emphasis was decidedly on rights rather than duties, with the result that the science of law tended to be divorced from ethics, and in a number of cases the decision became shocking to the moral sense of man. For the past seventy or eighty years Western jurisprudence has been moving steadily away from the amoral philosophy of law toward a healthy recognition of the social and ethical duties of man. During the same period, the legal thought of China, influenced as it was by its contact with the West in the nineteenth century, experienced at first a violent reaction against the old emphasis on duties, and moved toward a new emphasis on rights. This new vital tendency to Westernization, however, has been moderated by the ironic fact that the West is no longer so

"Western" as when the tendency first started. The East wanted to go the whole way in order to meet the West, but the West, without intending it, has met the East halfway. So far as legal thought is concerned, the East and the West have met in the zone of a happy medium.

But it is of more than historical interest to inquire how the relation between law and morality came to take the form it did in the old legal system of China after the days of the Han (206 B.C.– A.D. 220). In no other system has there been such a complete identification of law and morality. Whatever is immoral is a penal offense.[31] The underlying philosophy is that morality and law constitute the positive and negative phases of government.

This position was the end-product of a long evolution of ethical and legal philosophy before the Han period. Confucius and his followers advocated as principal methods of government the practice of virtue on the part of the ruler and the inculcation of good manners among the people. For Confucius, to rule is to rectify, and to rectify others presupposes rectitude in oneself.[32] If a ruler does not possess rectitude, he is not worthy of the name, nor can he ever hope to rectify his people, for the simple reason that you cannot impart something to others which you do not have in yourself. On the other hand, if the ruler cultivates the virtues and perfects his own person, the influence of his goodness will permeate the whole population. Once a corrupt officer of Confucius' own state came to ask him how to reduce the prevalence of thieves and robbers. Confucius' answer was: "If you, sir, are not covetous, the people would not steal, even if you should reward them for it."[33]

To Confucians, ethics and government are practically one and the same thing. If you cultivate your virtues so that harmony reigns in your own person, your goodness will radiate its influence around the fireside so that harmony will reign in the family. If one family is perfectly harmonious, it will gradually but surely influence other families. If all families are perfected, the state will enjoy peace and harmony. If all states are what they should be, they will be in peaceful relations with one another, and all under Heaven will enjoy universal peace and harmony.

No two schools of thought could be more completely antithetical to each other than the Confucians and the Legalists. Confucius says, "If you lead the people by political measures and regulate them by penal laws, they will merely avoid transgressing them but will have no sense of honor. If you lead them by the practice of virtue and regulate them by the inculcation of good manners, they will not only keep their sense of honor but will also be thoroughly transformed." [34] But Shang Yang (d. 338 B.C.) says, "If you govern by penal laws, the people will fear; being fearful, they will commit no villainies; there being no villainies, they will find peace and happiness. If, on the other hand, you govern by mere righteousness, they will be lax; and, if they are lax, there will be disorder and the people will suffer great miseries." [35]

Confucians maintain that good government depends upon the employment of good and capable men. But Shang Yang says, "It is the part of good government to set no store by the virtuous and the wise." [36]

Mencius says, "People tend to goodness as water tends downward." [37] But Shang Yang says, "People tend to self-interest, as water tends downward." [38]

Confucius was opposed to the promulgation of penal laws with a fixed and clear-cut tariff of penalties.[39] But Han Fei Tzu (d. 233 B.C.) says: "If a textbook is too summary, pupils will resort to ingenious interpretations. If a law is too general, litigations will multiply. Just as a wise man, when he writes a book, will set forth his arguments fully and clearly, so an enlightened ruler, when he makes his laws, will see to it that every contingency is provided for in detail." [40]

Confucians look to the ancient Sage-Emperors for models of rulership. But Shang Yang says, "Former generations did not follow the same doctrines, so which antiquity should we imitate? The emperors and kings did not copy one another, so what moral system can one follow?" [41]

Confucians lay greatest emphasis on the study of the *Odes* and the *History* and on the practice of moral virtues. These are all found in Shang Yang's list of "Pests," which includes "ceremony and music, *Odes* and *History*, care for old age, the cultivation of goodness, filial piety and fraternal affection, sincerity and good faith, purity and integrity, humanity and justice." [42]

Confucians have unbounded faith in the persuasive power of moral teachings and example. But Han Fei Tzu says:

Now take the case of a boy of bad character. His parents are angry with him, but he never changes. The villagers in the neighborhood reprove him, but he is not moved. His masters teach him, but he never reforms. . . . It is not until the district magistrate sends out police forces to search for wicked men in accordance with the law of the state that he becomes afraid and changes his ways and alters his deeds. So the love of parents is not sufficient to educate children. It takes the severe penalties of the district magistrate to accomplish what love cannot. This is because people are naturally spoiled by love and are obedient to authority.[43]

In deciding cases, Confucians would apply the spirit of the law, while the Legalists would adhere strictly to the letter. Han Fei Tzu relates approvingly an anecdote which seems typical of the Legalist position. "Marquis Chao of Han [reigned 509–495 B.C.] was drunk and fell into a nap. The crown-keeper, seeing the ruler exposed to cold, put a coat over him. When the Marquis awoke, he felt pleased. Afterward, however, he inquired of the attendants, 'Who put the coat on me?' 'The crown-keeper,' they answered. Thereupon the Marquis found both the coat-keeper and the crown-keeper guilty; the coat-keeper, because he neglected his duty, the crown-keeper, because he exceeded his office." Han Fei Tzu's comment on the case is interesting: "This was not because the Marquis did not mind catching cold, but because he considered trespassing upon the duties of another's office a more serious evil than his catching cold." [44] Confucians would have condemned this decision as repugnant to the natural dictates of the human heart. In fact, Confucius had said, "If morals and music are not promoted, penal laws will miss the just medium, and . . . the people will not know where to put their hands and feet." [45] The Marquis' decision is a good illustration of this point.

Confucians consider the family as the foundation of society. An unfilial son cannot be expected to become a loyal citizen. For the state to destroy the family is, therefore, suicidal, for it would be undermining its own foundations. That is why Confucius disapproved of the "straightforwardness" or uprightness of that son who stood forth to bear testimony to his father's theft of a sheep.[46] For him, true justice demands that the father and the son should shield each other's guilt. This philosophy is too much for the Legalists. Han Fei Tzu says:

In the State of Ch'u there was a certain upright man who, when his father had stolen a sheep, reported him to the law officer. The authorities said, "The son should be put to death." The reason was that, although the son was upright toward the prince, he was crooked toward the father, and therefore he should be charged with the father's guilt. Thus a dutiful subject of the prince becomes an unfilial son of his father.[47]

Confucians place the virtues of humanity and justice above all considerations of utility. Legalists base their whole system upon the "calculating minds" of the average people,[48] who would weigh in a sensible manner the pains and pleasures involved in the choice of a course of action and see the overwhelming advantage of obeying the laws. They would not expect even the ruler to be above average in virtue and in intelligence. An average ruler who is willing to let the law rule will accomplish more than a specially gifted ruler trying to do without specific rules of law.

All these antinomies may be reduced to a single issue, namely, whether the business of government depends upon good men or upon effective laws. The Confucian Hsün Tzu (fl. 298–238 B.C.) goes to the extent of saying that only the right men, not the right laws, can produce and maintain a good government.[49] Mencius is much more moderate. He says, "Goodness alone is not capable of governing; laws alone do not enforce themselves." [50] For him, therefore, it takes both the right kind of men and the right kind of laws to produce the right kind of government. His views are similar to those of William Penn, who, in his preface to *The Great Law*, writes, "Though good laws do well, good men do better; for good laws may want good men and be abolished or evaded by ill men; but good men will never want good laws nor suffer ill ones." Legalists, on the other hand, maintain that any government that depends in any way upon the existence of good men cannot be a good government, for the simple reason that it would be precarious, seeing that the existence of good men is a contingency and not a certainty. What they wished to produce was a system of laws built solidly upon the psychology of average rulers and average people, a system under which it would not pay anybody high or low to set the laws at defiance. They had such a narrow and mean conception of human nature that they thought that in order to produce an effective system of law only two motives needed to be reckoned with, namely, fear and profit. They ignored the facts that even terrorism and the inducement of reward have their limits, and that when men are dehumanized nobody is safe and secure. It is no accident that all the leading Legalists, Shang Yang, Han Fei, and Li Ssu (d. 208 B.C.) ended their lives tragically. It is to their credit that they saw the necessity of the Reign of Law; but they did a great disservice to the Reign of Law by conceiving it too narrowly and by attempting to build it upon force alone, and not upon justice, good faith, and the natural dictates of humanity. It was from Hsün Tzu that Han Fei and Li Ssu learned that human nature is evil. But Hsün Tzu's idea was that, since men are by nature evil, they should be made good by moral discipline. His Legalist pupils drew different conclusions from the same premise. They held that, since men are by nature evil, they should be taken for what they are and dealt with on that basis. They could see only two sanctions for law, force and profit, force to deter and profit to induce.

Hsün Tzu is at least partly responsible for the blunders of his disciples. In advocating the evil of human nature, he actually dug the grave for Confucian humanism and paved the way for the Legalist uprooting of humanity. He tried to demolish the doctrines of Mencius without understanding them. When Mencius said that human nature is good, he meant the *essential* nature of man is good, that nature which distinguishes man from the other animals. Hsün Tzu, on the other hand, was looking at men as they actually are. But, even then, he should have noted certain good qualities and tendencies along with the evil ones. In saying that men are by nature evil, and that all the good comes only from the teachings of the sages, he actually makes the sages rise above humanity, so that they become superhuman beings. Of all the Confucians, Hsün Tzu is the most superficial, but his influence was great upon the Legalists.

If the Legalists had been more moderate and less intolerant of other schools of thought, they would have succeeded in establishing a stable Rule of Law, comparable to what the Common Law countries have achieved. As it is, they ruined their cause by wedding the Rule of Law to a radically positivistic and materialistic point of view, and by identifying the concept of law exclusively with the positive statutes of the State. Their exclusion of the Natural Law element from the conception of law led to the Han scholars' exaggerated claims for Natural Law.[51]

Taking the tragic failure of the Legalists as a warning, the Han rulers and scholars worked out a penal system in which the polarity of law and morality is embodied, with morality as the positive element and law as the negative element. The result was a legalization of morality. They adopted from Confucianism the substance of moral duties, and at the same time adopted from the Legalists the procedure of enforcing them. The Emperor became the Pope and the Monarch combined in one person. If we can imagine a Church with police forces to enforce its precepts and to punish infractions, we can approximate the actual system under which the Chinese people lived for almost two thousand years, until it collapsed in the Revolution of 1911.[52]

But the Revolution was not entirely unprepared for by the revival of the philosophy of Mencius and of some later Confucians such as Huan Tsung-hsi (1610–1695), whose political treatise, *Ming-i tai-fang lu*,[52a] seems to sum up all that is best in the traditional political thought of China. It contains, among other things, essays on the Prince, on Ministership, and on Law. The essay on law is particularly valuable as a contribution to Chinese legal philosophy. It starts with a bold statement: "Until the end of the Three Dynasties [Hsia, Shang, and Chou, 2183–256 B.C.] there was law. Since the Three Dynasties there has been no law." The reason for this astonishing statement is that the Sage-Emperors of old made the laws entirely with the common good in mind; while the later kings made their laws mainly for preserving the Throne. The whole essay is worth serious study, but here I must content myself with one passage:

The law of the Three Dynasties safeguarded the world for the people. The prince did not monopolize all the wealth of the land nor did he jealously keep the right to punish and reward out of the people's hands. Position at court was not particularly considered an honor; to live an obscure life in the country was not particularly a disgrace. Later, this kind of law was criticized for its looseness, but at that time the people were not envious of those in high place, nor did they despise humble status. The looser the law was, the fewer the disturbances which arose. It was what we might call "Law without laws." The laws of later times safeguard the world as if it were something in the [prince's] treasure chest. It is not desired that anything beneficial should be left to the lowly, but, rather, that all blessings be reserved for the one on high. If the prince employs a man, he is immediately afraid that the man will act in his own interest, and so another man is employed to keep a check on the first one. If one measure is adopted, there are immediate fears of its being abused or evaded, and so another measure must be adopted to guard against abuses or evasions. All men know where the treasure chest lies, and the prince is constantly fretting and fidgeting out of anxiety for the security of the treasure. Consequently, the laws have to be made more comprehensive and detailed, and, as they become more detailed, they become the very source of disorder. These are what we might call "unlawful laws." [53]

I should like to point out that, although Huang Tsung-hsi was a Confucian, his was a Confucianism which had been "baptized" by the spirit of Taoism, with its emphasis on the cultivation of non-attachment and selflessness. If the Han scholars had wedded their Confucianism to Taoism, instead of placing it in the framework of the Yin-Yang philosophy and concentrating their efforts on the institution of court ceremonies, if they had seen eye-to-eye with Ssu-ma T'an (d. 110 B.C.) in his appraisal of the relative merits of the schools, both ethics and jurisprudence would have found a freer course of development in later generations.[54] As it is, law and morality have been identified with the *yin* and *yang* phases of one and the same process of government, and neither of them has been able to transcend the half-mythical and half-human cosmogony. By moralizing the external universe, this cosmogony has irrationalized the interior world of the spirit. Instead of achieving a true synthesis of the two by transcending both, what the Han and later Confucians have left us is a promiscuous blending of man and Nature. Nature is the macrocosm, while man is the microcosm, and so is everything human. Running through all is the polarity of *yin* and *yang*. This philosophy underlies the typically Chinese view of the relation between law and morals, as articulated in a commentary on the *Code of T'ang* (*T'ang-lü shu-i*): "Virtue and morals are the foundation of government and education, while laws and punishments are the operative agencies of government and education. Both the former and the latter are necessary complements to each other, just as it takes morning and evening to form a whole day, and spring and autumn to form a whole year." [55]

III. Harmony As the Goal of Human Society

I do not believe, with the German jurists of the historical school, that each nation has a soul of its own called the *"Volks-seele."* But I do believe that every nation has a way of living and thinking which is more or less peculiar to it, constituting, as it were, its distinctive spirit. This spirit permeates all the main channels of its activities, such as law, politics, social economy, literature, social etiquette, and even athletics. For instance, the American way of life is marked by the spirit of democracy and fair play. The spirit may not be fully realized in actual practice, but that makes no difference, so long as it is persistently there, ready to assert itself whenever it can and to the extent it can. The sense of fair play is the spirit of America. It says, "Every dog has his day, and every man his say."

China, too, has her spirit, formed long before the days of Confucius. The most deep-rooted desire of the Chinese people is for harmony. Whether they are speaking of self-cultivation or dealing with the affairs of the world, harmony is the keynote of all their thinking. In the practice of virtue, they aim at the harmony of body and soul. In the family, they aim at the harmony of husband and wife and of the brothers and sisters. In the village, they aim at the harmony of neighbors. Even the Golden Rule of Confucius and his principle of reciprocity are little more than an expression of the spirit of harmony. When Confucius says that in a country what is really to be worried about is not the scarcity of goods but the lack of proportion in their distribution, he is aiming at socio-economic harmony. When he says that in hearing litigations he is no better than other people, but that the important thing is to cause litigations to cease, it is very plain that he prefers social harmony, which would prevent any conflicts of interest from arising, to a just resolution of actual conflicts. *The Book of Changes* contains a hexagram called "*Sung*," [56] meaning litigation, contention, and controversy. The explanation is significant: "*Sung* intimates that, although there is sincerity and justice in one's contention, he will yet meet with opposition and frustration. If he cherish an apprehensive caution, the outcome will be auspicious; but, if he prosecutes the ligitation to the end, there will be evil." In summarizing the comments of Confucian scholars on this hexagram, Richard Wilhelm writes, "If a man is entangled in a conflict, his only salvation lies in being so clear-headed and inwardly strong that he is always ready to come to terms by meeting the opponent halfway. To carry the conflict to the bitter end has evil effects even when one is in the right, because the enmity is then perpetuated." [57] This represents the typical Chinese attitude toward lawsuits. How different in spirit from Rudolf von Jhering's fiery doctrine of the struggle for law and his advice: "Bring suit, cost what it may!" [58]

For better or for worse, the fact is that practically all the Chinese sages are more or less of the mind of Lao Tzu, who says, "The man of virtue attends to his duties; while a man of no virtue attends to his rights." [59] Real strength of character reveals itself in self-conquest, not in the conquering of another.

In the earliest extant literature of China, we note the Chinese predilection for peace and harmony. I need only to quote the beginning paragraph of *The Book of History*, giving a characterization of Emperor Yao of antiquity in these terms: "He was reverent, enlightened, refined, and mild. He was most courteous and capable of yielding. . . . By spreading the splendor of his noble virtues, he made affectionate the nine branches of the family. When harmony reigned among the nine branches of the family, he adjusted peacefully the relations of the hundred families. When the hundred families were well regulated, the myriad states were harmonized, and universal order and concord prevailed among all the people." [60] This may have been a myth, but a myth is a very real thing in the life of a nation. It reveals basic evaluations.

It is indeed remarkable that in the very first cabinet recorded in Chinese history there was included a Minister of Music, K'uei, whom Emperor Shun charged with the duty of teaching music to the eldest sons of the leading families so as to make them "upright and yet mild, big-hearted and yet circumspect, strong without being violent, simple and free in manners without being arrogant." [61]

In other words, the emperor wished the musical master to infuse into the hearts of future leaders the spirit of harmony.

But, although the idea of harmony is richer than the idea of justice, it nevertheless includes justice. At any rate, lack of justice bespeaks lack of harmony. In fact, injustice was considered the surest way of breaking the harmony of the universe and thereby calling down calamities from Heaven. For instance, a poet complained of the injustice of King Yu (reigned 781–771 B.C.) of Chou (1111–256 B.C.) as follows:

> *Lands owned by your people*
> *You have occupied by force.*
> *Men that belong to the lords*
> *You have robbed from their hands.*
> *This one should be declared innocent,*
> *Yet you have put him in jail.*
> *That one should be found guilty,*
> *Yet you have shown favors to him.*[62]

This is one form of injustice that disturbs the harmony of the universe. Another form consists in the lack of proportion in the distribution of burdens and benefits among the people, as is graphically described in the following verses:

Some people live comfortably at home:
Others wear themselves out in public service.
Some lie supinely in bed:
Others are always on the move.

Some never hear a clamorous sound:
Others are never relieved of toil and moil.
Some enjoy the pleasures of leisure:
Others chafe under the load of the king's business.

Some feast and drink in carefree joy:
Others live in constant dread of blame.
Some do nothing but talk and find fault:
Others are doomed to do all things.[63]

Occasionally, a poet would sing the praise of a just man:

Among the people goes the saying:
"Eat the soft, throw out the hard."
It is not so with the Venerable Chung-shan,
Who eats not the soft nor spares the hard.
For he had no fear of the powerful great;
Nor lorded it over the lonely and poor.[64]

The Chinese think of justice and harmony dynamically. The empty is to be filled, and the full is to be diminished. The low is to be exalted, while the high is to be leveled down. In the words of Lao Tzu, "To be great is to go far, and to go far is to return." [65] Many modern thinkers of China are returning to the ancient ideal of the Grand Harmony, as presented in *The Book of Rites:*

When the Great Way prevailed in the world, all mankind worked for the common good. Men of virtue and ability were elected to fill public offices. Good faith was universally observed and friendly relations cultivated. People's love was not confined to their own parents and their own children, so that all the aged ones were enabled to live out the natural span of their lives, all the young ones were brought up in the proper way, all the widows and widowers, the orphans and childless persons, the crippled and the sick, were well taken care of. Each man had a definite work to do, and each woman a home of her own. The people were loath to let the natural resources lie undeveloped in the earth; but they did not desire to hoard riches in their own houses. They were ashamed to be idle; but they did not labor for their own profit. In this way, the source of all greed was stopped up, and there was no occasion for the rise of theft and banditry, nor was there any need to lock the outer door of one's house. This is called the Age of Grand Harmony.[66]

Neither Confucius nor Mencius was an impractical visionary. They realized very well that, although cultural and spiritual life is of infinitely greater value than physical life, yet the latter must first be taken care of before the people could be expected to devote time and energy to self-cultivation. Confucius once entered a populous city, and uttered a spontaneous exclamation, "Oh, what a population!" A disciple asked him, "Given a multitude of people, what next?" He said, "Enrich them!" "After enriching them, what next?" He said, "Teach them!" [67] This, roughly, represents his program.

Mencius is even more explicit and emphatic on the importance of securing for all the people a regular livelihood. He pointed out that only scholars will be able to adhere unswervingly to the path of virtue even in the absence of economic security. As for the rank and file of the people, their hearts cannot be fixed on goodness as long as their livelihood is not secure. Therefore he proceeds to say,

. . . an intelligent ruler will regulate the livelihood of the people, so as to make sure that, above, they shall have sufficient wherewithal to serve their parents, and, below, sufficient wherewithal to support their wives and children; that in good years they shall always be abundantly satisfied, and that in bad years they shall not be in danger of perishing. After this, he may urge them, and they will proceed to what is good, for in this case the people will follow after that with readiness.[68]

It is only upon this condition that the Confucians set forth their truly thoroughgoing program of the moral reformation of the world with one's own moral transformation as the starting point. Let me quote the opening passage of *The Great Learning*, which seems to me to belong to the perennial philosophy and to contain a message for the modern world:

The goal of Great Learning consists in the elucidation of Bright Virtue, in renewing the spirit of the people, and in resting in the Supreme Goodness. When a man knows where to rest, his heart is fixed; when the heart is fixed he can really be quiet; when he is quiet, he can enjoy peace; when he enjoys peace he can think for himself; when he thinks for himself he can attain true insights. Things have their root and their branches. Affairs have their end and their beginning. To know what is first and what follows after is to be near to the attainment of Truth.

The ancients who wished to spread the knowledge of Bright Virtue to the world, first ordered well their own states. Wishing to order well their own states, they first regulated their families. Wishing to regulate their families, they first cultivated their persons. Wishing to cultivate their persons, they first rectified their hearts. Wishing to rectify their hearts, they first sought to be sincere in their thoughts. Wishing to be sincere in their thoughts, they sought after true knowledge. The attainment of knowledge depends upon the investigation of the nature of things and relationships.[69]

To put it the other way around, the investigation of the nature of things and relationships leads to true knowledge, which leads to sincerity in thought, which leads to purity of heart, which prepares for the perfection of the whole person, which conduces to an orderly family, which helps to make a well-governed state, which contributes toward the peace of the entire world. In fact, the whole process is a continuous harmonious movement from the innermost harmony to the outermost harmony. For the investigation of things and knowledge represent the harmony of subject and object; sincerity in thought and purity of heart represent the harmony of intellect and will; personal perfection represents the harmony of body and soul; while the orderly family, the well-governed state, and the peaceful world form a progressive series of concentric expansions of transpersonal harmony.

Although in ancient China the "world" designated no more than the whole of the then-known empire, this does not prevent modern Chinese thinkers from extending their mental horizons *pari passu* with the growth of the actual horizons of the world. Thus, Chinese ideology envisages an open society rather than a closed one. Nor does it consider the authority of the state in terms of absolute sovereignty. The family and the state are but stations, albeit necessary stations, to a harmonious world. When the head of the Chinese delegation to the United Nations Conference in San Francisco said, "If there is any message that my country . . . wishes to give to this Conference, it is that we are prepared . . . to yield if necessary a part of our sovereignty to the new international organization in the interest of collective security," he was but voicing the traditional spirit of China, the idea of universal harmony.

The Chinese idea of harmony comprehends not only unity but utmost diversity. It is something cosmic. Let me borrow a magnificent description of it from Chuang Tzu (399–295? B.C.). "The breath of the universe is called wind. At times, it is inactive. But, when active, every aperture resounds to the blast. . . . Caves and dells of hill and forest, hollows in huge trees of many a span in girth; these are like nostrils, like mouths, like ears, like beam-sockets, like goblets, like mortars, like ditches, like bogs. And the wind goes rushing through them, sniffing, snoring, singing, soughing, puffing, purling, whistling, whirring, now shrilly treble, now deeply bass, now soft, now loud, until, with a lull, silence reigns supreme. . . . The effect of the wind upon these various apertures is not uniform. But what is it that gives to each the individuality, to all the potentiality, of sound? Great knowledge embraces the whole: small knowledge, a part only. Great speech is universal: small speech is particular." [70]

The interesting point is that it is precisely thanks to the utmost oneness and impartial universality of the breath of the universe that all the diversities of sound are given the fullest expression. It is only when a particular part in the human world claims to be the universal whole that disharmony appears on the scene of history, disfiguring even the cosmic harmony. But cosmic harmony cannot be disturbed for long without avenging itself by disharmonizing the disharmony, until the original harmony is restored.

Chinese historians conceive of the process of history as consisting in an unending series of cycles of ups and downs. They take the moon as a symbol of human affairs with its unceasing successions of waxing and waning. The sages have drawn from this *Weltanschauung* some wisdom of life peculiarly Chinese. We are not to be elated when the winds are with us, nor are we to despair when the winds are against us. But we are tempted to fold our arms and hide our heads during the stormy days, in the confidence that by virtue of the cosmic dialectic the storm will soon blow over. Fatalism is our besetting sin.

I cannot help thinking that the Chinese conception of harmony is not entirely adequate. We are inclined to think of it too exclusively in terms of concord or a succession of concords. Whenever there is a discord, our harmony is disrupted. In other words, we seldom if ever think of a discord as an opportunity for rising to a new concord. The West is more adept in the art of resolution of discord, thus continuing the harmony through the discordant interval. When confronted with such a discordant interval, the Chinese too often feel utterly at a loss as to what to do except to wait patiently for the turning of the tide, and, when patience is exhausted, to burst out in uncontrollable passion and emotion. We have much to learn from the West in the way of resolution of discord. On the other hand, the West should remember that the discordant intervals are, after all, not the norm and that we cannot rest in restlessness.

The present crisis of the world in general and of China in particular calls for a revival of faith in the super-eminent justice and humanity of God as against the belief in the stars and the blind operations of dialectical materialism. No astral destiny or dialectical process can decide the fate of a nation and of mankind. In Western history, as Mircea Eliade has pointed out in his *Cosmos and History: The Myth of the Eternal Return,* "Christian thought tended to transcend, once and for all, the old themes of eternal repetition, just as it had undertaken to transcend all the other archaic viewpoints by revealing the importance of the religious experience of faith and that of the value of the human personality." [71] It is submitted that Confucian humanism, before it had degenerated into a kind of anthropomorphic cosmogony by being wedded to the philosophy of Yin-Yang and the mechanical alternation of the Five Elements (metal, wood, water, fire, earth), comes very near to Christian thought in its rational conception of the Mandate of Heaven and in its emphasis on the value of the human person.

In conclusion, I should like to call your attention to one more contrast between the East and the West. The East generally puts the Golden Age at the beginning, the West at the end. The East is Epimethean, while the West is Promethean. It makes little or no difference whether one looks backward or forward, so long as one looks far enough, for, ultimately, the alpha and the omega are absolutely one.

QUESTION: There is some agreement that "mediational law," in which cognizance is taken of the unique factors of a situation, has been paramount in China (through Ch'ing times, 1644–1912). Such "law" seems to contrast with the law of the Ch'ing written penal code, in which comparatively less concern is paid to the unique factors pertaining to the individual's commission of an act even than in many Western codes. For example, the fact that an act was accidentally caused is often of small matter in regard to legal guilt, and there is frequent legal guilt by mere implication. The fact that there was an act, plus its consequences, seems to be more the center of focus.

Do you feel that such a contrast (exceeding the normal one

between "mediational law" and determinate written rules) actually existed? If so, how do you reconcile the two interpretations? Is it that the written code embodies the strict focus on commission of the act of the legalist tradition, while the Confucian tradition of applying the spirit of the law is embodied in "mediational law"?

ANSWER: Strictly speaking, so-called "mediational law" is not law, but merely a certain attitude on the part of the Confucian magistrates in the administration of justice, especially in cases involving family relations.

It is not quite true to say that in the old penal system even an accidental act, that is, an act which is neither intentional nor negligent, could constitute the basis of criminal responsibility. In fact, from the earliest classics, it is clear that the greatest emphasis was laid on the presence of intention as the most essential element of a crime. Two basic legal maxims stand out prominently in *The Book of History:* (1) "An intentional act should be punished, however small the injury: but an unintended mishap should be excused, however great the harm." (2) "Better miss the guilty than slay an innocent person."

In all the penal codes of the different dynasties, the distinctions between intentional wrong, negligence, and pure accident are carefully preserved.

Mediation came into play when no grave wrongs were involved and the litigation concerned property rights between members of a family or between neighbors. Only in such cases would a magistrate advise the parties to forget about their rights and wrongs and to reach an amicable settlement.

Notes

1. *Shu ching (The Book of History)* has been translated into several European languages. The passages quoted in this paper are my own rendering, but I have consulted the translations of Legge, Couvreur, Old, and Karlgren.
2. T'ang was the founder of the Shang Dynasty (1751–1112 B.C.).
3. See "The Oath of T'ang" in *The Book of History.*
4. See *Chung-hui chih kao* (The Counsels of Chung-hui), *ibid.*
5. See *The Book of Mencius,* IB.5.
6. King Wu ascended the throne in 1121 B.C.
7. See "The Grand Oath" of King Wu, second part, in *The Book of*

History. It may be of interest to note that these words were quoted by Mencius.

8. *Book of Mencius,* IB.2. For a general discussion of Mencius' political and legal philosophy and its metaphysical foundations, see John C. H. Wu, "Mencius' Philosophy of Human Nature and Natural Law," *Chinese Culture Quarterly,* I, No. 1 (July, 1957), 1–19.

9. *Tao-te ching,* XIII.

10. *Ibid.,* LXXVIII.

11. See "The Songs of Five Brothers," in *The Book of History.* The translation is by Herbert Giles; see Giles, *History of Chinese Literature* (New York: D. Appleton & Co., 1931), p. 9.

12. *Tao-te ching,* XXXIX.

13. Kao Yao was the chief judicial officer under Emperor Shun, who reigned, probably, in the twenty-third century B.C.

14. This song of Kao Yao is found in "The Counsels of I and Chi," in *The Book of History.*

15. *Lun yü (The Analects),* XV.4.

16. *Ibid.,* VIII.18.

17. In ascetic life Lao Tzu advocated extreme renunciation of sensual enjoyment, while Confucius preached only moderation and propriety.

18. According to Hu Shih, in China the appeals to the Higher Law or Natural Law have taken five different forms: (1) the authority of the ancient sage-rulers, (2) the Will of Heaven or God, as with Mo Tzu, (3) the Way of Heaven, as with Lao Tzu, (4) the Canon of the Sacred Scriptures, as with the Han Confucians, and (5) Universal Reason or Natural Law, as with the Sung (960–1279) and Ming (1368–1644) Confucians. See Hu Shih, "The Natural Law in the Chinese Tradition," *Natural Law Institute Proceedings,* V (1951), 199–153. If we add to these five Mencius' view of human nature as instituted by Heaven and its fundamental tendencies as the basis of Natural Law, the list would be complete. See Paul K. T. Sih, "The Natural Law Philosophy of Mencius," *New Scholasticism,* XXXI, No. 3 (1957), 317–337.

19. *Analects,* XIII.25.

20. *Tao-te ching,* XXXVI.

21. "The King's Speech to Chün-ch'en," in *The Book of History.* Chün-ch'en was appointed by King Ch'eng (who ascended the throne in 1115 B.C.) to govern Hsia-tu, which was a colony of people of the superseded dynasty.

22. *Analects,* XX.2.

23. Lao Tzu seems to have had the same thing in mind when he declared: "The Sage-Ruler has no heart of his own: he takes the heart of the people for his heart." *Tao-te ching,* XLIX.

24. This stanza is quoted in *The Book of Mencius,* VIA.3.

25. See Y. P. Mei, trans., *The Works of Motse* (London: Arthur

Probsthain, 1929). In his *Chinese Political Philosophy* (London: K. Paul, Trench, Trübner & Co., Ltd.; New York: Harcourt-Brace and Company, 1930), p. 105, Liang Ch'i Ch'ao (1873–1929), while highly critical of Mo Tzu for his condemnation of music, expresses his admiration for him in these terms: "Nevertheless no one can deny the fact that Motse attained spirituality in an extraordinary degree. To do this, he suppressed his material life to the point of zero. For depth of sympathy, for vigour of altruism, and for the richness of the spirit of self-sacrifice there is none like him, save Christ, in the whole world."

26. *Tao-te ching*, XLIX.
27. *Ibid.*, LXXVII.
28. Y. P. Mei, trans., *The Works of Motse*, p. 152.
29. For an English translation of the whole passage, see John C. H. Wu, *Cases and Materials on Jurisprudence* (St. Paul: West Publishing Co., 1958), p. 159.
30. *Ibid.*, p. 160.
31. As Wigmore puts it, the reason for this is that "if a rule has become so settled and obvious that it has arrived at a place in the code, it *ought* morally to be obeyed by all; and the few who may resist must naturally be coerced by a penalty; they merit it." Quoted in John C. H. Wu, *The Art of Law* (Shanghai: Commercial Press, 1936), pp. 47–48.
32. *Analects*, XII.16.
33. *Ibid.*, XII.17.
34. *Ibid.*, II.3.
35. *Book of Lord Shang*, VII.
36. *Ibid.*, XXIV.
37. *Book of Mencius*, VIA.2.
38. *Book of Lord Shang*, XXIII.
39. The idea is that to have a tariff of penalties might relativize the notion of right and wrong, and might lead the people to think as though the government were setting forth definite prices for the privilege of committing certain crimes, thus giving rise to a commercial spirit.
40. *Han Fei Tzu*, XLIX.
41. *Book of Lord Shang*, I.
42. *Ibid.*, XIII.
43. *Han Fei Tzu*, XLIX.
44. *Ibid.*, VII.
45. *Analects*, XIII.2.
46. *Ibid.*, XIII.12.
47. *Han Fei Tzu*, XLIX.
48. *Ibid.*, XLVI.
49. *Hsün Tzu*, XII.

50. *Book of Mencius*, IIIA.1.
51. Even occasional sayings of Confucius came to be regarded as precepts of Natural Law by the Han (206 B.C.–A.D. 220) scholars.
52. For a more detailed account of the history of legal thought in China, see John C. H. Wu, "Chinese Legal Philosophy," *Chinese Culture Quarterly*, I, No. 4 (April, 1958), 7–48.
52a. That is, a treatise on government for use by future rulers.
53. I am using here a translation in Wm. Theodore de Bary, Wing-tsit Chan, and Burton Watson, eds., *Sources of Chinese Tradition* (New York: Columbia University Press, 1960), pp. 591–592.
54. For a translation of Ssu-ma T'an's discussion of the essentials of the Six Schools, see Burton Watson, *Ssu-ma Ch'ien: Grand Historian of China* (New York: Columbia University Press, 1958), pp. 43–48.
55. *Code of T'ang with Commentaries and Annotations*, reprinted in Peking in 1890, Vol. II, p. 14.
56. See Carl F. Baynes, trans., *The I ching, or Book of Changes*. The Richard Wilhelm translation rendered into English by Carl F. Baynes. Foreword by C. G. Jung. Bollingen Series, IX. 2 vols. (New York: Pantheon Books, 1950), Vol. I, pp. 28–32; II, pp. 51–56.
57. *Ibid.*, I, p. 29.
58. Rudolf von Jhering, *The Struggle for Law* (Chicago: Callaghan & Company, 1915), p. 26.
59. *Tao-te ching*, LXXVIII.
60. See "Canon of Yao."
61. See "Canon of Shun."
62. *Book of Odes*, ode no. 264.
63. *Ibid.*, no. 205.
64. *Ibid.*, no. 260.
65. *Tao-te ching*, XXV.
66. See "Evolution of Rites" in *The Book of Rites*. For a modern interpretation, see L. G. Thompson, *Ta T'ung Shu: The One-World Philosophy of K'ang Yu-wei* (London: George Allen & Unwin Ltd., 1958).
67. *Analects*, XIII.7.
68. *Book of Mencius*, IA.5.
69. For another translation, see E. R. Hughes, *The Great Learning and the Mean-in-Action* (New York: E. P. Dutton & Co., 1943), pp. 146 ff.
70. Herbert Giles, *Chuang Tzu* (Shanghai: Kelly and Walsh, 1926), pp. 12–13.
71. Mircea Eliade, *Cosmos and History: The Myth of the Eternal Return* (New York: Harper and Brothers, 1959), p. 137.

THOMÉ H. FANG   *The World and*
the Individual in Chinese Metaphysics *

I

THE TRENDS of Chinese metaphysical thought, taken in its entire
range, may be roughly likened to the bar-lines across the stave.
At regular or irregular intervals, different modes of speculation are
marked out in bars, each running in compound triple time with
beats in varying accentuation. From time immemorial to the middle of the twelfth century B.C., the metaphysical moods would be
the chords sounded in the triads of myth, religion, and poetry.
Thenceforward, until 246 B.C., for a creative period of more than
nine hundred years, there came to be the articulation of primordial
Taoism, Confucianism, and Moism. This period was followed by a
long epoch (246 B.C.–A.D. 960) of fermentation and absorbent
creation, tending to bring forth eventually a type of highly creative
speculation in Chinese Mahāyānic Buddhism. From A.D. 960 down
to the present day, we have had a re-awakening of metaphysical
originality in the form of Neo-Confucianism somewhat imbued
with the spirit of Taoism and Buddhism. In this period of
regeneration, there have come into prominence three trends of
metaphysics: (a) Neo-Confucianism of the realistic type; (b) Neo-
Confucianism of the idealistic type; and (c) Neo-Confucianism of
the naturalistic type.

* In this paper, except in some of the notes, the author's capitalization, in
the large, has been retained, despite some inconsistencies.

II

Let us now proceed with a discussion of the three major systems of Chinese metaphysics in successive order.

Two important features may be discerned in the metaphysical system of Confucianism. The first asserts the creative power of the heavenly *Tao*, whereby the dynamic world of all beings comes into existence; the second emphasizes the intrinsic value of human nature in congruence with the cosmic order. These two, together, constitute the architectonic structure of Confucianism from classical antiquity to the present day. The most important embodiment of this mode of thought is found in *The Book of Change* to be supplemented by *The Book of Mencius* and *The Works of Hsün Tzu*, which, apart from re-enforcing a set of original metaphysical ideas, elucidate the cardinal doctrine of a philosophical anthropology.[1]

The Book of Change is a formidable historical document. There are involved in it (1) a very complicated stratified historical frame, (2) a complete system of symbolic constructions based upon strict rules of logic, and (3) a set of interpretations making out the meanings of these symbolic constructions, expressible in the systematic syntax of language. All these three are the prelude to a theory of time conducive to the working out of a set of metaphysical principles explanatory of the cosmic order.

The revolutionary philosophy of change, initiated by Confucius (551–479 B.C.) himself and, upon the evidences [2] of Ssu-ma T'an and Ssu-ma Ch'ien further elaborated by Shang Chü (b. 522 B.C.) and others, was a long evolutionary product. Its new features might be diversified into four different forms: (1) A new philosophy of enlivened Nature permeated with the dynamic confluence of Life. Nature is power, or vital impetus, creative in advance and conducive to the fulfillment and consummation of Life capable of being partaken of by all beings.[3] (2) An exposition of intrinsic moral goodness in human life adorned with beauty. Such a moral-aesthetic perfection was characteristic of the unique human personality.[4] (3) A general theory of value in the form of the Supreme Good assimilating into it all the relative ranks of values prevalent in the entire universe.[5] (4) The final formulation of a value-centric ontology asserting the fullness of Being in its entirety.

The archetypal time-man, represented by the Confucians, deliberately chooses to cast everything—whether it be the life of

Nature, the development of an individual, the frame of society, the achievement of value, the attainment to the fullness of Being—into the mold of time in the order of its authentic existence.

The question is, What is time? [6] The essence of time consists in change; the order of time proceeds with concatenation; the efficacy of time abides by durance. The rhythmic process of epochal change is wheeling round into infinitude and perpetually dovetailing the old and the new so as to issue into interpenetration which is continuant duration in creative advance. This is the way in which time generates itself by its systematic entry into a pervasive unity which constitutes the rational order of creative creativity. The dynamic sequence of time, ridding itself of the perished past and coming by the new into present existence, really gains something over a loss. So, the change in time is but a step to approaching eternity, which is perennial durance, whereby, before the bygone is ended, the forefront of the succeeding has come into presence. And, therefore, there is here a linkage of being projecting itself into the prospect of eternity. Hence, in the nexus of the dynamics of time, "*The Book of Change* contains the measure of Heaven and Earth, enabling us to comprehend the all-pervasive *Tao* and its order." [7]

Based upon the concept of time, three metaphysical principles may be set out.

(1) The principle of extensive connection: Three essentials are involved in its formulation. Logically, it is a system of consistent deduction demonstrated rigorously.[8] Semantically, it is a syntax of language in which the rules of formation and transformation of significant statements indicate unerringly a relation of coordination and a relation of dovetailing and mutual relevance so as to discriminate what is licit from the illicit and to change the latter into the former.[9] Metaphysically, the philosophy of change is a system of dynamic ontology based upon the process of continuant creativity in time, as well as a system of general axiology wherein the origin and development of the idea of the Supreme Good is shown in the light of comprehensive harmony. Thus, the principle of extensive connection asserts at the same time that the confluence of life permeating all beings under Heaven and on Earth partakes of the creative nature of time and achieves, as a consequence, the form of the Supreme Good.

(2) The principle of creative creativity. Confucius in *The*

Book of Change—the philosophical part of it designated as the *chüans*—and his followers in *The Book of Propriety*—including *The Doctrine of the Mean*—diversified the all-pervasive *Tao* [10] into (a) the *Tao* of Heaven as the primordial creative power, giving rise to all creatures, comprehending them in the cosmic order of dynamic transformation conducive to a perfectly harmonious fulfillment, and issuing in the attainment of the Supreme Good; (b) the *Tao* of Earth, which, as the power of procreation, is a continuation and extension of the creative origination, sustaining all forms of existence; and (c) the *Tao* of man, who, with an assured status at the center of the universe, in communion with the creative and procreative power of Heaven and Earth should come to the full awareness of the Spirit and thereby become co-creative agents in the perpetual continuance of Life as a whole. With the Confucians, this spiritual awareness has given rise to a sense of individual moral excellence, a fellow-feeling of the intrinsic worth of other forms of existence, as well as a rational insight into the identifiable unity of the equitable Being of all beings.

(3) The principle of creative life as a process of value-realization. In the "Hsi tz'u" we find a theory set out by Confucius that "what is called *Tao* operates incessantly with the rhythmic modulation of dynamic change and static repose, thus continuing the creative process for the attainment of the Good and completing the creative process for the fulfillment of Nature, which is Life. . . . It manifests itself in the rational sentiment of humanity, but conceals its great function unawares, propelling all beings in a swing of vitality without inciting the anxieties of the holy. Its richness of virtue, its grandeur of enterprise is of all things the most sublime. Superabundance is what is called the deed-act; forevermore creativeness is what is called the supreme value. . . . The unfathomed mystery underlying the rhythmic modulation of the dynamic energy and of peaceful repose is what is called the divine." [11] Elsewhere Confucius said: "Embracing all in its comprehensiveness and investing each with its magnificence, it ensures that anything and everything will enjoy the concordant bliss of well-being." [12] "Of all values, the Good exhibited in the primordially creative-procreative is towering in its supremacy. Concordance in the sport of bliss is the convergence of all that is beautiful. Benediction in the realm of Life is the pervasiveness of all that is righteous. Consummation in the deed-act is the fundamentum of the world of enterprise." [13]

In the light of the above principles, the objective order of the universe is constituted by the superabundant power of creativity in the dynamic process of time. The human individual is thus confronted with a creative world. He must be equally creative in order to fit in with it. And, therefore, the Confucian dynamic value-centric ontology, once completed, evoked a system of philosophical anthropology. It was averred in *The Doctrine of the Mean* that the most truthful and sincere man in all the world, after completely fulfilling his own nature in the course of life, would extend his boundless sympathy by doing the same with other men, as well as with all creatures and things. In doing so, he could participate in the cosmic creation through the process of transformation and thereupon become a *co-creator* with Heaven and Earth.[14]

As the natural and moral order of life was initiated by the creative power of Heaven, so man can cope with the most high in creative potency. In some such way the Confucians developed a homocentric conception of the world as a prelude to the value-centric conception of man. This is why Mencius (372–289 B.C.) maintained that the spiritual stream of a superior man's life was concurrent with that of Heaven and Earth. He went further in asserting that a real man, relying upon his own intrinsic goodness, could, in virtue of his beautiful endowment, develop himself to the utmost into a great man. This greatness of character, enhanced by a subtle touch of spiritual exaltation in the process of transformation, would make him, first, a sage and, finally, a holy man invested with inscrutable magnificence.[15]

Not only Mencius. Even Hsün Tzu (313–238 B.C.), who started with the empirical observation of the ill nature of man, ventured to assert that man through a course of perseverent endeavor of cultivation could come to achieve greatness. Among the primordial Confucians, Hsün Tzu was the only one who seemed to be "fed up" with the value-centric conception of Heaven. Just for this reason, he wanted to set up the supremacy of man apart from unnecessary complication with Nature, which is nothing more than a neutral order [16] with physical energies in store for human utilization. According to Mencius, man, by virtue of his inborn goodness, is spontaneously great. In the opinion of Hsün Tzu, man's greatness is cultured in the best sense of the word. Allowing this difference between them, man is ultimately great just the same.

What, after all, is the rationale of human greatness? In *The*

Book of Propriety [17] compiled by Senior Tai Te, Confucius is reported to have said, in reply to the queries of Duke Ai of Lu, that there are five types of men in a rational linkage of development. Among (1) the common run of men, the individual can be educated to be (2) a learned and enlightened person who, with an insight of knowledge and with sagacity in action, issuing in the noble art of life, will become (3) a superior man, adorned with beauty of character and balance of mind. Through further edification he can come to be (4) a man of excellence. His choices and forsakings are in accord with the high standard of values acceptable to mankind as a whole. He always tries to act in the right without sacrificing the least part of the fundamental principles. His utterance of truth sets a good standard to the world without the loss of his own integrity. Finally, he becomes (5) a sage, or holy man. With perfect wisdom at his command, he acts in congruence with the ways of the great *Tao,* adapting himself to any circumstance of life in the flux of change without confronting any crises of danger or encumbrance. This he does because he thoroughly understands the true nature and disposition of all things. In virtue of such perfect understanding, all his decisions of value are made in accordance with the great function of reason. And, therefore, the achievement of greatness knowingly keeps abreast of Heaven and Earth in creativity. This development of man from the natural capacity to the ideal perfection by way of the function of reason is the Confucian rationale of human greatness. In the light of this rationale man copes with the most high in potency.

All of this leads to the natural conclusion that the world and the individual must always be in reciprocal communion.[18] In such communion, the cosmic status of the individual is firmly established for the reason that the full capacities constitutive of his personality are, now, developed to the utmost.

To the Chinese, the Confucian type of man is near and dear, like an ideal figure who has been cut by his own noble art of life in a set of expanding spheres representing gradually enlarged and qualitatively perfected humane relations, and toward whom all other persons, intimate in spiritual linkage and sympathetic in moral aspirations, are subtly attracted in such a way that there is always an interfusion and interplay of exultation in the influence of exalted personality. This is what makes of the Chinese world and Chinese society a natural domain of moral democracy incessantly leveling up to a higher plane of ethical culture which has sustained the Chinese national state ever since Confucianism came into vogue.

III

But, when we come to a consideration of the Taoists, we are suddenly transferred to a different world—a visionary dream-world. The Taoists make the best type of space man. They are wont to take flights into the realms unfrequented by the common run of people, in which they uplift us, level after level, each more exalted and mysterious than the last. From their vantage point at a height, unafraid, they gaze disinterestedly upon the stratified world below in which the tragi-comic persons are involved in the regressive lapse into folly and wisdom, illusion and truth, appearance and reality, all falling short of supreme Perfection, the Truth, and Reality.

Tao is the supreme category in the system of Lao Tzu (561?–467? B.C.). It may be diversified into four cardinal points.

(1) Ontologically, *Tao* is the infinite ontic substance which was multifariously characterized by Lao Tzu (a) as the fathomless unity of all beings, prior in existence even to God; [19] (b) as the fundamental root of Heaven and Earth, infinite in nature, invisible in shape, but really great in function because all creatures are begotten from it; [20] (c) as the primordial One having ingression into all forms of beings; [21] (d) as the unique pattern of all kinds of activities, discursive but wholesome, twisted around but straight-forward, emptying out but remaining full, worn out but forever renovating, eventually comprehensive of all perfection; [22] (e) as the Great Form, or the receptacular Matrix, wherein all creatures are embraced, free of harm, and full of peace, like babies held close to the bosoms of their mother; [23] and (f) as the final destiny whereto all creatures, after emptying out every kind of "quixotic" energetic activities in the course of life, will return for the ease and peace of rest conceived under the form of eternity and achieved in the spirit of immortality [24]—thus, on the score of eternity, consciously discerned, all come to be complaisant, equitable, noble, natural, and spontaneous, in full accord with the imperishable *Tao*.

(2) Cosmogenetically, the infinitely great *Tao* is the all-pervasive function with an inexhaustible store of powerful energy exerting itself in two different ways. On the one hand, being in-

visibly subsistent up in the transcendental realm of Nothingness and deeply sheathed back in the noumenal realm of unfathomed Mystery, it darts itself out and down into the realm of Being. Thus we can say that in the beginning there was Being, and Being was with Nothingness.[25] Henceforward, the *Tao* is the primordial begetter of all things. On the other hand, the supplied energy, within the bounds of Being, may be spent and exhausted through dispersion and waste. The immanent world of Being, in a state of urgent want, will resort to the transcendental world of *Tao* for a fresh impartation of energy. Hence, Lao Tzu has every reason to lay emphasis upon "the reversal of procedure in the dynamic transformation of *Tao*."

The function of *Tao* is dyadic in track. Progressively, the fundamental Nothingness in *Tao* gives rise to the being of all forms in the world,[26] whereas, regressively, the immanent Being in the whole world depends upon the Nothingness of the transcendental *Tao* for the performance of adequate function. Hence the pronouncement: "The fulfillment of Being leads to eudaemonia, whereas the attainment to Nothingness fulfills the performance of function." [27]

(3) Phenomenologically, the attributes of *Tao* can be classified under two headings, namely, natural attributes and arbitrary attributes. The natural attributes are discerned as so many properties inherent in the *Tao* conceived under the form of eternity. They may be enumerated as follows:

1) Integrity of *Tao* revealing itself as substance in the realm of Nothingness and as function in the realm of Being;
2) Conformation of non-action in which nothing is left undone;
3) The primordial incentive in the begetting of all things with no claim of origination;
4) Accomplishment of work on the cosmic scale with detachment;
5) Sustenance of all things without domination;
6) Creation without possession;
7) Energizing activity with no egocentric claim of merit.

On the contrary, the arbitrary attributes are those which are affirmed from the subjective viewpoint of men and inappropriately portrayed in terms of inadequate human language. Apart from these, the *Tao* conceived *per se* is the really real Reality, or, what is the same thing, the mysteriously mysterious Mystery intelligible only to men of supreme wisdom like the sage.

(4) Characterologically, the supreme excellences, manifested

as the natural attributes, originally pertain to the nature of *Tao* but will come in ingress into the integrity of the sage, who is really the exemplar of the *Tao* in this world. The sage, as an ideal man, has transcended all limitations and weaknesses by reason of his exalted spirit and by virtue of his assessment of ever higher worth. He knows how to gain a world of love and reverence by employing himself generously for the world. Having lived for the benefit of other men, he is richer in worth; having given all he has to other men, he is more plentiful in being. "And, therefore, the sage is always skillful and whole-hearted in the salvation of men, so that there is no deserted man; he is always skillful and whole-hearted in the rescue of things, so that there is no abandoned thing." [28] Thanks to Lao Tzu, we have come to the consciousness that the essence of each individual man, when realized in full, consists in an endeavor to attain to the ideal of the sage. Man's mission is constantly to make a campaign for the realization of this ideal. Thus the "wages" of winning a sure status in the world is his own inward sageliness.

Many perplexities in the system of Lao Tzu came to be cleared away by Chuang Tzu (b. 369 B.C.) in an attempt to push through the nullifying process far back into mystery after mystery, so that there would be no final Nothingness in the serial regress. Similarly, what was posited in the being of Being could be infinitely iterated, back and forth, thus forming a set of endless bilateral processes of progression and retrogression. The original antithesis between Nothing and Being was theoretically reconciled inasmuch as both Being and Nothing should merge into the profound mystery in such a way as to form an interpenetrative system of infinite integral Reality.[29] Finally, Chuang Tzu brought out the chief tenet of Lao Tzu as positing both the eternal Nothing and the eternal Being predominated over by the supreme unity, thus affirming the authentic Reality in the form of vacuity, which would not destroy the reality of all things.[30] For the same reason and in the same sort of way, the discrepancy between eternity and temporality was dissolved.[31]

Chuang Tzu could accomplish so much because, besides being a great Taoist, he was also much influenced by Confucius and Mencius,[32] as well as by his bosom friend, Hui Shih, from the logico-analytical camp. In the philosophy of change, Confucius thought of time as though it had a definite beginning in the past but an indefinite progression into the future. Chuang Tzu, however, accepted the indefinite stretch into the future but denied the definite origination in the past through the agency of creation. This is because he knew how, on the basis of "the reversal of procedure" in the function of *Tao*, to probe mystery after mystery without coming to a standstill in the remote past. Thus, time is literally infinite in respect to the past as well as to the future. Time is a long-enduring natural process of transformation without any beginning and ending. Hence, the Confucian assumption of the primordial power of creation—in fact, all necessity for the cosmic creation—is theoretically extirpated.

Not only is time infinite in span; space, likewise, is infinite in scope. Furthermore, with the metaphysical acumen of his poetic vision, he transformed, by a subtle touch of imagination, the obstructive mathematico-physical space into the infinite "painterly" space as a liberated realm of spiritual exultation whereunto he is to infuse "the wondrous proceeding of the *Tao*" in order that his own exalted "soul" may reach the most sublime for its ultimate acquirement. In a word, the metaphysics of Chuang Tzu is an elaboration of the great *Tao*, projected into the frame of infinite space and time, into a way of exalted spiritual life.

Such is the metaphysical import implied in the story of "A Happy Excursion" described in poetico-metaphorical language. Like the great magic bird, *p'eng*, Chuang Tzu could lift himself up into an intellectual solitude unafraid and exulting insofar as the greatness of his liberated nature would partake of the omnipotent with the support of the infinite *Tao*.

The "most fantastic" story of "A Happy Excursion" has been variously interpreted by different thinkers. The true meaning should be made out in the light of the philosophy of infinity under discussion by following up the clues indicated by Chuang Tzu himself in the context of the relevant chapters.

(1) It is asserted that the supreme man should lead his own spirit up to the primordial in its infinite regress, reposing blissfully in the realm of Nowhere, doing away with all petty knowledge about lowly things and getting entirely free from the bother of their burdens.[33] (2) At the culmination in the realm of perfect truth and in abidance by the fundamentum of the eternal *Tao*, his elevated spirit, being thus estranged from the physical world and disencumbered of all material allurings, would become independent and free from all restraint.[34] (3) Upon entering the gate of infinitude, and having an excursion in the realm of supreme bliss,

he would immerse his unique spirit in the exuberant light of the celestial and lose his identity in the eternal harmony of cosmic order.[35] (4) At the attainment to sagehood, he would abandon himself to the vast concord of all perfection. He is, now, the archetype of man in the full capacity of the omnipotent (*Tao*) to be cast into the mold of cosmic life as a whole wherein he gains nothing in particular and loses nothing in full. He forgets himself and forgets that he is really immersed in the bliss of *Tao*, just as fish swim in the river and sea and forget all about it.[36] (5) The perfected and perfect man is now what he is by virtue of his identifiability with the "Creator," imparting his potency to all the world without becoming the center of fame, the contriver of plans, the director of works, and the claimer to knowledge. He embraces infinity within the range of his experience and rambles in the realm of the infinite with levity and freedom.[37] He fulfills all that is natural in him without a sense of gain. In the spirit of vacuity, he employs his mind and heart like a mirror, impartially reflecting all that there is in the world without showing a trace of lure, dejection, or injury. It is then, and only then, that the final status of his exalted individuality is firmly established in the infinite world of *Tao*.

All these spiritual modes of life are, as it were, the rockets that launch the Taoistic type of space-man into the realm of the infinite, in which he is to find a vantage point called by Chuang Tzu "the acme of the Celestial" whereon he can survey the World-All from height to height, from width to width, and from depth to depth. The happy excursion into the realms of the infinite all along embodies Chuang Tzu's philosophy of spiritual liberation in the course of life. This is the Taoist temper of mind, which has incited the best of Chinese poetry as an expression of inspiration.

The exalted individual, once achieved, becomes a true sage, who, upborne by the wondrous procedure of *Tao*, can penetrate in insight into the Very One Truth comprehending the entire universe. All partial appearances, viewed from different angles in varying heights, will be facet-symbols for beauty susceptible of being interfused into the integral whole of reality. All differences in viewpoints will be reconciled in the over-all perspective which forms a complementary system of essential relativity, going anywhere and anywhen, as well as everywhere and everywhen, with the full swing of the all-pervasive *Tao*.

This is the pivotal point of his theory of leveling up all things.[38] Thus it is that the system of essential relativity is an all-inclusive system in which everything can find a place of its own fitness and in which no one thing can claim to have an especially privileged position so as to impose its surreptitious importance upon all others. At the same time, the system of essential relativity is an interpenetrative system wherein all entities come to be what they are by interlacing their own essences with one another so that nothing in it can stand alone in complete isolation. It is a system of interrelatedness and mutual relevance in which any one thing has its own intrinsic importance that will bear out valuable results as unique contributions to the make-up of any other. Furthermore, it is a system in which the infinite *Tao* operates as the unconditioned that will embrace all the conditions originally uncontrollable by any one individual outside the system. Especially the human individuals before their entry into this infinite system have suffered limitation, restraint, and bondage. Now that they, through the spirit of liberation, being aware of what ridiculous figures they have cut within the bounds of contracting narrowness, have discovered the authentic sagely Self by sharing the nature of *Tao,* they must cry for joy in uniting with the Ineffable and Inscrutable in the realm of the infinite, which breaks forth entirely from the limitations of any arbitrary scheme of thought, feeling, and action in life. As a result of all these characteristics exhibited in the infinite system of essential relativity, Chuang Tzu has set out a great theme: "The universe and I sustain a relation of co-existence; I and all beings have the same entry into the One." [39] Thus, being most inward with the Infinite, the individual in the exalted mode of life has well established himself in the world in congruence with all others.

IV

For an epoch of some five hundred years (241 B.C.–A.D. 240) China in the Asian world was not unlike Rome in the West. People of all ranks were busy doing work in the conquest of the practical world. Speculative interest waned in the intellectual realm.

The real revival of metaphysical contemplation dated from the year 240, when Ho Yen (190–249) and Wang Pi (226–249) made an attempt to reconcile the differences between Confucius and Lao

Tzu by laying importance upon the category of Nothingness for the interpretation of *Tao*.⁴⁰ Historically, Ho Yen was primarily a Confucian in that he tried to absorb Taoism into the system of Confucianism,⁴¹ whereas Wang Pi was essentially a Taoist with an intention of assimilating Confucianism into the system of Taoism. What was common in them consisted in an attempt to bring forth the unity of infinite substance as the core of metaphysical inquiry.

In his Commentary on the *Lao Tzu*, Wang Pi elucidated the central theme that all things considered as Being, taking shape in manifolds subject to limitation, should be, in the last resort, redeemable by the integral *Tao*, which, though designated as Nothing, is really everything transmuted into infinite perfection. It is in this light that he came to see the import of the philosophy of change. The whole world of dynamic being, begotten by the creative power exhibited in a plenitude of incessant change and variegated transformation, must revert to the fundamentum of *Tao* for its primordial unity, which, reposing in the form of Reason and in the spirit of eternity, will prevail over all multiplicities. Confucianism, as understood by Wang Pi, reveals only the origin of all things in the world of Being, while Taoism helps it to see into the ultimate destiny in which all of Being in every mode of change is brought back to a final consummation of perfection, which is Nothing, that is, nothing in particular but everything in full.⁴² It is the end result of all changes, borne out by the inexhaustible richness of function, that should be grasped as the infinite substance.

The spirit of Buddhism encompasses two alternative realms of thought: one conceived under the form of incessant change and the other conceived under the form of eternity. Should we include Hīnayāna Buddhism, we would find more causes to fight against the fluctuating mundane world, in which bigoted individuals plunge themselves into the deep waters of miserable blunders and sufferings. The vehicle of deliverance would have to bear them up through the fluctuations of time before reaching the other shore. In this sense, the Buddhist is a time-man, and he is such not in the blessed spirit of a Confucian. But, if we should take Mahāyāna Buddhism into consideration, the enlightenment it attained would illuminate before us an upper world of *Dharma* and *Dharma*-fulfillment in which the tragic sense of life in the process of time would be superseded by the bliss of eternity.⁴³ So, in this way the liberated spirit of a Mahāyānist would undertake a happy excursion into the poetically inspired space-world with the Taoist. He could, now, afford to forget the tragic sense of life enmeshed in the wheel of changing time. Under this circumstance, the spirit of a Buddhist was quite congenial with that of a Taoist.

V

It had taken a long epoch of more than seven centuries (67–789) for Chinese Buddhism to run its course of full development, which was, of course, conditioned by the continual works done in translation [44] and by the creative works done in system-building. From 789 onward until 960, the Buddhist tradition only went on and slid down in elaboration. Chiefly in the sixth century, the forerunning sects were to be formed and eventually in the period of Sui-T'ang (581–960) the ten different schools of Chinese Buddhism were completed. I cannot here attempt to outline their systematic theorizings, which, because of their doctrinal complexity and elaborateness, should form an independent study by themselves.[45] The most I can do now is select some features of Buddhism as ways of expressing the singular power of the Chinese mentality.

Upon being first introduced Buddhism could have taken deep root in the Chinese mind only by coming under the dominant influence of Chinese thought. It goes without saying that Chinese Buddhistic metaphysics was evoked and re-enforced by the spirit of Taoism and not vice versa.[46] The Taoists all along had claimed fundamental Nothingness to be a supreme category in their own system. And Buddhists such as Lokāksin (resident in China during 176–189), Chih Ch'ien (192–252), and K'ang Seng-hui (d. 280) continually laid extreme importance upon the category (thusness) of fundamental Nothingness, which they took to be equivalent to *Tathatā*.[47] During the fourth century, the impact of Taoism upon the philosophy of *Prajñā* was most obvious in the school of Tao-an (312–385) and his contemporaries.

As regards the controversies about *Wu* and *Yu* (Nothingness and Being), there were, then, six or seven schools [48] diversified into twelve trends [49] of thought discriminating the genuine truth from mundane creeds. On the evidences successively given by monks Tan-chi (*ca.* 473), Seng-ching (302–475), Hui-ta (*ca.* 481), and Yüan K'ang (*ca.* 649) and on the further evidence [50] of Chi-tsang (549–623), the above set of theories may be tabulated as follows:

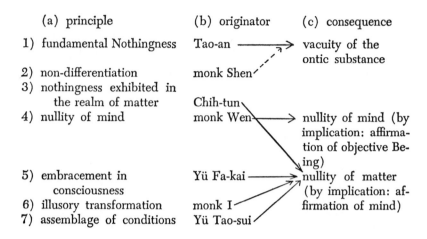

	(a) principle	(b) originator		(c) consequence
1)	fundamental Nothingness	Tao-an	→	vacuity of the ontic substance
2)	non-differentiation	monk Shen		
3)	nothingness exhibited in the realm of matter	Chih-tun		
4)	nullity of mind	monk Wen	→	nullity of mind (by implication: affirmation of objective Being)
5)	embracement in consciousness	Yü Fa-kai	→	nullity of matter (by implication: affirmation of mind)
6)	illusory transformation	monk I		
7)	assemblage of conditions	Yü Tao-sui		

In the above tabular scheme, (1) is more fundamental than the other six, which are all derived therefrom. According to Tao-an, "The fundamental Nothingness is the prius of all transformations, and vacuity is the beginning of all the visible world." All modes of the true *Dharma* are by nature vacuous and pure, spontaneously ensured from, and essentially identifiable with, the *Bhūta-tathatā* (Thatness of Being) denuded of any contamination by defiled elements. The trends of thought in the seven schools of Chinese Buddhism during the fourth and fifth centuries were centered around the metaphysical thesis which advocated the importance of Nothingness. From now on, the Buddhists would join hands with the Taoists and form a united front against traditional Confucianism.

The influence of Chuang Tzu is even more prominent in the school of Kumārajīva (343–413). His contribution lay in the field of the philosophy of *Śūnyatā* (Emptiness). Ultimate Reality is that which has emptied out all fantastic whims so as to show its own purity of essence in the form of Thusness. Among a great number of his pupils, Seng-chao (384–414) and Tao-sheng (374?–434) stood out as the twin stars never waning in their spiritual illuminancy.

The synoptic visions of Seng-chao are diversified into three cardinal theses: [51] (1) correlative motion and rest; (2) reconcilable Being and Nothing, or inseparable substance and function; and (3) the dovetailing of knowledge and "no-knowledge" transmuted into supreme wisdom.

(1) I have no time here to go into his penetrative arguments in this regard except to call attention to the two conclusions he arrived at. (a) Men of the world, engulfed in the flux of change, would have no sense of assurance, inasmuch as life in a shifting course of action would lead to death likely to destroy everything achieved in life. They are always sick of life and sick for unattainable *Nirvāṇa*. (b) The man of wisdom can discern permanence in the midst of change. He knows how to remain non-active in a state of spiritual repose and yet will not dispense with the world of action. It is only he who, being immortal in spirit, can plunge into the deep waters of life with no danger of annihilation. In his approach to *Nirvāṇa*, he has attained it, yet he will not stand attached to it, out of keeping with the changing world.

(2) Tao-an and his associates relied too much upon the fundamental Nothingness by asserting the vacuity of the ontic substance, or the nullity of matter, or the illusiveness of mind. Seng-chao, however, dissented strongly from all of them. Generally, in the usage of linguistic expressions or "ostensible names" we talk about an "objective" which is neither simply real as posited in Being nor simply unreal as denied in Not-Being or Nothing. The said "objective" may be either, and it may be both. In the light of the *Mādhyamika-śāstra*, to be or not to be: that is the *one-sided* question. It takes a man of supreme wisdom to discern Nothing in all modes of Being and to observe Being in the midst of Nothing. The ontic substance and the complete truth thereof cannot be rent into grotesque pieces.

(3) Seng-chao's metaphysics is a philosophy of the supreme wisdom which is concerned with Ultimate Reality, *Nirvāṇa*, the *Dharma-kāya* (Law-body), the *Bhūta-tathatā*, and *Dharmatā* (Reality as such). All of these are to him different names of the same "objective." In order to avoid misunderstanding, however, a distinction should be made between supreme wisdom per se and wisdom in the form of *upāya-kauśalya*, i.e., expedient wisdom. The power of the former penetrates deep into the objective, whereas the function of the latter adapts itself to all beings in the changing world. In virtue of wisdom per se, we are to illuminate the nature of the Void, while, by means of the expedient wisdom we are to launch into the world of fluctuating being. In dealing with Being in full, we shall have no misgivings with the nature of the Void. And, therefore, we can encounter the realm of Being without attachment. That being the case, we can illuminate what

is essentially vacuous without falling back upon it tenaciously. In the midst of knowledge in acquaintance with the world we shall arrive at a wondrous state of the liberated spirit with no knowledge whatever. The reason is that, if you know something in particular, there will be numberless other things that you do not know. Just because the spirit of the divine is with no knowledge in particular, there will be nothing that it does not know, freely and all-pervasively. Hence, the knowledge of no-knowledge embraces all that there is to be known. This may sound perplexing, but men of great genius, e.g., Shakespeare in the West, have understood it quite well.

> *O, out of that "no hope"*
> *What great hope have you! No hope that way is*
> *Another way so high a hope that even*
> *Ambition cannot pierce a wink beyond,*
> *But doubt discovery there.* [52]

The objective of the knowledge of no-knowledge is intent on the spirit of the divine. The divine spirit reposed in a state of vacuity, having no fumblings to get rid of, can be said to possess no knowledge. No knowledge that way is not the same as the supposed knowledge about Nothingness, which is something nullified into nothing. It is far above mere knowledge correlative with the limited modes of being. It is completely denuded of nescience, which is sheer ignorance. In a word, it is Enlightenment and *Prajñā* fused into the One. Enlightenment shades off what is extrinsic to itself and is essentially inner light in the form of no-knowledge, while *Prajñā* is an out-pouring of the inner light over the world-all by denuding it of fallaciousness.

I have mentioned Seng-chao and Tao-sheng as the twin stars in the ethereal sky of Chinese Buddhistic speculation. But there is a difference between them. Seng-chao formulated a system of principles explanatory of the nature of wisdom, whereas Tao-sheng turned the Mahāyānic theory into a way of spiritual life wherein human nature is fulfilled to the extent that it can partake of *Buddha*-nature.

Hitherto, Chinese Buddhists had looked upon the mundane world as a case of malady and thought about the actual individual as a source of blunder. Any acceptance of the world in its illusory appearances and any affirmation of the individual in his fantastic grimaces would indicate a silliness of view. But monk Hui-yüan

(334–416) had a different turn of mind. The world could exist in the form of permanence constitutive of Ultimate Reality. The human being could come to the possession of a real Self in intimacy with the Buddha. This line of thought had quite an influence upon Tao-sheng in formulating his philosophy of *Buddha*-nature. For brevity's sake, his fundamental ideas [53] in this regard may be enunciated as follows:

(1) The all-pervasive function of *Prajñā* and the substantial nature of *Nirvāṇa* are inseparable in the make-up of Ultimate Reality, which will embody the true *Dharma* and the perfect *Buddhatā* (*Buddha*hood) in the unity of *Buddha-dharma*.

(2) The ideal of *Nirvāṇa* is realizable in the midst of fluctuating life and death. Hence, the pure land of the Buddha is not different from the existent realm of all creatures. By way of moral purification, all creatures dwelling in the defiled world of blunders will be reinstated in the world of the noble and sublime, won over through the employment of Reason. Abidance in the enlightening Reason of the Buddha enables each and all to see every facet of the world as pure as it can be.

(3) The conquest of the darkened mind by the potency of Reason is the only way to emancipation. In pursuance of this, the real self of spontaneous freedom is achieved by the righteous mind which has been restored to the original purity of Nature through the exertion of Reason. Thus all human beings—not even excepting the *icchantika* (forsaken one)—endowed with intrinsic Reason, can come to share equally the ubiquitous *Buddha*-nature and to unfold the illuminating *Buddha*-wisdom implicit in their own conscience. In this sense, human individuals are spiritual comrades, equal in cosmic importance with the Buddha.

(4) As the light of supreme wisdom has a most direct penetration into his own rational essence, each man through devout devotion can come to a *sudden awakening* of the *Buddha*-nature within the inner constitution of his own nature and achieve *Buddha*hood on his own accord. This is the chief tenet of Mahāyāna Buddhism.

Tao-sheng's philosophy of *Buddha*hood is of great importance for several reasons. (a) It evoked a number of interpretations of *Buddha*-nature during the fifth and sixth centuries. (b) His emphasis on the perfectibility of human nature after the model of *Budda*-nature is quite congenial with the Confucian theory of the original goodness of man. This is evidenced by the fact that the poet-philosopher, Hsieh Ling-yün (385–433), in hearty sympathy with Tao-sheng's idea of sudden awakening, made a very favorable comparison of the spiritual achievement of Confucius with that of the Buddha.[54] (c) His theory of sudden awakening by reverting to the inmost nature of the mind anticipated the later philosophy of Ch'an (Zen). (d) His concept of the importance of Reason in gaining an insight into Ultimate Reality even anticipated the Neo-Confucianism of the Sung Dynasty (960–1279). In short, Tao-sheng was, on the one hand, the culmination of the line of thought in the linkage of Buddhism with Taoism, and, on the other, a bridge over which several schools of Buddhism were to make headway in alliance with some schools of Confucianism.

In the epoch of Sui-T'ang (581–960) ten different schools of Buddhism flourished in China. "A beggar of time" like me, finally, cannot refrain from mentioning, in particular, the categorical scheme of Hua-yen—the Avataṁsaka school—as a powerful expression of Chinese comprehensive harmony. Theoretically, if not entirely historically, the Hua-yen school may be made the line of convergence along which many systems of Buddhistic thought would have their confluence.

The categorical scheme of Hua-yen[55] was an attempt to integrate all the differentiating worlds, all the noble deed-acts, and all the achieved end results of the *buddhas* in the past, present, and future into a sum total of the True Realm of *Dharma* in the form of supreme perfection with a view to showing that each human being, inherently possessed of wondrous excellences, could awaken in himself, all at once, *buddha*-nature, adequately, spontaneously, and congruently. The one real Realm of *Dharma* is not far from this actual world of man, if everyone knows thoroughly how to live and act wisely by way of participation in the fundamental wisdom of the Buddha. *Buddha*-nature *in toto* has the potentiality of coming in ingress into the perennial spiritual constitution of man. This is the equality and equanimity of *Dharma*. The spiritual sun sheds its exuberant light over and into all living beings, and all living beings, in turn, assimilate and reflect and interfuse and re-enforce this spiritual light uniquely and reciprocally. Thus, all modes of the spontaneous function of reason, manifesting themselves in infinite varieties, would, at the same time, be actuated into a concert of life activities, in unison with the One True Realm of *Dharma*, equanimous in essence. In the midst of enriched varieties, the light of *Tathatā* (Thusness) radiated by the Buddha and witnessed and shared by all men alike will gladden the differentiating minds and the differentiating worlds into the non-differentiation of Reality perfectly embedded in the integral truth, which is Enlightenment, inherent in each and interpentrative into all.

Taken in its all-inclusive unity, this One True *Dharma-dhātu* (Realm of *Dharma*, or Law) evinces the omnipresence and omnipotence of Mind constitutive of the noumenon of all the phenomenal worlds, diversifying itself into (a) the differential Realms of Events, (b) the integrative Realm of Reason, (c) the interpenetrative Realm of Reason and Events, and (d) the interlacing Realm of all Events.

The theoretical formulation of the categorical scheme,[56] initiated by Tu-shun (557–640), developed by Chih-yen (602–668), elaborated by Fa-tsang (643–720), and further expounded by Ch'eng-kuan (760–820) and Tsung-mi (d. 841), embraces three grand views,[57] i.e., (1) of the true Void, (2) of the congruence of Reason and Events, and (3) of the dovetailing of all events in the form of universal coherence.

In the first view, an attempt is made to show (a) that the worlds of physical properties can be dissolved into the nature of the Void, just as phenomena are transmutable into the noumenon; (b) that the Void as the Ultimate Reality is constitutive of, and identifiable with, the assemblage of purified physical phenomena; (c) that the Void and the physical are mutually congruent; and (d) that, eventually, after the impenetrable inertia of the physical is explained away in terms of the efficacy of mental and spiritual transmutations and through the insinuation of the ontic essence— the true nature of the Void—into the physical, all one-sided characterizations in respect of the physical and the Void are transcended in the highest integral truth of the middle path.

In the second view, it is maintained that reason and events can be melded in a perfect manner. Reason is the wondrous function deeply rooted in the *Bhūta-tathatā* and has its efficacy anytime anywhere in virtue of the omnipresence of the Buddha. This can be accounted for in the following ways: (a) Reason as a whole, denuded of any specification, is universally present in all the worlds of events, however differentiated the latter may be, inasmuch as the *Dharmatā* is manifesting itself incessantly without limitation. And, therefore, even the minutest event-particles are immersed in the integral truth and imbued adequately with Reason. (b) The items of events which, as such, are differentiated must be restored into unity in the integration of Reason, just as the wavicles, spreading forth far and away, are losing their own unique momenta and can be re-enforced and saved only by taking up continually with the oceanic ingratiation. Hence, it may be asserted that events, each and all, are constituted according to the Reason which is exhibited thereof. Though they are interrelated, the truth, however, is not simply events which, once constituted, would overshadow the Reason inherent in them, and the events are not simply the truth which, if verified, would supersede the events limitative in their differentiation.

In the third view, it is asserted that the dovetailing of all events will vindicate the universal coherence of truth. This can be shown as follows: (1) Reason operates for the sake of events. It makes the events what they are in the mode of existence, in the way of differentiation, qualitatively as well as quantitatively, and in the process of change and transformation. Hence, the function of Reason issuing in truth will come in ingress into all the differentiating worlds of events. (2) The events, each and all, abide by Reason in virtue of which they would go through the process of change in incessant successions and remain permanent in the realm of eternity. And, therefore, the events in observance of Reason would permeate all modes of *Dharma*. (3) The events, as implied in Reason, would bring forth the following modes of implication: (a) one implicates another; (b) one implicates every other; (c) one implicates all others; (d) all others implicate one; (e) all others implicate every other one; and (f) all others implicate all others. Thus, the whole and the parts, the one and the many, as well as the universal and the particular, will be intertwined.

The above consideration brings into prominence the principle of mutual implication, the principle of mutual relevance, and the principle of all-pervasive coherence. All these principles, taken together, are explanatory of the integral infinite *Dharma-dhātu*. In the way of mutual implication, any one (*dharma*) can gather up any other one unto itself and enter into the constitution of that one; any one can gather up all others unto itself and enter into the constitution of that one; all others can gather up all others unto themselves and enter into the constitution of those others. Hence, the principle of mutual relevance needs no further elucidation. Furthermore, the principle of all-pervasive coherence holds on the following conditions: (a) one *dharma* gathers up another one into itself and enters into that one; (b) one gathers up all other *dharmas* into itself so as to enter into that one; (c) one gathers up another one so as to enter into all others; (d) one gathers up all others in order to enter into all others; (e) all other *dharmas* gather up one so as to enter into another one; (f) all other *dharmas* gather up all others so as to enter into any one; (g) all others gather up one so as to enter into all others; and (h) all others gather up all others in order to enter into them all. When all of these are melded together, the ultimate result is the integrity of the infinitely perfect *Dharma-dhātu*. If the above conditions are fulfilled, then the ten approaches to the metaphysical profundity and the six characteristics of all *Dharma* will be clear in the light of day without further elucidation. In view of such a philosophy, if any person is to gain a firm footing in the One Real *Dharma-dhātu*, he must live and have his being in the spirit of infinity.

In the above I have tried to depict tersely the ways in which the Chinese contemplative minds have been fascinated with the world and the human individual, which are taken, however, not so much in natural as "in dramatic regard." [58] The world and the individual, taken "in natural regard," would be the exhibitions of related facts, definite in content, determinate in nature, specific in conditions, articulate in forms, full in being, or substantial in essence. All of these, characteristic of scientific explanations, are, of course, very important for the understanding of man and the world. But Chinese philosophers choose to take a step further than this in their modes of contemplation. From their viewpoints, the world, taking shape in Ultimate Reality, must transcend the limitations of these relatively specific characterizations before all of its complete nature can come to the light of day. The actual world, strictly philosophically conceived, should be transformed into an ideal pattern adorned with the axiological unity of supreme perfection. The Chinese always aspire toward the transfigured world of liberating art, of edifying morality, of contemplative truth, and of religious piety. Any other world short of these will be a realm of anxiety making us look pale and tired. This is why Confucians have craved so much for the continually creative potency of the heavenly *Tao* in the shaping of the cosmic order as a whole. This is why the Taoists have whole-heartedly cherished the ideal of Nothingness for its coming to the rescue of all things relative in the realm of Being. And this is also why Chinese Buddhists have vehemently struggled for the partaking of the *Buddha*-nature embedded in the integral truth of the ultimate spiritual Enlightenment.

As to the nature and status of man, the Chinese, either as a unique person or as a social being, takes no pride in being a type of individual in estrangement from the world he lives in or from the other fellows he associates with. He is intent on embracing within the full range of his vital experience all aspects of plenitude in the nature of the whole cosmos and all aspects of richness in the worth of noble humanity. Anything different from this would be a sign of the impoverishment in the inner constitution of personality which is miserably truncated in development. This accounts for the concerted efforts of Chinese philosophers to advocate the exaltation of the individual into the inward sageliness and the outward worthiness which together make up the intrinsic greatness of man as Man.

Notes

1. Cf. my *Chinese View of Life* (Hong Kong: The Union Press, 1957), chap. 3, pp. 87–115, especially pp. 99–115.
2. In the *Shih-chi* (General History, Royal Library edn., 1746), Vol. 57, p. 8, and Vol. 130, p. 2, Ssu-ma Ch'ien clearly stated that his father, Ssu-ma T'an, learned the philosophy of change from Yang-hu, whose intellectual heritage was traced back to Confucius through an unbroken lineage of eight generations.
3. This cardinal doctrine was set forth by Confucius in the "Tuan" *chuan* (Compendiums), in the "Hsi tz'u" *chuan* (Conspectus), and in the early section of the "Shuo-kua" *chuan* (Scholia on the Hexagrams).
4. This idea was first formulated by Confucius in the "Wen yen" *chuan* (Corollaries to the Hexagrams *"Ch'ien"* and *"K'un"*) and more systematically in the "Shang" *chuan* (Symbolics).
5. The idea of value and the consequential value-centric ontology are developed in the "Hsi tz'u" *chuan.*
6. I attacked this problem in my *Sheng-ming ching-tiao yu mei-k'an* (The Sentiment of Life and the Sense of Beauty), National Central University Monograph on Art and Literature, Vol. 1, No. 1, 1931, pp. 173–204, especially pp. 192–203.
7. "Hsi tz'u" *chuan,* chap. 4.
8. Cf. my essay, "Logical Formulations of the Philosophy of Change," in the *I-hsüeh-t'ao-lun-chi* (Joint Studies on *The Book of Change*). (Changsha: Commercial Press, 1941), pp. 31–54.
9. Cf. Chiao Hsün, *I-t'u lüeh* (Logical Structures and Syntactical Scheme Exhibited in *The Book of Change*) (8 vols., 1813), Vol. I, p. 4; Vol. II, pp. 13–14; *I hua* (Talks on the Philosophy of Change) (2 vols., 1818), Vol. I, pp. 3, 12; *I t'ung-shih* (General Commentary

on *The Book of Change*) (20 vols., 1813); and *I chang-chü* (*The Book of Change: A Study in Syntax*) (12 vols., 1815).

10. Cf. the "Tuan" *chuan*, the "Wen yen" *chuan*, and the "Hsi tz'u" *chuan*, chaps. 5, 7; *The Doctrine of the Mean*, XXII. See also Tai T'ung-yüan, *Yuan-shan* (Treatise on the Good), chap. 1.
11. "Hsi tz'u" *chuan*, chap. 5.
12. "Tuan" *chuan*.
13. "Wen yen" *chuan*.
14. Cf. *The Doctrine of the Mean*, XXII.
15. Cf. *The Works of Mencius*, VIIB.25.
16. Cf. *The Works of Hsün Tzu* (Chekiang: Chekiang Book Co., 1876), Vol. II, chap. 17, pp. 11–16, 18.
17. Cf. Tai Te's version of *The Book of Propriety*, edited by Lu Chien-tseng, 1758, Vol. I, pp. 4–6.
18. Cf. the "Wen yen" *chuan* in *The Book of Change*.
19. *The Book of Lao Tzu* (Chekiang: Chekiang Book Co., 1875), IV.
20. *Ibid.*, VI.
21. *Ibid.*, XXXIX.
22. *Ibid.*, V, XXII.
23. *Ibid.*, XXXV, XXVIII.
24. *Ibid.*, XVI.
25. *Ibid.*, LX–LXI, LXV.
26. Cf. *ibid.*, LX.
27. *Ibid.*, XI.
28. *Ibid.*, XXVII.
29. Cf. *The Works of Chuang Tzu*, Vol. I, chap. 2, p. 24; Vol. V, chap. 12, pp. 6–7; Vol. VI, chap. 17, pp. 9–12; Vol. VIII, chap. 23, pp. 9–10.
30. Cf. *ibid.*, Vol. X, chap. 33, p. 25. Also cf. Ma Hsü-lun, *Chuang Tzu i Cheng* (Verifications of Meanings in *Chuang Tzu*) (Shanghai: Commercial Press, 1930), Vol. 33, pp. 18–19.
31. Cf. *ibid.*, Vol. III, chap. 6, pp. 7, 10; Vol. VI, chap. 17, p. 10; Vol. VII, chap. 21, p. 24; Vol. VII, chap. 22, pp. 36, 39, Vol. VIII, chap. 23, p. 9; Vol. VIII, chap. 25, p. 34.
32. Cf. *ibid.*, Vol. VIII, chap. 24, p. 22; Vol. X, chap. 31, p. 9 (Kuo Hsiang's notes). The monk Te ch'ing, in the Ming Dynasty (1368–1643) in a commentary on the *Chuang Tzu*, said emphatically that Mencius had a tremendous influence upon this great Taoist.
33. Cf. *The Works of Chuang Tzu*, Vol. X, chap. 32, p. 12.
34. *Ibid.*, Vol. V, chap. 13, p. 24.
35. *Ibid.*, Vol. IV, chap. 11, p. 26.
36. *Ibid.*, Vol. III, chap. 6, pp. 7, 9–10, 15–16.
37. *Ibid.*, Vol. III, chap. 7, pp. 22–26.
38. Cf. Chang T'ai-yen, *Ch'i wu lun shih* (Commentary on the Theory of Leveling All Things), pp. 1, 3, 11, 14, 18–19, 21–25, 51–55.

39. *The Works of Chuang Tzu*, Vol. I, chap. 2, p. 25.

40. *Chin shu* (History of the Chin Dynasty) (Shanghai: Commercial Press, 1934), Vol. 43, p. 8.

41. Cf. Chang Chan's citations from Ho Yen in the commentary on *The Works of Lieh Tzu* (Chekiang: Chekiang Book Co., 1876), Vol. I, chap. 1, pp. 4–5; Vol. IV, chap. 4, pp. 4–5.

42. Cf. Wang Pi and Hang K'ang-po, commentaries on *The Book of Change* (Shanghai: Chung Hua Book Co., 1922): (a) Wang's portion in Vol. III, p. 4; Vol. I, pp. 2, 5–6; Vol. II, p. 11; Vol. IV, pp. 2–3; (b) Han's portion in Vol. VII, pp. 3–4, 6–9; Vol. VIII, pp. 5–6. See also Wang Pi, *Chou-i-lüeh-li* (Sketchy Exemplifications of the Principles of Change) in the same edn., Vol. X, pp. 1–3, 6–8.

43. Cf. the *Mahā-parinirvāṇa-sūtra* in Chinese trans. (Shanghai: 1913, 1926), Vol. II, chap. 2, pp. 11, 19; chap. 3, pp. 23–25, 28; Vol. III, chap. 4, pp. 11, 15; and the *Mahā-prajñā-pāramitā-sūtra*, in Chinese trans., portion 16 (published in Ssuch'uan, 1940), Vol. 596, pp. 4–6.

44. Cf. *Liang jen-kung chüan-chi* (Collected Essays of Liang Ch'i-ch'ao), 1st series (Shanghai: Commercial Press, 1923), pp. 1–23; 81–134; 155–254.

45. See Junjirō Takakusu, *The Essentials of Buddhist Philosophy* (3rd edn., Honolulu: Office Appliance Co., 1956), and Chiang Wei-ch'iao, *Fo-hsüeh kai-lun* (Introduction to Buddhism) (Shanghai, 1930).

46. T'ang Yung-t'ung has given ample evidences to demonstrate this fact in the *Han-Wei Liang-Chin Nan-pei-ch'ao fo-chiao shih* (History of Chinese Buddhism During the Period 67–588) (2nd edn.; Taipei: Commercial Press, 1962), Pt. I, chap. 6, pp. 89–111.

47. Cf. the *Tathatā-parivarta* of the *Daśāsahasrika* (*Prajñā-pāramitā-sūtra*) in different Chinese translations by Lokākṣin and Chih Ch'ien. See the *Taishō* edn. of the Buddhist Tripiṭaka in Chinese, no. 224, p. 453; no. 225, p. 474.

48. Cf. Hui-ta, *Chao-lun hsü* (Preface to Seng-chao's Discourses). See the *Taishō* edn. of the Buddhist Tripiṭaka in Chinese, no. 1858, p. 150.

49. Cf. Yüan K'ang, *Chao-lun su-hsü* (Commentary on Seng-chao's Discourses). See *ibid.*, no. 1859, pp. 162–163.

50. Cf. Chi-tsang, *Chung-kuan-lung shu* (Commentary on the Mādhya-mika-śāstra). See *ibid.*, no. 1824, p. 29.

51. Cf. his "Wu pu-chien lun," "Pu-jen-kung lun," "Pan-jou wu-chih-lun" (Discourses On the Perennial, On the Non-Vacuous, and On the *Prajñā* as No-Knowledge). See the Buddhist Tripiṭaka in Chinese, no. 1858, pp. 150–157.

52. *The Tempest*, Act 2, sc. 1.

53. Tao-sheng's ideas are scattered in the commentaries on the

Saddharma-puṇḍarīka-sutra, on the *Mahā-pārinirvāṇa-sūtra* and on the *Vimalakīrti-nirdeśa-sūtra.*

54. Cf. Hsieh Ling-yün, *Pien-cheng lun* (Essays on the Discrimination of Doctrines) in the Further Collection of Essays on Buddhism, Vol. 18, pp. 13–19.

55. Cf. Chieh-huan, *Hua-yen ching yao-chieh* (Essentials of the Avataṁsaka-sūtra) compiled in 1128. Nanking Centre for Buddhist Publications, 1872.

56. For the important literature on the Hua-yen school, see the *Taishō* edn. of the Buddhist Tripiṭaka in Chinese, no. 1836, pp. 71–76; nos. 1866–1890, pp. 477–792.

57. Here I am utilizing Tsung-mi's *Chu Hua-yen Fa-chieh kuan-men* (Elucidations of the Hua-yen View of the *Dharma-dhātu*), which is essentially more systematic than the earlier expositions by Tu-shun and Fa-tsang, (*ibid.*, No. 1884, pp. 684–692).

58. Cf. C. Lloyd Morgan, *Mind at the Crossways* (London: Williams & Norgate, 1929), pp. 2–4, 13–14, 20–21, 224–227, 230–235, 267–272.

The Individual and the World
in Chinese Methodology

Introduction

I SHALL LIMIT this paper to the four important typical ways of thinking about the individual and the world in Chinese epistemology:

1. To think of the individual as objectively existing as a part of the world.

2. To think of the world as a part of, or the content of, or identical with, the being of the individual subject.

3. To think that both the individual and world must be transcended, and that there is then in reality neither individual nor world.

4. To think that both the individual subject and the objective world are to be asserted positively as existing, yet neither is asserted as a part of, or the content of, or identical with, the other; nor are they asserted as mutually exclusive, because their mutual transcendence and mutual immanence are both accepted.

I. The Individual Known as Objectively Existing and as a Part of the World through Class Names, Pointing, Spatio-temporal Location, and Relational Thinking

First, the way of thinking of the individual as objectively existing and as part of the world is that way of thinking which *starts* from the world as the objective side of our knowledge (through the temporary forgetting of the individual as a unique knowing or acting subject and the conscious—though not self-conscious—activity of the objectivation of the subject as one of the individual things in the world) and *ends* in the assertion that I, as an individual, and all other individual things co-exist as parts of the world. The problem here—how I as an individual person can be objectively known or conceptually determined as an individual is included in the general problem as to how any individual thing is objectively known or conceptually determined as an individual. Since individual things are usually thought of objectively by general concepts or class terms, which are universal in meaning, the problems as to how the individuality of a particular individual can be conceptually determined and how the individual can be thought of objectively have been complicated and delicate problems from Plato to the present in Western thought. However, Chinese philosophers have not taken the problem so seriously as has the West, though we are not lacking in answers to the problem. These answers are represented by the Moists, the Logicians, Hsün Tzu (313–238 B.C.), and the Yin-Yang school in classical Chinese thought.

(a) Moists think of the individual objectively merely as a member of a class. They stress the idea of class (*lei*) earlier than Mencius (372–289 B.C.) and Hsün Tzu. Mo Tzu (468–376 B.C.) teaches universal love as based upon the idea that all human beings are of the same kind. He teaches also that one should love the father of another man as he does his own. Thus, Mo Tzu takes my father merely as one member of the class of fathers. So, when Moism is developed into a theory of epistemology and logic in Mo Pien, an individual thing is called an individual or an actuality (*shih*). A *shih* may have its proper name and class names such as species name and genus name. As a proper name is arbitrarily given to a *shih*, conceptual knowledge of a *shih* requires the use of a class name. However, Mo Pien did not discuss the problem as to how an individual can be conceptually determined by the class name, which expresses the universal concept only. In Mo Pien's thought, the use of a class name to denote an individual is a practical matter. If a genus name is not enough to express the peculiarities of an individual, then a species name or sub-species name is required to differentiate one individual from another of the same kind. As the process of using class names with more specified meanings goes on, there is no problem as to how the individual can be conceptually determined and expressed by a class name. Consequently, this problem is not raised and discussed by Moists. However, it has to be raised and discussed, because the process of using names with more specified meanings cannot go on indefinitely, since there is no infirm species or lowest subordinative class-name to use; and, even if there were, it would still be a class name, and, we could know the individual only as a member of the class.

(b) Another way to know the individual as existing objectively is represented by the Kung-sun Lung (498? B.C.) of the logician school of Pre-Ch'in (Ch'in, 221–206 B.C.) philosophy. This is the way of knowing an individual by pointing to it. Kung-sun Lung is famous for his insistence on the difference of meanings between species name and genus name. Thus, "White horse is not horse" is his slogan. If genus name is different from species name because it has a wider denotation, it is implied that the lowest class-name still can denote more than one individual, and so individuality cannot be expressed by any class-name as such. Thus, the individual can be pointed out or indicated only by names and not conceptually determined by them. These are the topics of his two other treatises, "Ch'i-wu lun" (On Pointing and Things) and "Ming-shih lun" (On Name and Actuality), which are less mentioned than his theory of the difference of species and genus as expounded in his treatise "Pai-ma-lun" (On White Horse). It is quite clear that Kung-sun Lung thinks that the actuality (*shih*) of an individual thing can be pointed to only by names and that the differences between species name and genus name are based upon their different functions in pointing.[1] We use names for pointing out the individual thing, and the individual thing is shown and known to us in the very act of pointing.

It is one thing to use a universal name to point to an individual thing, and another for a person to be understood by others, as when we use a certain universal name to point to a certain individual. If the individuality of an individual is not capable of being determined in some other way, where can one get the guarantee that one shall not be misunderstood? Thus, the third way of knowing the individual, as propounded by Hsün Tzu, needs consideration.

(c) The third way of knowing the individual as existing objectively is that of determining an individual in a spatio-temporal system. When Hsün Tzu discusses how an actuality or an individual thing is determined in his chapter of the *Cheng-ming* (Rectification of Names), he disagrees with the view that an individual is determined by its appearances or attributes, which are usually expressed by universal names. Two things may have the same appearances or attributes but be in different places. Thus, they have to be called two distinct actualities, two individual things. On the other hand, in the process of becoming, "one [individual] thing may have different appearances or attributes [at different times] but must still be called one individual." [2] An actuality, or an individual, is determined by its location in the spatio-temporal system, with emphasis laid on the different spatial locations of different individual things. However, when we differentiate the different things according to their different locations in space and time, we presuppose that the space-time system is already differentiated in its structure prior to the things in it. Here the epistemological problem is: if there are not things related differently to one another in space-time, how can space-time, which is simply extended in spatio-temporal dimensions and is thought to be homogeneous everywhere, be differentiated by itself into different locations. If we cannot find any other answer to this problem, we can look for the principle of individuality only in the different things as differently related to each other.

(d) As things which are similar in appearances or attributes and subsumed under a class name do not usually have the same relations, such as causal relations, with other things, so any two individuals can be differentiated according to their different relations with different things. The Yin-Yang school is representative of this way of thinking: the fourth way of knowing the individual, that of relational thinking, the way of knowing the individual in its many-sided relations with other things. This way, expounded first by the Yin-Yang school, was adopted by many Confucianists after the Han Dynasty (206 B.C.–A.D. 220).

The meaning of *yin* and *yang* are subtle and complicated.[3] Originally, "*yin*" meant what is concealed and unknown to us, and "*yang*" meant what is manifested and known to us. They were originally concepts of attributes of things based on their status relative to other things, and were not originally concepts of substance or force. According to their derivative meanings, anything which is in front of or before other things is called *yang*, and that which is in back of or after other things is called *yin*. Consequently, what is progressive or active or generative is *yang*, and what is retrogressive or passive or degenerative is *yin*. All these meanings are relative. Therefore, according to the Yin-Yang school, everything takes the role of *yin* or *yang* relatively to other things, and anything of the same class can be differently determined as having different relations of *yin* and *yang* to these other things. Even if we limit the meaning of "*yang*" to "active" and "*yin*" to "passive," it is not difficult to determine the things to which a certain individual thing is peculiarly related, actively and passively, and then to differentiate it from the other individual things of the same class, in order that the uniqueness of a certain individual can be expressed through this kind of relational thinking without confusion.

The way of relational thinking of the Yin-Yang school was originally a way of thinking of an individual thing as existing objectively in the natural world. Yet, it is exactly like the Confucian way of thinking of the status of the individual person through his ethical relations in the human world. When an individual person is seen as existing objectively in the human world, his action and personality are regulated and determined by his reciprocal relations with other persons. As there are no two individual persons who have the same ethical relations to the other persons around him, so the unique status of an individual person in the human world can be cognized and conceptually determined through knowledge of his peculiar ethical relations to others.

II. The Individual as a Self-Conscious Moral Subject and the World as Seen by Such a Subject

I myself as a subject am a self-conscious subject. When I am self-conscious, what I am conscious of can be known as the content of my consciousness, and comprehended by my self-consciousness, which therefore transcends the world, and can then include it as a part of itself. If we say that only the self-consciousness which immediately reveals itself to me exists, this is extreme individualism or solipsism; and, if we say that there are different worlds belonging to the different self-consciousnesses of different individuals, this is pluralistic idealism or pluralistic spiritualism, and is a kind of individualism, too.

But, how can we know that self-consciousness is itself an individual reality belonging to me exclusively or belonging to each person separately? It is quite possible that self-consciousness, revealed immediately as a self-conscious subject, is simply a subject without being an individual, or a part of, or an expression of, a universal self-conscious subject, which is the only reality, as objective idealism or absolute idealism contends. Nevertheless, we still have reason to call the self-conscious subject an individual, because the self-conscious subject, since it transcends the world, can differentiate itself from the world. Hence, it is a unique being and capable of being defined negatively as different from everything else in the world and from the world as a whole, and can be called an individual, because any individual thing in the ordinary sense is usually defined as that which is different from everything else. Although we may not be able to define the self-conscious subject positively as an individual in the ordinary sense, we should leave open the question as to whether it is a part of or an expression of a universal self-conscious subject. If it is legitimate to call the self-conscious subject an individual, then any thought which thinks the world-being as the content of, or a part of, or identical with, the subject is a process of thinking of the world subjectively.[3a]

There is no eminent philosophy of pure Chinese origin—other than Buddhist Vijñānavāda idealism, and it came from India—which argues for a subjective idealism or for individualism by taking the self-conscious subject as a purely knowing subject and taking the world simply as the object known. However, there is a very important trend of Chinese thought which takes the self-conscious subject as both acting and knowing, and thereupon thinks of the world-being as subjectively included or comprehended as a part of, or the content of, or identical with, the subject.

This trend of thought may be called a kind of ethical idealism. Mencius, Lu Hsiang-shan (1139–1192), and Wang Yang-ming (1472–1528) are the leading philosophers involved. All of them emphasize the self-consciousness of the subject as a moral subject, which is not purely a knowing subject but a subject which knows its moral ideal, acts in conformity with it, and then knows itself self-consciously as a subject of both knowing and acting. There is here the thesis that "the universe (the ten thousand things) is perfectible in myself," [4] and "The universe is my mind, and my mind is the universe," [5] and "Pervading Heaven and Earth, there is just this spiritual light . . . my spiritual light is the master of Heaven, Earth, and deities . . . leaving my spiritual light, there is no Heaven, Earth, deities, or ten thousand things." [6]

It would be quite misleading, however, to interpret this thesis from the point of view of epistemological idealism or ordinary mysticism. Chinese philosophers who have held this thesis have never stated in a strict sense their epistemological arguments for this kind of idealism, nor have they said that the meanings of their thesis are mysterious as beyond the reason of man.

In ethical idealism, we take those things which ought to be as our ideal. This ideal determines what we ought to do to realize the ideal, and then the realization of the ideal is itself a moral ideal and moral action. The way of thinking in ethical idealism begins, in its first step, with seeing the things of the world as what they ought to be as our ideal prescribes, and then they are seen as full of possibilities or potentialities. It then proceeds, in the next step, to seeing things through our moral ideal and moral action. Henceforth, things are seen as gradually transforming themselves and tending to be what they ought to be; and their possibilities, when realized by our moral action, are found as of the nature of what they ought to be and of the ideal; while, on the contrary, what they are in actual fact is thought of as not so in reality. Therefore, if the moral subject has a moral ideal and moral action which are so high and lofty as to realize the universal *jen* (the utmost goodness in the world) through the self-consciousness of our good nature, or our original mind, (*pen-shin*)—as held by Mencius, Lu Hsiang-shan, and Wang Yang-ming—then all things in the world will be seen through this high and lofty ideal and action of the moral subject, and all things and the whole world will be seen as acted upon by the subject's moral action and as tending to realize its moral ideal, and will be thought of as of the same nature as the moral mind. Consequently, it is quite natural for Mencius to think that the ten thousand things are perfectible by me as a moral subject, for Lu Hsiang-shan to think that the universe is my mind, and for Wang Yang-ming to think of *liang-chih* (intuitive knowledge) as the spiritual light of Heaven, Earth, deities, and the ten thousand things.

The expression "see the world through the ideal and action of the moral subject" states a way of thinking by a fully self-conscious moral subject as a moral individual. It is not a way of thinking of the world as an object opposite to the subject. It is a way of thinking which begins by withdrawing the light in the ordinary outward-knowing process back to our inner self; and then throwing the light out again, along the very line of the extending of our moral ideal and our moral action; and knows the world as mediated by that very ideal and action, and as the realm for the embodiment of that ideal and action. Here, the seeing "eye" of the moral subject is immanent in the extending of the ideal and moral action, being acted upon by the action and transformed by the action. As the world is itself transformed to conform to the ideal, the "eye" will see the world as absorbed into the action and the ideal of the subject, and will experience it as one in being with the subject. When the subject is self-conscious and knows itself as transcending the world as experienced, the "eye" will see the subject as above the world, and the world will be seen as just a part of, or the content of, the subject as an absolute individual or an absolute I. This is the reason Liu Chi-shan (1578–1645), a great Neo-Confucianist in the late Ming Dynasty (1368–1644), gives so high a place to the idea of *tu* or *tu-chih*—the awareness of the solitary individual in absolute morality.[7]

III. The Individual and the World as Transcended in Vacuity and Receptivity of Mind and in Enlightenment and Spirituality

The third typical way of thinking of the individual and the world in Chinese philosophy is to think that both the individual and the world have to be transcended, such that there is in reality neither world nor the I as an individual. This is the same type of thinking as that of Western and Indian mystics and philosophers who think of "before the day of creation," but with different emphasis about the way in which the world and the I, or the self as an individual, are to be transcended.

Chuang Tzu (369? B.C.), one of the two most important Taoistic philosophers, is representative of this way. He has a spiritual vision which is beyond the sense of self as an individual and of the world as opposite to the self. "Forgetting of myself," "loss of myself," "forgetting the world under Heaven," and "out of the world under Heaven" are pertinent sayings of his. When Chuang Tzu talked about the "upward wandering with the creator [and] downward having friends who are beyond death and life and of no beginning and ending," [8] he was using a metaphor for the expression of his spiritual vision. His spiritual vision orginates from his profound wisdom, aesthetic enjoyment, and inner spiritual cultivation, rather than from his primary belief in the existence of a mystic state.

Chuang Tzu has three ideas about the mind which are closely related to the experience of "forgetting the world and the self as an individual." The first idea concerns the nature of mind as *hsü* and *ling*. "*Hsü*" means to be vacuous and receptive. Confucius and Lao

Tzu spoke of *hsü* mainly as a moral teaching. Chuang Tzu, followed by Hsün Tzu and the Neo-Confucianists, takes *hsü* as one fundamental nature of the mind and connects it with the word *"ling,"* which means knowing freely, spontaneously, and without attachment. When the nature of the mind is seen as both vacuous and receptive, the sense of ego or of self as an individual differentiating itself from other things is uprooted in the depth of the mind.

The mind can be receptive without being a positive receiver. When the mind is vacuous and receptive, all things of the world can be received by it, and then pass through it without meeting any barrier. This self-forgetting can be cultivated and continued in principle. Here, the most important thing is that the mind will be revealed to itself as both vacuous and receptive simultaneously. When it knows, it is receptive. But, if it is not simultaneously vacuous, then what is received is attached to the mind, and the mind is in turn attached to things. This is the ordinary way of knowing with attachment. On the contrary, if the mind is revealed to itself as both receptive and vacuous simultaneously, it can know things without attachment.

Secondly, Chuang Tzu uses the idea of *ming*, which means the lasting actual state of the mind when its nature, as purely vacuous and receptive, is fully realized in its knowing. Literally, *"ming"* means "light." As a state of mind, it is enlightenment of mind. When Western religious thought talks about enlightenment of mind, it usually means that the mind is enlightened by something above. It is not so in Chinese thought. All Taoists, Confucianists, and Buddhists use the word *"ming"* as self-enlightenment or enlightenment without self. For Chuang Tzu, enlightenment is *a state of mind* which is purely transparent, and this transparency of mind, which comes from that nature of the mind as both purely vacuous and purely receptive, is fully realized in its knowing. Ordinarily, we know things through concepts and names. When the concepts and names are applied to the things coming to our attention, we meet the things halfway. Here the mind is not purely receptive. The only remedy for such ordinary thinking is to transcend and withdraw our ordinary concepts and names and let the vacuity of mind be realized. Then the mind becomes purely receptive, and is willing to welcome things wholeheartedly, and all the things are thus transparent to us. Here we have enlightenment and also self-forgetting. Nevertheless, the enlightenment of the mind is difficult to achieve, because before things come to attention we already have habits from the past, ready concepts or subconsciousness. These are waiting for our use, and, when things come to us, they pour out like fluids and fill the vacuity of mind and sentence it to death, as it were. Chuang Tzu said that the death of the mind is the greatest lamentation.[9]

According to some philosophies and some religious thought, as, e.g., in Buddhism, we must engage in practice of inner meditation and concentration of mind to enlighten what is dark in our foreconsciousness and subconsciousness. It is not clear whether Chuang Tzu has the same point of view. In Chuang Tzu's philosophy, besides the dialectic thinking used for canceling our presupposed judgments, ready concepts, and names and habits of the past, there is a third important idea about the mind, the idea of *shen* as the function of mind which is complementary to the idea of *ming*. Meeting things with *shen* is Chuang Tzu's way for attainment of the state of self-forgetting and enlightenment. This is quite different from the way of quiet meditation or serious concentration of mind as generally understood. The word *"shen"* originally meant deity or spirituality. *Shen* is usually connected with—sometimes synonymous with—the word *"ling,"* as explained above. Chuang Tzu uses it to indicate a function of the mind which is not a definite psychological process such as willing, feeling, perceiving, imagining, conceiving, or reasoning, but one which is pervading, and meets the things in their changing processes with intuitive and sympathetic understanding but without attachment. *Shen* is a function of the mind when the mind is permeated with fully living life. *Shen* is always characterized by freedom and spontaneity and is never contracted and reflexive. When *shen* is extended and meets things with intuitive and sympathetic understanding, we have self-forgetting immediately, and we transcend any things which fill our mind. Thus, vacuity of mind can be realized, and enlightenment can be attained through the very extending of *shen*.

In view of Chuang Tzu's three ideas of the mind, it is quite clear that self-forgetting is possible of achievement. When such self-forgetting is achieved, the sense of the self as an individual is gone, and since, the world is correlated with the individual self, the sense of the world can thus be forgotten also.

As self-forgetting and world-forgetting are both stressed by Chuang Tzu, we call his way that of transcending the sense of both the individual self and the world as dualistically related, and as thinking that there is, in reality, neither world nor individual. We may, interpret this as the way of experiencing the two as one. Chuang Tzu says, "I am living with Heaven and Earth; I am one with the ten thousand things." [10] However, experiencing the two as one is not necessarily to be thought of or talked about. If it is thought of or talked about, the very thinking or talking has to be transcended again. Here we have paradoxical thinking and talking. This is because, when the mind is vacuous, receptive, and knowing without attachment, and enlightenment and spirituality of the mind are realized, the concept "one" cannot be used. It, too, has to be enlightened through and passed by the extending of spirituality, and so the sense of the world and the individual as one has to be transcended, too. Therefore, according to this type of thinking, there is neither world nor individual. The state of mind of this type of thinking is thus neither subjective nor objective. Instead, it resides in the center of subject and object, and, hanging *in vacuo,* escapes from the duality of these two.[11]

When Lin-chi I-hsüan (785–867?), the Ch'an master, talks about his way of teaching disciples, he says: "Sometimes I cancel the [idea of] 'person' [as subjective], but not the idea of 'world' [as objective]; sometimes I cancel the [idea of] 'world' [as objective] but not the [idea of] 'person' [as subjective]; sometimes, I cancel both the 'person' and the 'world'; and sometimes I cancel neither the 'person' nor the 'world.'" [12] His first way of teaching corresponds to the first way of thinking described above, with the difference that the latter positively asserts the individual person as existing in the objective world. His second way of teaching corresponds to the second way of thinking mentioned above, with the difference that the latter asserts positively the being of the objective world as identical with, or part of, or the content of, the being of the individual as subject. His third way of teaching is more like the third way of thinking, as discussed in this section; it is a synthesis of the earlier two, and rightly represents the spirit of Ch'an. Therefore, the way of thinking of Ch'an also belongs to this type. His fourth way of teaching is the negative of the third way in its logical form, and is actually the same in the spirit of negativity. "I cancel neither the person nor the world" is not the same as "I assert positively both the existence of the subjective person as an individual and the objective world." This will be discussed next.

IV. The Individual and the World Known as Mutually Transcendent and Immanent Through Knowledge of Virtuous Nature and Sense-Knowledge

The fourth way of thinking of the individual and the world—that both exist—is a general tendency of Chinese thought. Even those thinkers who have been classified above as belonging to the other three types never deny this explicitly. However, only the Confucianists take the co-existence of individual and world seriously, and only in Confucianism do we get the philosophical basis of this way of thinking, a view of the mind which is more synthetic than the other three views.

This fourth view takes the mind as both receptive cognitively and active and creative morally, and insists that, when its nature is realized authentically, enlightenment (*ming*) and spirituality (*shen*) can be included. This view originated with Mencius and was developed in *The Doctrine of the Mean (Chung yung)* and the Commentaries on *The Book of Changes* (*I ching*), which can be supposed to be later than Mencius, and was further developed by Neo-Confucianism in the Sung and Ming dynasties (960–1644). It is sometimes neglected by some Confucian thinkers who are more practically oriented.

In this trend of thought, when the mind knows cognitively and becomes intelligent or wise, it should also be as vacuous as it can be. When the mind is vacuous, it is purely receptive and can become transparent and enlightened. In this respect there is no fundamental difference between Confucianism and Taoism. Yet, on the other side, the mind has its activity and creativity, and it can be self-conscious of itself as an acting subject or a creative subject. When the mind knows the objective world cognitively and has no reflection of itself or thinks of its knowing subject or itself as a thing existing in the world objectively, then we have the first type of thinking, which neglects the subject as an individual which is incapable of being objectified as one among the other things in the world. When the mind is self-conscious of itself as a knowing and acting subject, and thinks of the world-being as identical with its own being or as the content or a part of itself, we have the second way of thinking, which neglects the independent and transcendent existence of the objective world. The first way of thinking may lead man to lose the sense of individual dignity and go astray in the myriad things of the world. The second way of thinking may lead man to assert his self as an absolute and in that case may engender the sense of pride, which is contrary to the moral sense of man. The third way of thinking considers the mind as vacuous, and then self-pride is eradicated. The shortcoming of the third way is its neglect of the mind of the individual self as a subject which is active and creative and self-conscious of itself as such. As it is active and creative, it is not simply vacuous as non-being, but is being and existence also. As it is self-conscious of itself, it can know itself as being an existing self-conscious individual self. On the other side, as the mind is receptive and can know things other than itself, the things also can be self-consciously known as existing. As it is possible also for the mind to forget itself as self-conscious, it is not necessary for it to see things existing merely as a part of, or the content of, or identical with, its being, and it is quite possible for the mind in its self-forgetting to assert the existence of the world and to see it as independent existence.

When the existence of the mind of the individual self and the existence of the things of the world are both asserted, we have the fourth way of thinking of the individual and the world. In this fourth way, Confucianists have the idea of enlightenment and spirituality, which are connected with the mind as active and creative more than with the mind as vacuous and receptive.

According to Mencius, the mind is active and creative, because it has moral nature, which is essentially good, with an inner light. When man fully realizes his good nature and has sageliness, which is unfathomable by knowledge, he has spirituality or holiness.[13] As Mencius' thought is developed into the thought of *The Doctrine of the Mean* and the Commentaries on *The Book of Changes,* ideas about enlightenment and spirituality become more important. In the former, the virtue of human nature is called "*ch'eng,*" which means "creating and accomplishing oneself and all the things of the world." [14] *Ch'eng* is *Tao,* the principle of the world as well as of man. The highest *ch'eng,* as it is realized by the sage, is a way of everlastingly creating and accomplishing, which is the same as everlastingly creating and accomplishing Heaven and Earth. When *ch'eng* is realized and is expressed, there is light or enlightenment, and from enlightenment one can also realize *ch'eng.*[15] Therefore, the "everlastingly creating and accomplishing" is not only a process of continuous activity; it is also a process illuminated by light and transparent from beginning to end; it is the same as the way of the deity, which is a way of spirituality.

In *The Doctrine of the Mean,* one's inner self and outer things are harmonized in the idea of *ch'eng* as a universal principle. This is rightly called the way of thinking whereby both the individual and the world exist in one ultimate harmony (*t'ai ho*), with light illuminated through it. The inner self as subjective and outer things as objective are then mutually reflected, as mutually creating, mutually accomplishing, and interdependent in a common spiritual enlightenment. In the Commentaries on *The Book of Changes,* the principle of Heaven is called "*ch'ien,*" which is a principle of knowing and creating, and the principle of Earth is called "*k'un,*" which is the principle of realization and accomplishment.[16] These two principles are embodied in man as his human nature, in which intelligence or wisdom, and *jen,* generating love, originated. Here intelligence or wisdom is receptive in knowing, and, at the same time, knowing is an act and is creative also. Generating love is creative, and, at the same time, is receptive to what is loved. The mind as receptive may be called its *yin* aspect, and as creative may be called its *yang* aspect.[17] As *yin* and *yang* are two principles or two aspects of the one ultimate *Tao,* and are mutually rooted in each other, therefore the creative aspect and the receptive aspects of mind are mutually rooted in its nature, and the mind, as knowing and acting, or as intelligence or wisdom, and generating love (*jen*) are mutually implied in their meanings.

In the Commentaries on *The Book of Changes,* the idea of enlightenment (*ming*) and the idea of spirituality (*shen*) are also emphasized. *Ch'ien,* a universal principle of knowing and creating, is also characterized as a "great enlightenment from beginning to end,"[18] and spirituality is taken as "pervading all things of the world" and "without particular direction."[19] Here enlightenment is not merely a static state of mind; it also resides in a dynamic process of changing life; and spirituality is not only meeting things with intuitive and sympathetic understanding and without attachment, but also "pervading in creating and accomplishing all things according to their particularities without remainder."[20] As spirituality and enlightenment exist in man, what should be sought is the "preservation of them in silence and the realization of them in virtuous action."[21] Thus, the "human nature of oneself is realized" and "Heaven's decree is attained or fulfilled."[22] This is a way of

thinking which puts emphasis on both oneself as an individual subject and other individual things of the world as objects, and all
of them are seen as organically related in one ultimate harmony,
a universal principle of man or of human nature and of all things
in the world, and the co-existence of the world and the individual
was thus established in classical Confucianism.

Its development in the Neo-Confucianism of the Sung and
Ming dynasties consists in the clearer elucidation of the thoughts of
classical Confucianism with some new interpretations. One new
idea agreed to by almost all Neo-Confucianists of the Ch'eng-Chu
school is the idea of "one principle (or one reason) participated
in by different things," which is a metaphysical idea for the synthesis of the one and the many, identity and difference, and the
universal and the particular individual. It is also closely related to
a new theory of mind and knowledge. As Chang Tsai (1020–1077)
and the Ch'eng brothers classify man's kinds of knowledge into
sense-knowledge (*chieh-wen chih-chih*) and knowledge of virtuous
nature (*te-hsing chih-chih*), the latter is always taken as universal,
self-identical, and one, and the former is always taken as particular
and as differentiated according to the many sensed objects.

As knowledge of virtuous nature can be expressed through
sense-knowledge, we have an example of "one principle participated in by different things." According to Chang Tsai and the
Ch'eng brothers, "knowledge of virtuous nature" is quite different
from "sense-knowledge." One of the differences is that we can have
knowledge of virtuous nature which comprises spirituality and enlightenment,[23] but we cannot attain to spirituality and enlightenment through sense-knowledge alone. The reason knowledge of
virtue can comprise enlightenment and spirituality is based upon
the fact that knowledge of virtuous nature is not merely knowledge
which takes virtuous nature as its object.

Knowledge of virtuous nature is knowledge through the very
virtuous practice of the moral mind. More adequately, it is not
knowledge about anything else; it is only self-knowledge of the
moral mind as such, or of the moral mind self-conscious of itself
as such, or the moral mind as transparent to itself as such, and
this is self-enlightenment. As the self-conscious moral mind is active, creative, and pervading all things in the world, it knows no
limits in its creative and active extending, and it acts like deity
and comprises spirituality. However, sense-knowledge is directed to
the sense-object, which is opaque by itself, but can, so to speak,

absorb the light radiated from our minds. Therefore, when isolated from the knowledge of the virtuous mind, it does not comprise self-enlightenment, and thus we can never attain spirituality through it alone.

Sense-knowledge is distinctly different in kind from self-knowledge of virtuous nature or spiritual enlightenment, but they are not necessarily separated in existence and can co-exist. In fact, they ought to co-exist, and the knowledge of virtuous nature can fully exist only through sense-knowledge. This is because the virtuous nature ought to be realized in moral action, and moral action is purposive in creating and accomplishing objective things, which can be known only through the senses. So far as our knowledge of virtuous nature is realized and expressed in the outer world through sense-knowledge about outer things, the knowledge of virtuous nature is taken as one, and sense-knowledge about outer things varies according to the differences of things. We thus have an actual exemplification of "one principle expressed (and participated in) by different things." Since knowledge about outer things is the necessary condition for the expression of our knowledge of virtuous nature, it ought to be sought and stressed even from the point of view of the knowledge of virtuous nature. Since things known by sense-knowledge are all individuals, "investigation of individual things one by one" is included in the teaching of the "investigation of things" as expounded by Ch'eng I (1033–1107) and Chu Hsi (1130–1200).

Furthermore, since these two kinds of knowledge are related and are differentiated only by their directions as outer-oriented and inner-oriented, what is known through them as "I as self-conscious moral subject" and "individual things of the world" should both be posited as really existing. Here we have four points of view about the mutual transcendence and immanence between the world and individual self.

First, when I am known by myself mainly through my sense-knowledge as an individual existence, I then co-exist with other outer things and persons in one objective world, and I as one individual and all other individuals are immanent in one objective world.

Second, if all outer things, including my body and other persons and things known as outer things, are taken as nothing but those known only through my sense and immanent in my world of sense, and, if I am convinced also that I have knowledge of virtuous nature, which belongs to a higher level above my knowledge of outer things, then I, as an individual self-conscious moral subject, can be taken as transcendent to all things of the world known as outer, and, similarly, can be looked upon as transcendent to the whole outer world.

Third, from a higher point of view, I know also that I am not the only individual self-conscious moral subject, and that other individual persons whom I know through sense as existing in the outer world are each actually having their knowledge of virtuous nature, and each is an individual self-conscious moral subject as well as I am; and I as an individual am known by others through their sense and by being seen by them as existing in their outer worlds also; therefore, I have to acknowledge their transcendence to me and that I am immanent in their sense of the outer world. Thus, I am immanent in the outer worlds of others, which are transcendent to me.

Fourth, from a still higher point of view, we should have the self-conviction that I know all that has just been said. I know that each person has the same self-conscious moral mind and knowledge of virtuous nature. I know also that I have to act toward them with respect and love. I know all of these through the reasoning of my moral mind (also the rational mind), which is based on the knowledge of my virtuous nature. Consequently, nothing is transcendent to this reasoning of my moral mind, which is based on the knowledge of my virtuous nature. Thus, the reasoning of my moral mind is without doubt mine. However, this reasoning leads me to the acknowledgment of others as having the same moral mind, the same outer world, and the same reasoning as mine. It is, then, a transcendental reasoning which leads me to transcend the "very reasoning as only mine," and such reasoning should be taken as self-transcending reasoning and not only as belonging to me but also as revealed to me. Thus it may be taken as heavenly reasoning, or the heavenly principle, as participated in by me and flowing in my mind. As heavenly, the reasoning or principle is universal and of the world as well as mine. It is revealed to me and participated in by me as an individual, as well as revealed to, and participated in by, any different individual who is a self-conscious mind or moral subject, as I am. Hence, we have an ultimate belief in "one principle" or "one reason" participated in by different individuals, which is closely related to the above ideas about the nature of moral mind, the knowledge of virtuous nature, and sense-knowledge.

In conclusion, though the world and the individual are either immanent or transcendent to each other from the different points of view of different levels of thinking, they are ultimately included as moments of one idea of an ultimate harmony of mind and Heaven, or one vision of the ultimate harmony of the individual and the world which expresses "one principle expressed by (or participated in by) different things," as in the Ch'eng-Chu school.

As the fourth way of thinking about the individual and the world is not denied explicitly by other schools of Chinese thought, the relation of the individual subject and the objective world is usually thought of by Chinese thinkers as in one ultimate harmony.

The Chinese translation of the words "subject" and "object" of Indian and Western philosophy are *"chu"* and *"pin,"* or *"jen"* and *"ching,"* or *"chien"* and *"hsiang"*. Originally *"chu"* means host, and *"pin"* means guest; *"jen"* means man, and *"ching"* means environment or things in vision; *"chien"* means seeing, and *"hsiang"* means what is seen and taking the role of assisting in the seeing. The three pairs of words are reciprocally complementary as in a harmonious whole or a harmonious experience. Taking the subject as host, the object is the guest who is invited and loved by the host (this symbolizes the object's immanence in the subject), and also respected and sent out by the host (this symbolizes the object's transcendence to the subject). On the other hand, the world can be seen also by the poets and philosophers as host, and then the man (or I as an individual) is guest of the world and is entertained by the hospitality of the world. It is quite clear that there is no dualism between host and guest. This metaphor is the best symbol for Chinese thought about the relation of the subjective individual and the objective world as mutually immanent and transcendent in an ultimate harmony.

QUESTION: In Section III of your paper you have quoted the sayings of Lin-chi I-hsüan and have translated the fourth sentence as "I cancel neither the person (as subject) nor the world (as object)." The same sentence is translated by Suzuki as "to make both the subject and the object remain." Which of the two translations is closer to the original, or do they both have the same meaning?

ANSWER: According to the Chinese original, Lin-chi I-hsüan used the expression *"ch'u-pu-to"* in the fourth sentence, which means to "cancel neither," as I have translated it. Suzuki's translation has converted the negative sentence into a positive one, as if to "cancel neither" may imply to "assert both." Nevertheless, in the spirit of Ch'an, a double negation does not necessarily imply an assertion; therefore, to "not cancel" or to "cancel neither" may simply imply the negation of canceling, and nothing more. So, I think my translation may be closer to the original.

QUESTION: You have classified Chinese thought about the individual and the world according to four types, yet most of your illustrations are taken from the schools of pre-Ch'in philosophy. I would like to know how you classify the different schools of Chinese Buddhism of the Medieval Ages and Neo-Confucianism of the Sung-Ming and Ch'ing dynasties according to these four categories.

ANSWER: The reason most of my illustrations of the categories come from schools of the pre-Ch'in period is that the thoughts of these schools are more original and purer in type, and their essential ideas are more easily grasped. As to the classification of Chinese Buddhism and Neo-Confucianism, the problem is somewhat complicated. Roughly speaking, in the different schools of Buddhism, the Mādhyamika school, which takes *śūnyatā* as objectively pervading all individual things, is a way of thinking belonging to the first category in a superseded form; the Vijñānavāda school, which begins with epistemological idealism and ends in a kind of ethical idealism through the transformation of *vijñāna*, has to be classified as beyond the individual and the world, and belongs therefore to the third type. The schools of Hua-yen and T'ien-t'ai, which are schools of Buddhism created by Chinese monks and which emphasize, not only the teaching of co-existence of the one and the many, of the world and the individual, but also their mutual inclusion and interreflexive relations in a most comprehensive and subtle metaphysical system, may be taken as a Buddhist version of the *Chung yung* and *The Book of Changes,* and thus belong to the fourth type.

After the Sung Dynasty, the thoughts of Chou Tun-i and Chang Tsai, who take the cosmological approach to philosophy and see man as part of the objective world, which is not pervaded simply by *śūnyatā* but exists objectively, belong to the first category. The Lu-Wang school and the Ch'eng-Chu school are classified as belonging to the second and third types, respectively, as explained in my paper. Some thinkers of the Lu-Wang school, such as Yang Chien and Wang Chi, who emphasize the sense of "beyond the self as individual ego and the world as opposite to the self," and some forerunners of the Ch'eng-Chu school, such as Shao Yung, who, in his philosophical poems expresses his pure contemplation of the changes of the universe without recognition of the individual or the world, are all of the third type of thinking.

At the end of the Ming Dynasty and the beginning of the Ch'ing Dynasty, there was Wang Fu-chih, who went back to Chang Tsai's way of thinking and emphasized the status of the individual against the background of an objective, natural, histori-cal world. Tai Chen, Yen Yüan, and many scholars of the Ch'ing Dynasty all laid emphasis on the knowledge of individual things as objectively determined by their spatio-temporal locations, their ac-tual functions of and relations to other things of the world, and thus encouraged the study of history, ancient classics, and historical remains. It seems that, in the later period of the Ch'ing Dynasty, the profound Chinese philosophical wisdom sank to acceptance of what is actually existing in the objective historical world. The reason the historical materialism of Marx and Engels could conquer the mind of recent China is that it takes advantage of this trend of thought, though the other three typical ways of thinking in tradi-tional philosophy will come back again, according to the historical fluctuations of Chinese thought.

Notes

1. He begins his treatise "On Pointing and Things" with the statement that nothing is incapable of being pointed to, but that the pointing (with the names we use for pointing understood) is not being pointed to. *Kung-sun Lung*, III.

2. *Hsün Tzu*, XXII, "Rectification of Names." For detailed discussion on Hsün Tzu's theory of names, see my paper "Hsün Tzu chen-ming yü ming-hsüeh *san tsung*" (Hsün Tzu's Rectification of Names and Three Schools of Logicians in Pre-Ch'in Philosophy), *Hsin-ya hsüeh-pao* (*New Asia Journal*), V, No. 2. (August, 1963), 1–22.

3. For the original meaning and the derivative meanings of the words "*yin*" and "*yang*," consult my book *Che-hsüeh-kai-lun* (A Treatise on Philosophy) (Hong Kong: Mencius Educational Foundation, 1961), Vol. II, Part III, chap. 5, sec. 3; also chap. 9, sec. 1.

3a. As for individualism, we have Yang Chu (400–? B.C.) in the Pre-Ch'in period, who insists on the theory of one self (*wei-wo*), and who is as influential as the Moist school was in the Mencius age. However, we know nothing clear about all his arguments for individualism. He does not expound any solipsism or subjective idealism in the epistemological sense.

4. *Mencius*, VIIA.4.

5. *Hsiang-shan ch'üan-chi* (*The Complete Works of Lu Hsiang-shan*) (Shanghai: Chung Hua Co., 1935), Vol. 36, p. 37.

6. *Yang-ming ch'üan-shu* (*The Complete Works of Wang Yang-ming*) (Shanghai: Chung Hua Co., 1935), Vol. III, p. 26.

7. Liu Chi-shan's discussion on the ideas of *tu* and *tu-chih* is available in the last volume of *Ming-ju hsüeh-an* (Anthology edited and written by Huang Tsung-hsi and Critical Accounts of the Neo-Confucians of the Ming Dynasty) (1610–1695). For a contemporary exposition, see Mou Tsung-san's article "Liu-Chi-shan chih ch'eng-i-chih-hsüeh" (Theory of Authenticity of Will of Liu Chi-shan), *Tzu-yu hsüeh-jen* (Free Thinker), I, No. 3 (October, 1956), 9–24.

8. *Chuang Tzu*, XXXIII.

9. *Chuang Tzu*, II.

10. *Ibid.*

11. The second chapter of the *Chuang Tzu* begins with talking about "loss of reason," which can be rightly explained as getting out of the duality of subject and object.

12. "Chih-wu lun" (Records of the Pointing of the Moon), edited by Chu Ju-chi (Taipei: Far East Book Co., 1959), Vol. 14, p. 5.

13. *Mencius*, VII.

14. The word *"ch'eng"* is sometimes translated as sincerity. This is quite misleading and does not conform to the text of the *Chung yung*. It is better to define it as "creating and accomplishing oneself and all the things of the world" than to follow a literal translation.

15. *Chung yung*, XXI. (Shanghai: Commercial Press edition, 1937), p. 12.

16. The best exposition of *ch'ien* as principle of knowing and creating and of *k'un* as principle of realization and accomplishment is available in the *Hsü-t'an-chih-chüan* (Looking around the Altar with Straightforward Illustrations) of Lo Chin-ch'i (1515–1588). See my essay "Lo Chin-ch'i chih li-hsüeh" (On the Philosophy of Lo Chin-ch'i) Special issue for one hundred issues of *Min-chu p'ing-lun* (Democratic Review), V, No. 6 (March, 1954), 2–10.

17. See my book *A Treatise on Philosophy*, Vol. II, Part II, chap. 19, sec. 6.

18. See "Ch'ien wen-yen" (Commentaries on *Ch'ien* as a Principle of Heaven), in *The Book of Changes*.

19. Commentaries on *The Book of Changes*.

20. *Ibid.*
21. *Ibid.*
22. *Ibid.*
23. The ideas of *shen* (spirituality) and *ming* (enlightenment) are two very profound ideas of Neo-Confucianism which are closely related to the knowledge of virtuous nature, but are usually neglected by contemporary scholars of Confucianism. I have given some hints on the significance of these two ideals of Confucianism in my book *Chung-kuo-wen-hua chih ching-shen chia-chih* (The Spiritual Worth of Chinese Culture) (Hong Kong: Cheng Chung, 1953), chap. 4. Further study of their meanings in Neo-Confucian thought is needed.

WING-TSIT CHAN   *The Individual*

in Chinese Religions

THERE ARE conflicting phenomena in Chinese religions, especially where the individual is concerned. On the one hand, in
popular religions the life of the individual is strongly influenced,
if not controlled, by his ancestors and other spiritual beings. In
ancestor worship, his duty is to serve the deceased, and he sub-
merges himself in group ancestral rites, in which the spirit of the
ancestor is central. He believes in fate, which is beyond his control.
The government used to regulate the number of temples, appoint
and dismiss priests, and even promote or demote the gods he
worshipped. On the philosophical level, the Confucianist aspires
to be one with Heaven; the Taoist aims at identification with
Nature "without differentiation"; and the Buddhist hopes to enter
nirvāna, where all individual characteristics and differences disappear.

On the other hand, aside from ancestral rites, group worship
has never been an institution in China, worship being largely a
personal matter. Even in religious festivals, worship is individual.
There has never been a central religious authority to dictate to
conscience, regulate the beliefs, or control the destiny of the individual. National religious organizations were unknown until 1929,
when the Chinese Buddhist Society was established. That organization was entirely for the purpose of the protection of temple
properties and for social and intellectual reforms, however, and had
nothing to do with personal beliefs or practices. It was not intended
to be a national church. In the Taoist religion, there was not even

an attempt at a national organization until 1958, when the National Taoist Society was formed in Peking, obviously for political control. The so-called Heavenly Teacher, presumably the head of the Taoist religion, had no more than local contact with Taoist priests and had very little influence over the faithful. His very title implies that he was custodian of a body of religious knowledge but was not an arbiter of morals or an authoritative spiritual leader. The last Heavenly Teacher merely conducted a school in the bastion of the religion, the Dragon and Tiger Mountain area in Chiangsi, and acted as an astrologer and a miracle performer, believed by some to be able to "command the wind and produce the rain." The Taoist or Buddhist priest was essentially a technician and a consultant whose duty it was to advise on and to perform ceremonies, usually for a consideration. He was in no sense an agent of the worshipper before the gods or a link between them. The worshipper's approach to the gods was his own—direct, individual, and personal.

These facts clearly show that there are conflicts in the Chinese religious picture, particularly with respect to the individual. However, these conflicts are more apparent than real. When the fundamental aspects of Chinese religious life and thought are understood, these conflicts will be resolved.

The best way to understand the status of the individual in Chinese religions is to see, first, what the goal in Chinese religions is; secondly, the way to achieve that goal; and, thirdly, the position of the individual in relation to ultimate reality, namely, Heaven in Confucianism, *Tao* in Taoism, and *Nirvāṇa*, or Thusness, in Buddhism.

The Goal of Self-Realization

Like any other people, the Chinese aim at many things in their religious beliefs and practices, but their ultimate goal is simply the survival of the individual and the realization of his nature. Historically, the question of survival came first—we shall consider it later.

From the very early days of Chinese history, the Chinese believed in personal survival. Records found in the oracle bones dating back to the Shang Dynasty (1751–1112 B.C.) contain numerous references to sacrifices to ancestors, with offerings of food and other daily necessities and luxuries. Daily utensils and, in extreme cases, their bodyguards or even concubines were buried with them so that they could be served. These sacrifices, however barbaric, clearly indicate a definite belief in individual survival after death. Gradually the concept of the Highest God, *Ti*, or the Lord, developed. The interesting thing is that illustrious ancestors were believed to co-exist with *Ti* in Heaven. As *The Book of Odes* says of the founder of the Chou Dynasty (1111–256 B.C.), "King Wen is above On the left and right of the Lord." [1]

During the Chou Dynasty, another practice became common, that of recalling the soul of the individual. After a person died, his family immediately went up to the roof and, waving some of his clothing, called, "So-and-so, please come back," and then descended to the house to offer him food.[2] The assumption was that the man's soul ascended to the sky and could return to receive the offerings. Ancient Chinese literature, especially that of the fifth and fourth centuries B.C., is fairly rich in essays and poems devoted to recalling the soul. The soul is called "*hun-p'o*." According to ancient belief, at death a white (*p'o*) light leaves the human body and joins the moon's light. To this was later added the concept of *hun*, which etymologically includes the element of *yün* (cloud), which is more active than light. Thus, according to the traditional theory, *hun* is the soul of man's vital force, which is expressed in man's intelligence and his power of breathing, whereas *p'o* is the spirit of man's physical nature expressed in his body and his physical movements. At death, *hun-p'o* survives.

This strong belief in personal survival after death certainly affirmed the importance of the individual after death, but at the same time tended to undermine his importance before death. In the Shang Dynasty no important activity was undertaken without first obtaining the approval of spiritual beings. Holes would be drilled halfway through the oracle bones. They would then be thrown into fire, and priests would interpret the message of spiritual beings by the cracks.

This practice continued into the Chou Dynasty, which succeeded the Shang, but a radical change began to take place. The new dynasty needed human talents to build a new state. When irrigation produced more water than prayer for rain, man naturally assumed an increasing importance over spiritual beings. Man came to the fore, and spiritual beings were kept more and more at a distance. As *The Book of Rites* says, "The people of Yin (Shang) honored spiritual beings, served them, and put them ahead of ceremonies. . . . The people of Chou honored ceremonies and valued highly the conferring of honors. They served the spiritual beings and respected them, but kept them at a distance." [3]

This trend was highly accentuated by Confucius (551–479 B.C.). He would not discuss spiritual beings.[4] He told one of his pupils that "to honor spiritual beings and keep them at a distance may be regarded as wisdom." [5] When he was asked about serving spiritual beings, he replied, "If we are not yet able to serve man, how can we serve spiritual beings," and, "If we do not yet know about life, how can we know about death?" [6] Actually, Confucius neither denied the existence of spiritual beings nor ignored ancestors. He declared, "How abundant is the display of power of spiritual beings. . . . Like the spread of overflowing water, they seem to be above and to be on the left and on the right." [7] He taught people "to serve the dead as they were served while alive, and [to] serve the departed as they were served while still with us." "This is the height of filial piety," he added.[8] But his way of serving was radically different from the traditional. Even during his lifetime there were two cases of human sacrifice.[9] He bitterly denounced such an inhuman practice and even the use of dummies to bury with the dead.[10] What he wanted was to replace such barbaric customs with moral principles and social decorum. He urged his pupils to serve parents according to the rules of propriety while they are alive, bury them according to the rules of propriety when they die, and sacrifice to them after death according to the rules of propriety.[11] Since his emphasis was on rules of propriety, spiritual beings came to occupy a secondary position. In this way, whether Confucius meant to or not, he weakened, if not destroyed, the belief in personal survival after death.

But the chief rivals of the ancient Confucianists, notably the Moists of the fifth and fourth centuries B.C., strongly attacked them and upheld the belief in spiritual beings. Mo Tzu (fl. 468–376 B.C.) defended the belief on the grounds that people had actually heard the voices of spiritual beings, that their existence had been recorded, and that belief in spiritual beings was helpful to personal conduct and national peace.[12] In his basic doctrine of promotion of welfare and removal of evil, he always insisted that what was beneficial to Heaven, spiritual beings, and man is good.[13] Although he never proved the existence of spiritual beings, nowhere else in ancient China was the belief in personal immortality more strongly held.

Eventually, this belief grew in two different directions, namely, in the Taoist religion and in Buddhism. The Taoists wanted immortality on earth, while the Buddhists wanted it in paradise.

Eventually, this belief grew in two different directions, namely, in the Taoist religion and in Buddhism. The Taoists wanted immortality on earth, while the Buddhists wanted it in paradise.

The Taoist search for earthly immortality goes back to antiquity. Chuang Tzu (b. 369 B.C.) mentioned immortals.[14] From the first to the sixth century, Taoist priests pushed this search with great effort. They practiced alchemy, promoted exercises, developed medicine, and delved into breathing, concentration, and sex techniques, all in an attempt to achieve immortality on earth. Until recently, to become immortals remained a fervent hope for many of the faithful in the Taoist religion.

In about the same period, Buddhism began to flourish in China. One of its greatest attractions to the Chinese was its promise of eternal life in paradise, for there had been no such idea in China. The belief in paradise was especially strong in the Pure Land school founded in China in the fourth century. It has been the most popular Buddhist sect in China for the last 800 years, testifying to the strong belief in and the earnest hope on the part of millions of Chinese for rebirth in the Pure Land. So far as the masses are concerned, there is no question that the individual continues to live after death.

The story with the intellectuals, however, has been entirely different. With a few exceptions, such as the Moists, they have been consistent in rejecting belief in personal survival after death.

In the first century A.D., Wang Ch'ung (27–100?), one of the most rationalistic and critical philosophers in Chinese history, and one of the most influential, wrote a treatise to disprove the existence of spiritual beings. He argued that "the dead do not become spiritual beings, do not possess consciousness, and cannot harm people." [15] "When a person dies," he said, "his blood becomes exhausted. With this, his vital forces are extinct, and his body decays and becomes ashes and dust. What is there to become a spiritual being?" [16] Furthermore, "If a spiritual being is really the spirit of a dead man, then, when people see it, they ought to see the form of a nude. . . . Why? Because garments have no spirit." [17] He offered other reasons against the existence of spiritual beings. While they sound very naïve, for almost 2,000 years no one in Chinese history has successfully refuted him.

Just as Wang Ch'ung criticized the traditional belief in spiritual beings, Fan Chen (b. 450) attacked the Buddhist belief. He argued that physical form and spirit were identical and that, as the physical form disappears, so does the spirit, as the sharpness of a knife disappears with the knife.[18] Later, Neo-Confucianists, from the twelfth century on have unanimously attacked both the Taoist and the Buddhist belief in everlasting life. Wang Yang-ming (1472–1529), for example, said, "The Buddhists lure people into their way of life by the promise of escape from the cycle of life and death, and the Taoists, who seek immortality, do so with the promise of everlasting life." [19] To him, as to other Neo-Confucianists, the motivation is selfish and immoral. For them, as for Chinese intellectuals from the sixth century B.C. on, immortality consists in social immortality, or immortality of influence. When the question was asked in 546 B.C. about what the ancient saying, "dead but immortal," meant, the answer was that "the best course is to establish virtue, the next best is to establish achievement, and still the next best is to establish words. When these are abandoned with time, this may be called immortality." [20] Confucius certainly contributed to this feeling, and it has been the feeling of the intellectuals ever since.

Does this mean that the intellectuals reject the individual? Not in the least. They, like the masses, firmly believe in the central importance of the individual, but in another way, namely, full realization of one's nature, instead of everlasting life on earth or eternal existence in paradise.

The Confucianists were the first in ancient China to propagate the doctrine of fulfillment of human nature. Mencius (371–298? B.C.) said, "He who exerts his mind to the utmost knows his nature. He who knows his nature knows Heaven. To preserve one's mind and to nourish one's nature is the way to serve Heaven. Not to allow any double-mindedness regardless of longevity or brevity of life, but to cultivate one's person and wait for destiny (ming, fate, Heaven's Decree or Mandate) to take its own course is the way to fulfill one's destiny." [21] This doctrine reached its zenith in the Ch'eng brothers and Chu Hsi (1130–1200) and has remained central in the Confucian tradition. Ch'eng I (1033–1107) said, "The investigation of principle to the utmost, the full development of one's nature, and the fulfillment of destiny are one thing. As principle is investigated to the utmost, one's nature is fully developed, and, as one's nature is fully developed, one's destiny is fulfilled." [22]

His brother, Ch'eng Hao (1032–1085), said, "The investigation of principle to the utmost, the full development of one's nature, and the fulfillment of one's destiny—these three are to be accomplished simultaneously. There is basically no time sequence among them. The investigation of principle to the utmost should not be regarded merely as a matter of knowledge. If one really investigates principle to the utmost, even one's nature and destiny can be fulfilled."[23] Chu Hsi considered preserving the mind and nourishing one's nature, and cultivating and controlling them, to be "the fundamental task," and it must be thorough.[24]

This trend of thought finds its modern expression in the contemporary Neo-Confucianism of Professor Fung Yu-lan (1890–) and Hsiung Shih-li (1885–). Fung said, "People in the moral sphere fulfill human relations and human duties. In doing so, they investigate human principle to the utmost and fulfill human nature. People in the transcendental sphere serve Heaven and assist in the natural transformation of things. In doing so they investigate the principle of the universe and fulfill the nature of the universe. . . . To penetrate the mysteries and to know the transformation of the universe are to complete the work of the universe. . . . And this is serving Heaven."[25] Hsiung has expressed the same idea succinctly, saying, "One's self-nature is true and real. There is no need to search for a heavenly Lord outside oneself. One can develop one's own nature to the fullest extent. One need not desire nirvāṇa."[26]

The word "hsing," meaning the nature of man and things, is not mentioned in the Lao Tzu, but it runs through the Chuang Tzu.[27] In both, the ultimate goal is to preserve the essence and vitality of man. Consequently, in the Taoist religion the aim is to realize the Three Original Principles—Essence, Vital Force, and Spirit. From the third through the seventh century, both the development of ideas and the practice of alchemy were directed to this goal. In the Southern school of the Taoist religion, the emphasis is on the cultivation of one's nature, while in the Northern school it is on the cultivation and development of one's vital power.[28] This is one reason why the Taoist religion has paid special attention to the human body. It has promoted exercises, refined Chinese cooking, and developed medicine, all dedicated to the fulfillment of human nature.

In Buddhism, the idea of the realization of one's nature was not prominent. In the quest for rebirth in paradise, the chief methods were to repeat the name of the Buddha and to express faith by making offerings, reciting scripture, etc. The Buddhists said, "Take refuge in the Buddha." While the ultimate objective, rebirth in paradise, was centered on the individual, the method certainly was not. In the seventh century, a revolt arose and demanded the shift to self-effort, and that was the realization of one's own nature.

The movement was led, or probably started by Hui-neng (638–713), generally regarded as the founder of the Southern school of Buddhist Meditation (Ch'an, or Zen). In his famous *Platform Scripture,* he emphatically urged his followers to take refuge in the nature within oneself instead of taking refuge in the *buddhas* outside, for what is called the great wisdom by which to reach the Pure Land is nothing but this self-nature, and all *buddhas,* all *dharmas* (elements of existence), and all scriptures are immanent in it. Reading scriptures, building temples, doing charitable acts, making offerings, reciting the name of the Buddha, and praying to be reborn in the Pure Land are all useless. The Pure Land is nothing but the straightforward mind. If one sees his own nature, he said, one will become a *buddha.*[29]

The Way to Self-Realization

So far we have dealt with the goal of self-realization in Chinese religions and have said something about the way to achieve that goal, but much more can be added. Each of the three religions has its own way, but in each case the way can be summed up in one word, namely, vacuity (*hsü*) in Taoism, calmness (*ting*) in Buddhism, and sincerity (*ch'eng*) in Confucianism.

The term "vacuity" (sometimes translated as "emptiness") is not to be taken in the literal sense of being empty. Rather, it means absolute peacefulness and purity of mind and freedom from selfish desires and not being disturbed by incoming impressions or allowing what is already in the mind to disturb what is coming into the mind. As a feature of reality, it means a profound and deep continuum in which there is no obstruction. Lao Tzu taught people to "keep their minds vacuous," "attain complete vacuity," and "maintain steadfast quietude" in order to become enlightened and to be in accord with *Tao.*[30] Elaborating on this theme, Chuang Tzu said, "Do not be the possessor of fame. Do not be the storehouse of schemes. Do not take over the function of things. Do not be the master of knowledge [to manipulate things]. Personally realize the infinite to the highest degree and travel in the realm for which there is no sign. Exercise fully what you have received from Nature, without any subjective viewpoint. In a word, be absolutely vacuous." [31] Chuang Tzu called this state of vacuity "fasting of the mind." [32] Later, in the Taoist religion, quiet sitting, which is Taoist "fasting of the mind," re-enforced by Buddhist meditation, became an institution. It was the Taoists' chief way of preserving one's nature and nourishing the spirit.

For a similar reason, the Buddhists advocated calmness. In *The Platform Scripture*, Hui-neng repeatedly asserted that one's self-nature is originally pure, and when one becomes calm he will see this pure nature and attain *buddha*hood. Calmness will be achieved when one is freed from thoughts, from the characters of things, and from attachment to them. This does not mean not to think at all or to have nothing to do with the characters of things. Rather, it means not to be carried away by thoughts in the process of thought, to be free from the characters of things while in the midst of them. [33] Thus, the conventional method of sitting in meditation, in which one attempts to eliminate thoughts, is not good. One should not sit motionless trying to look at his own mind or his own purity. [34] Imperturbability is not motionlessness but freedom from attachment to erroneous thought. [35] When no erroneous thoughts arise, there is calmness, and, when one's inner nature is unperturbed, there is true meditation. [36] If one sees his own nature, he will become enlightened, that is, achieve *buddha*hood, suddenly.

This is the new and radical doctrine of sudden enlightenment of the Ch'an school. One can easily detect the Taoist elements of naturalness and individualism in this doctrine, but the Ch'an school has pushed the individual element much further. One of the most famous sayings of Ch'an is, "Everyone will be self-contained, and everyone will be perfectly realized." [37]

This Ch'an saying should remind one of Mencius' well-known sayings. "All things are already complete in oneself" and "All men may be Yao and Shun [sages]." [38] In the Confucian school, the doctrine of self-realization is just as strong and was developed much earlier. There the method is neither vacuity nor calmness but sincerity. The thesis is very simple. When one's will becomes sincere, one's feelings will be correct and one's moral life will be perfect. As said in *The Great Learning*, attributed to the Confucian pupil Tseng Tzu (505–*ca.* 436 B.C.), "When the will is sincere, the mind is rectified; when the mind is rectified, the personal life is cultivated; when the personal life is cultivated, the family will be regulated; when the family is regulated, the state will be in order; and, when the state is in order, there will be peace throughout the world." [39]

The Doctrine of the Mean, attributed to Confucius' grandson Tzu-ssu (492–431 B.C.), goes even further. It says, "Only those who are absolutely sincere can fully develop their nature. If they can fully develop their nature, they can then fully develop the nature of others. If they can fully develop the nature of others, they can then fully develop the nature of things. If they can fully develop the nature of things, they can then assist in the transforming and nourishing process of Heaven and Earth. If they can assist in the transforming and nourishing process of Heaven and Earth, they can thus form a trinity with Heaven and Earth." [40]

The reason for the all-importance of sincerity is that it makes things real. Significantly, the word *"ch'eng"* means both sincerity and realness. It contains as its basic element *ch'eng*, an independent word meaning "to complete." According to *The Doctrine of the Mean*, "Sincerity means the completion of the self, and the Way is self-directing. Sincerity is the beginning and end of things. Without sincerity there would be nothing." [41] As Chu Hsi explains it, "In the moral realm, there can be the deed of filial piety only if there is first of all the mind sincerely devoted to it." [42] "If every word comes from the bottom of one's heart," he said, "what is said is true. On the other hand, if one tells a lie, what he says amounts to nothing. This is why it is said that sincerity is the completion of things." [43] Wang Yang-ming also said that, if there is sincerity in being filially pious to one's parents, filial piety will take care of itself. One of the most important passages in his *Instructions for Practical Living* says, "If it is the mind that is sincere in its filial piety to parents, then in the winter it will naturally think of the cold of parents and seek a way to provide warmth for them, and in the summer it will naturally think of the heat of parents and seek a way to provide coolness for them. These are all offshoots of the mind that is sincere in its filial piety." [44]

But sincerity is not only the way to realize one's own moral nature, but also to realize the nature of things. *The Doctrine of the Mean* says, "Sincerity is not only the completion of one's own self; it is that by which all things are completed." [45] Thus, sincerity has a metaphysical meaning. Perhaps the best illustration for it, so far as we here are concerned, is religious sacrifice.

Curiously enough, Confucius had very little to say about sincerity in *The Analects*. The word hardly occurs there. However, it is recorded there that, when he offered sacrifice to his ancestors, he felt as if the ancestral spirits were actually present. When he offered sacrifice to other spiritual beings, he felt as if they were actually present. He said, "If I do not participate in the sacrifice, it is as if I did not sacrifice at all!" [46] Commentators agree that what Confucius wanted was to be sincere. As Chu Hsi remarked, "This means that, when it is time to offer sacrifice, if one cannot do so personally because of one reason or another, but asks someone else to do it for him, it will be impossible for him to extend his sincerity to the point of feeling that the spiritual beings are actually there." [47] In the case of Confucius, the idea is that he was so sincere that, when he offered sacrifices to spiritual beings, he felt as if they were really there.

Sincerity, however, not only makes spiritual beings seem real to the person who offers the sacrifice, but also makes the spiritual beings themselves real. To explain this, we have to explain what spiritual beings are.

The Chinese words for spiritual beings are *"kuei"* and *"shen."* Etymologically, *"kuei"* means "to return to the source," and *"shen"* means "to expand," but in ancient times, and for the masses even today, *"kuei-shen"* means merely spiritual beings. We have seen how important they were in the Shang Dynasty, how Confucius avoided discussing them, and how Chinese intellectuals have persistently denied their existence for the last two thousand years. To them, *kuei* and *shen* are cosmic forces, more especially the activity of the negative cosmic force, *yin,* and the positive cosmic force, *yang.* As the Neo-Confucianist Chang Tsai (1020–1077) put it, "Kuei and *shen* are but the spontaneous activity of the two material forces (*ch'i*)," that is, *yin* and *yang.* [48] In the Neo-Confucian view, everything is the product of the interaction of these two material forces. In the case of the human being, for example, innumerable elements of the two forces integrate, culminating in the father and the mother, and a person is born. As these elements disintegrate, he dies, and the material forces return to where they came from or expand. He has ceased to exist as a human being, and does not continue to exist as a ghost, but his forces continue to operate. This is the philosophical basis of the theory that sincerity can make the objects of religious sacrifice real.

Confucius said in *The Doctrine of the Mean,* "How abundantly do spiritual beings display the powers that belong to them! We look at them, but do not see them. We listen to them, but do not hear them. Yet, they enter all things, and there is nothing without them. They cause all the people in the kingdom to fast and purify themselves, and array themselves in their richest clothing, in order to attend their sacrifice. Then, like overflowing water, they seem to be above the heads and on the right and left of their worshippers. *The Book of Odes* says, "The coming of spiritual beings cannot be surmised. How much less can we get tired of them.' [49] Such is the impossibility of suppressing the outgoing of sincerity." [50] To the Neo-Confucianists, this does not mean that there are ghosts that go around and possess things. Rather, it means that the forces that used to constitute ancestors pervade everything. Sincerity can cause them to interact and integrate, even to the point of being like real persons.

Chu Hsi was once asked whether, in sacrificing to Heaven, Earth, and the spirits of mountains and rivers with offerings of silk, meat, and wine, it was merely to express one's sincerity or whether some force actually comes to receive the sacrifice. He answered, "If you say that nothing comes, then why sacrifice? What is it that is so solemn above that causes people to make offerings with awe and reverence? But, if you say that some spirit comes riding in a chariot, that is just wild talk." [51] What he meant was that, while no force comes like a ghost, certain forces are affected by one's sincerity, and so they react as if spiritual beings were coming to accept the sacrifice. In other words, although the forces of ancestors have scattered, one can, through his will to practice sincerity, cause them to come together.

The reason this is possible is that the material force of one thing is basically the same as the material force of another. The material forces of *yin* and *yang* interact, and integrate and disintegrate, in countless ways, thus producing an infinite number of things, but the material forces of these things are essentially the same. This being the case, there is a continuity between the one who offers the sacrifice and the object of his sacrifice. As Chu Hsi said, ancestors and descendants share the same material forces.[52] There is not only common blood. There is also the family heritage, which is also a kind of force combining ancestors and descendants.[53]

The continuity of a family is very much like the sea, to use Chu Hsi's analogy. Each generation is comparable to a wave. The wave in the front and the wave behind are different, and yet the water pervading both is one.[54] Just as the wave behind can affect the wave in front, so people offering sacrifice to ancestors can affect them.

In the act of sacrifice, then, if sincerity is extended to the utmost, the spirit of the ancestors can be collected. This means that the condition of the spirit of one's ancestors depends very much on one's sincerity. Chu Hsi said, "Wherever the human mind concentrates, there is the spirit." [55] As another Neo-Confucianist put it, "When there is sincerity, there will be the spirit. When there is no sincerity, there will not be the spirit." [56] A third Neo-Confucianist even went so far as to say, "Whenever we want spirit, there it will be. Whenever we do not want spirit, there it will not be." [57]

The Individual in Relation to Ultimate Reality

From the foregoing, it is clear that Chinese religions are based on the sincerity of the will, and that means the individual's own will. In this sense the individual is of great importance in Chinese religions. The question inevitably arises, however, since the goal of self-realization and its methods of vacuity, calmness, and sincerity are only for the ultimate purpose of serving Heaven in the case of Confucianists, identification with Nature, or *Tao*, in the case of Taoists, and *buddha*hood in the case of Buddhists, does this not mean that in the ultimate state, whether it is Heaven, *Tao*, or *nirvāṇa*, the individual is in the end dissolved or absorbed, since in that state all distinctions and differences, and thereby all individuality, disappear? This is the question of the relationship between the undifferentiated continuum, so to speak, and the specific, individual, differentiated units. In other words, it is the question of the relationship between the one and the many, a basic question in Chinese philosophy, of which religion may be regarded as only a part. It is not within the scope of this paper to go into this question at length. Suffice it to say that in all the three systems, Confucianism, Taoism, and Buddhism, the solution of the apparent conflict between the one and the many is essentially the same, namely, that each involves the other. In none of the three systems is the one understood as absorbing and thereby obliterating the many, or vice versa. The common conviction has been that each requires the other.

In Taoism, the question arose with the Neo-Taoists, notably Wang Pi (226–249) and Kuo Hsiang (d. 312). To Wang Pi, ultimate reality is original non-being (*pen-wu*). According to his thinking, which is developed in his Commentary on the *Lao Tzu*, original non-being transcends all distinctions and descriptions. It is the One, pure and simple, which underlines and combines all things. To Kuo Hsiang, on the other hand, ultimate reality is Nature. According to him, things exist and transform according to principle, but each and every thing has its own principle. This doctrine is fully developed in his Commentary on the *Chuang Tzu*. His emphasis is the many rather than the one. He and Wang Pi seem to stand at opposite poles, with no possibility of reconciliation. But the many of Kuo Hsiang all function according to principle, and, for Wang Pi, both function and substance, that is, the one and the many, are identified. The one and the many are not mutually exclusive, after all.[58]

The point is more clearly made in the Buddhist view, in which the one and the many explicitly involve and penetrate each other. In his famous treatise on the golden lion, Fa-tsang (643–712) says, "The gold and the lion are mutually compatible in their formation, the one and the many not obstructing each other. In this situation, the principle and the facts are different, but, whether the one or the many, each remains in its own position. This is called the gate of mutual compatibility and difference between the one and the many." [59] That is to say, in the case of the golden lion, the lion and every part of it involve the gold, and, at the same time, the gold involves the lion. Neither can exist without the other in the golden lion. Fa-tsang was using this simple and crude analogy to explain the one and the many, or the individual person and *buddha*hood. When the Ch'an school reiterates that all people have *buddha*hood in them or that the Buddha and the common people are not different, they are expressing the same idea.

The Buddhists had a decided influence on the Neo-Confucianists, whose solution of the seeming conflict between the one and the many follows the same pattern. The founder of Neo-Confucianism, Chou Tun-i (1017–1073), said, "The many are ultimately one, and the one is actually differentiated into the many. The one and many each has its own correct state of being. The great and the small each has its definite function." [60] This is the famous Neo-

Confucian doctrine that principle is one but its manifestations are many. As Ch'eng I said, "Principle in the world is one. Although there are many roads in the world, the destination is the same, and, although there are a hundred deliberations, the result is one.[61] Although things involve many manifestations and events go through infinite variations, when they are united by the one, there cannot be any contradiction." [62] In Chu Hsi's words, "Fundamentally, there is only one Great Ultimate [the sum total of principles], yet each of the myriad things has been endowed with it and each in itself possesses the Great Ultimate in its entirety. This is similar to the fact that there is only one moon in the sky, but, when its light is scattered upon rivers and lakes, it can be seen everywhere. It cannot be said that the moon has been split." [63] Chu Hsi seems to be arguing for the oneness of principle, but it must not be forgotten that he said that each thing has in itself the Great Ultimate. One is reminded of Leibniz' monad. Chu Hsi's analogy of the moon is probably a specific, though indirect, borrowing of the famous Buddhist metaphor of the ocean. The Buddhists, especially of the Hua-yen school, were fond of saying that the ocean consists of many waves, and the many waves form the ocean, each involving the other, and one cannot be fully realized without the other's being fully realized also.

This metaphysical principle definitely lies behind the ancestral group-rites, for example. These rites involved all male descendants of an ancestor, each in his proper position according to seniority of generation and age, and performing under the direction of a master of ceremony, who was often a scholar in the clan. These rites were traditionally directed by the head of descent of the clan, but he was neither an authority nor an agent, but a symbol of the unity of the clan. It may be argued that, since the scattered forces of the ancestor required the total sincerity of the whole clan before there could be enough influence on them to gather, the head of descent was an authority insofar as he was a necessity. It is certainly true that he was a necessity, but the necessity was sociological rather than religious. The system of heads of descent goes back to Chou times. By the eleventh century, it had ceased to function. Neo-Confucianists, such as Ch'eng I, strongly urged its revival. He said, "In order to control the mind of the people, unify one's clan, and enrich social customs so that people will not forget their origin, it is necessary to clarify genealogy, group members of the clan together, and institute a system of heads of descent." [64]

His interest was mainly sociological. While in these rites the clan acted as a group, each person had his unique place and function, and his sincerity toward his ancestor was personal and direct.

Government regulations and control of temples, priests, and even gods were not regular practices, nor did they have any direct relationships with the individual's religious beliefs and behavior. The measures were mostly economic and political, treating temples, priests, and even gods as civil matters. Undoubtedly there were abuses and corruption. But, even in these matters, there is something very interesting, philosophically speaking. For instance, only a higher official could promote or demote an inferior deity. The assumption was that, just as waves can affect the ocean, so human beings can influence the spiritual world, and in this case it happens that the human force is greater than that of the spirit. From the earliest times, it was the rule that the emperor worshipped Heaven, the feudal lords worshipped the spirits of mountains and rivers, higher officials worshipped the five deities, and the common people worshipped their ancestors. Scholars are not agreed what the five deities were. Up to the end of the Manchu (Ch'ing) Dynasty (1644–1912) the emperor alone could offer sacrifice to Heaven. During the Republic, President Yuan Shih-k'ai (1858–1916) once tried it. It has been suggested that the system shows that the Chinese believed simply that spiritual beings lived in exactly the same manner as human beings, so that, as there is a need for an official hierarchy in this world, so there must be one among the gods. This may well have been the case. But the philosophical implication is that Heaven required the sincerity of the whole state, of which the emperor was the symbol, to be activated. In other words, in religious worship, there is a correspondence, even in rank, between the worshipper and the worshipped. Put differently, the two parties are equally important.

What can we say about the belief in fate? Here it seems the influence comes from only one side. It is certainly true that many ignorant people believe that their lives are directed by spiritual forces beyond their understanding or control. In their ignorance and ineptitude, they have failed to realize the mutual influence of the one and the many. The educated, however, understand that *ming* does not mean fate in the sense of mysterious control by spiritual beings but means Heaven's Mandate, or Heaven's Decree, that is, what Heaven has given to a person, what Heaven has endowed him with. This is what *The Doctrine of the Mean* means when it says, "What Heaven imparts (*ming*) to man is called human nature." [65] This is the nature to be realized, and the way to realize it, as already brought out, is through one's own effort at moral cultivation, such as sincerity of will. This does not mean that the individual is the master of the universe, for there *are* things, such as life and death, and longevity or brevity of life, that are beyond his control. But, as we have learned from Mencius,[66] the Confucian injunction has been to cultivate one's moral life, develop one's nature, and let Nature take its course. The individual does not completely control his own destiny, but he is the master of his own ship in a sea that is not entirely devoid of uncertainties.

QUESTION: Is sincerity a material substance?

ANSWER: No. The translation of "*ch'i*" as material force is most unfortunate. The word *ch'i* involves, not material substance, but some force. It is translated as "breath" or "vital force" when related to the body. But when you talk about the *ch'i* of the universe, you cannot call it "breath" or "vital force." *Ch'i* in the universe is negative or positive force, or *yin* or *yang*, conditioned by material elements.

QUESTION: You say, "The Buddhist hopes to enter *nirvāna*, where all individual characteristics and differences disappear." But later you say, "In none of the three systems is the one understood as absorbing and thereby annihilating the many." Perhaps there is no conflict here, but some people might think that the Buddhists say that there is a change in China. Is that what you had in mind?

ANSWER: There was a change. In an earlier stage, *nirvāna* meant a state in which everything is transcended. But in the Huayen, or Kegon, school, which is based on the *Avataṁsaka-sūtra*, there was a distinctly Chinese development. This school developed the idea of the correlation of the one and the many. They penetrate each other.

QUESTION: Sometimes you use the word "fate," but sometimes you use "destiny." In English the word "fate" normally implies that life is somewhat blind, but on the whole nobody speaks of destiny as being blind. Now, which of the two would you like, or do you have both?

ANSWER: The word "*ming*" has not only both of these meanings but also the meaning of the verb to order, to give, to endow. To the ignorant, the uncertainty leads to superstitions. For them, the word *"ming"* should be translated as "fate." But, to the educated, the scholars, the word *"ming"* means "fate" only to the extent of covering life and death and the length and the shortness of life. It also covers success and failure, but not success and failure in the sense that we cannot do anything, but only ultimate success or failure. The general sense of *"ming"* is that, if you know what your nature is and if you do your best, you can fulfill it. The idea is that anybody trying his best can become a sage. In that sense, the word *"ming"* should be translated as "destiny."

QUESTION: What is the status of the individual woman in Chinese religious thought?

ANSWER: So far as salvation is concerned, woman is absolutely on a par with man. There has never been the idea that a woman could not become an immortal, or enter paradise.

QUESTION: Just what is the status of the individual in Chinese religion? You have spoken of individual perfection or the perfection of the capacities of human nature. Besides individual perfection, is there any such thing in Chinese religion as individual immortality? That is, if I were a sage and of perfect nature, when I die, will I completely disappear? Will I be immortal only through my influence on my society? So, religiously considered, is there any such thing in Chinese thought as individual immortality of the perfect sage?

ANSWER: For the uneducated there is belief in individual immortality, but immortality does not mean a ghost living in paradise, but social immortality, or immortality of influence.

QUESTION: The individual is eternal in the view of immortality in all the major religions, Hindu, Muslim, Christian. What about China?

ANSWER: The individual is neither eternal nor non-eternal in the absolute sense. He is a combination of many elements. The combination changes from time to time, most radically at what we call birth and death. But, even at death, certain things continue, like influence, work, children. A sage can organize the various elements in him and make himself into a perfect harmony, which can last for a long time, not in a physical sense, but in the sense of the influence of the individual.

QUESTION: How individual?

ANSWER: Confucius, for instance, is still considered to be living, not as a living person, but a living force.

You see, the idea of life among Chinese thinkers is not just one's body. We live not only as oneself but also as fathers to our children or as sons to our fathers. We live as members of society. We live in the exchange of ideas with others. At death, our bodies perish, but many other parts of our life will continue, like blood and flesh in our children, our interests, our words, and our contributions in society. Shall we say that we at death are no more or that we are still there? So, the word "immortality" as you people have been using it does not apply in the case of China.

Notes

1. Ode no. 235.
2. *I li* (Book of Ceremonials), "Shih-sang li" (Ceremonies in an Official's Funeral); and *Li chi* (Book of Rites), "Li-yun" (Evolution of Rites).
3. *Li chi,* "Piao chi" (Record of Examples).
4. *Analects,* VII.20.
5. *Ibid.,* VI.20.
6. *Ibid.,* XI.11.
7. *Doctrine of the Mean,* XVI.
8. *Ibid.,* XIX.
9. *Tso chuan* (Tso's *Commentary*), Duke Chao, 13th year, and Duke Ting, 2nd year.
10. *Book of Mencius,* IA.4.
11. *Analects,* II.5.
12. *Mo Tzu,* III.
13. *Ibid.,* XXXV, XLVII. See Wing-tsit Chan, *A Source Book in Chinese Philosophy* (Princeton: Princeton University Press, 1963), p. 226.
14. *Chuang Tzu,* II, XI, etc. Ssu-pu ts'ung-k'an (The Four Libraries Series) edition entitled *Nan-hua chen-ching* (True Classic of Nan-hua), I, pp. 12b, 40a–b; VI, pp. 36a, etc.
15. *Lun heng* (Balanced Inquiries), Ssu-pu pei-yao (Essentials of the Four Libraries) edition, 62. See Chan, *op. cit.,* p. 299.
16. *Lun heng,* XX, pp. 92, 14a. See Chan, *op. cit.,* p. 302.
17. *Ibid.* See Chan, p. 301.
18. "Wu-shen lun" (An Essay on the Absence of Spiritual Beings), in the *Liang shu* (History of the Liang Dynasty), XLVIII.

19. *Ch'üan-hsi lu* (Records of Instructions for Practical Living). See Wang Yang-ming, *Instructions for Practical Living, and Other Neo-Confucian Writings by Wang Yang-ming,* Wing-tsit Chan, trans. (New York: Columbia University Press, 1963), sec. 49.
20. *Tso chuan,* Duke Hsiang, 24th year.
21. *Book of Mencius,* VIIA.1.
22. Ch'eng I, *I shu* (Surviving Work), Ssu-pu ts'ung-k'an edition, XVIII, p. 9a.
23. *Ibid.,* II, pt. 1, p. 2b.
24. *Chu Tzu ch'üan-shu* (Complete Works of Chu Hsi), I, pp. 18a–19a.
25. *Hsin Yüan-jen* (A New Treatise on the Nature of Man), p. 94.
26. *Tu-ching shih-yao* (Essential Points in the Study of Classics), II, p. 53b.
27. *Chuang Tzu,* VIII–XVII, XIX–XX, XXIII–XXV, XXIX, XXXI–XXXII. The word is mentioned here many times.
28. See Wing-tsit Chan, *Religious Trends in Modern China* (New York: Columbia University Press, 1953), pp. 149–151.
29. Hui-neng, *The Platform Scripture, the Basic Classic of Zen Buddhism,* Wing-tsit Chan, trans. (New York: St. John's University Press, 1963), pp. 24–27, 29–31, 34.
30. *Lao Tzu,* III, XVI.
31. *Chuang Tzu,* VII, Ssu-pu ts'ung-k'an edition, III, pp. 5b–6a. See Chan, *Source Book,* p. 207.
32. *Chuang Tzu,* IV (*Nan-hua chen-ching,* II, p. 13a).
33. *The Platform Scripture,* 17.
34. *Ibid.,* 18.
35. *Ibid.,* 17.
36. *Ibid.,* 19.
37. A common Ch'an saying sometimes attributed to Bodhidharma (fl. 460–534), the First Patriarch of Ch'an in China, but actually its origin can no longer be traced. See Chan, trans., *Instructions for Practical Living, and Other Neo-Confucian Writings,* p. 68, note 31.
38. *Book of Mencius,* VIIA.4; VIB.2.
39. *Great Learning,* the text.
40. *Doctrine of the Mean,* XXII.
41. *Ibid.,* XXV.
42. *Chu Tzu yü-lei* (Classified Sayings of Chu Hsi), LXIV, p. 17a.
43. *Ibid.,* p. 19a.
44. *Instructions for Practical Living,* p. 8.
45. *Doctrine of the Mean,* XXV.
46. *Analects,* III.12.
47. *Lun yü chi-chu* (Collected Commentaries on *The Analects,* II, commenting on *The Analects,* III.12).
48. *Cheng-meng* (Correcting Youthful Ignorance), chap. I. See Chan, *Source Book,* p. 505.

49. Ode no. 256.
50. *Doctrine of the Mean,* XVI.
51. *Chu Tzu ch'üan-shu,* LI, p. 50b.
52. *Ibid.,* p. 41a.
53. *Ibid.,* p. 41b.
54. *Ibid.,* p. 43a.
55. *Ibid.,* p. 52b.
56. *Ibid.,* p. 46b.
57. *Ibid.,* p. 42a.
58. For Wang Pi and Kuo Hsiang, see Chan, *Source Book,* pp. 316–332, 326–335.
59. *Ching shi-tzu chang* (A Treatise on the Golden Lion), sec. 7. See Chan, *Source Book,* p. 411.
60. *T'ung shu* (Penetrating *The Book of Changes*), XXII.
61. Quoting *The Book of Changes,* "Appended Remarks," Pt. 1, chap. 5.
62. *I shu,* III, p. 3b.
63. *Chu Tzu ch'üan-shu,* XLIX, p. 11a.
64. *I shu,* IV, p. 6b.
65. *Doctrine of the Mean,* I.
66. See above, note 21.

HSIEH YU-WEI   *The Status of the Individual*

in Chinese Ethics

WHAT IS THE STATUS of the individual in Chinese ethics? As we all know, there are different systems of ethics in the history of Chinese thought: Confucianism, Buddhism, Taoism, Moism, and others. It is impossible to discuss all of them here. So, since Confucian ethics has always been the most influential and the most widely practiced ethics of the Chinese people, I shall answer the question from the standpoint of Confucian ethics.

Confucian ethics never downgrades the status of the individual; on the contrary, it always emphasizes the value and dignity of the individual. Confucius and his followers, in fact, recognized and asserted the equality of man's value in every individual. What the West calls "the equality of the individual," "the freedom of the individual," "the individual's relations to other individuals," and "the individual's relations to the community, i.e., to the family, the state, and to mankind," were all advocated in one form or another by Confucian ethics, too.

I. The Equality of All Individuals

The central idea of Confucian ethics is *jen*, "humanity." Confucian ethics could not ignore the significance of any individual; otherwise, it would be in conflict with *jen*. What is *jen*? In *The Analects* (*Lun yü*), "Fan Ch'ih asked about *jen*. The master said, 'It is to love all men.' "[1] Since *jen* is to love all men, the importance of the individual is necessarily emphasized. But, owing to historical accidents and to wrong interpretations by emperors for centuries, the importance of the individual in Confucian ethics was not always made explicit. Also, owing to the lack of clear discussion about the individual's equality, freedom, and rights in Confucian ethics, the suspicion naturally arose that it neglected the importance of the individual. But the implied affirmations of the importance of the individual, the individual's equality, freedom, rights, and duties, are clear.

Confucian ethics asserted the equality of all individuals, but what Confucius called equality is the equality of humanity. It is the equality of man's value insofar as man is man, equality a priori, that is to say, all men are born equal. In *The Doctrine of the Mean* (*Chung yung*), it is said, "What Heaven has conferred is called the nature," [2] and this "nature" is human nature. Human nature is what everybody has received from Heaven. And what everybody has received from Heaven must be equal. This is the justice of Heaven. It is the equality of every man's possibility, the opportunity to be a man.

How Confucius maintained the equality of "human nature" can be seen from the Confucian conception of *jen*. *Jen* is the reality of the universe, and also the essence of man, that which makes him man. In Chinese philology, man is defined as *jen*.[3] In *The Doctrine of the Mean*, it is said, "*Jen* is man, and the greatest exercise of it is in loving relatives." [4] And in the *Mencius* it is said, "*Jen* is the distinguishing characteristic of man. As embodied in man's conduct, it is called *tao* [the way]." [5] Thus, *jen* is clearly the distinguishing characteristic of man, according to the central idea of Confucian ethics.

But, how do we know that the distinguishing characteristic of man is *jen?* We know this by our own experience and by our own observation. As Mencius said,

The ability possessed by men without having been acquired by learning is intuitive ability, and the knowledge possessed by them without the exercise of thought is their intuitive knowledge. Children in arms know how to love their parents, and, when they have grown a little older, they all know how to love their elder brothers. Filial affection for parents is the working of *jen*. Respect for elders is the working of righteousness. There is no other reason for those feelings—they belong to all under Heaven.[6]

That is to say, the fact that every man has intuitive ability and intuitive knowledge, or the fact that every man has "*jen*," is a fact that can be verified by children's unquestionable love for their parents.

Furthermore, the fact that every man has *jen* can be verified by the feeling of commiseration that every man possesses. As Mencius said,

. . . if men suddenly see a child about to fall into a well, they will without exception experience a feeling of alarm and distress. They will feel so, not as a ground on which they may gain the favor of the child's parents, nor as a ground on which they may seek the praise of their neighbors and friends, nor from a dislike of hearing such a noise. From this case we may perceive that the feeling of commiseration [etc.] is essential to man. . . . The feeling of commiseration is the beginning of *jen*.[7]

This inability to bear to see the suffering of others, this feeling of commiseration, is a fact that we can see everywhere. How can we deny that men have *jen*?

But, though every man has *jen*, what a man has is merely the "beginning of *jen*," or just a seed of humanity. How, then, can we affirm the equality of all individuals? It was precisely in order to emphasize this seed of humanity that Confucius built up his ethical system. Confucius considered this seed of humanity as what is most valuable in men and what makes man man. The difference between men and animals lies in this seed of humanity. The dignity and value of man which enable him to achieve unity with Heaven also lie in this seed of humanity. If there were no such seed of humanity, ethical education would be impossible; but it is clearly possible to educate man as man, as wise man and sage.

Since every man has this seed of humanity, Confucian ethics claims that men are born equal refers precisely to the universal equality of this seed of humanity, though not equality in other respects. When man is born, he is in possession of this seed of humanity, and what he possesses is no more and no less than any other man.

Because of this seed of humanity Confucian ethics also maintained that every man can become a sage or can become Emperor Yao or Emperor Shun. It is clearly declared, "What a man is Shun? And what am I? All those who try can be the same." [8] If every man can be a sage—and to be a sage is the highest ideal of man—does this not demonstrate the basic equality of all individuals?

Of course, to say that every man can be a sage is not to say that every man is a sage. Only a few can be considered sages.

Hence, in fact, men are not equal. What is called equality is equality of opportunity or equality of possibility, and not equality of achievement. The highest ideal of Confucian ethics is to educate men to be sages, and, if every man has the possibility of becoming a sage, what more can we want or require?

Furthermore, the equality asserted by Confucian ethics is fundamental. All other equalities are implied by this one basic equality. Hence, the fact that other equalities, such as equality of rights, equality before the law, etc., were seldom discussed does not mean that they were denied. They were all clearly implied. At least, they are implied in principle, with this basic equality. The reason why Confucian ethics seldom talked about other equalities is that, if a man wants to become a sage, he should do his best by himself and should not depend on other men or other conditions. Even if all other conditions are unfavorable, if one does one's best, one can still become a sage. All other equalities are within this concept of *jen*. This interpretation is also asserted by most contemporary Chinese scholars. I may mention Ch'ien Mu [9] and T'ang Chün-i [10] as representatives.

Thus, since Confucian ethics has the spirit of "the great equality," the principle of equality in traditional Chinese ethics is undeniable.

II. The Freedom of the Individual

Confucian ethics also asserted the freedom of the individual. The meaning of freedom, as we all know, is very complex. Generally speaking, freedom means political freedom, such as freedom of thought, freedom of speech, freedom of belief, etc. Such freedoms were little or seldom discussed in Confucian ethics; hence, it is often suspected that Confucian ethics denied the freedom of the individual. In fact, the freedom asserted in Confucian ethics is also fundamental and can include or at least imply all other freedoms.

The freedom advocated in Confucian ethics is the freedom to do good or the freedom to choose what is good. It is ethical freedom of choice. But such freedom of choice has its own ground and its own limits. It is a limited freedom. There is no such thing as an unlimited freedom. "Free" does not mean "free from." To be free from everything—free from other men, free from law, free from morality, free from thought, free from sense—as F. H. Bradley points out, "is to be nothing." [11] Unlimited freedom is impossible in fact and should not be demanded by ethics.

The truth that the freedom which is possible and which ought to obtain must have some ground or limitation is recognized in Confucian ethics. This ground or limitation is goodness. One should choose good; one should not choose evil. If we grant that every individual has the freedom to choose evil, then the freedom of everyone will be threatened by the evil. If evil prevailed, freedom might disappear. Hence, *from the point of view of ethics,* we should allow only the freedom to choose good and not the freedom to choose evil. Confucius says in *The Analects,* "When I walk alone with two others, they may serve me as my teachers. Choose what is good and follow it, but avoid what is bad." [12] Again, he says, "Hear much and select what is good and follow it." [13] Such expressions clearly indicate the idea of freedom to choose good. Later, in *The Doctrine of the Mean,* such sayings as "Choose the course of the mean" [14] and "He who attains to sincerity is he who chooses what is good and firmly holds it fast" [15] indicate the same attitude. Freedom to choose is freedom to choose, within the complex of good and evil, what is good and not what is evil. This is man's freedom, and the only freedom which is permitted in Confucian ethics.

If freedom means freedom to choose good, then what is good? What is good in the opinion of Confucius is the same as *jen. Jen* is good, and good is *jen.* All values created by men will be affirmed and protected by *jen. Jen* is most unselfish and least obstinate. What is firmly upheld by *jen* is *jen* itself, and not just *any* man's private opinion. Confucius strongly opposed such obstinacy. Confucius was not obstinate in his own opinion. It is said in *The Analects,* "There were four things from which the Master was entirely free. He had no foregone conclusions, no arbitrary predeterminations, no obstinacy, and no egotism." [16]

Confucius did not like forced uniformity of belief or opinion— even in ethics. "The superior man is catholic and not a partisan." He said, "The mean man is a partisan and not catholic" [17] and "The superior man is seeking for harmony but not sameness. The mean man is seeking for sameness but not harmony." [18] Later, Mencius expressed the same attitude in saying, "The superior man seeks just for *jen* and cares not for sameness." [19] This means that, if one's words and actions are in accordance with *jen,* it is not necessary for them to be the same as mine. To choose good is to choose the good in accordance with *jen,* and not tne good in any man's private opinion. This is the true meaning of freedom to choose the good in Confucian ethics.

As indicated above, the freedom to choose the good implies or justifies the other important freedoms, *ethically.* To illustrate, Confucius traveled to different states during his lifetime. The purpose of his travel was to choose a good prince to serve. Now, the relation between prince and minister is a political relation. If one has the freedom to choose which prince to serve, one is not held in bondage by the relation between prince and minister but has political freedom. Such political freedom Confucius indicated in the following sayings: "My doctrines make no way. I will get upon a raft, and float about on the sea." [20] "When called to office, to undertake its duties; when not so called, to lie retired." [21] "When right principles of government prevail in the kingdom, he will show himself; when they are rejected, he will keep concealed." [22] "Some men of worth retire from the world. Some retire from particular states." [23]

Confucius also maintained, in social affairs, the freedom to choose friends. The saying quoted above—"When I walk along with two others, they may serve me as my teachers. Choose what is good and follow it, but avoid what is bad" [24] —indicates his attitude clearly.

The freedom to choose a place to live was also affirmed by Confucius. He said, "It is *jen* which constitutes the excellence of a neighborhood. If a man in selecting a residence does not fix on one where *jen* prevails, how can he be wise?" [25]

As to freedom of speech, Confucius affirmed this in his own deeds. Confucius himself was free to speak as he pleased. He edited *The Book of Odes* (*Shih ching*) and wrote *The Book of History* (*Shu ching*) in accordance with his own ideas. Certainly, he would not oppose freedom of speech. He would oppose only the speaking of bad words or empty words, that is, words without corresponding actions. Good words, or what should be said, one must say; otherwise, it is not ethically right. Confucius said, "When a man may be spoken with, not to speak to him is to err toward the man." [26] He also said, "What the superior man requires is just that in his words there may be nothing wrong." [27] Hence, the only condition for the freedom of speech is whether your speech is right or not. If it is right to speak, you should speak freely even to those high above you, such as the prince or your parents. To argue with prince or parents is permitted by Confucius. He said, "In serving his parents, a son may remonstrate with them, but gently." [28] Such freedom to argue with the prince constituted one of the most important kinds of political freedom under the Chinese political system. Mencius, too, enjoyed freedom of speech. Mencius argued freely with the princes of several states, and sometimes he even scolded them. But Mencius confessed that he did not like to argue. He argued because he had to.[29] It was under the compulsion of goodness, or *jen*, that Mencius felt he had to argue. Consequently, freedom of speech has its limitation, and that limitation is goodness, or *jen*. The saying "Speak not what is contrary to propriety" [30] demonstrates this attitude of Confucian ethics.

Thus, in view of the freedom to choose the good, we have freedom to choose our prince, freedom to choose our friends, freedom to choose our residence, and freedom of speech. On condition that we choose within the limits of goodness, we can choose freely. Outside the limits of goodness, one should not be free. This is the true meaning of freedom. Freedom to choose the good is thus the same as to assert all other freedoms. No other freedoms should be allowed to violate goodness. If you act in accordance with goodness, you are free. Otherwise, you may lose your freedom. Whatever freedom you want, you should not violate this ethical principle of freedom to choose the good.

This freedom to choose the good may also be interpreted as the freedom to develop one's humanity or one's true self. Every man has *jen*, and this constitutes his true nature or true self. But this true nature needs cultivation or development. And this must be done by oneself. It is said in *The Analects*, "Yen Yüan asked about *jen*. The Master said, 'To subdue one's self and return to propriety is *jen*. If a man can for one day subdue himself and return to propriety, all under Heaven will ascribe *jen* to him. Is the practice of *jen* from a man himself, or is it from others?' " [31] This state is one of freedom. For the flowing of *jen*, or humanity, is free. It comes from one's own self, and no outside force can interfere with it. Hence, such practice of *jen*, or the development of one's humanity, must of necessity be free. In *The Doctrine of the Mean* it is said, "It is only he who is possessed of the most complete sincerity that can exist under Heaven and can give full development to his nature. Able to give full development to his own nature, he can do the same to the nature of other men. Able to give full development to the nature of other men, he can give full development to the natures of animals and things. Able to give full development to the natures of animals and things, he can assist the transforming and nourishing powers of Heaven and Earth. Able to assist the transforming and nourishing powers of Heaven and Earth, he may with Heaven and Earth form a ternion." [32] When a man may with Heaven and Earth form a ternion, then he is really free. But it all depends upon the full development of his own nature.[33]

III. The Duties of the Individual

From the above we know that Confucian ethics called for the freedom of the individual. And freedom is one of—or expresses—the rights of the individual. Every individual has the right to be free, that is, free to choose the good. In this sense, Confucian ethics also asserted the rights of the individual. But, it was not the rights of the individual that were considered most important. Of most importance were the duties or obligations of the individual. According to Confucian ethics, in order to be a man or to be a sage, it is necessary, first, to perform one's duties, not to claim one's rights. It is the fulfillment of duties that can make a man into a man or into a sage.

The duties of the individual are the moral principles according to which one should act with regard to oneself and to others. In order to be a man or to be a sage, one must observe these moral principles in the cultivation and development of one's humanity. The equality and freedom that one enjoys are mere possibilities for becoming a man or a sage. They will not be realized unless one has done one's duties in accordance with these moral principles.

Every individual has duties, first of all, to himself. In order to fulfill one's duties to oneself, the important work one has to do is "self-inspection" (tzu-hsing). Self-inspection is what is nowadays called self-criticism or self-examination. The belief is that the individual himself has the clearest insight into what he has done and whether it has been done in accordance with jen.

If one fails to carry out self-inspection, the question as to whether or not one can fulfill other duties, or the question as to whether or not other duties one performs can be considered fulfilled, cannot be answered. The reason for those acts which deceive oneself, and others, derives precisely from the failure to carry out this first duty. So, Confucius emphasized this duty of self-inspection. In *The Analects*, it is said, "The philosopher Tsang said, 'I daily examine myself on three points—whether in transacting business for others, I may not have been loyal; whether in intercourse with friends, I may not have been sincere; and whether I may have mastered and practiced the instruction of my teacher.'" [34] This expression, "daily examine myself on three points" explicitly advocates self-inspection. It is also said, "When we see men of worth, we should think of equaling them; when we see men of a contrary character, we should turn inward and examine ourselves." [35] "Turn inward and examine ourselves" means "self-inspection," but also more than that.

Self-inspection is the inspection of actions that one has done. But Confucian ethics taught something more than "self-inspection," what is called "taking care of one's own will" (*shen-tu*) in *The Great Learning* (*Ta hsüeh*). It is said, "What is meant by making the will sincere is the allowing of no self-deception, as when we hate a bad smell and as when we love what is beautiful. This is called self-enjoyment. Therefore, the superior man must take care of his own will." [36] This "taking care of one's own will" is self-inspection before action. It is concerned with our will or intention rather than with our conduct. One's conduct can be seen by all, but one's will or intention is known to oneself alone. When action has taken place, although it is necessary to examine it by self-inspection to see whether it is in accordance with *jen* or not, it is too late to do anything when it is wrong. In order to avoid wrong action, self-inspection alone is not enough; the work of "taking care of one's own will" must be added. "Prevention is much better than cure." This taking care of one's own intention or making the will sincere constituted the outstanding characteristic of Neo-Confucianism in the Sung Dynasty (960–1279).

Self-inspection and taking care of one's own will are two important duties of the individual to himself. In regard to other men —between individual and individual—the relation should be that of "propriety" (*li*). This is of first importance—to treat others with propriety.

The most obvious meaning of "propriety" is respect of man for man. Each man should pay respect to other men because such respect is respect for man as man, for the humanity (*jen*) which is possessed by every man. Though this respect is paid to others, it is in fact paid to oneself, too. It may be called the self-respect of man as man. If one does not pay respect to other men, one does not care for the humanity possessed by other men. In that case, the humanity possessed by oneself may be questioned. If one really has humanity in one's heart, one will naturally pay respect to the humanity in other men. So, Confucius considered "self-control and return to propriety as *jen*." [37] In propriety we can see the manifestation of *jen*. The importance of propriety lies here. Propriety must be based upon *jen*. If not, it can hardly be called propriety. It is said in *The Analects*, "If men are without *jen*, what use is there for propriety?" [38] It is for the sake of *jen* that one should treat others with propriety. And in such propriety, in such respectful conduct toward other men, one affirms the personality, the value, and the rights of other men. If every man has such respectfulness in regard to other men, then the relation between man and man will be in perfect harmony and without conflict.

Propriety means, then, the cultivation of harmony between man and man. "Propriety" is always connected with "concession" (*jang*). If one knows propriety, one must also know concession. In case one does not know concession, and quarrels with other men, one still does not know propriety. But concession is concession of rights and not concession of duties. One should not concede one's duties, such as the duty to practice *jen*. "He may not yield the performance of *jen* even to his teacher." [39] In that case, if every man were to concede rights and not duties, there would be no basis for quarrels between man and man. So, it is said in *The Analects*, "In practicing the rules of propriety, harmony is to be prized." [40] Accordingly, the aim of propriety is peace among men.

Confucian ethics maintained propriety and concession as the duties of the individual toward others. Moreover, Confucian ethics also required loyalty (*chung*) and reciprocity (*shu*) as principles in one's conduct toward others. It is said, "The doctrine of our Master is nothing but loyalty and reciprocity." [41] But loyalty and reciprocity also come from *jen*.

For Confucian ethics, it is incorrect to interpret loyalty as loyalty to king or prince. Loyalty means self-devotion, that is, doing one's duty with all one's strength. Loyalty is loyalty to one's duty as prescribed by *jen*, or the humanity within oneself. It might be described as one's own conscience determining one's duty. And, in accordance with his conscience, or *jen*, every individual has the duty to help others. It is said in *The Analects*, "Now, the man of *jen*, wishing to be established himself, seeks to establish others;

wishing to be enlarged himself, he seeks also to enlarge others." [42] For the sake of carrying out this duty, one has to do one's best, that is, one must be loyal.

The word "loyalty" first appears in *The Analects* in connection with Philosopher Tsang's saying, ". . . whether in transacting business for others, I may not have been loyal." [43] This shows clearly that loyalty is not reserved for the king only; rather, it is an attitude toward all men. Though Confucius paid due respect to the king, his respect was paid to the position of the king, and not the king himself. The relation between the king and the minister, for Confucius, should be one of mutual respect. Hence, he said, "A prince should employ his minister according to the rules of propriety. Ministers should serve their prince with loyalty." [44] Loyalty may be paid to the prince, on condition that the prince treats his minister with propriety. Loyalty is self-devotion to the duties to other men; the prince is included, but not the prince alone.

Based upon *jen*, we have the duty of loyalty to other men. Also based upon *jen*, we have the duty of reciprocity toward other men. Loyalty and reciprocity go together in one's relationships with other men. The way to treat others is to be loyal, on the one hand, and to practice reciprocity, on the other. Reciprocity clearly comes from *jen*. It is the natural consequence of *jen*, when it is developed. A man of *jen*, in establishing himself, seeks to establish others, and, in enlarging himself, seeks to enlarge others. This is reciprocity. It consists in treating others in the same way as you treat yourself. It is the Golden Rule. It is said in *The Analects*, "Tzu-kung asked, saying, 'Is there one word which may serve as a rule of practice for all one's life?' The Master said, 'Is not reciprocity such a word? What you do not want done to yourself, do not do to others.' " [45] Reciprocity is a fundamental principle for the relations between man and man. If this principle is followed by all, then peace will be established among men.

IV. *The Individual and the Community*

For the moral duties of the individual to himself, Confucian ethics maintained self-inspection and taking care of one's own will; and maintained propriety, loyalty, and reciprocity as one's moral duties to others. But what about duties of the individual to the community? The duties which the individual should perform with respect to the community were expressed clearly in *The Great*

Learning. Here, it is said, "The ancients who wished to illustrate illustrious virtue throughout the world first ordered well their own states. Wishing to order well their states, they first regulated their families. Wishing to regulate their families, they first cultivated their persons." [46] This means everybody has the duty to regulate his family, to order the state, and to bring about peace in the world. Family, state, and the world (or mankind as a whole) are communities to which every individual owes a duty.

Though Confucian ethics called for duties of the individual to the community, it did not overemphasize the community and ignore the individual. In fact, Confucian ethics considered the individual even more important than the community. Confucian ethics regarded individuals as roots, and communities as leaves— or individuals as foundations and communities as roofs. The duty to cultivate oneself should come first; then come the duties of regulating the family, ordering the state, and making peace in the world. One's duties to the community depend upon one's duties to oneself. It is said, "From the Son of Heaven down to the masses of the people, all must consider the cultivation of the person the root of everything else. It cannot be that, when the root is neglected, what springs from it will be well ordered." [47] Hence, the cultivation of the person, or the individual, is fundamental. Without such cultivation of the person, or the individual, no other duties can be fulfilled by the individual.

But, before proceeding, let us see what duties of the individual to the community were prescribed by Confucian ethics. First of all, every individual has a duty to his family. Duty to the family was especially emphasized in Confucian ethics. But this emphasis on duty to the family was in fact for the good of the individual. The common mistaken view is that, since Confucian ethics emphasized the importance of the family, Chinese ethics took the family as the unit of its system, that Chinese ethics considered the family as the basis or the center to which all individuals must be subordinated, that the family is everything, and that individuals are nothing, that individuals must submit to the family and work for the family. This is not correct.

The importance of the family is specifically for the sake of realizing the individual, that is, for the fulfillment the seed of *jen* possessed by every individual. This seed of *jen* comes directly from the family. We all get our humanity originally from the family. Since we all get our lives from our parents and grow up in the family, the cultivation and development of our humanity must begin within the family. But how do we cultivate and develop our humanity within the family? Individuals should do their duty to the family. The two important duties of the individual to the family are filial piety (*hsiao*) and brotherliness (*ti*).

Filial piety and brotherliness are moral principles which teach men to love and respect their own parents and elder brothers. These principles were based upon the seed of humanity inborn in all men in loving their parents, and were intended to preserve and develop it by ethical education. Confucius considered the rudimentary instinct of loving one's parents as the root of *jen*. Without cultivation, it may wither away or disappear. In order to cultivate and develop such a root of *jen*, Confucius taught the doctrine of filial piety and brotherliness in the family. So, in *The Analects* it is said, "Filial piety and brotherliness—are they not the root of *jen*?" [48] For the practice of *jen*, filial piety and brotherliness should be practiced first. The reason is obvious. If a man does not love his own parents, can he be a man of *jen*? And, if a man has the duty to love men, whom should he love first? Is it not his own parents? The doctrine of filial piety and brotherliness is intended to teach men to love and respect their own parents and brothers first, and then extend their love and respect to the parents and brothers of others. This is the way to cultivate and develop one's own humanity. It is a way to educate men in the family, in order that they can develop and realize their true selves. What is important is individuals in the family and not the family as such.

As a matter of fact, Confucian ethics considered the individual and the family equally important and mutually dependent. Individuals cannot be separated from the family. The development of an individual's humanity must begin in and with the family. Without the family, or in neglect of the family, one's *jen*, or humanity, is rootless. Can those who do not love their own parents love other men? The importance of the family lies here. On the other hand, the family can be regulated only through the development of the individual. Without the development of the individual, the family cannot be regulated. Herein lies the importance of the individual.

Just as Confucian ethics asserted the mutual dependence of the individual and the family, it also asserted the mutual dependence of the individual and the state and the whole of mankind. Confucian conceptions of the state and of mankind were not too clear, but what is clear is that, as a community, the state is larger than the family, and the whole of mankind is larger than the state. But, no matter how large the community is, the status of the individual remains unchanged for Confucian ethics: what is all-important is the cultivation of the person, or the development of *jen* in the individual. Without such cultivation or development, one cannot talk about duties to the family, to the state, and to the whole of mankind. Since every individual has his duty to the family, naturally every individual also has his duty to the state and to the whole of mankind. This is due to the development of *jen* in the individual, which will not stop short at the family, but will necessarily extend to the state and to the whole of mankind.

Although Confucian ethics asserts the duties of the individual to the community, when conflicts arise between the individual and the community, the individual must maintain his own independent decision. The individual should decide by his own conscience whether he should obey the authority of the community or obey his own conscience. There were two cases in the works of Confucius and Mencius which showed the independence of the individual in conflict with the community. One case is: if one's father has stolen a sheep, one may conceal the misconduct of one's father.[49] The other case is: if Emperor Shun's father was a murderer, Emperor Shun might abandon his empire and run away with his father.[50]

This does not mean that the individual can be independent of the community. The individual needs the community, and the community needs the individual. The relationship between the individual and the community is one of mutual dependence and equal importance.

It is not a relationship of ends and means. One cannot say that the community is an end and that individuals are means only. Nor can one say that individuals are ends and that communities are means only. In fact, for Confucian ethics, the individual and the community are both ends and are realized throughout by the development of *jen* in the individual. The key lies wholly in *jen*. If *jen* prevails, then the importance of the individual and of the community will be equally affirmed.

QUESTION: Concerning the concept of freedom, do you use the word "freedom" in a different sense than its Western origin, for "freedom to choose what is good" is not freedom in the Western sense?

ANSWER: From the ethical point of view, we should allow only freedom to do the good and not freedom to do evil. No ethics of any kind would allow freedom to do evil. This is the meaning of freedom in Confucian ethics, and it is almost the same as self-determination in the Kantian sense.

QUESTION: Concerning the conflict of values, in Confucian ethics is there room for individual conscience against one's family? For instance, if a man's father stole a sheep, to use an example you cite, should he tell the truth to the police or not?

ANSWER: For Confucian ethics, there is no abstract standard by which to resolve the conflict of values. The only solution is that every man should decide by his own conscience, or *jen*. Whatever you do, you should do in accordance with *jen*.

Notes

1. *Analects*, XII.22.
2. *Doctrine of the Mean*, I.1.
3. *Shih ming* (Interpretation of Names) (Ssu-pu ts'ung-k'an—Collection of Four Kinds of Classic).
4. *Doctrine of the Mean*, XX.5.
5. *Book of Mencius*, VII.B16.
6. *Ibid.*, VII.A15.
7. *Ibid.*, II.A6.
8. *Ibid.*, III.A1.
9. *Ssu-shu shih-i* (Interpretations of the Four Books) (Taipei: United Publishing Center, 1953), II.77.
10. *Jen-wen ching-shen chih ch'ung-chien* (Reconstruction of the Spirit of Humanism) (Hong Kong: New Asia College, 1956), p. 410.
11. *Ethical Studies* (2nd ed.; Oxford: Oxford University Press, 1927), p. 56.
12. *Analects*, VII.21.
13. *Ibid.*, VII.27.
14. *Doctrine of the Mean*, VII.
15. *Ibid.*, XX.18.
16. *Analects*, IX.4.
17. *Ibid.*, II.14.
18. *Ibid.*, XIII.23.

19. *Book of Mencius,* VIB.6.
20. *Analects,* VI.6.
21. *Ibid.,* VII.10.
22. *Ibid.,* VIII.13.
23. *Ibid.,* XIV.39.
24. *Ibid.,* VII.21.
25. *Ibid.,* IV.1.
26. *Ibid.,* XV.7.
27. *Ibid.,* XIII.3.
28. *Ibid.,* IV.18.
29. *Book of Mencius,* IIIB.9.
30. *Analects,* XIII.1.
31. *Ibid.,* XII.1.
32. *Doctrine of the Mean,* XXII.
33. "Reconstruction of the Spirit of Humanism," p. 410.
34. *Analects,* I.4.
35. *Ibid.,* LV.17.
36. *Great Learning,* VI.
37. *Analects,* XII.1.
38. *Ibid.,* III.3.
39. *Ibid.,* XV.35.
40. *Ibid.,* I.12.
41. *Ibid.,* IV.15.
42. *Ibid.,* VI.28.
43. *Ibid.,* I.4.
44. *Ibid.,* III.19.
45. *Ibid.,* XV.23.
46. *Great Learning,* I.4.
47. *Ibid.,* I.6, 7.
48. *Analects,* I.2.
49. *Ibid.,* XIII.18.
50. *Book of Mencius,* VIIA.35.

Y. P. MEI   *The Status of the Individual*

in Chinese Social Thought and Practice

THE PREDOMINANT molding force of traditional Chinese society is Confucianism. Confucianism places dual emphasis on the importance of the proper development of the individual for the well-being of society, and, at the same time, on the importance of social responsibility for the perfection of the individual. While this double-barreled Chinese outlook on the status of the individual in society has been cultivated mostly by the teachings of Confucianism, its roots to a considerable extent go back to social thought and practices antedating Confucius. We shall take up some samples of pre-Confucian Chinese social thought and practice in the first section of the paper.

I. Early Chinese Social Thought and Practice

Valuable glimpses of the status of the individual in Chinese social thought and practice in its prototypal forms can be gained by consulting Chinese mythology and Chinese classical literature. Mythology is employed here, not for its religious significance, but as an expression of time-honored, deep-rooted, and widespread attitudes on the part of the Chinese people. We have in mind specifically the status of man in the concept of a cosmic triad as manifested in the legend of the Three Sovereign Groups. The Three Sovereign Groups, the earliest rulers China had, are said to have consisted of the Celestial Sovereign Group of twelve brothers, each reigning 18,000 years; the Terrestrial Sovereign Group of eleven brothers, each reigning 18,000 years; and, interestingly, the Human Sovereign Group of nine brothers, reigning for a total of 45,600 years in 150 generations. Of course, nobody believes in such tall tales, not even the Chinese. The thing that is notable in this legend is the Chinese insistence on the importance of the generic man. Man is so important that he is matched from the beginning of time with Heaven and Earth to make a cosmic triad. In Chinese, the term for the triad of Heaven-Earth-man is *san ts'ai*, meaning three powers, three forces, three origins, etc. Throughout the long history of Chinese thought, in the popular mind as well as in classical literature,[1] there has been persistent emphasis on the importance of man. Man is often spoken of in the same breath with Heaven and Earth. It is doubtful whether any other major world-civilization has laid emphasis to a comparable degree on the cosmic importance of man. The emphasis on the importance of the generic man in relation to Heaven and Earth has provided the undergirding, in Chinese thought and practice, for the collateral emphases on the importance of the common man in relation to his ruler, as well as the importance of the individual in relation to society.

The social significance of man and his life in the early Chinese tradition manifests itself further in the Chinese attitude toward immortality. Until the introduction of Buddhism and related ideas from India, the Chinese had only the vaguest ideas about heaven and hell and about future life in general. Insofar as they had any sense of or interest in immortality, it was mainly some form of social immortality. In the *Tso chuan* is kept the following record of a conversation on immortality:

> When Muh-shuh (P'aou) went to Tsin, Fan Seuen-tsze met him, and asked the meaning of the saying of the ancients, "They died but suffered no decay," . . . Muh-shuh said . . . "I have heard that the highest meaning of it is when there is established [an example of] virtue; the second, when there is established [an example of] successful service; and the third, when there is established [an example of wise] speech. When these examples are not forgotten with length of time, this is what is meant by the saying—"They do not decay." [2]

This conversation on immortality, which took place in 549 B.C., is instructive in itself and significant for the tremendous influence it has exercised. While the masses may be thinking about their future life in terms of heavens and hells, to this day educated Chinese are much more interested in "leaving behind a fragrance lasting for millenniums" (*liu-fang ch'ien-ku*). And the way to attain this distinction lies in one's achievement during one's lifetime, in virtue, in public service, and in teaching,[3] as stipulated in the conversation just quoted.

Among the pre-Confucian social practices in China, probably the most noteworthy for us is the trend of the gradual rise of the worth of the individual. In the dim, distant past, China had her share of inhumane social practices, including human sacrifice. When a great lord died, his harem of women and his household of servants were buried alive with his corpse. Eventually, clay figurines were used as substitutes for real people at these burials, and this type of human sacrifice became extinct. Prisoners of war at first were killed as a matter of course, but later they were enslaved rather than killed. At one stage there was the practice of what might be called "fixture slavery." Under this practice, the slaves were treated as part and parcel of the land they worked. When (and only when) the land changed hands, then did the slaves change hands. The eventual appearance of slave trade and the slave market was in fact a significant step in social and humanitarian reform. The scattered records of slave trade in ancient China showed a definite upward trend in the value of the slave. One bronze vessel of the reign of King Hsiao of Chou (909–894 B.C.) bears an inscription recording the exchange of five human beings for one horse plus one skein of silk. Some four hundred years later, Yen Ying (died 493 B.C.), the Prime Minister of Ch'i, offered one of his superb horses for a slave whose appearance impressed him.[4] The worth of the individual increased about five times over the period of four hundred years. These accounts are isolated instances, to be sure, but the trend of the rising worth of the individual in ancient China, as signified by his market price, is unmistakable.

By the time of Confucius, China was dominated by a number of powerful feudal states. The imperial house became more and more a figurehead as the rivalry among the leading feudal states became more fierce and militant. The condition of chaos and disunity in the empire, however, notably enhanced the increasing worth of the individual. The contending feudal lords were contending for power, and power consisted of troops and food, both of which depended in turn on the size of the population. Although the ambitious feudal lords uniformly regarded the views about government of Confucius and the other idealistic teachers as counsels of perfection and impracticable, they could well appreciate, from their own selfish interest, Confucius' yardstick of good government: "Good government obtains when those who are near are made happy and those who are far off are attracted." [5] The practice of a measure of benevolence in their despotic rule evidently became the best policy under the circumstances. Whatever the motivation, be it self-interest or human compassion, there was a decided trend of the rising worth of the common man in Ancient China.

II. Status of the Individual in Confucian Social Thought

Confucius (551–479 B.C.) lived in an age of growing confusion and chaos. Dedicating himself to the task of bringing order out of chaos, the sage became firmly convinced that a society could be only as good as its members. Even if it should be too much to expect every member of a community to be a superior man, at least the leaders and rulers must be exemplary individuals before the community could expect to achieve its well-being. The relation of the individual to society is here envisaged, not in terms of a collection of disparate atomistic units to form an aggregate, but in terms of a continuing permeation of the quality of the character of the individual throughout the ever-broadening circles of society. This qualitative relation of the individual to society is categorically stated in the celebrated passage of the *Ta hsüeh* (*The Great Learning*), as follows:

The ancients who wished clearly to exemplify illustrious virtue throughout the world would first set up good government in their states. Wishing to govern their states well, they would first regulate their families. Wishing to regulate their families, they would first cultivate their persons. Wishing to cultivate their persons, they would first rectify their minds. Wishing to rectify their minds, they would first seek sincerity in their thoughts. Wishing for sincerity in their thoughts, they would first extend their knowledge. The extension of knowledge lay in the investigation of things. For only when things are investigated is knowledge extended; only when knowledge is extended are thoughts sincere; only when thoughts are sincere are minds rectified; only when minds are rectified are our persons cultivated; only when our persons are cultivated are our families regulated; only when families are regulated are states well governed; and only when states are well governed is there peace in the world.

From the emperor down to the common people, all, without exception, must consider cultivation of the individual character as the root. If the root is in disorder, it is impossible for the branches to be in order. To treat the important as unimportant and to treat the unimportant as important—this should never be. This is called knowing the root; this is called the perfection of knowledge.[6]

This passage is important in several respects. Particularly noteworthy is the conclusion that everyone, whether he is in high place or low, must consider cultivation of the individual character as "the root" of social well-being and harmony. One of the outstanding characteristics in Chinese social thought is the emphasis on obligations rather than rights and prerogatives of the individual in relation to society. Do not ask what society can do for you; ask what you can do for society—exhortations such as this fall right in line with the Chinese spirit. And what can the individual do for society? Of course, the specific answers will vary with each individual. But there is a basic answer common to all men, and this is what the Chinese sages have been insisting upon, namely, the cultivation of one's character. The cultivation of the character of the individual, according to the *Ta hsüeh*, as quoted above, includes five inward steps of self-perfection and three outward steps of social extension spreading to the family, the state, and the whole world. This eight-step scheme has served in China as a master plan of moral and educational development as well as a blueprint for social and political administration.

While the individual in China does not ask what society can do for him, he cannot do without society for his achievement of the good life. The Chinese ideal for the individual is sometimes described as "sageliness within and kingliness without,"[7] a kind of double-barreled ideal. An individual is expected to be a man of enlightenment and a man of affairs. He is to be a citizen of the universe and at the same time a member of society. His is a life that is in the world and yet not of the world. It is in society that the individual lives, moves, and has his being, and, furthermore, grows into the fullness of his manhood, even sagehood. According to Confucian teaching, there is in some sense an identification of the sage with the universe, but the identification is here achieved by way of society and not in spite of it. Social well-being depends on the proper cultivation of the individual, to be sure, but the individual can achieve the full realization of his destiny only through public service and social participation. Social obligations and responsibilities of an individual are not chains and burdens to be escaped from, or to be borne and suffered. To the contrary, it is in the fulfillment of these social responsibilities that the individual realizes his complete personal fulfillment. In a very fundamental sense, the individual and society in Confucian social thought are mutually dependent.

While social service and participation are indispensable to the perfection of the individual, his status in society is defined, according to Confucianism, not by social esteem or other external circumstances, sometimes in spite of them, but by one's inner sense of personal integrity and dignity. "Man is born for uprightness," [8] said Confucius. It is well known that the key concept in Confucianism is *jen*, or human-heartedness, or love, or, according to James Legge's translation, virtue. I presented a summary statement on this central concept of Confucianism earlier in this volume,[9] and repetition will be avoided here. Attention is directed specifically to the intuitive and spontaneous quality of *jen*. The following are some of the sayings of Confucius from *The Analects* (*Lun yü*):

Is virtue (*jen*) a thing remote? I wish to be virtuous, and lo! virtue is at hand.[10]

Is anyone able for one day to apply his strength to virtue (*jen*)? I have not seen the case in which his strength would be insufficient.[11]

Thus it is evident that *jen* is not the special endowment of some privileged class, but the "spark of divinity" planted in every man without exception. For the seed of *jen* to grow into the full-blown virtue of *jen*, it takes, of course, cultivation and education. Confucius declared in feudalistic China, some two thousand five hundred years ago, "In teaching there should be no distinction of classes." [12] No one could have said such a thing under the circumstances of Confucius' day, if he did not have an unswerving conviction in the native integrity and dignity of the individual. Both Mencius and Hsün Tzu, the great followers of Confucius, maintained that every man on the street could become a sage-king like Yao and Shun, according to Mencius, and like the Great Yü, according to Hsün Tzu. Chinese thinkers have not interested themselves in human rights as such. But the conviction of the inviolable worth of the individual lies at the heart of Confucian teaching and accounts for a good measure of the democratic spirit in Chinese life.

The character of integrity and the dignity of the individual gives him a sense of confidence and serenity. He is not easily swayed, or ruffled, or affected by the fortunes of the day. He has an inner frame of reference and scale of values, and his life is ordered through self-control. In one passage in *The Analects* of Confucius several of Confucius' sayings on this point are recorded, and we quote some of them as follows:

The Master said, "The commander of the forces of a large state may be carried off, but the will of even a common man cannot be taken from him" (chapter XXV).

The Master said, "Dressed himself in a tattered robe quilted with hemp, yet standing by the side of men dressed in furs, and not ashamed— ah! it is Yü who is equal to this!" (chapter XXVI).

The Master said, "When the year becomes cold, then we know how the pine and the cypress are the last to lose their leaves" (chapter XXVII).

The Master said, "The wise are free from perplexities; the virtuous from anxiety; and the bold from fear" (chapter XXVIII).[13]

This ancient list of three freedoms of Confucius should be heeded, we submit, as much as the contemporary list of "Four Freedoms." Similarly, both Mencius and Hsün Tzu left a description of the great man, and what they considered as the great man was the man of integrity. In spite of the radical disagreements between these two great Confucian teachers on several basic subjects, the two descriptions are almost identical. We quote first Mencius and then Hsün Tzu as follows:

He who dwells in the broad house of the universe, stands firm on the true base of the universe, walks in the great way of the universe, if successful, walks in the way for the good of the people, if unsuccessful, walks in the way all alone; he whom riches and honor cannot corrupt, poverty and obscurity cannot move, threats and violence cannot make bend—he it is that may be called a great man.[14]

Therefore, power and gain cannot influence him; mobs and multitudes cannot sway him; the whole empire cannot move him. By this [perfect character] he will live and by it he will die, and this is what is meant by moral integrity. With moral integrity one could achieve firmness, and with firmness one could achieve flexibility. Possessing firmness as well as flexibility, he may be said to be a perfect man. Heaven is prized for its brilliance; the earth is prized for its vastness; the superior man is prized for his perfection.[15]

III. Status of the Individual in Non-Confucian Social Thought

Chinese social thought is not limited, of course, to Confucian thought. Mo Tzu (470–391? B.C.), for instance, taught the doctrine of universal love. On appearance, this teaching might be expected to uphold egalitarianism of all individuals. But, in social and political thought, Mo Tzu actually advocated "identification with the superior," i.e., submission of one's individual will in conformity with that of one's superior.

The Taoists had little use for society, and were completely indifferent about the social status of an individual. Organization of any kind was regarded by the Taoists as anathema, and social participation as an impediment to the life of freedom and spontaneity.

The Legalists placed the state above the individual, and the status of the individual was determined solely according to his usefulness to the state, that is, the sovereign.

Buddhism, with its monastic order, introduced what might be called extra-societal egalitarianism of the individual. In the eyes of the Buddha, all men are blinded by their passion and ignorance and are equally in need of compassion and enlightenment. The status of the individual in ordinary society is immaterial, except as an indicator of the desert of his accumulated past deeds, according to the Law of *Karma*.

While these various systems have exercised their influence in various degrees, the main current of Chinese social thought has been Confucian social thought since the second century B.C., when in the early Han Dynasty (206 B.C.–A.D. 26) Confucianism began to assume supremacy over indigenous systems.

IV. Status of the Individual in Chinese Social Practice

The phenomenon of the status of the individual in Chinese society extends over a broad spectrum. Topics like slavery, prostitution, women, children, the aged, etc., would all make interesting material for discussion, but such discussions belong more naturally elsewhere.

Concerning the more relevant considerations regarding the status of the individual in social practice, this paper will confine itself to the two outstanding Chinese characteristics of social cohesion and social fluidity. Generally speaking, it is the family system and the civil service examination system that over the centuries have fostered, respectively, these qualities of Chinese society, and cast a unique light over the status of the individual in society. We shall proceed to consider these two institutions briefly.

The central position of the family in Chinese society is well known. The family in China is not only the primary social group, as it is everywhere, but it is also the prototype of all social organization. The term for emperor in Chinese is "Son-of-Heaven," the local magistrate is addressed by his charges as "parent-official," and good friends become sworn brothers.[15a] Social organizations and social relations in China are patterned after the family. A system of five social relations—those between father and son, sovereign and subject,[16] husband and wife, brother and brother, and, finally, friend and friend—together with the respective obligations pertaining to each relation has been developed. The individual achieves his inner stature as well as his social status through his participation in the social process and his contribution to society, and the family is the point at which to begin. Take, for instance, the basic virtue of *jen,* or human-heartedness, of Confucius. While the seed of *jen* is inborn in all men, its flowering and flourishing depend on proper cultivation. The family situation provides the first and most favorable opportunity for the exercise and development of this virtue, a sort of nursery for nurturing the seed of *jen.* If battle was to Homer the furnace for the forging and testing of heroes, then the family must be to Confucius the gymnasium for the developing and the perfecting of men of *jen.* Looked at in this light, filial piety is but an expression of *jen* in the specific context of the child-parent relation. The cultivated individual is prepared for regulating the family, and thereby governing the state, and then, in turn, bringing peace to the world, according to *The Great Learning,* as we have learned. Chinese society might be said to be a system of "familiocracy," and the basis for familiocracy lies in *jen* and agape.

For ordinary purposes, an individual is a member of a family, i.e., a father, a son, a brother, etc. An individual is an individual only rarely and by abstraction, as it were. A wedding in China, for instance, is as much an exciting affair for the young man's family (clan) as for the two individuals involved. But, since it means an addition of a permanent member to a close-knit intimate group, which only death can alter, all members of the group might well take a personal interest in the occasion. Divorce is provided for only on the strictest conditions, and is resorted to very rarely indeed. The family shares in the successes of its members and is held responsible for their failures. Hence the widespread practice of nepotism and the feature of family-group responsibility in the administration of law and social justice in China.

Such a family system has naturally generated a high degree of cohesion and stability. An individual thinks twice in making a decision—once about the consequences to himself and once about the consequences to the family. The quality of social cohesion in traditional Chinese social practice makes itself conspicuous in Chinese communities located in a contrasting cultural setting, such as the Chinatowns of New York and San Francisco. During the year 1955, for instance, the phenomenon of the absence of juvenile delinquency among the Chinatown teenagers in the United States was discussed in three popular American magazines, namely, *Saturday Evening Post, America,* and *Coronet.*[17] In these articles, the point is repeatedly made that the Chinese children keep off the streets and keep out of trouble because they feel that the home, no matter how humble, is the place for them to live in and because consideration for their folks and family is in their minds whenever they have to decide what to do and what not to do. Lately, however, we begin to hear of isolated cases of "Chinese-American J. Ds." Perhaps some Chinese youths are beginning to "progress" away from the traditional "social stagnancy," terms not infrequently used by modern Western observers in discussing Chinese society.

The force of modernization has, of course, already affected the family system in China considerably, and it will influence it much more in the years ahead. Modernization, however, is a universal phenomenon affecting for better or for worse everyone without exception, with a stronger impact on the older societies, to be sure, than on the newer ones. The problem everywhere is one of devising a structure of family organization that will permit a large degree of initiative and freedom of thought and action on the part of the individual and yet assure a proper measure of family cohesion. Individuals crave not only freedom but also belongingness, togetherness. Robinson Crusoe, until the appearance of Friday, was completely free and completely miserable. Human rights should indeed be emphasized and fought for where necessary, but human rights are only the minimal conditions for man. Human obligations should be at least equally emphasized, because they are essential for the fulfillment of the supreme mission of man, for man to break out of his individual shell and become completely social, human, and therefore divine—a point that Confucius realized clearly two thousand five hundred years ago, and a point that the Chinese have learned to insist upon ever since.

Finally, a few remarks on social mobility in China and the operation of the Chinese civil service examination system. Chinese society is said to consist of four classes, namely, the scholar, the farmer, the artisan, and the merchant. It is to be noted that this fourfold classification is nothing more than an indicator of the profession of the individual at the moment. It is entirely possible for people to change their profession and classification, and this is done all the time. There are the natural factors of inertia, tradition, and material advantage for the son to follow the profession of the father, but there is little in the form of arbitrary barrier preventing anyone from making a change. The degree of social mobility in China is remarkable. The American cliché "from shirt sleeves to shirt sleeves in three generations" is not inapplicable to the Chinese social scene.

Probably the most potent factor contributing to social fluidity and mobility in China is the politico-educational institution of civil service examinations.[18] According to Confucianism, some men, because of their talent and virtue, are fit to lead and some to follow. That the leaders should be given the responsibility of government is a matter of natural law as well as one of *noblesse oblige*. But how are such men to be discovered and identified? This was a perplexing problem even in Confucius' day.[19] The Confucian doctrine of government gave rise to the institution of the civil service examination system in China. The first attempts at discovering men of virtue and talent and appointing them to public office go back to 165 B.C. The full-fledged system of examinations had operated in China for well over a thousand years before it was abolished in 1905 in favor of the modern Western-styled school system. While the examination system was in operation, it occupied the center of attention of all young men of ambition in the land. The competition was keen, but the reward, in honor, glory, riches, and beautiful wives was high. Over the centuries, the system brought about a unity of culture for the nation, and produced a class of government leaders and an intellectual élite who stood at the top of the list of the four social classes.

The remarkable feature about the civil service examination system for our purpose is the fact that, by and large, it operated as an open system. With minor exceptions varying from dynasty to dynasty, the examinations were open to all men who had properly prepared themselves. Youths of well-to-do families and children of degree-holders had an advantage over boys from poorer families, to be sure, but Chinese folklore is filled with success stories of self-made men. The Chinese self-made men were the successful candidates, who, coming from destitute families, had prepared themselves by studying under moonlight and even by the light of fireflies kept in a bag of gauze. The civil service examination system served as a social equalizer, and contributed to social mobility in China through the ages. This means there has been a considerable degree of fluidity in the status of the individual in Chinese society.

Certain modern investigators have questioned such assumptions by enlarging upon the differences of opportunities between children of the high-born and of the low-born, and the tendency of the degree-holders to attempt the perpetuation of special privileges within their own families and class. Such phenomena are present in every land. They are not completely absent in China. The important point is, however, that these open examinations in China served to an appreciable degree as a corrective to such tendencies and as an agent for social equalization. The signal significance of the examination system in itself and in relation to the social history of China is evidenced by the recent publication of several English-language studies on this problem within a period of two years.[20] The most thoroughgoing work is the one by Professor Ping-ti Ho, from which we quote one of the author's noteworthy conclusions as follows:

> So common was the fact that trade and other productive occupations either alternated or were synchronized with studies that many Ming-Ch'ing [1368–1911] social observers were of the impression that the status distinction among the four major occupational categories (scholars, farmers, artisans, and merchants) was blurred. What is more, all types of literature agree that the most striking characteristic of the post-T'ang [ca. 900–] society was that, on the one hand, social success depended more on individual merit than on family status, and that, on the other hand, high-status families had little means of perpetuating their success if their descendants were inept.[21]

The phenomena of social cohesion and fluidity are outstanding features of Chinese life, and they are factors that should not be lost sight of in any consideration of the individual and society in China. The status of the individual in Chinese social thought and practice admittedly leaves room for improvement, particularly in the context of modern life. However, while we stress the importance of independence for the individual, we should not overlook the importance of interdependence for his happiness and perfection. In this respect, the relation between the individual and society rather resembles that between the individual nation and the "family of nations," a term and a notion with a noticeable Chinese flavor, and a note on which it would not be inappropriate to conclude a paper on Chinese social thought.

QUESTION: Do you want to comment on alleged authoritarianism in Confucian social thought?

ANSWER: One might speak of a degree of authoritarianism in Confucius in the same way, and only in the same way, as one might speak of a degree of authoritarianism in Immanuel Kant. The authority lies within the individual with Confucius as it does with Kant. The Categorical Imperative indeed carries authority with it, but this authority is self-realized and is in no way externally imposed.

QUESTION: Since there is the conviction of the inviolable worth of the individual at the heart of Confucian teaching, why is it that Chinese thinkers have not interested themselves in human rights as such?

ANSWER: The difference between Western thinkers, who have placed a great deal of emphasis on human rights, and the Chinese thinkers, who have been interested in the inviolable worth of the individual, is mainly a difference of idiom. The idiom of thought and expression is, of course, a growth out of a whole cultural background. It would not be very rewarding to expect every culture to be employing the same idiom, even when these cultures are directing their attention to the same human experience. It is possible, for instance, to conceive of formulating a set of philosophical concepts and issues in the idiom of, say, Indian philosophy and require Western writers to discuss Western thought in terms of that idiom. There would then be a good deal of embarrassment and perhaps not much enlightenment. My plea here is for a readiness on the part of participants in a discussion of East-West philosophy to appreciate and, insofar as possible, translate the other man's philosophical idiom into his own.

QUESTION: What has been the status of freedom of thought in your tradition? Or, expressed otherwise, has there ever been any serious curtailment of freedom of thought—either in theory or in practice—in the Chinese tradition?

ANSWER: The problem of freedom of thought has many facets. Religious and political freedom ranks perhaps ahead of social freedom in importance. Within the sphere of social thought and practice, there was a remarkable measure of freedom of thought in traditional China. The classical period of Chinese philosophy, from the time of Confucius to the unification of the empire in the late third century B.C., is referred to among the Chinese as the "Period of the Hundred Philosophers." (Curiously, the 1957–1959 period of communist rule in China is now known as the "Bloom-Contend Period." This is because Mao Tse-tung, in urging the nation to speak out their criticisms of the communist administration, used two of the popular sayings among the Chinese: "Hundred flowers bloom together" and "Hundred philosophers contend together.") Historically, the "hundred philosophers" did contend together, and taught a great variety of doctrines. The worst punishment that could happen to a thinker was to be considered a queer fellow and to have few listeners. If a teacher, like Confucius, did not get the proper kind of attention and respect from one feudal lord, he proceeded to the next feudal state and tried his luck with the next ruler. Confucius did not emerge supreme among the "hundred philosophers" until several centuries after his death. Eventually there developed an orthodoxy, i.e., Confucianism, as the ruling ideology of the nation, and the civil service examinations were tailored very closely along orthodox Confucian lines. But, then, not everyone needed to take up civil service, and no one was subjected to these examinations just to be tested on the point of orthodoxy. Actually, dissidents existed in China in large or small numbers in every age.

In the course of Chinese history, there have been religious persecutions and literary proscriptions. The actual causes for these limitations of freedom have usually consisted of political threats to or economic encroachment upon the authority of the throne. Such discussions, however, belong elsewhere in this volume.

QUESTION: In the American social tradition, the concept of "equality of opportunity" plays a very prominent role. Is this concept equally prominent in Chinese social thought, and equally emphasized in Chinese social practice?

ANSWER: Yes. I have quoted the saying of Confucius, "In education there should be no discrimination." (The wording I actually used was the standard translation by James Legge, which says, "In teaching there should be no distinction of classes.") This saying should be read together with another by the Master, "By nature all men are pretty much alike; it is by custom and habit that they are set apart." [22] (Significantly, this quotation is used, and is the only one used, in UNESCO's pamphlet, *The Race Question*,[23] published in 1950.) In a popular rhymed primer, which for centuries countless Chinese school boys have been made to commit to memory in traditional China, there are these lines: "Generals and high ministers do not come from designated stocks;/Every man should exert himself to the utmost," *Hsün-meng yu-hsüeh shih* (Rhymed Primer for the Training of Beginners). There is a deep-rooted and widespread conviction among the Chinese, since Confucius' day, that, with the necessary effort on the part of the individual himself, any man should and could have the opportunity to "make good." The most effective and influential Chinese institution giving expression to the conviction of the potentiality and educability of the individual, is, of course, the wide-open civil service examination system.

One has to admit that traditional China did not develop the idea or institution of universal education, i.e., the requirement by law that all boys and girls must attend school for so many years. But, then, universal education is a very recent phenomenon everywhere in the world and is operating in contemporary China, but our business here is to discuss characteristics of traditional cultures.

Notes

1. See, for instance, James Legge, trans., *The Yi King* (*The Classic of Changes*), X. 63. Sacred Books of the East, Vol. XVI. (Oxford: The Clarendon Press, 1899), p. 402.
2. The *Tso chuan*, the 24th Year of Duke Hsiang (549 B.C.), James Legge, trans. The Chinese Classics, Vol. V, the *Tso chuan* (London: Henry Frowde [China, 1939]), p. 507.
3. Dr. Hu Shih used "worth, work, and word" as English equivalents for the three items, and called the idea the Chinese three-W theory of immortality. See Hu Shih, "Concept of Immortality in Chinese Thought," in *The Harvard Divinity School Bulletin*, 1945–1946, pp. 40–41.
4. This incident is recorded in the biographical essay on Yen Ying in

the *Shih chi* (Historical Records) by Ssu-ma Ch'ien. Both of the incidents referred to in this paragraph are cited in Kuo Mo-jo, *Shih p'i-p'an shu* (Collection of Ten Critical Essays) (rev. ed.; Peking: Hsian Hua Book Shop, 1954), p. 41.

5. James Legge, trans., *Confucian Analects,* XIII.16. The Chinese Classics, Vol. I (Oxford: Clarendon Press, 1893), p. 269.

6. *Ta hsüeh* (*The Great Learning*), Y. P. Mei, trans., in William T. de Bary, ed., *Sources of Chinese Tradition* (New York: Columbia University Press, 1960), p. 129.

7. The first appearance of this ideal in Chinese literature is to be found in Chapter 33, the last chapter, of the *Chuang Tzu.* For a recent discussion of this ideal in relation to Taoism and Confucianism, see Y. P. Mei, "Ancient Chinese Philosophy According to the *Chuang Tzu,* Chapter 33," in *The World of Thought,* with an English Translation of the Chapter, with the Chinese text, *Tsing* (*Ch'ing*) *hua hsüeh-pao, Tsing* (*Ch'ing*) *Hua Journal of Chinese Studies,* New Series, IV, No. 2 (February, 1964), 186–211.

8. James Legge, trans., *Confucian Analects,* VI.17, The Chinese Classics, Vol. I, p. 190.

9. Y. P. Mei, "The Basis of Social, Ethical, and Spiritual Values in Chinese Philosophy."

10. James Legge, trans., *Confucian Analects,* VII.29; Legge, Vol. I, p. 204.

11. *Ibid.,* IV.6; Legge, Vol. I, p. 167.

12. *Ibid.,* XV.38; Legge, Vol. I, p. 305.

13. *Ibid.,* IX.25–28; Legge, Vol. I, pp. 224–225.

14. *Mencius,* IIIB.2, 3. Translation by Y. P. Mei, *Tsing Hua Journal of Chinese Studies,* New Series, II, No. 2 (June, 1961), 367. James Legge's translation is to be found in The Chinese Classics, Vol. II, *The Works of Mencius* (Hong Kong, Lane, Crawford & Co., 1861), p. 141.

15. *Hsün Tzu,* I, "An Exhortation to Learning." Translation by Y. P. Mei in *Tsing Hua Journal of Chinese Studies,* New Series, II, No. 2 (June, 1961), 375–376. H. H. Dubs's translation is to be found in *The Works of Hsüntze* (London: Arthur Probsthain, 1928), p. 41.

15a. The *China News Analysis,* a weekly report on all significant developments in Communist China, published in Hong Kong, contained in No. 416, April 13, 1962, pp. 6–7, a brief article on "Filial Piety." It is mostly a summary of an article on the same topic published in *Chung-kuo ch'ing-nien pao* (Chinese Youth Daily). One of the key sentences, perhaps the concluding sentence, runs as follows: "Indeed, our Socialist Fatherland is a great happy family of the people!"

16. The relation between sovereign and subject since the overthrow of

the imperial dynasty of the Manchus in 1911 has been replaced by that between the state and the citizen.

17. "No Chinese American J. Ds.," *America*, 93 (July 23, 1955); James C. G. Coniff, "Our Amazing Chinese Kids," *Coronet*, 39 (December, 1955), 31–39; "Why No Chinese-American Delinquents?" *Saturday Evening Post*, 227 (April 30, 1955), 12. Two other magazine articles might be mentioned: William A. McIntyre, "Chinatown Offers No Lesson," *New York Times Magazine*, October 6, 1957, pp. 49 ff.; Chandler Bossard, "Americans without a Delinquency Problem," *Look*, XXII (April 29, 1958), 75 ff.

18. For a compact description of the Chinese civil service examination system, see Teng Ssu-yü, "China's Examination System and the West," in H. F. MacNair, ed., *China* (Berkeley: University of California Press, 1946), pp. 441–451.

19. See James Legge, trans., *Confucian Analects*, XIII.2; The Chinese Classics, Vol. I, pp. 262–263.

20. We cite here three items as follows: Robert M. Marsh, *The Mandarins, The Circulation of Elites in China, 1600–1900* (New York: Free Press of Glencoe, 1961); Wolfram Eberhard, *Social Mobility in Traditional China* (Leiden: E. J. Brill, 1962); Ping-ti Ho, *The Ladder of Success in Imperial China, Aspects of Social Mobility, 1368–1911* (New York: Columbia University Press, 1962).

21. Ho Ping-ti, *ibid.*, p. 257.

22. *Analects*, XVII.2.

23. *Unesco and Its Programme III*, Unesco Publication 791.

JOHN C. H. WU   *The Status of the Individual*

in the Political and Legal Traditions

of Old and New China[1]

I. The Individual and the State: A Diversity of Views

How does the individual in China stand vis à vis the state? Here
we meet with a refreshing diversity of views.

The Taoists set the highest value on individual freedom. For
them, that government is the best which meddles and taxes the
least. The ancient "Chi-jang kou" (Song of Mud Balls) [2] was evidently of Taoist inspiration:

> *As the sun rises I get up.*
> *As the sun sets I go to rest.*
> *I dig a well for my drink.*
> *I till the fields for my food.*
> *What has the power of the emperor to do with me?*

This love of personal freedom is well exemplified in the life
of Chuang Tzu (bet. 399 and 295 B.C.),[3] the greatest Taoist after
Lao Tzu.[4] Once a certain king sent some emissaries to invite him to
be his prime minister. He declined because he wanted to "wag
his tail in the mud" like the tortoise.[5] On a similar occasion he said
that he would rather be a free bird seeking its food in the hills
than be domesticated and petted to death.[6]

To the Taoists, then, everybody is free to lead the quiet tenor
of his life, and no government has the right to interfere with his
freedom, much less to compel him to take office. They chose to
be recluses.

Confucius (551–479 B.C.) was of a different mind. When some

recluses [7] warned him against his vain attempts to turn the current of the age, he said with a sigh, "It is not in the nature of man to find his social life among the beasts and birds. If we do not remain in the society of men, with whom else can we associate ourselves? Moreover, if the world were in good order, I should not be trying to change it." [8]

However, to remain in human society is one thing, but to join a government is another thing. Confucius would serve only a prince whom he considered worthy of his service. He traveled from one state to another for many years in search of a princely prince who would go along with his principles and ideals.[9] As he found none, he returned a disappointed man to his native state, where he continued to teach his pupils and compile his books.

In this connection, two points are worthy of note. First, both Confucius and the rulers seem to have taken for granted that an individual was free to choose the prince he would like to serve, and that he was even free to leave his office if he was displeased with the prince's ways.[10] Second, in all his travels from state to state, there is no record to show that there was any need of a passport and a visa. This shows that in those days there was complete freedom of movement among the states.

In *The Book of Changes* we find this significant saying: "Absorbed in the high and noble interests of his own, he refuses to serve the prince and duke." [11] The book was a common source of inspiration for Taoists and Confucians alike, although in this particular instance the Taoists followed its teaching more unconditionally than the Confucians. Later, when Buddhism came to China, it re-enforced the Taoist stand. The Buddhists went to the extent of declaring that "monks owe no veneration to the king." [12]

Thus, the three main traditions of Chinese thought and religion have, each in its way, upheld the freedom of the individual vis-à-vis the state, because all of them recognized a sort of Natural Law which derives its authority from a higher source than the state. For the Confucians, this higher source is found in Heaven and Heaven-ordained human nature.[13] For the Taoists, it lies in *Tao*, the Law of Nature. For the Buddhists, *Buddha-dharma* is the Supreme Law transcending the laws of this world. Taoists are *in* the world, but not *of* it. Buddhists consider themselves as neither *of* nor *in* the world, but *out* of the world, the world being, in their view, an impermanent phenomenon.[14] As to the Confucians, they are both *in* and *of* the world. They are resolutely involved in human relationships and wholeheartedly committed to the fulfillment of all the duties entailed. Still, they are not without a transcendental dimension in their total involvement, for the Law which ordains those duties is not made by man but by Heaven. The Buddha and Lao Tzu soared into the heights and dived into the deeps, but Confucius walked on the solid ground, coping with all situations of life according to the dictates of his conscience. He did not withdraw from the world, but played the part of a "mu-to" (wooden bell), "i.e., a teacher and a conscientious objector." [15]

Mo Tzu [16] (470–391? B.C.) was even more positive in spirit than the Confucians. He was willing to sacrifice himself for the welfare of others, and worked most strenuously to stop the states from going to war. Like Confucius, he found the Higher Law in the will of Heaven, and he preached the noble doctrine of universal love. But it is regrettable that he seems to have by-passed human nature and the family.[17] With vigorous logic he stressed uniformity at the expense of diversity.

If the Taoists tended to ignore the state, the Legalists [18] tended to ignore the individual. To them, the state is the all-important thing. The state is the end, while the people are merely means to the end. They rejected all private standards of right and wrong. They recognized no authority above the state, nor any law higher than the positive laws of the state. Theirs was a radical positivism. To them, "right" meant what the rulers want, and "wrong" what the rulers do not want.[19] Under their Rule of Law, all individuals are indeed equal; only, they are equal in being slaves of the state. They denounced and outlawed all the traditional moral virtues as subversive of the public order of the state. Nor did they tolerate the traditional emphasis on family relationships. In their ideology, the individual does not belong to the family or even to himself. He belongs exclusively to the state. They wanted the people to work, fight, and die for the state. In the words of Lord Shang (d. 338 B.C.), "A people that looks to warfare as a ravening wolf looks at a piece of meat is a people that can be used. In general, fighting is a thing that people detest. A ruler who can make the people delight in war will become the king of kings." [20] It was by means of the Rule of Law, with its system of penalties and rewards working as inexorably as fate, that they succeeded in expanding the State of Ch'in (255–207 B.C.) into an empire. But, by isolating the Rule of Law from the fundamental humanity of men, they foredoomed it to a catastrophic collapse.

It is a pity that the Rule of Law should in the hands of the Legalists be wedded to a totalitarian, materialistic, and militarist ideology, so that, instead of securing the rights and freedom of the individual, as it normally should, it became actually a ruthless instrument for dehumanizing the people and turning them into tigers and wolves. So far as China was concerned, this unhappy wedding spoiled the chance of a genuine balanced Rule of Law for over two millenniums.

Of all these lines of thinking, the way of Confucius would seem to be the most balanced. It excels Moism by its catholicity, and excels Buddhism by its sense of reality. It steers between the anarchistic tendencies of Taoism and the totalitarianism of the Legalists. It recognizes the need of unity, but at the same time it sees the desirability of diversity. As Confucius himself put it, "Men of superior quality aim at harmony, not uniformity; while the small-minded aim at uniformity, not harmony." [21] This is in the best tradition of political wisdom, and is still a living ideal.

At this point I wish to enter a caveat. In this paper I will speak rather critically of the "legalization of Confucianism," or, what amounts to the same thing, the "Confucianization of the law." [22] This must not be taken to indicate criticism against Confucius and his teachings. He would be the last person to approve of the legalization of Confucianism. He was a great teacher and respected the personal ideals of each of his pupils.[23] He often asked them to tell him their aspirations, and never tried to impose upon them his own ideals, still less to reduce the diversity of their wishes into a dead monotony. He saw clearly that each individual had his unique qualities and peculiar faults, which were but the defects of his qualities.[24] He was a pioneer of individualization in pedagogy. Extremely many-sided in his interests, he was appreciative of different types of excellence in others.[25] He had an almost religious respect for the free choice of each and every individual.[26] Even in inculcating moral principles in the minds of his pupils, he would use only the method of dialogue and persuasion.[27] Compulsive morality would be inconceivable to him.[28]

It is true that Confucius laid great stress on the rites and rules of propriety, but his attention was focused on the underlying spirit rather than on the formalities and the letter of specific rules.[29] Confucius knew that the basic principles of morality, e.g., the Golden Rule, are immutable and of universal validity. But he also knew that their applications and expressions must vary according to the changing conditions and circumstances of life.[30] It was for this that Mencius called him the "Sage of Timeliness."[31] Solid like a mountain, he was yet as flexible and adaptable as water.[32] He was too broadly human to be a mere familist, too pure to be puritanical, too moral to be moralistic, too reasonable to be rationalistic, too thoroughgoingly moderate to be immoderate even in the virtue of moderation, and, finally, too genuine and well-integrated an individual person to be an individualist.[33] It is most regrettable that his moral teachings have been distorted beyond recognition and rigidified into an official system since the period of Han, (206 B.C.–A.D. 220), when Confucianism was wedded to the cosmic philosophy of the Yin-Yang school and lost its original rationality, purity, and flexibility.[34]

II. The Status of the Individual Under the Old Legal System

The old legal system of China began to take form in the Former Han period (206–23 B.C.), came to its maturity under the T'ang Dynasty (618–907 A.D.),[35] and remained stagnant through the succeeding dynasties until the end of the nineteenth century, when the legal-reform movement was set on foot. This defective system of law was formed under the influence of "Yin-Yang Confucianism," which polarized morality and law as the positive and negative aspects of government.[36] Morality sets up the norm of conduct; law sanctions it by penalizing its violation. When morality and law are thus wedded, the result is a system of compulsive morality, under which individual freedoms and rights can hardly be developed. What the Yin-Yang Confucianist brought about was the enforcement of Confucian social ethics, as they interpreted or, rather, misinterpreted it, by the machinery set up by the Legalists. Confucius himself would have condemned such a queer combination. Not that there was nothing good in it, but it could have been much better.

Let us look at some of its characteristic features insofar as they bear upon the status of the individual.

1. *All law was penal in nature.* There was no civil law. Even breaches of contract and injuries by negligence were penalized. The underlying philosophy was that law is the handmaid of ethics, and that any acts which are morally wrong constitute crimes, which it is the function of the law to inhibit and punish. In all the codes

from T'ang (618–907) to Ch'ing (1644–1911), there is a general provision to the effect that *whoever does what ought not to be done shall be punished.*[37] Although in practice this article was rarely invoked, in theory at least it must have been like the sword of Damocles hanging over the head of everybody.

2. *The problem of equality.* Were all persons equal before the law under the old system? Yes and no. Yes, in the sense that all persons, including the emperor himself, were required to respect and observe the law as it was. In an early case, Chang Shih-chih,[38] the Commandant of Justice under the reign of Emperor Wen of Han (reigned 179–156 B.C.), maintained the sovereignty of law against the Emperor's wish to impose a heavier penalty than was prescribed by the law, and uttered these unforgettable words: "The law must be upheld by the Son of Heaven as by everyone in the whole empire. Seeing that the penalty that I have imposed in the present case is what the law prescribes, to impose a higher penalty would be to discredit the law in the eyes of the people. . . . It is the duty of the Commandant of Justice to hold the scales of justice even and equal for the whole empire. If once the scales were overturned, the entire legal system of the empire would fall into confusion, and the people would not know where to put their hands and feet. May I ask Your Majesty to give serious consideration to this?" After a long silence, the Emperor said, "I believe you are right." [39] Chang Shih-chih established the principle of judicial independence, which became a sacred tradition for the judges of succeeding generations; and the good example set by Emperor Wen was seldom if ever departed from by later sovereigns.

Although there was no written constitution like the Magna Charta, the powers of the emperor were severely restricted by immemorial constitutional customs and by the unquestioned authority of the Confucian classics, effectively sanctioned by the fear of being called a "wicked monarch" in the ages to come.[40] From the Hans to the Manchus, there were some mediocre and weak monarchs, but there have been no despots or tyrants who placed themselves above the law. In this sense, it can be truthfully asserted that under the old system all persons were equal before the law.

Yet, in another sense, not all persons were equal before the law. For, although no one was above the law, yet the law itself created categories of people for special treatment. Prominent in all the codes were the eight categories of persons who were entitled to special consideration when guilty of crimes not of a treasonable nature.[41] They were: (1) relatives of the sovereign, (2) old friends of the sovereign, (3) persons of great virtue, (4) persons of great ability, (5) persons who had achieved great merit, (6) high-ranking officials, (7) persons who had served the government with exceptional zeal and diligence, and (8) the guests of the dynasty, that is, the descendants of the superseded dynasty.[42] Now, what were the privileges they were entitled to? For one thing, they could not be arrested or investigated before special permission was granted by the emperor. In some dynasties, they could not be fettered.[43] In other words, they were not privileged to commit crimes, but only to have their cases reported to the emperor for his final decision, and be immune to certain procedures and methods of trial. Taken all in all, these privileges did not amount to much.

3. *The legal status of the individual in the family.* Traditionally, a Chinese seldom thought of himself as an isolated entity. He was his father's son, his son's father, his elder brother's junior—in other words, an integral member of his family. He was a concrete individual person who moved, lived, and had his being in the natural milieu of the family. The ties of blood and, to some extent, of marriage created for him a network of human relationships in which he had his proper place. Each family had a head, to whom his wife, his children, his daughters-in-law, his grandchildren, and the domestics owed unquestioning obedience. I know of no other system of law which is so meticulous in enforcing the duties of filial piety. So long as the parents were living, it was a crime for the sons, including those who were married, to set up a separate household.[44] Children were betrothed by the mutual agreement of the heads of the families involved, and the parties themselves had no voice in the choice.[45] Nor were the young man and girl supposed to see each other before their wedding. Marriage within the period of mourning for one's parents entailed heavy penalties and was null and void.[46] It was a crime for a married son to beget a child within the mourning period.[47] This rule was in force for many centuries until it was abolished at the instance of Emperor T'ai-tsu of Ming (reigned 1368–1399), who held that it was against human nature and therefore could not be the teaching of Confucius.[48]

Confucius himself would have seen eye-to-eye with Emperor T'ai-tsu. Confucius was indeed insistent on the three-year mourning for parents, but his epigones have out-Confucianized him in this, as in so many other respects. When we speak of the "Confucianization of law," we must take care not to think that Confucius would have been happy to see some of the extremities to which his teachings were made to go at the hands of his later followers. For instance, Confucius did say that it was all right for father and son to conceal each other's crimes.[49] If the father had committed a crime, the son had no duty to testify against him. This privilege not to testify against one's parent was extended after the T'ang Dynasty to all members of the family living under the same roof, and the prosecutor was forbidden to ask anyone who was thus allowed to conceal the crime to bear witness.[50] So far, this seems to be reasonable, and it has its counterparts in other systems of law. But what was peculiar to Chinese law was the rule that anyone who accused his parents should be put to death, even if the accusation proved to be true.[51]

In all crimes of one member of the family against another, the degrees of relationship between the offender and the victim were used as an index to the degrees of punishment. Generally speaking, in crimes against the person, such as killing and wounding and slandering, the closer the relationship the higher the punishment; while in crimes against property, such as stealing and embezzlement, the closer the relationship the lighter the punishment.[52]

Chinese law was so geared to the idea of the family that it treated even religious communities as families. The relationship of master and novice was assimilated to that of uncle and nephew. The objects of worship were probably regarded as ancestors, as may be inferred from the following provision of the Code of T'ang (T'ang-lü shu-i): "Whoever steals or destroys an image of the Lord of Heaven (the supreme deity in Taoism) or the image of the Buddha shall receive three years' imprisonment. If a Taoist priest or nun should steal or destroy an image of the Lord of Heaven, or if a Buddhist monk or nun should steal or destroy an image of the Buddha, the penalty shall be banishment with penal labor. If the image in question is that of a True Man, or a bodhi-sattva, the penalty shall in each case be reduced by one degree." [53]

From the above examples, it is easy to see the legal status of the individual in the family. Each family was a little kingdom, which may be called a "familiadom," in which each member occupied a unique status different from all the others.[54] He might be superior to some and inferior to others, but never altogether equal to anyone, for the simple reason that even brothers were classified into elder and younger with important legal differences. But this does not mean that their status was static; for, if the sons survived their parents, they could set up their separate households and thus become family heads themselves.

4. *Inequality between sexes*. Under the old legal system, the status of woman left much to be desired. In the eye of the law, a woman was under a perpetual coverture. According to an old saying, a woman was subject to threefold dependence. Before her marriage, she was dependent on her father; after marriage, on her husband; when widowed, on her sons. But nowhere is the inequality more glaring than in the law of divorce. The wife could under no circumstance divorce her husband, but the husband could divorce his wife on no fewer than seven grounds, namely, childlessness, adultery, negligence in serving her husband's parents, loquacity, stealing, jealousy, and loathsome disease.[55] Some of these grounds, as you will see, are simply ridiculous. Especially negligence in serving the parents-in-law as a ground of divorce became a prolific source of heart-rending tragedies in family life. In some cases, the husband and wife were in perfect harmony with each other, but they were forced to be divorced because her mother-in-law did not like her. A story of this kind is told in the well-known poem, "The Peacock Flies to the Southwest." [56] And Lu Yu, a great poet of the Sung period (960–1279), divorced from his beloved wife at the instance of his mother, continued to exchange love poems even after she was remarried into another family.[57]

However, the law enumerated three conditions under which the wife could not be divorced on any of the seven grounds, except adultery. The conditions were (1) that she had no close relatives to whom she could return, (2) that she had worn three years' mourning for her husband's parents, or (3) that her husband's family was poor at the time of their marriage but had grown prosperous afterwards.[58] The third condition is particularly significant, for it indicates that the law was not blind to the fact that the building up of a home usually depended upon the co-operation of the wife.

In actual life, the Chinese woman's role was as important as her legal status was low. There is no telling how many monarchs and statesmen and scholars have attained greatness with the silent help of their wives and their mothers.[59] There was a popular proverb on the lips of everybody: "The mother is as lovable as the sun in winter; the father is as severe as the sun in summer." Poor man, what he had gained in legal authority was more than offset by his loss in spontaneous affection and devotion on the part of his children.

5. *Equality as the rule.* From the above, one may have been led to conclude that there are no general principles of law and justice underlying the legal system of Old China which are applicable *equally* to all persons. This would be an erroneous impression. Although family relationships did modify the general principles to a notable extent, they did not exclude them altogether. It would not be far from the truth to observe that particular relationships and general principles formed the warp and woof of the law. Then, too, we must realize that most cases that came before the magistrate were between parties not in any way familially related to each other, and they were governed by the general rules of the law. In all such cases, there was perfect equality of all persons before the law.

As the magistrates were drawn from the ranks of Confucian scholars, they were, as a rule, steeped in the spirit of classical teachings. Two passages in the ancient classics seem to have had the greatest influence on their minds. One is a saying of Tseng Ts'an as recorded in *The Analects.* A friend of his, newly appointed to a judicial office, came to call on Tseng Ts'an and asked for some words of advice. Tseng Ts'an said, "The rulers have departed from the right Way, and the people have been demoralized for a long time. In trying a case, if you should get at the truth of the charge, cherish a sense of sorrow and compassion for the culprit and by no means feel elated." [60] It seems as though Heaven itself were speaking through the mouth of honest Tseng Ts'an.

But the *locus classicus* of the fundamental principles of criminal justice is to be found in a dialogue between Emperor Shun and Kao Yao as recorded in *The Book of Documents.*[61] This remarkable dialogue between a sage-emperor and a sage-minister presents in a nutshell all the essentials of the Chinese philosophy of penal justice. It teaches that penal law is a subsidiary means of education, that the ultimate end of punishment is to bring about the cessation of all punishment, that intention is an essential element in a crime, and that, although an act may fall within the letter of the law, one should sacrifice formal regularity rather than run the risk of punishing an innocent person. All these ideas would seem to belong to the perennial philosophy of justice, springing directly from the natural reason of man. They constitute the living fountain from which Confucian magistrates through the ages have drawn their inspiration and their guidance. Even Su Tung-p'o, who used to declare airily that he had never in his life set his eyes upon the statutes, wrote a beautiful eulogy of Kao Yao's ideas of justice.[62]

6. *A touch of humanity in the judges.* Although Confucian scholars did nothing to develop the law, they had the merit of not forgetting that the law was made for man and not man for the law, and that punishment was but a means of education. That is why, in hearing litigations between family members on property rights, for example, the first impulse of a magistrate would be to try to reconcile the parties. Let me relate a typical case. Two brothers were disputing for farms. Su Ch'iung, the magistrate, said to both of them, "The most precious thing in the world is brotherly affection, and the least precious is a piece of land. Why should you quarrel over the least precious at the expense of the most precious?" Moved by this sagacious admonition, the brothers embraced each other and, after ten years of estrangement,[63] were reconciled. In this kind of atmosphere it was impossible to develop a rigid law of property. Instead of trying to solve the case by threshing out the rights and wrongs involved in the dispute, the magistrate simply disposed of it by dissolving the dispute itself. Nevertheless, this typical way of settling a case of this nature has an irresistible charm which will cast such a spell upon one's mind that one would sooner have a judgment like that than read a dozen learned treatises on the law of property.

Another case is even more interesting. When Chen Shih was a magistrate in a certain district, a thief entered his house one evening and hid himself on the top beam. Chen Shih espied him but pretended not to notice him. He called the members of his family together and began to preach a moral lesson to them. "Each of you," he said, "must diligently attend to his duties. You should know that robbers and thieves are not bad by nature. They become such only through the habit of laziness. For example, the gentleman on the top beam is a case in point." The burglar was so frightened that he fell to the ground. Chen Shih spoke gently to him, "Judging by your appearance, you are not a bad man. I only hope you will correct your mistakes and do good. Probably your wrong-doing is due to your poverty; I here give you two pieces of silk to help you start anew." The gentleman was profoundly moved and after that became a reformed man. When this was known to the public, all the people were converted by the report of Chen Shih's kindness and magnanimity.[64] There was neither thief nor robber in his district after that. The Chinese have a euphemism for thief: "The gentleman on the top beam." After all, Old China had its unique qualities, and the lack of legal experts was but a defect of its qualities.

III. The Status of the Individual under the New System

1. *The Influence of the West.* Communications between China and the West began long before the last century, but China did not feel the real impact of the West until the latter part of the century, the heyday of Western individualism. The good Emperor Kuang-hsü (reigned 1875–1908) saw the urgent need of a thoroughgoing overhauling of the old institutions. He wanted to introduce a constitutional monarchy after the pattern of England and Japan. Unfortunately, this was frustrated by the infamous Empress Dowager. But the Emperor's initiative in the reform of the criminal law proved fruitful. In 1902, he issued an edict appointing a commission to revise the laws "on the basis of a comparative study of the laws of all nations, to the end that our new laws may be applicable both to our own people and to foreigners, and that our administration of justice may be improved." [65]

In the end, the penal system was considerably modernized. The new penal code was promulgated in 1910, but the Emperor did not live to see it. Although it has been superseded by later codes, it marked the beginning of the new legal system.

There was also some attempt to produce a code of civil law, though it did not pass beyond the drafting stage. But the very fact that the law was now divided into penal and civil was a tremendous gain for the rights of the individual. Moreover, the legal profession was for the first time recognized by the law, and law schools began to appear.

2. *The "San-min chu-i" as the Foundation of the Present System.* As we have seen, the old legal system was based upon the Yin-Yang philosophy. It was not until this all-embracing cosmology was replaced by the *San-min chu-i*,[66] the philosophy of the threefold well-being of the people—the people's nationhood, the people's political powers and legal rights, and the people's livelihood—that a truly Chinese system of law could be established. The *San-min*

chu-i, which Sun Yat-sen formulated, was based, on the one hand, upon Lincoln's idea of government "of the people, by the people, for the people," [67] and, on the other hand, upon the best political, legal, and economic traditions of China from the earliest times to the present day. Horizontally, it draws from the collective experience of Western democracies. Perpendicularly, it makes itself heir to the inexhaustible legacy of Old China. Consequently, it is broad and cosmopolitan in spirit; and, at the same time, is deeply-rooted in the native soil. It represents a magnificent harmony between the one and the many, doing justice at once to the urgent claims of unity and universality and to the vital urges of diversity and uniqueness.

In the present Constitution, a whole chapter is given to the formulation of the basic rights and duties of the people. It begins with a declaration of the equality of all citizens before the law, "irrespective of sex, religion, race, or party affiliation." [68] Time does not permit me to enumerate here all the freedoms and rights guaranteed by the Constitution. The author of the first draft made it a special point to incorporate the institution of *habeas corpus* in his draft; and it has been preserved in the permanent Constitution.[69] Only two duties are mentioned, namely, paying taxes and performing military service in accordance with law. Another noteworthy point is that the constitutionally guaranteed rights cannot be restricted by law "except by such as may be necessary to prevent infringement upon the freedoms of other persons, to avert imminent crisis, to maintain social order, or to advance public welfare." [70] This is similar to the "Due Process Clause" of the American Constitution.

All these provisions, inspired by the spirit of the *San-min chu-i*, would seem to furnish a firm legal foundation for the development of a vibrant and full-blooded individual person and a working democracy.

3. *The Civil Law*. Although the civil law as an independent branch of the law had emerged in the early years of this century, it was not until 1930 that the civil code was promulgated. This code is a major accomplishment in the history of modern Chinese law. With the *San-min chu-i* for its guiding spirit, it embodies general principles drawn from comparative law, and at the same time it gives specific articulation to many of the prevailing customs and attitudes of the people.[71] Thus, both the universal and the

unique have found a hospitable abode in its spacious premises, in which every individual in China may feel at home.

a) *The Place of Good Morals in the Civil Law.* To turn a moral wrong as such into a crime would constitute a great threat to individual integrity; but to turn a moral wrong into a civil wrong, or a tort, would involve, at most, a question of compensation. This is why the civil law can afford to be more hospitable to moral considerations in the determination of liability. There is a plethora of provisions in which "good morals" is made a decisive criterion of civil liability or of the validity of a transaction. Let two samples suffice: "A juristic act which is contrary to public order or good morals is void." [72] "A person, who, intentionally or by negligence, unlawfully infringes upon the rights of another is bound to compensate him for any damage arising therefrom. The same applies when the injury is done intentionally in a manner contrary to good morals." [73]

It is true that many such provisions are adopted from modern European codes. But the Chinese legislators have done so not blindly but selectively. They have selected precisely those new principles of Western law which are most congenial to the spirit of Chinese tradition. By a fortunate coincidence, the Chinese civil code was produced at a time when Western juristic thought had for several decades been turning away from the extreme individualism of the nineteenth century and heading steadily toward a humanistic and sociological position strikingly similar, in spirit, to the Chinese philosophy of the human-minded and well-integrated individual, who thinks of his duties more than his rights.

b) *The Equality of the Sexes Before the Law.* The most revolutionary feature of the civil code was the complete legal equality between men and women. In the first place, all provisions of the code applied to both sexes alike. In the second place, for the first time in the history of China, women were entitled to inherit in equal shares with men in the law of intestate succession.[74] In this, the principle of *agnatia*, which had prevailed for at least three millenniums, was replaced by the principle of *cognatia*.

Marriage is no longer a matter arranged between two families, but is based strictly upon the mutual consent of the parties themselves.[75] Only when a minor makes an agreement to marry or concludes his marriage is parental consent required.[76] The only material difference that the law makes between the sexes is with regard to the marriageable age, which for a man is eighteen and for a woman sixteen.[77] In all other ways, they are equal before the law.

4. *The Penal Law.*

a) The present criminal code starts out with a recognition of the democratic principle of *Nulla poena sine lege:* "An act is punishable only if expressly so provided by the law at the time of its commission." [78] This means that, however evil the act may be from a moral point of view, it is not subject to punishment as long as there is no explicit prohibition by the law. The object of this law is not to encourage the people to do evil, but to secure their freedom from the possibility of arbitrary judgment of the court.

b) While all the old codes highlighted the eight classes of persons entitled to special consideration, the new code puts all offenders on an equal basis. The law has equal respect for all persons, special respect for none. If there is special respect at all, it is for certain persons against whom a crime has been committed, as may be seen from Article 116, which provides that any crime against the person or reputation of the chief executive of a friendly state or its duly accredited representative is subject to a higher punishment than that which is provided for a crime of the same nature committed against other persons.[79]

c) It is interesting to note that family relationships still play an important part in the measurement of punishments in certain situations. This serves as a link between the old system and the new.

The accusing of one's family relatives is no longer prohibited as in the old law; but in a number of situations the existence of family relationships controls the degree of punishment. In offenses such as false testimony, malicious prosecution, profaning the dead, homicide, causing bodily injury, and abandonment, the presence of a family relationship between the offender and the victim raises the degree of punishment.[80] On the other hand, in offenses such as fraud, breach of confidence, theft, and embezzlement, the presence of a family relationship reduces the punishment. In some cases the judge is authorized even to remit the punishment.[81]

In all such cases, the law is doing nothing more than being responsive to the realities of human relationships and family solidarity so deep-rooted in the Chinese tradition.

d) The last but not the least significant feature of the criminal code is the large scope of discretionary powers it gives to the judges in meting out punishment. In almost all cases, the law prescribes a maximum punishment and a minimum; between these limits there is often a large leeway, thus making possible the individualization of punishments.[82] Besides, the code permits suspension of punishment in cases where the sentence is no more than two years' imprisonment.[83] It has also adopted a system of parole.[84]

But the most typical example of individualization of punishment is to be found in Article 16: "Criminal responsibility may not be avoided on the ground of ignorance of the law, but punishment may be reduced according to the circumstances. If a person believed with good reason that his act was permitted by law, punishment may be remitted." In this, the Confucian empathic principle of consideration toward every individual finds a happy expression.[85]

While the whole movement of the individualization of punishment is one of the most advanced developments in Western jurisprudence, it accords surprisingly well with the old Chinese tradition of fitting the punishment to the concrete individual person rather than to the abstract nature of his crime. This is but an instance of the intriguing paradox that the East in seeking to be Westernized has often encountered its dormant self, just as in some other spheres, especially in philosophy of life and spiritual cultivation, the West is beginning to discover its original self in exploring the profundities of the Eastern mind.[86] In each case, the excursion is really a homecoming.

The East and the West so closely interpenetrate each other that one is often tempted to say that East is West and West is East. Perhaps it is more accurate to say that, while East is East and West is West, there is East in the West and West in the East. Each instinctively seeks the other for its own completion and fulfillment. Let us therefore treasure their differences; for, without differences they would not be able to enrich each other. And let us also treasure their essential oneness, without which their existential differences would not be able to evolve into a harmony. But, thanks to their real unity and real diversity, there is great reason to hope that all the bewildering multiplicity of cultural processes can be an inexhaustible source of counterpoints to feed an ever-expanding and ever-deepening symphony of humanity, in which unity becomes infinitely vital and rich and diversity acquires eternal meaning and significance.

QUESTION: In the last part of your paper, where you speak of the features of the present criminal code of China, you cite

Article 16 as an example in which the Confucian principle of consideration finds a happy expression. Now, the legal principle underlying this provision is familiar to all students of modern criminology. My question is: Is this Article an original Chinese invention or is it adopted from the West?

ANSWER: It is not a Chinese invention, but an adoption from the West. But, although it is not original with the Chinese, the choice is conditioned by Chinese preferences, which are Confucian.

QUESTION: Your description of the legal system of modern China is particularly interesting to me as a student of Japanese law. You point out that, even in the modern modifications of the old legal tradition, Chinese lawmakers managed to preserve a certain continuity with the spirit of the past. What strikes me is that these modifications coincide on so many points with the Japanese modifications. This must be because there is a fundamental similarity in the social structures of the two countries which condition their choice of exactly the same elements from the legal systems of the West. Or, is it because there have been mutual influences between China and Japan?

ANSWER: The similarity of social structures of the two countries can be traced to a great extent to the fact that in her formative days Japan absorbed Confucianism quite thoroughly. Of the contemporary Chinese lawmakers, not a few received their juristic training in Japan, although a greater number have studied in the West. Anyway, mutual influences between China and Japan have been inevitable. However, the greatness of a nation does not depend so much on its originality as on its capacity to assimilate congenial ideas from others.

QUESTION: You mention the eight categories of privileged persons, giving the impression that under the old Chinese legal system not all persons were really equal before the law. Were there no counterbalancing responsibilities against those privileges? For instance, there was a well-known maxim prevailing in olden times: "When those who should know the law transgress it, the punishment should be doubly severe." That is to say, the greater your knowledge, the greater your responsibility. Now, the privileged classes are usually more educated than the unprivileged ones. So, in fact, the inequality was not as great as your presentation would make it seem to be.

ANSWER: There is a point in your question. But there is a distinction between *"de jure"* and *"de facto."* I have pointed this out in connection with the legal inequality of the sexes: "In actual life, the Chinese woman's role was as important as her legal status was low." Similarly, on this question of privileged classes, there were certainly some counterbalancing responsibilities. Politically and constitutionally, for instance, the supreme privilege of the emperor was coupled with his supreme responsibility, to such an extent that in case of grave breaches of the trust imposed upon him by the Mandate of Heaven, the leaders of the people had not only the right but the sacred duty of revolution. But there is one thing I have to bring out in connection with your question, and that is that, although many persons belonging to the privileged classes were educated, not all educated persons belonged to the privileged classes.

In this connection, let me introduce a pet theory of mine—the *principle of neutralization.* Where, for instance, the starting point is equality, inequalities creep into the system in practice, thus neutralizing the official theory. On the other hand, where the starting point is inequality, equalities creep into the system in practice, thus toning down the harsh consequences of the theory. Truly, as Justice Holmes once remarked, the life of the law has not been logic; it has been experience.

The same is true of women's "right of inheritance." Legally, it is absolutely correct to say that a woman had no right of inheritance. Yet, this does not mean that therefore all women were in danger of starvation. In fact, rich families as a rule provided fine dowries for their daughters on their marriage; and although a girl did not inherit from her father, she "inherited," together with her husband, from *his* father. Of course, in a legal sense, she could not be said to "inherit," but, if the husband became rich, she could not remain poor in fact, at least in normal cases.

Notes

1. This paper is strictly confined to the question of individual freedom and equality. For a general background of legal and political thought and institutions, the reader is referred to my article on "Chinese Legal and Political Philosophy," in Charles A. Moore, ed., *Philosophy and Culture East and West* (Honolulu: University of Hawaii Press, 1962), pp. 611–630; also this volume, pp. 213–237.

2. See Shen Te-ch'ien, *Ku-shih yüan* (Origins of Ancient Poetry, An Anthology of Old Poems). This anthology was first published in 1719, but has been reprinted innumerable times. The song quoted in the text is the first poem in the anthology. It is purported to date from the third millennium B.C. This is of more than doubtful authenticity. The first two lines of the poem are found in *Chuang Tzu* XXVIII with reference to any such song. It is likely that the song was produced after the time of Chuang Tzu. But, whatever the date, it was certainly of Taoist inspiration.

3. Chuang Tzu.

4. Lao Tzu, author of the *Tao-te ching*, was, traditionally, an elder contemporary of Confucius. His dates have been perhaps the most controversial question in the history of Chinese philosophy. Some scholars have put him even later than Chuang Tzu. But the latest tendency among Chinese scholars is toward a confirmation of the traditional date.

5. *Chuang Tzu*, XVII.

6. See, for instance, the *Chuang Tzu*, XVIII, containing the following story: "Formerly a sea-bird alighted in the suburbs of Lu. The marquis went out to meet it and brought it to the ancestral temple, where he treated it to a banquet. Exquisite ancient music was played for it; an ox, a sheep, and a pig were killed to feed it. The bird, however, looked at everything with dim eyes, and was very sad. It did not venture to take a single bit of meat, nor drink a single cupful; and in three days it died."

7. Several such encounters are recorded in *The Analects*. See, for instance, *Analects*, XIV.34,41,42; XVIII.5,6,7.

8. *Analects*, XVIII.6.

9. Confucius had great confidence in his statesmanship. "Were any prince to employ me, in a twelvemonth something could be done, and in three years there could be some worth-while result" (*Analects*, XIII.10). This does not mean that he would accept any kind of employment. When he was in the State of Wei, Duke Ling asked him about military tactics. He replied curtly, "With sacrificial rites I have indeed an acquaintance, but as to military matters I have never studied them" (*Analects*, XV.1). The next day he left the state (*ibid.*).

10. When he was the Minister of Crime in Lu, as the Prime Minister, the neighboring state Ch'i was afraid that Lu would grow so strong as to constitute a menace to its safety. So, Ch'i presented a company of eighty beautiful dancing girls as a token of homage to the ruler of Lu, with the result that the latter neglected to attend to the business of government. Eventually, Confucius went abroad. (See Ssu-ma Ch'ien, *Shih chi*, XLVII, "Confucius: His Life and His Family.")

11. *I ching*, under the *Ku* (eighteenth) Hexagram. The quoted words

constitute the oracle attached to the sixth and topmost line.

12. See *Hung-ming chi* (An Anthology of essays in defense of Buddhism, compiled by Seng-yu of the Liang Dynasty [502–556]). Book 5 contains a thoroughgoing exposition by Hui-yüan (344–416) of the reasons why Buddhist monks do not venerate the king.

13. The *Chung yung* opens with a clear-cut statement: "What is ordained of Heaven is called 'Nature.' The following of this 'Nature' is called 'Tao,' or 'Moral Law.' The refinement of the *Tao* is called 'Culture.'"

14. This does not mean that Buddhists believe this world to be nothing. It is a conglomeration of elements which is only temporary. Because of its intrinsic impermanence, human existence is not real in the same sense as *nirvāṇa* is.

15. "Wooden bell" (*mu-to*) is really a metal bell with a wooden tongue. Its function was to awaken people and call them together, especially in times of danger at night. *Analects,* III.24.

16. See Yi-Pao Mei, trans., *The Ethical and Political Works of Motse* (London: Arthur Probsthain, 1929). Refer also to *A Source Book in Chinese Philosophy,* translated, compiled, and edited by Wing-tsit Chan (Princeton: Princeton University Press, 1963), pp. 211 ff.

17. His doctrines suffered from excessive asceticism. For instance his wholesale condemnation of music ignored the fact that music is a necessity of life and can be turned into a potent factor of education. His exaltation of uniformity of thought at the expense of salutary diversity unwittingly paved the way for the Legalists' unification of thought by the force of the state.

18. See J. J. L. Duyvendak, trans., *The Book of Lord Shang* (London: Arthur Probsthain, 1928), and W. K. Liao, trans., *The Complete Works of Han Fei Tzu* (London: Arthur Probsthain, 1939).

19. See Arthur Waley, *Three Ways of Thought in Ancient China* (London: George Allen & Unwin Ltd., 1929), p. 200.

20. *Ibid.,* p. 221.

21. *Analects,* XIII.23. In this, as in so many other aphorisms, Confucius' merit did not lie in originality but in his unsurpassed gift of expressing a whole tradition in a living epigram. Yen Tzu, an elder contemporary of his, had eloquently said the same thing to Duke Ching of Ch'i by means of some interesting illustrations, such as the preparation of a soup and the composition of music. "If water is flavored with water, who can enjoy its taste? If the lute and the harp had but one note, who could enjoy their music? Such is the undesirability of uniformity!" See *Ch'un ch'iu, Tso chuan,* under year XX of Duke Chao (522 B.C.).[2]

22. See Ch'ü T'ung-tsu, *Law and Society in Traditional China* (Paris: Mouton & Co., 1961), pp. 267 ff.

23. *Analects,* XI.25, where Confucius was asking his disciples to state

their ideals of life. When one of them hesitated to speak, because his ideal of life was so different from those of the others, Confucius urged him on, saying, "What does it matter? After all, each of us may speak of his own ideals."

24. For instance, *Analects*, XVII.16, where he pointed out that, even though the ancients, too, had their defects, those were the defects of their qualities, while the moderns have the same defects without any corresponding qualities to counterbalance them. Also in *Analects*, XVIII.10, Confucius quoted the advice that the Duke of Chou gave to his son that he must not seek perfection and all-aroundness in any one man.

25. See, for instance, *Analects*, XVIII.8, where he praised the different types of excellence among ancient worthies, while admitting that he himself was different from all of them, since he refused to be pinned down to any definite pattern. The important thing is to be true to oneself: in the choice of styles, there is "no *must* and no *must-not*."

26. *Analects*, IX.25: "You can take away the commander from the forces of a large state, but you cannot take away the free will from a person, however humble he may be."

27. Cf. *Analects*, III.7; I.15.

28. It is well known that Confucius laid emphasis on the transforming influence of virtuous example; he would be the last person to try to reform popular morals by resorting to legal measures and punishments.

29. *Analects*, III.3: "If a man is not human, what has he to do with rites? If a man is not human, what has he to do with music?"

30. According to Confucius, one must, first of all, have a sincere desire to learn; then he must be able to stand on the principles he has learned; finally, in applying the principles, he must be able to weigh the exigencies of the times and circumstances. See *Analects*, IX.29.

31. *Book of Mencius*, VB.I.

32. According to Confucius, the good take delight in the mountains, while the wise take delight in the waters. (*Analects*, VI. 21.) Confucius himself seems to combine the two.

33. Just as true virtue is not self-righteous, so a truly integrated person cannot be deliberately individualistic.

34. Confucius' conception of Heaven (*T'ien*), like those of Mo Tzu and Mencius, was fundamentally theistic. When, in the Western Han period (206 B.C.–A.D. 25), Confucianism was wedded to the Yin-Yang philosophy, Heaven-and-Earth began to take the place of Heaven, and there emerged what may be called a cosmic pantheism. In the hands of Confucius and Mencius, "*T'ien-ming*" was Divine Providence. With the Han scholars, it became equated with fate.

35. The *T'ang-lü shu-i* (*The Code of T'ang with Annotations*), which was drafted by a committee consisting of eight high-ranking

ministers and ten Doctors of Law (under the chairmanship of Ch'ang-sun Wu-chi) was submitted to the Throne in 653. It contains 502 articles divided into twelve parts. Each article is followed by annotations, which were considered an integral part of the Code. The Code summed up the best elements handed down from the previous dynasties after the Han, and served as the model for later codes.

36. In the introductory commentaries to Book I of the Code, we find the polarity of law and morality formulated in these words: "Virtue and morals are the foundation of government and education, while laws and punishments are the operative agencies of government and education. The former and the latter are necessary complements to each other, just as it takes morning and evening to form a whole day, or spring and autumn to form a whole year." However excellent the *Code of T'ang* was, it was limited by the cosmological framework of Yin-Yang Confucianism, which was by that time deeply intrenched in the Chinese mind.

37. See Article no. 450 of the *Code of T'ang*. All the later codes contain a similar provision. See, for instance, *Ta Tsing Leu Lee*, Sir George Thomas Staunton, trans. (London: T. Cadell & Davies, 1810), p. 419: "Whoever is guilty of improper conduct, and such as is contrary to the spirit of the laws, though not a breach of any specific article, shall be punished, at the least, with 40 blows; and when the impropriety is of a serious nature, with 80 blows."

38. Ssu-ma Ch'ien's biography of Chang Shih-chih has been translated by Burton Watson in his *Records of the Grand Historian* (New York: Columbia University Press, 1961), Vol. I, pp. 533–539.

39. Cf. *ibid.*, pp. 536–537.

40. An important branch of Chinese literature consists of memorials to the Throne. This forms an inexhaustible source of history and wisdom which is still little explored.

41. For a detailed treatment, see Ch'ü T'ung-tsu, *op. cit.*, note 22, pp. 177 ff.

42. *Ibid.*

43. *Ibid.*, p. 178.

44. See the *Code of T'ang*, Article No. 55.

45. Under the old law, to disobey the will of one's parents would be an act of filial impiety, which was listed as one of the ten gravest crimes. Marriage was primarily the concern of the family, meant to continue the family lineage and traditions. To the Western reader, this system must seem incredibly cruel; he is apt to think that every marriage must have been a mockery of marital happiness. But, in fact, unhappy marriages were the exception rather than the rule. On the whole, parents were very careful in choosing spouses for their children. Their children had implicit confidence in their judgment,

and would feel too bashful to comment, even if they were consulted. In Confucius' day, marriage was not primarily a matter for the family. The parties knew each other before the wedding. This can be inferred from the considerable number of poems on courtship and marital happiness in *The Book of Songs*, which Confucius loved so much that he set every one of the three-hundred-odd odes to music, and never wearied of encouraging his pupils and even his own son to read them. Confucius was certainly much more modern than his later epigones. In this paradox lies the key to a proper understanding of the cultural history of China.

46. See the *Code of T'ang*, Article no. 179.
47. *Ibid.*, Article no. 156.
48. *Ming T'ai-tsu hsiao-tz'u lu hsü* (Emperor T'ai-tsu of Ming, Preface to Models of Filial Piety and Paternal Affection), quoted in Yang Hung-lieh, *Chung-kuo fa-lü ssu-hsiang shih* (History of Chinese Legal Thought) (Shanghai: Commercial Press, 1936), Vol. II, p. 290.
49. *Analects*, XIII.18.
50. See T'ung-tsu Ch'u, *op. cit.*, note 22, pp. 70–71.
51. *Ibid.*, p. 72.
52. This is a beautiful expression of humanism in the law, laying greater emphasis on the integrity of the person than on material interests.
53. *Code of T'ang*, Article no. 276.
54. This unique status is not fixed once and for all in its content. It may vary from day to day, from year to year. Let us suppose a family of seven members, consisting of the parents and five grown-up sons. The father is the head of the family. If the father dies, the sons cannot yet establish their separate families, because the mother is still living. The eldest son becomes the legal head of the family, possessing an authority over his younger brothers similar to that of the father. So far as the eldest son is concerned, his status has undergone a radical change following the death of his father. If the eldest son dies, the second son takes his place as the head of the family. If the mother dies, all the sons are free to establish their separate households. Thus, at any moment the status of each member is determined by the law; but, at the happening of an external event, he may be transposed from one status to another.
55. See the *Code of T'ang*, Article no. 189 *et seq.*
56. *K'ung-chüeh tung-nan fei.* For an English translation, see Robert Payne, ed., *The White Pony: An Anthology of Chinese Poetry* (New York: Mentor Books, 1960), pp. 117–125.
57. For an English translation of Lu Yu's poem and his former wife's response, see Teresa Li, (Li Te-luan), "Fifty Poems from the Chinese," *T'ien Hsia Monthly*, IX (1939), 286, 304–306.
58. *Code of Tang*, Article no. 189.

59. For some illustrious examples, see Albert O'Hara, S.J., *The Position of Woman in Early China: Including Translation of Lieh-nü chuan* (Hong Kong: Orient Publishing Co., 1955).

60. *Analects*, XIX.19.

61. See "Ta-Yü mo" (Counsels of the Great Yü), in *Shu ching.*

62. See his famous essay, "Hsing-shang chung-hou chih-chih lun" (The Acme of Clemency in Punishment and Reward), in which he expounded the principle laid down by Kao Yao that in doubtful cases the sovereign should err on the side of leniency and generosity rather than try to follow the strict letter of the law. This essay is included in many popular anthologies.

63. See *Pei-Ch'i shu* (History of the Northern Ch'i Dynasty), Bk. 46.

64. See *Hou-Han shu* (History of the Later Han Dynasty), Bk. 92.

65. See Yang Hung-lieh, *Chung-kuo fa-lü ssu-hsiang shih* (History of Chinese Legal Thought), Vol. II, p. 305.

66. Commonly translated as "Three Principles of the People."

67. See "Wu-ch'üan hsien-fa," in *Kuo-fu ch'üan-chi*, Chang Ch'i-yün, ed., (Taipei: United Publication Center, 1960), p. 165.

68. Constitution of the Republic of China, Article 7. On the spirit of the present constitution, see Sun Fo, *China Looks Forward* (New York: John Day, 1945).

69. *Ibid.*, Article 8.

70. *Ibid.*, Article 23.

71. For a more detailed account, see my article, "Chinese Legal Philosophy: A Brief Historical Survey," *Chinese Culture Quarterly*, I, No. 4 (April, 1958), 7, 39 ff. The Constitution of the Republic of China, The Criminal Code, and the Civil Code are available in English translation in *Laws of the Republic of China: First Series— Major Laws*, (Taipei: Government of Taiwan, 1961).

72. Civil Code, Article 72.

73. *Ibid.*, Article 184.

74. *Ibid.* The expression "lineal descendants" (Article 1138) denotes both males and females without distinction. Even in the case of a will, the testator has no power to deprive any heir of his or her "compulsory portion," which is one half of what he or she would have received in the absence of a will.

75. *Ibid.*, Article 972.

76. *Ibid.*, Article 974.

77. *Ibid.*, Article 980.

78. Criminal Code, Article 1.

79. This, of course, is motivated by the national solicitude to keep peace with other nations.

80. The *Code of T'ang*, Articles 170, 251, 272, 280, 295, etc.

81. *Ibid.*, Articles 162.v, 324, 343, etc.

82. *Ibid.* Some general standards are laid down for the guidance of the

judge in meting out punishment; but these standards are flexible in their application. See Article 57.

83. *Ibid.*, Article 74.

84. *Ibid.*, chap. X, on "Conditional Release"; also see Articles 77–79.

85. The Confucian doctrine of *shu* (which has been translated as "mutual consideration" or "reciprocity") finds its expression, negatively, in the formula: Not to do to another what you would not like to have done to you (*Analects*, XV.23). On the positive side, it finds its expression in the formula: Try to extend to others what you desire for yourself (*ibid.*, VI.28). These are the substantial principles of *shu*, which merges in its farthest reaches into *jen*. In its strict sense, *shu* is the functional aspect of *jen;* it is the "art of *jen*," which consists in the ability "from one's own self to draw a parallel for the treatment of others" (*ibid.*). This means that one must step into the shoes of another in order to understand him by seeing things from his standpoint. The ideal judge should be able to do so with the parties before him. Only thus can he avoid rash judgment and render a truly impartial and fair decision.

86. I have adopted the term "aboriginal Self" from Emerson's essay on "Self-Reliance," where he says, "What is the aboriginal Self, on which a universal reliance may be grounded? What is the nature and power of that science-baffling star, without parallax, without calculable elements, which shoots a ray of beauty even into trivial and impure actions, if the least mark of independence appear? The inquiry leads us to that source, at once the essence of genius, of virtue, and of life, which we call Spontaneity or Instinct. We denote this primary wisdom Intuition, whilst all later teachings are tuitions. In that deep force, the last fact behind which analysis cannot go, all things find their common origin." In this he anticipated the upsurge of interest, in the contemporary West, in Far Eastern traditions, especially in Zen, and the philosophical Taoism of Lao Tzu and Chuang Tzu.

Romanization and Corresponding

Chinese Characters

Ai (Duke of Lu) 魯哀 (公)
an 安

Ch'an 禪
ch'an 讖
Chan, Wing-tsit 陳榮捷
Chang Carson 張君勱
Chang Chan 張湛
Chang Ch'i-yün 張其昀
Chang Heng 張衡
Chang Heng-ch'ü hsien-sheng ch'üan-chi 張橫渠先生全集
Chang-san Wu-chi 長孫無忌
Chang Shih-chih 張釋之
Chang T'ai-yen 章太炎
Chang Tsai (Chang Heng-ch'ü) 張載 (張橫渠)
Chao 昭
Chao (Duke) 昭公
"Chao-lun hsü" 肇論序
che 哲
Che-hsüeh kai-lun 哲學概論
chen-jen 眞人
Ch'en Shih 陳寔
Ch'en Ti 陳第
Ch'en Tu-hsiu 陳獨秀

Chen-yen 眞言
Ch'en (Tschen) Yin-k'o 陳寅恪
ch'eng 誠
ch'eng 成
Ch'eng 程
Ch'eng (King) 成
Cheng Ch'iao 鄭樵
Ch'eng-Chu (School) 程朱學派
Ch'eng Hao (Ch'eng Ming-t'ao) 程顥 (程明道)
Cheng Hsüan 鄭玄
Ch'eng I (Ch'eng I-ch'uan) 程頤 (程伊川)
Ch'eng-kuan 澄觀
Cheng-meng 正蒙
Cheng-ming 正名
Ch'eng-shih 成實
Ch'eng-shih i-shu 程氏遺書
Ch'i 齊
ch'i 氣
"Chi-jang ko" 擊壤歌
Chi-lu 季路
Chi-tsang 吉藏
"Ch'i-wu lun" 齊物論
Ch'i-wu lun shih 齊物論釋
ch'i-yün 氣運

Chia li 家理
Chiang Wei-ch'iao 蔣維喬
Chiang Yu-kao 江有誥
Chiang Yung 江永
Chiao Hsün 焦循
Chiao Hung 焦竑
Chieh (King) 桀
Chieh-huan 戒環
chien 見
ch'ien 乾
chien-ai 兼愛
Ch'ien Mu 錢穆
Ch'ien Ta-hsin 錢大昕
chien wen chih-chih 見聞知之
"Ch'ien wen-yen" 乾文言
chih 質
Chih Ch'ien 支謙
Chih-lüeh lu 指月錄
chih-jen 至人
Chih-tun (支遁)
Chih-wu lun 指物論
Chih-yen 智儼
Ch'in (Dynasty) 秦
Chin shih-tzu chang 金獅子章
chin shih 近世
Chin shu 晉書
ching 敬
ching 經
ching 境
Ch'ing (Dynasty) 清
Ching (Duke of Ch'i) 齊景公
Ch'ing-hsüeh 清學
Ching-i shu-wen 經義述聞
ching shuo 經說
Ching-t'u 淨土
Chou (Dynasty) 周
Chou (Duke of) 周公
Chou (King) 紂
Chou (Duke of Han) 韓昭侯
Chou-i lüeh-li 周易略例
Chou Tun-i (Chou Lien-hsi) 周敦頤 (周濂溪)

Ch'u (State) 楚
ch'ü 取
chu 主
Chu Ch'ien-chih 朱謙之
Chu Hsi (Chu Yüan-hui) (Chu Wen-kung) 朱熹 (朱元晦) (朱文公)
Chu Hua-yen fa-chieh kuan-men 註華嚴法界觀門
Chu Ju-chi 瞿汝稷
chü-pu-to 俱不著
Chü-she 俱舍
Ch'ü T'ung-tsu 瞿同祖
Ch'u tz'u 楚辭
Ch'u-tz'u chi-chu 楚辭集註
Chu Tzu ch'üan-shu 朱子全書
Chu Tzu yü-lei 朱子語類
Ch'üan-chou 泉州
Ch'uan-hsi lu 傳習錄
ch'üan-li i-i 權立疑義
Ch'üan-shu 全書
Chuang Chou (Chuang Tzu) 莊周 (莊子)
Chuang Tzu i-cheng 莊子義證
Chün-ch'en 君陳
Ch'un ch'iu 春秋
Ch'un-ch'iu fan-lu 春秋繁露
Ch'un-ch'iu Tso-chuan 春秋左傳
chün-tzu 君子
chung 忠
chung 中
"Chung-hui chih kao" 仲虺之誥
chung ku 中古
Chung-kuan lun-shu 中觀論疏
Chung-kuo ch'ing-nien pao 中國青年報
Chung-kuo fa-lü ssu-hsiang shih 中國法律思想史
Chung-kuo jen-wen ching-shen chih fa-chan 中國人文精神之發展
Chung-kuo ssu-hsiang tui-yü Ou-chou wen-hua chih ying-hsiang 中國思想對於歐洲文化之影響

Chung-kuo wen-hua chih ching-she chia-chih 中國文化之精神價值
Chung-shan 仲山
Chung yung 中庸

en 恩
en-i 恩義
Erh-Ch'eng ch'üan-shu 二程全書

Fa-hsiang 法相
Fa-tsang 法藏
Fa Yen 法言
Fan Chen 范縝
Fan Ch'ih 樊遲
Fan Seuen-tsze (Fan Hsüan-tzu) 范宣子
Fang Thomé H. 方東美
Fang Tung-shu 方東樹
Fo-hsüeh kai-lun 佛學概論
Fu 伏 (生)
fu 服
Fu Hsi 伏羲
Fung Yu-lan 馮友蘭

Han (Western) 西漢
Han (Eastern) 東漢
Han Fei Tzu 韓非子
Han-hsüeh 漢學
Han K'ang-po 韓康伯
Han-Wei liang-Chin Nan-pei-ch'ao fo-chiao shih 漢魏兩晉南北朝佛教史
Han Yü 韓愈
Ho Kuan Tzu 鶡冠子
Ho Ping-ti 何炳棣
Ho Yen 何晏
Hou-chi 后稷
Hou-Han shu 後漢書
Hsi (or I) (monk) 喜 (法師)
Hsi-shih 西施
"Hsi-tz'u" *(chuan)* 繫辭傳
Hsia (Dynasty) 夏朝
hsia ku 下古

Hsia-tu 下都
hsiang 相
hsiang 象
Hsiang (Duke) 襄公
Hsiang-shan ch'üan-chi 象山全集
hsiao 孝
Hsiao (King of Chou) 孝王
Hsiao ching 孝經
Hsiao T'ung 蕭統
Hsieh Ling-yün 謝靈運
Hsieh Yu-wei 謝幼偉
hsin 心
Hsin-hsueh 心學
Hsin-ya hsüeh-pao 新亞學報
Hsin Yüan-jen 新原人
hsing 性
hsing 行
Hsing-li-hsüeh 性理學
Hsing-shang chung-hou chih chih lun 刑賞忠厚之至論
Hsiung Shih-li 熊十力
hsü 虛
Hsü Ch'an 徐蔵
Hsü P'eng-chüng (P.C.) 徐彭春
Hsü-tan-chih-chüan 盱壇直詮
Hsüan (King of Ch'i) 宣
Hsüan-hsüeh chia 玄學家
Hsüeh Kuang-chien (Paul K. T. Sih) 薛光前
Hsün Ch'ing (Hsün Tzu) 荀卿 (荀子)
Hsün-meng yu-hsüeh shih 訓蒙幼學詩
"Hsün Tzu cheng-ming yü ming-hsüeh san tsung" 荀子正名與名學三宗
Hu Shih 胡適
Hu Shih lun-hsüeh chin-chu 胡適論學近著
Hua Heng-fang 華衡芳
Hua-yen 華嚴
Hua-yen ching yao-chieh 華嚴經要解
Huai-nan Tzu 淮南子

Huang-chi ching-shih 皇極經世
Huang-Lao 黃老
Huang Siu-chi 黃秀璣
Huang-ti 黃帝
Huang Tsung-hsi 黃宗羲
Hui-neng 惠能
Hui Shih 惠施
Hui-ta 慧達
Hui-yüan 慧遠
hun 魂
hun-p'o 魂魄
Hung-ming chi 弘明集

i 異
I (river) 沂
i 易
i 義
I chang-chü 易章句
I ching 易經
I-hsüeh t'ao-lun chi 易學討論集
I hua 易話
I li 儀禮
I shu 遺書
I-t'u lüeh 易圖畧
I t'ung-shih 易通釋
I t'ung-shu 易通書

jang 讓
jen 仁
jen-sheng 人生
jen-tz'u 仁祠
Jen-wen ching-shen chih ch'ung-chien 人文精神之重建
ju 儒
Ju-chia che-hsüeh 儒家哲學

kai 蓋
K'ang Seng-hui 康僧會
K'ang Yu-wei 康有爲
k'ao-cheng 考證
k'ao-chü 考據
Kao Yao 皋陶

Kao-yu 高郵
ko-chih 格致
Ko Hung (Pao-p'u Tzu) 葛洪 (抱扑子)
ko wu 格物
ku 故
ku 蠱
Ku Chieh-kang 顧頡剛
Ku Hung-ming 辜鴻銘
Ku-shih yüan 古詩源
Ku Yen-wu 顧炎武
kua 卦
Kuan-yin 觀音
kuang chih 廣智
Kuang-hsü (Emperor) 光緒
K'uei 夔
kuei-shen 鬼神
k'un 坤
K'ung-ch'üeh tung-nan fei 孔雀東南飛
K'ung Fu Tzu 孔夫子
Kung-sun Lung 公孫龍
Kung-sun Lung Tzu 公孫龍子
Kung-yang 公羊
Kuo-fu ch'üan-shu 國父全集
Kuo Hsi 郭熙
Kuo Mo-jo 郭沫若
Kuo Hsiang 郭象

Lao Tan (Lao Tzu) 老聃 (老子)
lei 類
li 里
li 理
li 禮
Li Ao 李翱
Li chi 禮記
Li hsüeh 理學
Li-huo lun 理惑論
Li Kung 李塨
Li Shan-lan 李善蘭
Li-shih che-hsüeh 歷史哲學

Li Ssu 李斯
Li Ssu-kuang 李思光
Li Te-lan (Teresa Li) 李德蘭
"Li yün" 禮運
Liang (Dynasty) 梁
Liang Ch'i-ch'ao 梁啟超
liang-chih 良知
Liang jen-kung ch'üan-chi
　梁任公全集
Liang shu 梁書
Liao Wei-kuei (W. K.) 廖文魁
Lieh-nü chuan 列女傳
Lieh Tzu 列子
Lin-chi I-hsüan 臨濟義玄
Lin Yutang 林語堂
Ling (Duke) 靈公
ling 靈
Liu Chi-shan 劉蕺山
Liu Chi-shan chih cheng-i-chih-hsüeh
　劉蕺山之誠意之學
liu-fang ch'ien-ku 留芳千古
Liu Hsieh 劉勰
Lo Chin-ch'i 羅近溪
"Lo Chin-ch'i chih li-hsüeh"
　羅近溪之理學
Lo Ken-tse 羅根澤
Lo Nien-an 羅念菴
Lu (State) 魯
Lu Chi 陸機
Lu Chein-tseng 盧見曾
Lu Chiu-yüan (Lu Hsiang-shan)
　陸九淵 (陸象山)
Lu Hsiang-shan ch'üan-chi
　陸象山全集
Lü Tsu-ch'ien 呂祖謙
Lu-Wang (School) 陸王 學派)
Lu Yu 陸游
lun 倫
Lun heng 論衡
Lun yü 論語
Lun yü chi-chu 論語集註

Ma Hsü-lun 馬叙倫
Manchus 滿洲 (淸)
Mao (School) 毛家
Mao-shih ku-yin k'ao 毛詩古音考
Mao Tse-tung 毛澤東
Mei Tsu 梅鷟
Mei Yi-pao 梅貽寶
Meng Tzu 孟子
Meng Tzu tzu-i shu-cheng
　孟子字義疏證
Min-chu p'ing-lun 民主評論
Ming (Dynasty) 明
ming 明
ming 命
Ming-chia 名家
Ming-ch'ing 明淸
Ming-i tai-fang lu 明夷待訪錄
Ming-ju hsüeh-an 明儒學案
Ming-shih lun 名實論
Ming T'ai-tsu hsiao-tz'u lu hsü
　明太祖孝慈錄序
Ming-t'ang 明堂
Mo chia 墨家
Mo Pien 墨辯
Mo Ti (Mo Tzu) 墨翟 (墨子)
Mou Tsung-san 牟宗三
Mou Tzu 牟子
Mu-shuh (shu) 穆叔
mu-to 木鐸

Nan-hua chen-ching 南華眞經
neng-jen 能仁
nien 駑

Ou 偶

"Pa-pen se-yüan lun" 拔本塞源論
"Pan-jo wu-chih-lun" 般若無知論
p'ang-cheng 旁證
pao 豹
Pao-p'u Tzu 抱朴子
Pei-Ch'i shu 北齊書
pen-cheng 本證

pen-hsin 本心
pen-wu 本無
p'eng 鵬
pi-ch'eng 筆乘
piao 表
"Piao chi" 表記
p'ien 駢
Pien-cheng lun 辯正論
pin 賓
p'o 魄
"Po-ma lun" 白馬論
po shih 博士
"Pu-chen-kung-lun" 不眞空論
P'u hsüeh 樸學

san chiao 三教
San-lun 三論
San-min chu-i 三民主義
san-ts'ai 三才
Seng-chao 僧肇
Seng-ching 僧鏡
Seng-yu 僧祐
"Shang" *(chuan)* 上卷
Shang (Yin) (Dynasty) 商
Shang Chü 商瞿
Shang-chün shu 商君書
shang ku 上古
Shang-ti 上帝
Shang Yang 商鞅
Shao Yung (Shao K'ang-chieh)
　邵雍 邵康節)
shen 神
Shen (Monk) 琛 (法師)
shen-jen 神人
Shen Te-ch'ien 沈德潛
shen-tu 愼獨
shen-yü 神遇
sheng 生
Sheng-ming ch'ing-tiao yü mei-k'an
　生命情調與美感
shih 事

Shih chi 史記
Shih ching 詩經
shih-fei 是非
shih i 是以
"Shih-jen p'ien" 識仁篇
Shih ming 釋名
Shih p'i-p'an shu 十批判書
"Shih-sang li" 士喪禮
shu 恕
Shu ching 書經
Shun (Sage-Emperor) 舜
Shuo-ju 說儒
"Shuo-kua" *(chuan)* 說卦傳.
"Ssu hsüan" 思玄
Ssu-ma Ch'ien 司馬遷
Ssu-ma T'an 司馬談
Ssu-pu pei-yao 四部備要
Ssu-pu tsung-k'an 四部叢刊
Ssu-shu shih-i 四書釋義
Su Ch'iung 蘇瓊
Su Shih (Su Tung-p'o) 蘇軾 (東坡)
Sui-T'ang 隋唐
Sun Fo 孫科
Sun Yat-sen 孫逸仙
Sung (Dynasty) 宋
Sung hsüeh 宋學
Sung-Ming 宋明

ta
Ta chuan 大傳
Ta hsüeh 大學
Ta Tsing lu lee (Ta Ch'ing lü-li)
　大清律例
Ta t'ung shu 大同書
"Ta-Yü mo" 大禹漠
T'ai 泰
Tai Chen (Tai Tung-yüan)
　戴震 (戴東原)
T'ai-chi 太極
T'ai-chi t'u shuo 太極圖說
t'ai ho 太和

T'ai-hsüan 太玄
ta-i mieh-ch'in 大義滅親
T'ai-p'ing yü-lan 太平御覽
T'ai Shang 太上
Tai Te 戴德
T'ai-tsu (Emperor of Ming) 太祖(明)
Tan-chi 曇濟
T'an Ssu-t'ung 譚嗣同
T'ang (Dynasty) 唐
T'ang (Emperor) 湯
T'ang Chün-i 唐君毅
T'ang-lü shu-i 唐律疏義
T'ang Yung-t'ung 湯用彤
Tao 道
Tao-an 道安
Tao-chia 道家
Tao hsüeh 道學
Tao-sheng 道生
Tao-te ching 道德經
te 德
Te-ch'ing 德清
te-hsing chih-chih 德性之知
Teng Hsi 鄧析
Teng Ssu-yü 鄧嗣禹
Ti 帝
t'i 體
ti 弟
t'i-jen 體認
t'i-yen 體驗
T'ien (Heaven) 天
T'ien-chu shih-i 天主實義
T'ien-ming 天命
T'ien Hsia (Monthly) 天下
T'ien-t'ai 天台
Ting (Duke) 定
ting 鼎
"Ting-hsing shu" 定性書
tsai 災
Tsai shen-ching sheng-huo fa-chan chung chih hui-yü i-shih 在神精生活發展中之毀譽意識
tsao-wu-che 造物者

Tseng Hsi 曾晢
Tseng Tien (Tien) 曾點
Tseng Ts'an (Tseng Tzu, or Tsang) 曾參 (曾子)
Tsin (Chin) (Dynasty) 晋
Tsin 晋
Tsing Hua Hsüeh-pao (Ch'ing-hua Hsüeh-pao) 清華學報
Tso 左
Tso chuan 左傳
Tsou-i 奏議
Ts'ui-yen 粹言
Tsung-mi 宗密
tu 獨
tu-chih 獨知
Tu-ching shih-yao 讀經示要
Tu I Hsi-tz'u lun-hsing 讀易繫辭論性
Tu-shun 杜順
Tuan *(chuan)* 段傳
Tuan Yü-ts'ai 段玉裁
T'ung chih 通志
Tung Chung-shu 董仲舒
T'ung shu 通書
Tzu-chih t'ung-chien 資治通鑑
Tzu-hsia 子夏
tzu-hsing 自省
tzu jan 自然
Tzu-kung 子貢
Tzu-ssu 子思
tzu-te 自得
Tzu-yu hsüeh-jen 自由學人

wan wu 萬物
Wang Chi 王畿
Wang Ch'ung 王充
Wang Fu-chih 王夫之
Wang Lung-ch'i 王龍溪
Wang Nien-sun 王念孫
Wang Pi 王弼
Wang Shou-jen (Wang Yang-ming) 王守仁 (王陽明)

Wang Yang-ming ch'üan-chi
王陽明全集
Wang Yin-chih 王引之
Wei (State) 衞
wei 緯
Wei-shih 唯識
wei-wo 爲我
Wen (King) 文 (王)
Wen (Monk) 溫 (法師)
wen 文
Wen-chi 文集
Wen-hsin tiao-lung 文心雕龍
Wen hsüan 文選
wen shih 文士
Wen-ti (of Han) 文帝
"Wen yen" *(chuan)* 文言傳
wu 無
wu 物
Wu (Emperor of Liang) 梁武帝
Wu (King) 武
"Wu-ch'eng" 武成
Wu Ch'eng 吳澄
wu ching 五經
Wu Ching-hsiung (John C. H.)
  吳經熊
"Wu-ch'üan hsien-fa" 五權憲法
"Wu-pu-ch'ien-lun" 物不遷論
"Wu-shen lun" 無神論
wu t'a 無他
"Wu-te chung-shih shuo-hsia te
  Cheng-chih ho li-shih" 五德終
  始說下的政治和歷史
wu-wei 無爲
Wu Yü 吳棫

yang 陽
Yang Chu 楊朱
Yang Chien 楊簡
Yang Hsiung 楊雄

Yang Hu 楊虎
Yang Hung-lieh 楊鴻烈
Yang-ming ch'üan-shu 陽明全書
Yao (Sage-Emperor) 堯
Yen Hui 顏回
Yen Jo-chü 閻若璩
Yen Tzu 晏子
Yen Ying 晏嬰
Yen Yüan 顏淵
yin 陰
Yin (Shang) (Dynasty) 殷
Yin-hsüeh wu-shu 音學五書
Yin-ping-shih ho-chi 飲冰室合集
Yin-Yang (school) 陰陽家
yin-yang 陰陽
Yü (Emperor of Hsia) 禹
yu 有
yü 友
yu 幽
Yu (King of Chou) 幽王
Yü Fa-k'ai 于法開
Yü-lei 語類
Yü Tao-sui 于道邃
Yu Tzu 有子
yu-tz'u kuan-chih 由此觀之
Yüan (Dynasty) 元
Yüan K'ang 元康
Yüan-shan 原善
yüan-sheng 緣生
Yüan Shih-k'ai 袁世凱
Yüeh (state) 越
yüeh 悅
yün 雲
"Yün pu" 韻補
yung 用
Yung 庸
Yung-chia (School) 永嘉
Yung-k'ang (School) 永康

Who's Who

WING-TSIT CHAN

Anna R. D. Gillespie Professor of Philosophy, Chatham College, and Adjunct Professor of Chinese Thought, Columbia University.

A.B., Lingnan University, Canton; M.A. and Ph.D., Harvard University; A.M. (honorary), Dartmouth College.

Formerly Dean of Faculty and Professor of Philosophy, Lingnan University; Professor of Chinese Philosophy, University of Hawaii; Chairman, Division of The Humanities, Dartmouth College; Visiting Professor, New York University Teachers College; Summer Session, University of Hawaii, Michigan State College, and Smith College.

Guggenheim Fellow, 1948–1949; Honorary Research Fellow, Institute of Far Eastern Research, Chung Chi College, Hong Kong, 1963 to present; Honorary Fellow, Institute of Oriental Studies, University of Hong Kong, 1964; Honorary Research Fellow, New Asia College Institute of Research, 1963 to present. Has held research grants from many societies and foundations.

Goldwyn Smith Lecturer, Cornell University, 1943; Class of 1907 Lecturer in Oriental Civilization, Bryn Mawr College, 1943; Mayling Soong Foundation Lecturer, Wellesley College, 1948; American Council of Learned Societies Lecturer on Chinese Religion, 1949–1950; Haskell Foundation Lecturer, University of Chicago, 1950; Machette Foundation Lecturer, Wesleyan University, 1950. Has also lectured at many American colleges and universities and at Naval War College, Brooklyn Institute of Arts and Sciences, and Foreign Policy Association.

Member, American Council of Learned Societies Committee on Far Eastern Studies, 1950–1953.

Panel Member, East-West Philosophers' Conference, 1939, 1949, 1959, 1964.

Author of *Religious Trends in Modern China; Historical Charts of Chinese Philosophy;* and *An Outline and an Annotated Bibliography of Chinese Philosophy.* Translator and compiler of *A Source Book in Chinese Philosophy.* Translator of *Instructions for Practical Living and Other Neo-Confucian Writings by Wang Yang-ming; The Way of Lao Tzu; The Platform Scriptures;* and *Reflections on Things at Hand, Neo-Confucian Anthology.* Co-editor with Charles A. Moore, Junjirō Takakusu's *The Essentials of Buddhist Philosophy;* and co-editor and author, with William Theodore de Bary and Burton Watson, *Sources of Chinese Tradition.*

Associate Editor, *Lingnan Journal,* 1929–1936; Contributing Editor, *Philosophical Abstracts,* 1940–1947; Member, Board of Editors, *Philosophy East and West,* 1951 to date; Consulting Editor, *Tsing-Hua University Journal of Chinese Studies,* 1955; Editor for Chinese Philosophy, *Encyclopedia of Philosophy,* 1963 to date.

THOMÉ H. FANG (Fang Tung-shu)

Professor of Philosophy, National Taiwan University. Visiting Professor of Philosophy, Michigan State University (1964–1966).

Educated at the University of Nanking, Ohio State University, and the University of Wisconsin.

Professor of Philosophy, the Central Institute of Political Sciences, 1927–1936 and 1945–1948; the University of Nanking, 1927–1932; and the National Central University, 1929–1948. Director of the Institute of Advanced Studies in Philosophy, National Central University, 1938–1948.

Visiting Professor of Philosophy, State University of South Dakota and University of Missouri. Has lectured at several American colleges.

Awarded the Medal of Distinguished Service Professor by the Chinese Ministry of Education, 1956 and 1964.

Panel Member, Fourth East-West Philosophers' Conference, 1964.

Principal writings: (in Chinese) *The Sentiment of Life and the Sense of Beauty; Essentials of the Chinese Philosophy of Life; Science, Philosophy, and the Significance of Human Life—A Study in the History of European Ideas; Joint Studies in the Philosophy of Change* (in collaboration with Professor Li Cheng-kang); *Collected Poems* (1938–1953); *Philosophy of Hegel,* 2 vols. (with several co-authors); (in English) *Chinese View of Life: the Philosophy of Comprehensive Harmony.*

HSIEH YU-WEI

Professor of Philosophy and Dean of the Research Institute, New Asia College.

B.A., Soochow University, 1926; M.A., Harvard University, 1931.

Formerly Professor, National Kwangtung Law College, Canton; Professor and Chairman of the Department of Philosophy, National Chekiang University, 1937–1948; Professor of Philosophy, National Cheng Chi University, 1954–1959.

Panel Member, East-West Philosophers' Conference, 1959, 1964.

Publications (in Chinese): *An Introduction to Ethics: A Critical Exposition of Major Contemporary Philosophical Works; Lectures on Philosophy; The Spirit of Chinese Culture; The True Meaning of Freedom; Mankind and Culture; On Whitehead's Philosophy; The Metaphysics of F. H. Bradley; On Hegel's Dialectic; The Logical Theory of F. H. Bradley; On Bertrand Russell's "Prejudice" and Western Philosophy; History of Western Philosophy,* Vol. I. Editor-in-chief, *Hsin Pao,* Batavia, Java; *The Free Press,* Djakarta, Indonesia; and Editorial Director, *The Central Daily News,* Taipei.

HU SHIH

President, *Academia Sinica* (until his death in 1962).

B.A., Cornell University; Ph.D., Columbia University. Recipient of over thirty honorary degrees from American and European universities.

From 1917, a leading figure in the Literary Revolution of China.

Professor of Philosophy and, later, Chairman, Department of English Literature, National Peking University, 1917–1927; President of the China National Institute, 1928–1930; Dean of the College of Arts, National Peking University, 1930–1937; Ambassador to the United States, 1942–1945; Chancellor of the National Peking University, 1938–1942.

Major publications: (in Chinese) *A History of Chinese Philosophy; History of Vernacular Literature; The Philosophy of Tai Chen; Collected Essays; Recent Essays on Learned Subjects; Forty Years: An Autobiography;* (in English) *The Development of the Logical Method in Ancient China; The Chinese Renaissance.*

Died February 24, 1962.

E. R. HUGHES

Formerly Visiting Professor of Chinese, Claremont Graduate School; missionary in the interior of China, 1911–1929.

Reader in Chinese Religion and Philosophy, Oxford, 1934–1941; Acting Professor of Chinese Language and Literature, Oxford, 1941–1947.

M.A., Oxford.

Panel Member, East-West Philosophers' Conference, 1949.

Author, editor, and translator of numerous works on Chinese thought. Recent publications: *The Invasion of China by the Western World; The Individual in East and West* (editor and contributor);

Chinese Philosophy in Classical Times; The Great Learning and the Mean-in-Action; The Spirit of Chinese Philosophy (translator); *Religion in China* (co-author); *The Art of Letters: a Chinese Point of View.*
Died in October, 1956.

Y. P. MEI (Mei Yi-Pao)

Professor of Oriental Studies, Chairman of Chinese and Oriental Studies, and Director of Center for Far Eastern Studies, State University of Iowa.

B.A., Oberlin College; Ph.D., University of Chicago. Studied at the University of Cologne. Honorary degrees: LL.D., Oberlin College; L.H.D., Wabash College.

Professor of Philosophy, Dean of the College of Arts and Letters, and Acting President, Yenching University, Peiping, 1928–1949. Visiting Professor of Philosophy: University of Chicago, University of Hawaii, Indiana University, University of Cincinnati, Princeton University, Wabash College, Bowdoin College, and Oberlin College.

Panel Member, East-West Philosophers' Conference, 1949 and 1964. Formerly member, Chinese Cultural Mission to U.S.; President, Oberlin-in-China; President, American Association of Teachers of Chinese Language and Culture, 1961–1962.

Major Publications: *The Ethical and Political Philosophy of Motse; Motse, The Neglected Rival of Confucius;* and numerous articles in major encyclopedias and in several scholarly journals. Member, Editorial Board, *Tsing-Hua University Journal of Chinese Studies.*

T'ANG CHÜN-I

Dean of the Faculty of Arts, New Asia College.

Educated at Sino-Russian University, Peking University, and National Central University.

Formerly, Lecturer, West China Union University; Professor of Philosophy, National Central University, 1945–1949.

Helped to found New Asia College, at which he has served as Dean since its beginning.

Member, Philosophical Association of China and of Oriental Idealistic Humanists Society; Advisor, Buddhistic Cultural Association.

Panel Member, East-West Philosophers' Conferences, 1959 and 1964.

His major publications (in Chinese) are: *Comparative Studies in Chinese and Western Philosophies; Reconstruction of the Moral Self; Experience of Human Life; Spiritual Values in Chinese Culture; Reconstruction of the Humanistic Spirit;* and *Cultural Consciousness and Moral Reason.*

JOHN C. H. WU

Professor of Asian Studies, Seton Hall University.

LL.B., Comparative Law School of China, Shanghai; J.D., Michigan University School of Law. Honorary degrees: LL.D., University of Oregon, Boston College, and St. John's University; Litt.D., Rockhurst College.

Formerly Professor of Law and, later, Principal, Comparative Law School of China; Professor of Law, Seton Hall University School of Law.

Judge, Chief Justice, and President, successively, of the Provisional Court (later, Special High Court), International Settlement of Shanghai; Member, Legislative Body of National China, 1933–1946; Advisor, Chinese Delegation to the first General Assembly of the United Nations, 1945; Envoy Extraordinary and Minister Plenipotentiary of China to the Holy See, 1946–1949; Member, The Permanent Court of Arbitration, The Hague, 1957–.

Panel Member, East-West Philosophers' Conference, 1959 and 1964.

Major publications: *Chinese Versions of The Psalms and The New Testament; Beyond East and West; The Interior Carmel; Fountain of Justice;* translator, *Tao Te Ching.* Managing editor, *T'ien Hsia Monthly,* 1935–1941.

Index

PREPARED BY E. MURIEL MOYLE

perspective, 92
pessimism, 8, 49
Petrarch, 108
*Phenomenological Study of the
Consciousness of Praise and
Defamation in the Development
of Spiritual Life* (Tang Chün-i),
211 n
philology, 129
philosophy: comparative, 106 f;
Chinese: basic principles, 4 ff;
and divination, 16; legal, 6; political, 6; practical character of,
11 f; and religion, 1, 6; and social
affairs, 17
*Philosophy and Culture, East and
West,* v n, 357 n
Philosophy—East and West, v n,
vii, 103 n, 131 n
*Philosophy of Human Nature by
Chu Hsi* (J.P. Bruce), 75 n,
166 n
Philosophy of Wang Yang-ming
(F.G. Henke), 166 n
phonetics, 126 f
phonology, 121, 123, 126 f
physics, 95, 97, 105, 107
p'ien ("double-harness writing"),
88
Pien-cheng lun, see *Essays on the
Discrimination of Doctrines*
Platform Scripture, 293 f, 305 n
Plato, 83, 94 f, 99, 151, 190, 192,
265
Plato's Earlier Dialectic (R. Robinson), 83, 102 n
pluralism, 139, 268
po shih, 84
poetry, 22 f, 35, 56, 94, 101, 238,
248
political authority, 213 ff
political life, 182
Position of Woman in Early China:

*Including Translation of Lieh-
nü chuan,* 363 n
positive law, see law
positivists, 90
posterity, 180 f
postulation, concepts by, 94 ff, 105
praise, desire for, 193 f
prajñā (insight), 61, 251, 254 f
Prajñā-pāramitā-hṛdaya-sūtra,
148 n
prayer, 180, 196
Preface to Seng-chao's Discourses,
262 n
priests, function of, 287
"A Primer on the Study of the
I Ching," 120
primitivism, 48 f
Princeton Institute of Advanced
Studies, 101
principle, see *li*
prisoners of war, 325
privileged classes, 356 f
prognostication, see omens
pronunciation, ancient, 121, 123 ff,
129
property rights, 24, 350
propriety, see *li*
Protestant reform, 101
psychology, and Confucius, 35
P'u-hsüeh (Concrete Philosophy),
74 n
"Pulling up the Root and Stopping
up the Source," 17
punishment, 216, 220 ff, 224 ff,
233 f, 236 n, 342, 344 ff, 349 f,
354 ff, 360 n, 361 n, 364 n
Pure Land school (Buddhism), 21,
55, 290, 293
Pure Words, 28 n, 29 n, 75 n

quietism, 49, 56, 207

Rabelais, 108
The Race Question, 337